THE
CHRISTIAN CHURCH
IN CANADA

H. H. WALSH, M.A., S.T.M., Ph.D.

Associate Professor of Church History
McGill University, Montreal

THE RYERSON PRESS – TORONTO

Published December, 1956
Paperback Edition, 1968

To

ELIN AND GEORGE

PRINTED AND BOUND IN CANADA
BY THE RYERSON PRESS, TORONTO

PREFACE

ABOUT FORTY years ago, Dr. A. G. Doughty, one of the editors of *Canada and Its Provinces*, made a forceful appeal for a study of Canada's spiritual resources. Commenting on the prominence of the physical in Canadian national development, he ventured the following prediction: "The physical may appear for the present to have supremacy. Soon, it may be, the desire for something more enduring which has always been manifest, will assert itself, and then Canada will have attained, to the full extent, national self-consciousness."[1] As a contribution to this end, two volumes of the justly famous history of the Canadian people and their institutions were devoted to a study of missions, arts and letters. Prominent members of the various churches in Canada were assigned the task of writing the history of their own particular denominations. These contributions gathered together in one volume constitute the first attempt to give an over-all picture of Canadian church development.

The project, however, suffered from one serious defect, in that most of the histories were written in a denominational spirit. This, as Professor W. W. Sweet, an eminent authority on American church history, has said, is the wrong way to write church history. "Taken by themselves," he says, "all the incidents which go to make up the life of a denomination do not mean much in gaining an understanding of the total religious life of a nation." Indeed he regards the "history of one church taken by itself as probably misleading."[2] Dr. Doughty seems to have been well aware of this danger, as he urges students of *Canada and Its Provinces* not to be content with reading the story of one denomination, but to read them all in order to get a complete view of the religious development of Canada.

It is to help provide such a view that the author has written this book. Although I write from within one Church I have endeavoured to avoid any denominational presuppositions and to set forth as objectively as possible the total religious life of Canada. In doing so I have been greatly helped by Dr. Lorne Pierce for the constant encouragement he has

[1]Shortt and Doughty, *Canada and Its Provinces* (Toronto, 1914), XI, p. 3.
[2]W. W. Sweet, *The Story of Religion in America* (New York, 2nd rev. ed. 1950), p. 1.

given me while the work was in progress.   I am also much indebted to the Rockefeller Foundation for making it possible for me to visit many church archival centres across Canada and to Dean Thomson and the authorities of McGill University for a six-months leave of absence to complete the work.   My thanks are also due to many librarians across Canada for their kindly attention and to several of my students at Divinity Hall for help in research work.

The author acknowledges the courtesy of the editors of *Church History*, *The Canadian Historical Review*, *Queen's Quarterly* and *The Bulletin* of the Committee on Archives of The United Church of Canada in permitting him to reprint portions of articles that have already appeared in those journals.   A special word of thanks is due to the editor of *Encyclopedia Canadiana* for permission to use in my introductory chapter material originally prepared for the *Encyclopedia*.   Above all I wish to express my gratitude to my wife for her encouragement and assistance.

H. H. WALSH.

Divinity Hall, Montreal.
May, 1956.

PREFACE TO SECOND PRINTING

THE PUBLICATION of the first edition of this book in 1956 has been credited with arousing considerable interest in research in the field of Canadian church history.   Perhaps one of its most notable fruits was the publication of a symposium edited by J. W. Grant, entitled *The Churches and the Canadian Experience* (Ryerson, 1963).   This interest in Canadian church history has been kept alive from year to year by the proceedings of the Canadian Society of Church History founded in 1959, and which produced the authors who have embarked upon a comprehensive account of the history of the church in Canada based upon past studies but also supplemented by original research.   The first volume of this work written by the author *The Church in the French Era* has already appeared (Ryerson, 1967) and is to be followed by two others under the general editorship of John Webster Grant.   It is hoped that when this project is completed it will be a worthy memorial to Dr. Lorne Pierce whose constant encouragement made this book possible, as well as the formation of the Canadian Society of Church History.

During the twelve years that have elapsed since the publication of *The Christian Church in Canada* little has occurred within the contemporary Canadian church scene to require any radical revision or modification of views expressed in 1959; nor does one find any great change emerging in the pattern of Canadian church development. There has been of course some slight change in the relative strength among the various churches and sects. The 1961 census reveals that Protestants and Roman Catholics are now nearly equal in numbers: the latter represents about 45.7 per cent of some twenty million Canadians, compared with 43.3 per cent in the previous census; the United Church of Canada remained the second largest denomination, accounting for 20.1 per cent of the population, compared with 20.5 per cent ten years earlier, representing a growth of 27.3 per cent; the Anglican Church increased its membership by 16.9 per cent, but declined in its share of the population, moving from 14.7 per cent down to 13.2; a like fate befell the Presbyterian Church which has declined from 5.6 to 4.5 per cent of Canadians; the Lutheran Church showed a remarkable growth by increasing its total membership by 49 per cent; even more significantly the Pentecostals continued to be the fastest growing religious group in Canada, with an increase of 51.2 per cent.

Despite the great increase in the strength of the Pentecostals and allied fundamentalist sects there is little doubt that the three churches that dominate the Canadian scene are the Roman Catholic, the United and the Anglican; they also follow a common pattern that gives its own shape to Canadian ecclesiastical life, since eight out of ten Canadians belong to one or other of these churches. That this common pattern will be followed even more rigorously in the future seems evident from the fact that two of these churches have recently announced their intention to proceed towards organic union on the basis of a document entitled: The Principles of Union between the Anglican Church of Canada and the United Church of Canada. This document has been hailed by a prominent Canadian theologian as "a second break-through" . . . "almost forty years to the day—June 1, 1966—after the first act in the drama of Canadian ecumenism." [1]

It does not appear that the Roman Catholic Church will be as seriously troubled over the prospect of a united Protestantism during this second round of church union as was the case in the first round; for as Father Gregory Baum has pointed out, through a "shift of perspective

[1] J. C. McLelland, *Toward a Radical Church* (Ryerson, 1967), p. 134.

the Catholic Church has caught up and joined other Christian Churches in the ecumenical movement."[1] This "shift of perspective" is probably the most significant event that has occurred, not only within the Canadian Christian community but in the whole Christian world since the first publication of this volume.

As part of this ecumenical development it is interesting to note that when the union of the Anglican and the United Church is consummated, the newly united churches and the Roman Catholic will be numerically dominant in each province of Canada: the Roman Catholic will have 46 to 88 per cent of the population of three provinces while the new United Church will have from 40 to 53 per cent of the remaining seven; further evidence that despite the vigorous sectarianism that continues to thrive in Canada, churchism is strongly entrenched in Canadian national life.

In the field of theology there is little notable change to record in the Canadian interpretation of the Christian gospel. No doubt some Canadian theologians have been greatly influenced by the Death of God theology, but one is hesitant as a historian to make any comment on this remarkable phenomenon of doubt that has arisen within the household of faith. Whether the so-called new theology is a temporary phase in the history of Christianity or is leading the church dramatically into the intellectual climate of the twentieth century is a question that must be answered by some future historian writing from the perspective of the mid-twenty-first century.

H. H. WALSH.

Weymouth, Nova Scotia.
July, 1968.

[1] *The Church in the Modern World, Essays in Honour of James Sutherland Thomson* (Ryerson, 1967), p. 89.

CONTENTS

I

Introduction

THERE is general agreement among Canadian historians that writing a history of Canada is an unusually difficult task. A dual culture and geographical barriers which have fostered regional development are two of the chief obstacles in the way of a unified story. There is also the great divide: before and after the British Conquest. All the problems which the secular historian faces as he tries to organize his material into a connected story are intensified in the field of ecclesiastical history, and up to the present no one has ventured to do more than to trace "the sociological significance of certain general movements of religion in Canadian social development." [1]

There are, of course, several denominational histories available and a few regional church histories, but no serious attempt has been made to fuse the religious story of Canada into one integrated history. But despite the difficulties in the way of a unified Canadian story we now possess some very excellent political and social studies covering the whole period of Canada's existence; so it ought not to be impossible to set forth our religious heritage in more universal terms than is usually the case in a denominational monograph. It is the purpose of this introductory chapter to point out some of the historical factors around which Canadian church history can be organized and to indicate how these factors have been responsible for certain distinctive trends in Canadian ecclesiastical development.

I

All our historians are in agreement that the most determining factor in Canadian development is the existence of two major cultural groups within one national framework. The clash of culture is the great Canadian theme. It is this clash which gives a sense of continuity to Canadian history before and after the British Conquest, as it was present in the first French settlements on the North American continent when Huguenot and Catholic attempted to co-operate in the founding of a French empire in the New World. But this co-operation took an ominous turn on the docks of Dieppe, when, according to one chronicler, "the heretic merchants" [2] refused to give passage on their ships to some Jesuit missionaries assigned to Port Royal, Acadia (now Annapolis Royal, Nova Scotia). The upshot of this dispute was the banishment of the "heretic merchants" from New France until their return as the camp followers of a conquering British army. Nevertheless, during the one hundred and fifty years in which the Jesuits and other orders dedicated to the ultramontane principle were building a model Catholic state in North America, sheltered from all heterodox opinion, they could never lose consciousness of the existence of a rival Zion to the south of them which was far more successful in a material way than their own theocracy. As the main preoccupation of the civil authorities at Quebec was to prevent this vigorous mercantile community from intruding into the trading preserves of New France, so the church leaders at Quebec were equally alert to prevent their flock from being contaminated by what they considered to be the dangerous heretical views of these theologically-minded traders. After the Conquest, when the "heretic merchants" returned once again to take over the commercial interests of New France, the pattern of life for the faithful hardly changed. Though the hierarchy immediately proceeded to discourage any intimate mingling of Protestant and Catholic, nevertheless, there was still the same consciousness of an ideological conflict or, as it has been well expressed, ". . . even in the remote countryside of Quebec today where a word of English is hardly ever spoken, and few Protestants exist, the Roman Catholic never loses consciousness of the aggressive Protestant world just over the horizon." [3]

There was, however, a bleak moment for the hierarchy when by the Treaty of Paris (1763) sixty thousand French Canadians were embodied into the British North American Empire of two million English-speaking Protestants. Already some ten thousand Acadians from Nova Scotia had been dispersed throughout the Thirteen Colonies; assimilation of the French into the larger racial group seemed inevitable. Then the unexpected happened: the emergence of a sharp division within the English-speaking group gave the Roman Catholic minority a new lease of life. This division within the ranks of the English first became evident to the French in the Quebec Act of 1774; for the Act was an overture on the part of British officialdom at Quebec to the French Canadians for an alliance against the republican sentiment already becoming vocal in the older colonies and which was even affecting the mercantile community at Quebec. By creating a new province in which the French were in a majority, and by granting the church permission to tithe its people, the British authorities laid the foundations for the dual culture of Canada.

But the hierarchy was not yet secure. Another bad moment followed after the American Revolution, when Canada began to be overrun by a great influx of refugees—the Loyalists, as they are called in Canadian history books—from the former Thirteen Colonies. Once again the British authorities came to the aid of the harassed French with the Constitutional Act of 1791, dividing Canada into two parts: the upper half to be given to the Loyalists, where they could enjoy English laws and customs; the lower half to retain French civil law and the feudal practices of the old regime. Thus was created within Canada itself the same alert tension that had previously existed between New England and New France, and often seemed destined to break out into open warfare. But with a constant threat of assimilation by the United States, which became very real during the War of 1812, both the Loyalists and the French were compelled by their mutual antipathy for their southern neighbours to find some ideological basis upon which to build a nation that might survive "the pull to the south."

It is beyond the scope of this introductory chapter to discuss in any detail the British North America Act of 1867, the foundation charter of Canada. But it may be noted in passing that this fundamental instrument of government does reflect the religious struggle that had been going on between the two cultures of Canada, and in some respect it points back to the earlier frontier experiences of New England and New France. This is most clearly seen in the fact that it left to the provinces jurisdiction over municipalities, giving to Quebec the right to base local self-government on parochial experience, while Ontario could continue the New England type of local government the Loyalists had never abandoned.[4] The emphasis here seems to be on the side of isolating the two cultures of Canada into incompatible groups; yet it would be wrong not to see in this pact some common ideals; if not, there could have been no hope of the new nation surviving.

Fortunately for Canada, there are some similarities in the two cultures that have been compelled to live together in one house, affinities that can be traced back to the spiritual progenitors of the two faiths. The most conspicuous of these is an austere philosophy of life, early adopted by both New England and New France as necessary for the hard struggle of building a new civilization in the forests of North America.

The frontier also left a similar impress upon the two cultures. Both the authoritative Roman Church and the patriarchal Congregational system had to make concessions to the democratic spirit of frontier settlements. The latter is reflected in the town meeting system of New England and carried by the Loyalists to Canada; the other is the parochial system of Quebec. As the present Archbishop of Quebec has pointed out,[5] the Quebec parish is unique in the Roman Catholic world, since it permits parishioners to elect wardens who are embodied in a *fabrique*, the church council which unites both the civil and religious aspects of the community into one corporation. In these two experiments in local self-government under ecclesiastical guidance, the two racial groups of Canada gained the necessary discipline for the successful conduct of parliamentary institutions. And though a middle wall of partition has been embodied in the constitution of the country, yet enough unity has been achieved to give Canada the unique distinction of having "two subordinate nationalisms existing within a supranationalism."[6]

II

As has already been intimated, it was a schism within the English-speaking community that permitted the French Canadians to retain their own traditional way of life after the British Conquest. This schism has played almost as significant a role in Canadian development as the clash between the Reformation and the Counter-Reformation. Since it occurred within the Reformation tradition itself, it might at first sight appear to be part of the age-long conflict between the church and sect forms of religious organization.[7] To some extent it was, and as such has been made the central theme of an important book on Canadian social development.[8] There can be no question as to the significance of sectarianism in creating new cultural and religious values on the North American frontier, as all American church historians are now aware; but sectarianism never attained the same chaotic proportions in Canada as in the United States, evidenced by the fact that there are now only some thirty separate denominations listed in the Canadian census,[9] whereas there are well over three hundred still listed as active denominations in the *Handbook of Denominations in the United States*.[10]

Without, however, minimizing the significance of the clash between church and sect in the social development of Canada, it does seem that the more permanent consequences are to be found in another controversy, free or established churches, which soon overshadowed the earlier clash. The real significance of this later development lies in the fact that it is the continuation on Canadian soil of the controversy behind the American Revolution.

Up to the time of the Revolution the British government had been quite tolerant towards religious diversity in its newly acquired French colonies, as it had previously been tolerant toward religious diversity in the Thirteen Colonies. Though the Church of England had been established in Nova Scotia by the first assembly meeting at Halifax in 1758, yet this very act of establishment assured religious freedom to all dissenting bodies, with the exception of the Roman Catholics, who were shortly thereafter surreptitiously tolerated. In fact the British government in its anxiety to resettle farm lands left vacant by the expulsion of the Acadians even went so far as to subsidize the construction of Congregational and Lutheran places of worship.

It was the American Revolution that brought this spirit of tolerance or indifference towards diversity of religious beliefs to an end, and caused the British authorities to embark on an entirely new religious policy for their overseas possessions. Sectarianism had now become identified with republicanism, and Anglicanism with loyalty to the British crown; therefore, the obvious way to retain what was left of British North America after the American Revolution was to establish an imperial church to teach proper respect for British institutions. It was during this period of reassessment that the British government set up two Anglican episcopates in North America: one in Nova Scotia in 1787, and another in Quebec in 1793, thus providing rallying points for all those who were determined that American democratic ideals should not take root in Canada. It was a desperate attempt to halt an inevitable trend, but it was persisted in for almost a half-century. The ensuing controversy gave to Canadian Christianity some of its most distinctive characteristics.

III

First among these is a close affinity of politics and religion. It began with the arrival of Loyalists, who immediately moved into the centres of power and with the aid of the established Anglican Church proceeded to organize tight little oligarchies, derisively known as "Family Compacts." Apart from the selfish interests involved in the formation of these compacts, all too evident to the mass of the people, there was the sincere conviction in the Tory ranks that a graded hierarchical society was the only hope of overcoming the lawlessness and disorder that was constantly emerging on frontier settlements. So the Anglican Church and the Tory party became firmly united in a pact which had for its highest motive the preservation of the traditional values and *mores* of eighteenth-century Europe; its lowest being snobbery and selfish class interest.

The alliance of an established church with the forces of conservatism is not difficult to understand, but what is not so obvious is the close association of otherworldly sects with the reform or liberal parties that began to emerge in Canada after the arrival of the Loyalists. It is sometimes customary to trace this alliance back to the early days of Nova Scotia, when Congregationalists in defence of their township system put up a strong resistance to an Anglican parochial system centralized at Halifax.[11] This can hardly be regarded as a liberal revolt against conservatism, but rather a struggle over the relative merits of two forms of church establishment. Though the charter of religious freedom that the New Englanders won from a Nova Scotian governor became a term of reference for the reform movement led by a daring young newspaper editor in Halifax, Joseph Howe, yet the spirit of non-conformity which created the social climate for a great victory over the Family Compact in Halifax must be sought in the Newlight movement originated by a young farmer from Falmouth, Henry Alline.

The Newlight movement was a radical revolt within the Congregational church similar to one that had occurred earlier in New England; but it had its repercussions in all the churches in Nova Scotia and stimulated in them a very subjective approach to religious problems, with a consequent depreciation of authorities. In the writing of British history it has become a commonplace to emphasize the kinship between English non-conformity and nineteenth-century liberalism, but there has been little attempt to bring out the full implications of a parallel phenomenon in Canada, even though E. M. Saunders, in his *History of the Baptists of the Maritime Provinces*, gave the clue when he pointed out that what Howe was to the state, so was Alline "in the realm of religion and church life."[12]

A similar pattern soon began to unfold itself in Upper Canada where the Methodists, who were closely allied to American conferences, tended to support Canada's famous rebel, William Lyon Mackenzie. The agitation for responsible government, however, in Upper and Lower Canada was far more turbulent than in Nova Scotia, and the ideals set forth by its leaders bear closer resemblance to Jacksonian democracy than British liberalism. But after two abortive rebellions in 1837 and 1838, the reform movement in the Canadas began to adopt the patient legal and parliamentary procedures that characterized Joseph Howe's crusade in Nova Scotia.

Since so many of the issues debated during the struggle for responsible government were closely related to church establishment, all denominations felt compelled to declare themselves politically. The Roman Catholic hierarchy was at first inclined to remain aloof from what it considered a domestic quarrel within the English-speaking family; but when it found that many of its own adherents were becoming imbued with American republicanism, it felt compelled to speak out on the side of the Tories, particularly after the rebellion of 1837. It remained firmly allied with the Conservative party until long after Confederation. The Presbyterians were usually divided in their political allegiance; the adherents of the established Church of Scotland being on the whole favourably disposed to the Tory party, while dissenting Presbyterians usually favoured the reform parties. A good many Methodists under the influence of British Wesleyanism deserted the reform movement to give their support to a moderate conservatism.

IV

One result of this intimate association of religion and politics has been to give Canadian church leaders a deep sense of responsibility for the national welfare of their country. Both in the formation of the federal constitution and the extension of the original four provinces westward, Canadian churchmen have played a conspicuous role. From the very beginning of Confederation they helped to give a substantial reality to an artificially contrived nation by fashioning their own indigenous church structures in accordance with the new national boundaries that began to take form after 1867. But what was more important, they actively co-operated in bringing about a *modus vivendi* between the two warring cultures that found themselves compelled to work together peaceably if Canada were to survive.

Next to Confederation, the opening up of the west ranks as one of Canada's greatest accomplishments, and not the least achievement of the Canadian churches has been the keeping abreast with Canada's immigrant population on the western frontier. In some respects it was the churches that prepared the way for Canadian administration of the northwest; for, long before the Canadian government felt ready to take over the responsibility from the Hudson's Bay Company of administering this difficult terrain, the churches were in continuous contact with frontier needs and conditions. When, finally, the Canadian government took over the control of the northwest, it was the missionaries, long familiar with the ways and manners of the Indians and Eskimos, who acted as intermediaries between the Canadian rulers and their new subjects. And when the half-breeds or *metis* were provoked into rebellion it was the Roman Catholic Bishop Taché and the Anglican Bishop Machray who followed the path of moderation while hotheads were courting disaster.

In view of this persistent interaction between church and state it appears self-evident that any comprehensive understanding of Canadian society and culture depends as much upon a familiarity with the religious as with the political history of Canada. Perhaps in no country in the world has the maintenance of the ties of nation depended so much upon the "maintenance of a system of ecclesiastical control."[13] In short, to know the Canadian community, it is of vital importance to know the Canadian churches.

REFERENCES

1. S. D. Clark, *Church and Sect in Canada* (Toronto, 1948), preface.
2. *Vide* R. G. Thwaites, ed., *The Jesuit Relations and Allied Documents* (Cleveland, 1896-1901, 73 vols), vol. 1, p. 133.
3. *Vide* article by A. R. M. Lower, "Religion and Religious Institutions" in *Canada* (United Nations Series, Toronto, 1950), ed. by George W. Brown, p. 459.
4. *Vide* article by K. G. Crawford, "Local Government" in *Canada* (United Nations Series), *op. cit.*, pp. 314-330.
5. Maurice Roy, *The Parish and Democracy in French Canada* (Toronto, 1950), p. 17.
6. W. S. Wallace, *The Growth of Canadian National Feeling* (Toronto, 1927), p. 13.
7. For a detailed study of these two forms of religious organization *vide* Ernest Troeltsch, *The Social Teachings of the Christian Churches* (trans. by Olive Wyon, London, 1931, 2 vols.).
8. S. D. Clark, *Church and Sect in Canada, op. cit.*

9. The Canadian Census has ignored some very small sects.   The registration forms at the Prairie Bible Institute, Three Hills, Alberta, indicate a student body representative of 47 religious denominations or sects.   W. E. Mann in his study of *Sect, Cult, and Church in Alberta* (Toronto, 1955) has identified 35 fundamentalist sects in Alberta, p. 30.

10. F. S. Mead, *Handbook of Denominations in the United States* (New York and Nashville, 1951).

11. *Vide* D. C. Harvey, *The Struggle for the New England Form of Township Government in Nova Scotia* (Report of the Canadian Historical Association, Ottawa, 1933).

12. E. M. Saunders, *History of the Baptists of the Maritime Provinces* (Halifax, 1902), p. 23.

13. *Vide* article by S. D. Clark, "The Canadian Community," in *Canada* (United Nations Series), *op. cit.*, pp. 375-389.

II

Religious Background

THE STORY of religion in Canada necessarily begins in sixteenth-century Europe where John Calvin and Ignatius Loyola outlined the unyielding dogmas that created "Canada's Problem." If we accept these two men as the spiritual progenitors of the two antithetical systems that early evolved on the American continent, it will be important to notice their similarities as well as their differences, for it is their mutual agreements that have made possible, to some extent, the present accommodation of Protestant and Catholic in Canada. As a matter of fact there are striking resemblances in the careers and purposes of Calvin and Loyola. Both of them were greatly concerned over the religious void in Europe that followed upon the collapse of the Medieval church. They were both equally determined to restore the values of an earlier day and they recommended a revival of asceticism as one way of achieving their goal.[1] Though there are important differences in Calvinistic and Ignatian asceticisms, yet their ultimate effects in the New World were strikingly similar, and the Province of Quebec today has as large a legacy of blue laws as any New England state.

Again, Loyola and Calvin were at one in their abhorrence of the scepticism of the Renaissance, but their reaction to it was different; and it is in their divergent responses to the challenge of sixteenth-century scepticism that the deepest cleavage between the Reformation and the Counter-Reformation emerges—particularly on the American continent. Loyola regarded the spirit of intellectual curiosity the Renaissance had engendered as the real enemy of the religious spirit[2] and he sought to repress it by the re-establishment of an hierarchical church whose pronouncements were to be accepted without question, even if it should assert that "white was black."[3] Calvin, because of the assurance that had come to him through "justification by faith," felt free to allow his great intellectual powers full scope. His followers in New England did likewise, and as a consequence Harvard College, founded in 1636, was soon producing scholars with an international reputation for creative thinking; while New France, carefully shielded from all "heretical thought," produced little native scholarship to compare with that of New England.

It would, however, be an oversimplification of our European background to regard Loyola and Calvin, alone, as the chief sources of the two cultures that grew up in constant rivalry to one another in the New World; for it was by no means a pure Ignatianism that finally emerged in New France, nor a pure Calvinism that took root in New England. The former had been mediated to New France through the crucible of French piety, best exemplified in a Fénelon or a François de Sales which greatly soften the harsher aspects of Spanish mysticism. It was this great-hearted piety of French mysticism that inspired an unusual devotion to the welfare of the aborigines who came under the French rule. Calvinism reached New England through the medium of English Separatism in which it acquired a social irresponsibility that led almost to the complete extermination of the Indians. In this further contrast of the two systems, the laurels must go to New France rather than to New England.

I

Of significant importance to the ecclesiastical history of French Canada is the great religious revival of seventeenth-century France. This revival drew heavily upon Spanish mysticism for its inspiration, and from the same source that brought about the Ignatian revival throughout Roman Catholic Europe. But it is necessary to draw a distinction between the thoroughly-drilled and well-organized attempt of the Ignatian Order to reimpose upon the social life of Europe the world view of the Medieval Church, and the more mystical piety found in the writings of St. Teresa of Avila and St. John of the Cross.[4] These contain far more intense mysticism than that practised by the Jesuits, and there is a spontaneity about it lacking in the *Spiritual Exercises* of St. Ignatius, particularly in the practice of mental prayer. This mental prayer became the germ of a mystical theology which was carried to France by Anne of Jesus, who was just as saintly and strong willed as St. Teresa.

St. Teresa's works had been read in France by a Madame Acarie, who was instrumental in stirring up a great interest in the work of the Reformed Carmelites of Spain. Her home became the centre of a religious revival[5] and with the co-operation of St. François de Sales she decided to get a branch of the Reformed Carmelites established in Paris. De Marillac, the Chancellor of France, was persuaded to give some assistance. With this semi-official approval Madame Acarie set sail for Spain in 1603 to study the life of the Reformed Carmelite Order at its source. On this visit she met Anne of Jesus, whom she persuaded to come to Paris in company with her Carmelite sisters to give direction to the new religious life that was obviously coming to birth in France.

It was not to Madame Acarie, however, that the title "the French Teresa" was given by Bossuet, but to a member of the teaching order of the Ursulines, none other than Madame Martin, better known to French Canadians as Marie de l'Incarnation. Since so much of Madame Martin's career is bound up with the early development of church life in New France it is sometimes forgotten that she was one of the more important figures in a spiritual revival in old France. As a young widow she had had an unusual religious experience which led her to abandon her ten-year-old son to the care of a monastery and enter the Ursuline convent at Tours, where she assumed the name Marie de l'Incarnation. It was here that she became acquainted with Madame de la Peltrie, with whom she was to share so many vicissitudes on the shores of the St. Lawrence.

Vincent de Paul, one of the most notable products of the mystical revival in France, was a close friend of these two women. His greatest contribution to the revival was in the realm of social welfare, since the poor and the sick were his constant concern. The members of the Confraternity of Charity, which he founded in 1617, were to be practitioners of the mystical way of life, since they were to care for the souls of men as well as their bodies.[6] In preparing his novices for their two-fold task, St. Vincent de Paul insisted that they must become intimately acquainted with St. François de Sales' *Introduction à la Vie Dévote*, a book of mystical piety still treasured by the Sisters of Charity in French Canada.

It was out of this religious ferment, standing in such utter contrast to the political and economic life of seventeenth-century France, that the real drive came for the evangelization of the aborigines of Canada. When this project was, to a large extent, frustrated by the fury of the

Iroquois Indians, the missionaries turned to the task of building model Catholic states, based upon French colonization, both in Acadia and in the St. Lawrence Valley.

II

The religious background of English-speaking Canada is far more complicated and varied than that of French Canada. As has already been intimated, the early colonists in America even including the Anglicans in Virginia were very Calvinistic in outlook, but Calvinism is a mosaic of many colours. It was perhaps less emphasized in the Anglican Church than in most of the reformed churches in Europe, but even here it had strong representatives who were to take the lead in trying to overthrow the Elizabethan religious settlement worked out during the years of uncertainty in England after the national church had broken with Rome in the reign of Henry VIII.

The system of church government which these dissenters, or Puritans, as they were generally called, advocated during Elizabeth's reign was similar to a form that had been introduced into Scotland by the acceptance of Knox's *Book of Discipline* in 1560. They were also strict on matters of Sabbath observance and were constantly heard denouncing the immoralities and extravagances of the time. Most of them had no thought of doing away with an established state church or even of creating a schism.

However, there were among them some radicals who advocated the absolute independence of each congregation of believers. Most of these separatists were compelled to flee the country, taking refuge in Holland where, under the leadership of Henry Ainsworth, they put forth in 1596 a separatist creed.[7]

Ainsworth's first company was greatly disrupted by one of its members, John Smyth, who had come under the influence of some disciples of Arminius, the great critic of rigid Calvinism. These had led Smyth to the opinion "that valid baptism demands the assent of contemporaneous personal faith in the recipient."[8] Smyth now felt compelled to start a new congregation by baptizing first himself and then all those of Ainsworth's community who held the same opinion as himself. Thus began a long era of controversy, disruption and persecution within the ranks of Puritanism, passing from Amsterdam to England and thence to New England, echoes of which could still be heard as the New

Englanders began to emigrate to Nova Scotia after the expulsion of the Acadians.

Ainsworth took the initiative in disrupting the Amsterdam company by expelling Smyth's group from his church. The excommunicates returned to England in 1612 and established at Newgate, London, the first Arminian (General) Baptist Church of England, a church to be distinguished from the Calvinistic (Particularistic) Baptist Church which separated from an Independent Congregation at Southwark, England, in 1633. Both these congregations sent representatives to America and helped to create the religious turmoil that became so characteristic of all frontier settlements.

It wasn't long after the departure of Smyth and his followers that Ainsworth found himself out of sympathy with the majority of his congregation in the matter of church government and discipline. The majority, under the leadership of Francis Johnson, had reached the conclusion that the presbytery of elders constituted the church, and that "tell it to the church" meant "tell it to the elders."[9] Though Ainsworth had opposed this move towards what became known as the Presbyterian polity and seemed to favour a more democratic form of church government, yet he did not wish to be regarded as favouring a popular form of secular government, since he is credited with saying, "If the multitude govern, then who shall be governed?"[10]—a sentiment that was re-echoed by the famous New England divine, John Cotton. By leaving the issue between "the freedom of the membership" and "the autocracy of the elders" rather ambiguous, Ainsworth set the stage for a long-drawn-out controversy in the New England colonies.

In Leyden, however, there was another experiment in church government that was having a far more peaceful time than the one in neighbouring Amsterdam. Here was a congregation of English refugees who had wholeheartedly repudiated the idea that the elders were the church. According to the leader of this group, John Robinson, the function of eldership was the moral one of leading the membership in its action. It is to John Robinson that the meticulous historian of Congregationalism, H. M. Dexter, gives the honour of working out the Congregational church system that finally prevailed in the New England colonies. This seems to have been a precarious balance between Presbyterianism and extreme Separatism and was diligently expounded by John Cotton while acting as Teacher of the First Church in Boston, Massachusetts.[11]

The triumph of Puritanism in England during the Commonwealth regime under Cromwell only added to the difficulties of the New Englanders in their attempt to create for their new Zion a universal church polity. It was during this regime that there emerged numerous small sects, such as Millenarians, Quakers, Seekers, Levellers, etc., representatives of which were to find their way across the ocean to America and add to the religious diversity of the New World.

III

After the triumph of the Puritan cause in England, it was the Anglicans who began to leave the country in great numbers; some of them to settle in Virginia, Maryland and the Carolinas. Since the descendants of these settlers were to make up a large proportion of the Loyalist immigration to Canada, Anglican church development in the Thirteen Colonies is significantly related to Canadian church history.

As a matter of fact, the Church of England was conducting missionary work in America some time before the arrival of the Puritans. The chartered company which founded the Virginia Plantations (1607) attempted to provide for the religious needs of the settlers and to conduct missions to the Indians. Nicholas Ferrar, of Little Gidding fame,[12] who represented a more vigorous form of Anglicanism than that which survived the Cromwellian regime, was the man most responsible for this missionary effort. With the restoration of the Stuarts, the missionary zeal of Anglicanism seems to have disappeared for the time being, while the trading companies chartered under royal patronage had little thought for anything else than trade and profits.

The Virginia episode, however, is relevant to our story, as it established an Anglican tradition in North America which greatly influenced Anglican church development in Canada. This tradition was created chiefly by loyal Anglicans who had fled to Virginia during the Commonwealth era in England. One of these refugees wrote a pamphlet entitled *Virginia's Cure* in which he urged upon the bishop of London, who was in charge of all overseas churches, the necessity of sending out a bishop to America. Unfortunately for the Church of England in America, this suggestion was never taken seriously by the responsible authorities in England.

The bishop of London, however, attempted to give some authoritative leadership to the American church by appointing James Blair his commissary in Virginia (1690); later he appointed Thomas Bray to a similar post in Maryland (1696). With these appointments the commissary became the most important Anglican official in the American colonies until the establishment of an episcopate after the Revolution.[13]

Not much was achieved by the Anglicans in the way of extension until the rise of what has been designated "the Religious Society Movement of late seventeenth-century England." This was a religious revival in reaction to the "infamous clubs of Atheists, Deists, and Socinians,"[14] a precursor of a much greater revival under the leadership of John Wesley.

One of the leading spirits of the movement was Thomas Bray, the bishop of London's commissary in Maryland. Having learned at first hand of the dire need in the colonies for religious instruction, he organized the Society for the Promotion of Christian Knowledge (S.P.C.K.) with the object of building up parochial libraries. He also helped in organizing a Society for the Propagation of the Gospel in Foreign Parts (S.P.G.), as an adjunct to the S.P.C.K. It was also due to his efforts that this society received a royal charter (1701), thus securing for Anglican missionary work in North America a semi-official status.[15]

Very early in its career the S.P.G. began to agitate for an episcopate in North America, and it seemed so close to its goal in 1711 that an episcopal residence was set up at Burlington, New Jersey. In the midst of the negotiations Queen Anne, who had favoured the project, died (1715); and with the accession of George I the plan was quietly dropped. Puritan opposition to the appointment of a colonial bishop, particularly vehement in New England, may have had something to do with the government's failure to provide an episcopate for the church in America.

After the outbreak of the American Revolution the British authorities began to look more favourably upon a church that was unusually loyal to Tory principles. But it was too late to make amends for their former neglect. What remained of Anglicanism in America at the conclusion of the war was in desperate straits, since it was impossible for prospective candidates for the ministry in the separated colonies to be ordained in England unless they took an oath of allegiance to the British Crown. The archbishop of Canterbury was now ready to solve the problem by consecrating an American priest as bishop, but this could only be done with the approval of Parliament, which was not immediately forthcoming. The impasse was finally broken when Dr. Samuel Seabury of Connecticut proceeded to Aberdeen, Scotland, where on November 14, 1784, he was consecrated by three non-juring bishops of Scotland. Shortly after this consecration the British government passed the necessary legislation for the consecration of bishops outside of England (1787), making it possible to set up Anglican episcopates in Canada at the time of the Loyalist immigration.

IV

Scotch Presbyterianism, early upon the scene in British Canada, was long plagued by internal divisions inherited from various phases of the Scottish reformation. The first phase of this reformation was very similar to the Anglican revolt against the Medieval papacy; then it moved on to a more extreme form of Calvinism. The particular phase most relevant to Canadian church history belongs to an era of unrest connected with the church settlement that followed upon the advent of William and Mary to the throne of England (1688).

A great many members of the Church of Scotland were dissatisfied with this settlement because the sovereign had not subscribed to the Solemn League and Covenant. These dissidents formed themselves into societies of protest which came together in 1743 to create the Reformed Presbyterian Church of Scotland.[16] The most serious secession from the ranks of the established church occurred when Ebenezer Erskine, at the opening of the Synod of Perth and Stirling (1732), denounced the prevailing slackness of church discipline. Being deposed by the General Assembly, he secured enough followers to form an independent Associate Presbytery in 1733. This presbytery may be regarded as an evangelical revolt within the established Church of Scotland, similar to the contemporaneous Wesleyan revolt within the Church of England and the Newlight Movement of Jonathan Edwards within the framework of New England Congregationalism. It was chiefly missionaries from evangelical Presbyterianism that first appeared upon the scene in Canada, but not before the evangelical movement in Scotland had been severed into two wings. The division occurred over the matter of an oath required of citizens of corporate towns by the British authorities after the abortive Rebellion of 1745. Since the oath insisted upon an allegiance to "the true religion presently professed within this realm" and a repudiation of "the Roman religion called papistry," a good many adherents of the Associate Synod felt that it involved an acknowledgment of the Church of Scotland as the true religion of the country, and refused to take it. The non-jurors formed a separate group called the General Associate Synod, but more frequently known as the Anti-Burgher. The majority of the Associate Synod were of the opinion that the oath in dispute was hardly more than a conventional repudiation of the Roman Church and were willing to take it; for thus acceding to the government demand, they were dubbed Burghers. Shortly after this disruption, both the Burghers and Anti-Burghers began to send missionaries to North America, where they still continued to debate the merits of their respective points of view.

There remains to note still one more secession from the Church of Scotland, the Relief Presbytery, whose representatives in Canada also contributed to the din of controversy within the ranks of Canadian Presbyterianism. The Relief Presbytery originated out of a dispute caused by church authorities forcing unacceptable ministers upon protesting congregations. In 1752 Thomas Gillespie refused to take part in such a proceeding, and this led to his being ousted from the ministry of the Church of Scotland. Those ministers who agreed with Gillespie's remonstrance united to form a new presbytery (1761), assuming the name Relief, as its members were prepared to provide relief for "oppressed congregations."

An even more serious disruption over this same issue of forcing ministers upon protesting congregations occurred in the Church of Scotland in 1843, when Thomas Chalmers led a large following into the wilderness to form the Free Church of Scotland; but this is an event that may be considered integral to Canadian church history rather than to its religious background.

Not all Scots who came to Canada belonged to the Protestant churches. In the Highlands there remained a good many adherents of the Roman Catholic Church, whose faith had been sustained by intrepid Jesuit missionaries, though as late as the reign of Queen Anne "the offer of 500 marks for the capture of a priest or a Jesuit"[17] still remained upon the statute books of Great Britain. This church also followed its adherents to Canada and was to play a conspicuous role in the field of education both in Nova Scotia and Ontario.

V

Passing on to Ireland, we find a religious situation almost as confused as that of Scotland, producing even more bitter controversy in Canada than any of the religious heritages we have yet encountered in this review. Irish Roman Catholics who came to America carried with them bitter memories of Protestant persecution extending back to the Cromwellian regime and beyond. The period that most immediately concerns Canadian church history begins with the reign of William and Mary when there was introduced into the British Parliament a series of penal laws that were even increased during the reigns of Queen Anne and George II.[18] These laws literally reduced the Irish to "idleness and neglect of agriculture," and caused the flower of the nation to flee to the continent of Europe and to North America. Coupled with this attempt to destroy the economic life of the country was the endeavour to obliterate Irish learning and culture through the suppression of schools and the destruction of precious manuscripts. Though "hedge schools" secretly taught by lay teachers under the direction of priests did much to retain some relics of literacy among the peasants, most Irish parents who could afford it sent their children abroad for education, which accounts for the numerous eighteenth-century Irish schools conducted in Spain, Portugal, France, and the Netherlands.

The peopling of Ulster with Scotch and English Protestants during the reign of James I (1603-1625) led to cruel outrages upon one another by both Roman Catholics and Protestants in Ireland. Naturally, the Irish resented being dispossessed of their patrimony by these Protestant intruders, and tried to make life for them as difficult as possible. The Protestants, in turn, organized into bands known as the "Peep o' Day Boys," and began to carry out surreptitious raids upon their tormentors. Later (1795) they organized the Orange Lodge, whose members took an oath to exterminate Catholics as far as lay in their power. In answer to this threat the Roman Catholics brought into being an organization known as the United Irishmen, for the purpose of retaliation against the Orangemen. Both these orders found their way to Canada where they continued their rough and noisy quarrels, particularly during the celebrations of St. Patrick's Day and the Battle of the Boyne.[19]

The Scottish Presbyterians of Northern Ireland also held a particular grievance against the established Church of England and Ireland. They had failed to be included in the favoured position that had been granted during the reign of William and Mary to their co-religionists in Scotland, and were still subject to the legal disabilities imposed upon the non-conformists of England. Because of these disadvantages and other irritations, a large number of Irish Presbyterians emigrated to America in the eighteenth century; some of them found their way from Pennsylvania to Nova Scotia.   During the American Revolution their sympathies were on the side of the rebels.[20]

VI

Our review of the religious background of Canada would hardly be complete without some reference to the contribution of continental Europe. The most influential of these Europeans were the German Lutherans, some of whom arrived in Nova Scotia shortly after the founding of Halifax (1749). Others came from the United States, having fought on the losing side in the War of Independence and found themselves classed among the Tories in the United States. But not all the Germans were Lutherans; a great variety of German sects also reached Canada *via* the United States.

The reason for the migration of large numbers of Germans to British America in the late seventeenth and early eighteenth centuries may be attributed to the evil effects of the Thirty Years' War (1618-1648), a so-called religious war, perhaps one of the most brutal and economically destructive in all history.[21] The religious fervour behind it had almost disappeared towards its close, but in the beginning the avowed object on the part of the Roman Catholics was the destruction of Protestantism, while the Protestants in turn were determined to obliterate Catholicism from the face of the earth. The Treaty of Westphalia (1648) which brought this war of "unlimited ends" to a close was to create an era of religious toleration; yet individual princes were still inclined to interfere with the liberty of their subjects, and America appeared as the only hope of religious freedom to many oppressed groups. Moreover, the larger church groups such as the Lutherans, Reformed, and Roman Catholics showed little inclination to tolerate sectarian groups of Mennonites, Dunkers, Quakers, and numerous other dissenting bodies that had originated during the days of religious and civil turmoil. William Penn's state of religious freedom beckoned to these as well as to the larger denominations caught within the confines of an unfriendly principality. Nevertheless, during the War of Independence a good many of these continental emigrés remained loyal to the British Crown, thus becoming once more the victims of persecution and compelled to seek new homes in Canada.

There remains for consideration still another religious body from the continent of Europe which has played a prominent role in Canadian history. The Calvinists or Huguenots of France have had representatives in Canada from earliest days to the present time. Their early migration to America, particularly to Florida and Brazil, resulted only in their massacre by the fanatical Spaniards.[22] At the close of the Wars of Religion in France (1598), and with the Edict of Nantes, it looked as if the days of persecution were at an end.

It was during these favourable circumstances that several French Protestants gained valuable privileges for trading and colonization in North America.[23] One of these, M. Chauvin, in association with Pont-Gravé, a merchant of St. Malo, was given the exclusive right to trade in furs in America on the stipulation that he transport five hundred French colonists to the New World. Out of this agreement originated an attempt to found a French colony at Tadoussac on the lower St. Lawrence. Most of the settlers were Huguenots, but few of them survived the rigours of this northern latitude. Other almost equally abortive settlements under Huguenot leadership were attempted on the Bay of Fundy. A Huguenot, Sieur de Monts, a gentleman in ordinary of the King's chamber and a governor of Paris, was closely associated with Samuel de Champlain both at Port Royal and Quebec. Other Huguenots who played a prominent role in early French colonizations are De Caens, the Kirkes, and Charles and Claude de la Tour, names familiar to the students of French Canada.

The immigration of Huguenots to Canada was brought to an end by Cardinal Richelieu, the chief minister of France during the reign of Louis XIII. It was now France's policy that none but Frenchmen, and those Roman Catholics, were to be allowed to settle in New France, a policy that became even more rigid under Louis XIV.

Finally, in 1685 came the revocation of the Edict of Nantes and renewal of persecution in France, forcing hundreds of thousands of French Protestants to seek shelter in neighbouring European countries and in America.[24] After the British Conquest a great many of these displaced persons found their way to Canada once more, particularly to Nova Scotia, where along with the German Lutherans and Reformed they were quickly assimilated into the English-speaking cultural group.

THE CHRISTIAN CHURCH IN CANADA

REFERENCES

1. Ignatius wrote ". . . we must above all endeavour to establish in ourselves a complete indifference towards all created things, though the use of them may not be otherwise forbidden . . ." *Vide Manresa* or the *Spiritual Exercises of St. Ignatius* (London and New York, New Edition, n.d.), p. 20.
Cf. John Calvin, *Institutes of the Christian Religion* (trans. by John Allen, Philadelphia, 1848, 2 vols., 4th American ed., n.d.), I, pp. 68-69.

2. *Vide* H. D. Sedgwick, *Ignatius Loyola* (New York, 1923), p. 69.

3. *Ibid.*, p. 61.

4. *Vide* E. A. Peers, *Studies of the Spanish Mystics* (London, 1927, 2 vols.), I, pp. 25 *et seq.*

5. The story of this revival is well told by Henri Bremond, *Histoire Litteraire du Sentiment Religieux en France* (Paris, 1923, 6 tomes).
Vide also Lucy Menzies, *Mirrors of the Holy* (Oxford, 1928), pp. 229 *et. seq.*

6. *Vide* C. A. Jones, *The Life of St. Vincent de Paul* (London, n.d.), especially pp. 60-61.

7. The story of Congregationalism is fully told by H. M. Dexter, *Congregationalism of the Last Three Hundred Years as Seen in Its Literature* (New York, 1880).

8. *Ibid.*, p. 318.

9. *Ibid.*, p. 352.

10. *Ibid.*, p. 354.

11. *Vide* T. J. Wertenbaker, *The Puritan Oligarchy* (New York and London, 1947), p. 21.

12. *Vide* A. L. Maycock, *Nicholas Ferrar of Little Gidding* (London, 1938), p. 70.

13. *Vide* A. L. Cross, *The Anglican Episcopate in the American Colonies* (New York, 1902).

14. C. F. Pascoe, *Two Hundred Years of the S.P.G.* (London, 1902, 2 vols.), I, p. 2.

15. A copy of the original charter of the S.P.G. is to be found in C. F. Pascoe, *op. cit.*, II, pp. 932-938.

16. A useful reference work on Christianity in Scotland is Sir Thomas Raleigh's *Annals of the Church in Scotland* (Oxford, 1921).
William Gregg's *History of the Presbyterian Church in the Dominion of Canada* (Toronto, 1885) gives a brief summary of the religious background of Presbyterianism in Canada.

17. T. Raleigh, *op. cit.*, p. 285.

18. A good account of religious controversies in Ireland is to be found in Julius Pokorny's *A History of Ireland* (trans. by Dr. Deana D. King, London, New York, and Toronto, 1933).

19. For a sympathetic account of these clashes *vide* William Perkins Bull, *From the Boyne to Brampton* (Toronto, 1936), *passim.*

20. *Vide* I. F. Mackinnon, *Settlements and Churches in Nova Scotia* (Halifax and Montreal, 1930), pp. 92-97.

21. For a bitter estimate of the consequences of the Thirty Years' War *vide* H. A. L. Fisher, *A History of Europe* (London, 1935, 3 vols.), II, chap. XVII.

22. For a detailed study of the religious struggle between Catholic and Huguenot in France and America *vide* H. M. Baird, *History of the Rise of the Huguenots* (London, 1880, 2 vols.), especially pp. 199-202.

23. *Vide* F. X. Garneau, *History of Canada* (trans. by A. Bell, Toronto and Sydney, Nova Scotia, 1876, 3rd ed., revised, 2 vols.), I, p. 71 *et seq.*

24. *Vide* W. H. Foote, *The Huguenots* (Richmond, Va., 1870), part III, "Huguenots at Home in America."

III

The Beginnings of Christianity in Canada

THE YEAR Jacques Cartier sailed up the St. Lawrence River as far as Hochelaga (Montreal) may well be considered Canada's birth year. It was this second voyage of 1535 that first brought to the view of the French public the prospect of building a French empire in the interior of North America through the conversion of the aborigines to the Roman Catholic faith. Already the French had become intensely interested in the Indians of North America through contact with the captives Cartier had taken back to France in 1534.[1] No doubt commercial interests were dominant in the minds of those who first began to plan a permanent occupation of North America, and the exploitation of the Indians as primary producers, particularly in the fur trade, loomed large in all such planning.[2] Yet, in the writings of Samuel de Champlain, who was early associated with Sieur de Monts in founding colonies in North America, there appears a genuine interest in the moral and spiritual welfare of the original inhabitants of the continent.

In his memoirs he states that when he found the aborigines "living without God and without religion like brute beasts, I thereupon concluded in my private judgment that I should be committing a great sin if I did not make it my business to devise some means of bringing them to the knowledge of God."[3] His interest coincided with an unusual outburst of religious zeal in seventeenth-century France, much of which became concentrated on the conversion of the Indians of North America.

This zeal was embodied in a charter granted in 1604 to Sieur de Monts, in which it was stipulated among other things that in return for a monopoly of the fur trade in Acadia he was to propagate the Roman Catholic faith among the Indians.[4] Baron de Poutrincourt, who continued to administer Acadia from Port Royal (Lower Granville, Nova Scotia) after de Monts and Champlain had in 1608 transferred their interest to the St. Lawrence region, tried to discharge his religious obligation by bringing out from France a secular priest, Jessé Fléché, as a missionary to the Micmacs.[5]   There is some evidence that this priest was a little hasty in baptizing Indians; according to one Jesuit chronicler, he yielded to a thoughtless zeal and baptized a hundred savages without having sufficiently instructed and tested them.[6] His first convert, however, the Sagamore Membertou, was held in the highest respect by Fléché's successors, the Jesuits.

I

From the beginning of French colonization in North America, the Jesuits were impatient to undertake a missionary enterprise among the Indians, but they were to meet serious opposition from the Huguenot merchants who were financing the expeditions. These merchants well knew that their days were numbered if they allowed the Society of Jesus an entrance into their trading preserves. Their fears were lucidly expressed by Marc Lescarbot, a French lawyer who had spent a year at Port Royal (1606) in company with Pont-Gravé, second in command to Sieur de Monts and Champlain. In a report to the Queen Mother he describes rather fulsomely the missionary activity of Jessé Fléché and suggests that for the present at least there is no need in Canada for such learned doctors as the Jesuits, "who may be more useful in combatting vices and heresies at home."[7] His real opposition to sending out Jesuits is revealed, however, in his comment that "there is a certain class of men in whom we cannot have complete confidence, who are in the habit of censoring everything that is not in harmony with their maxims and wish to rule wherever they are."[8]

The plea of this early historian of Canada was in vain; partisans of the Jesuits, through the influence of the Queen Mother herself, were in a dominant position at the French court, and were resolved to put their favourites in control of the missionary work in North America. Though the Huguenot merchants were determined not to transport members of the hated order to Acadia, they were finally outwitted by a lady of honour to the queen, the Marchioness de Guercheville, who proclaimed herself "the patroness of American missions."[9] She then proceeded to buy up the dormant rights of Sieur de Monts in Acadia, and thus forced Poutrincourt to find passage to Port Royal for two Jesuit priests, Pierre Biard and Ennemond Massé. She also succeeded in compelling Poutrincourt's son, Biencourt, who for a time represented his father at Port

Royal, to provide subsistence for the missionaries out of the revenue from the fisheries and fur trade. As Lescarbot in his history points out, this levy was a severe strain upon the slender resources of the infant colony; he felt that "if a contribution of a seignorial nature were due to anyone, it certainly was due to Poutrincourt, and not to the Jesuits, who could not subsist without him."[10]

Even after gaining her way in the matter of subsistence for the missionaries, the marchioness was still dissatisfied with the co-operation she was receiving from the authorities at Port Royal, so she decided to establish a colony of her own firmly based upon an ecclesiastical foundation. Consequently there arrived at Port Royal in 1613 a small vessel under the command of a courtier, Saussaye, bearing forty-eight sailors and colonists, and accompanied by two Jesuit missionaries, Father Quentin and Brother Gilbert du Thet. The latter carried with him a royal commission "to establish a new settlement in a suitable place and to have a sufficient number of colonists to protect it."[11] Though the colonists at Port Royal expressed strong opposition to this new adventure, Fathers Biard and Massé immediately joined Saussaye's company, which proceeded to the Penobscot River in what is now the state of Maine, where a new colony named Saint-Sauveur arose on the Island of Mount Desert. But scarcely had the work of fortification begun when there appeared on the horizon a well-armed English ship from Virginia which immediately proceeded to bombard the fort. During the bombardment Brother du Thet was killed, being the first of a long list of Jesuit casualties in the attempt to build a French Catholic empire in North America.[12]

Captain Samuel Argall, in command of the English ship, carried most of the colonists back to Virginia as prisoners. When the governor of this first English colony in America learned that the French were trespassing beyond the forty-fifth parallel of north latitude, he became so indignant that he immediately sent Captain Argall back to Acadia to destroy all the French coastal forts.[13] These orders were scrupulously carried out, even to the extent of erasing what remained of an abandoned French settlement at St. Croix, as well as Port Royal. Thus early began a long and acrimonious struggle between the French and English settlers in the New World.

At the time the French colonists were more inclined to lay the blame for their misfortunes on the Jesuits than on the English, particularly when they saw Biard among their enemies. In this they were probably being unfair to the Jesuit priest, who had been compelled by his captors to guide them to Port Royal.   Nevertheless, for the time being the Society of Jesus was completely discredited in the eyes of the colonists, and it was over a decade before it was allowed to resume missionary work in New France.

II

Champlain, however, refused to give up the attempt to convert the Indians.   He still felt that it would be a great sin if he did not make it his business to find suitable missionaries to carry on the work that had already been started by the Jesuits.   To attain this end, he says, "I exerted myself to find some good friars, with a zeal and affection for the glory, whom I might persuade to send or come themselves with me to this country to try to plant there the faith."[14]   His search finally led him to the Récollets, a reformed branch of the Franciscan Order, who were ready to take up the challenge as presented to them by Champlain.

In 1615 three Récollet fathers, Denis Jamay, Jean d'Olbeau, Joseph le Caron and a lay brother, Pacifique du Plessis arrived at Quebec to initiate an ambitious missionary enterprise.[15]   Father Jamay, the commissary of the company, set up headquarters at Quebec and began to assign various Indian tribes to his colleagues.   Father d'Olbeau was sent to Tadoussac to seek out the Montaignais, who along with the Moskapi occupied most of the northern sections of what is now the Province of Quebec.   It was these Indians that the early French explorers had first met in Canada, but it was soon discovered that they were not the most promising subjects for conversion, as they stood lowest in the cultural scale of all the North American Indians.

Adjoining the Montaignais in the east were the Algonquins, who became the particular interest of Father Jamay himself.   Closely allied with the Algonquins were the Malecites, who lived along the St. John River in the present Province of New Brunswick, but also wandered over to the shores of the St. Lawrence, opposite Tadoussac, and even penetrated into the present state of Maine where they joined with several Algonquin tribes to form a loose confederacy known as the Abenaki.

Because of the migratory habits of these tribes, the Récollet fathers early began to despair of their conversion.   To add to their discouragement was a discovery made earlier by Father Biard that these coastal Indians were totally unprepared to understand even the rudiments of Christianity.[16]   In a letter to his provincial in Paris, Father Biard explains the difficulty of teaching Christian truths to Micmacs whose language lacked such words as fidelity, justice, mercy, and other abstract symbols.[17]   Such a lack was even more noticeable among the tribes with whom the Récollets first came into contact.   As a matter of fact none of the Canadian Indians, who numbered only some 220,000 in the seventeenth century,[18] had advanced beyond a neolithic type of culture before the arrival of the white man.   Life on the material side was about the same as northern Europe around 2000 B.C.

After a brief encounter with these migratory bands, the Récollets decided they must seek out tribes with more sedentary habits.   The nearest were the Iroquois, who dwelt in fairly well-organized settlements in the basins of the Genesee and Mohawk Rivers.   However, Champlain had early antagonized these Indians by giving aid to an Algonquin attack upon them.   Since the Iroquois were now the implacable enemy of the French, the missionaries began to look farther west to the Hurons, who had early become the middlemen in the French fur trade with the western Indians.

The Hurons, allied in origin and language to the Iroquois, dwelt in several large villages between Lake Simcoe and the Georgian Bay of Lake Huron.   They appeared at first inaccessible to the French missionaries; nevertheless Father Jamay assigned the Hurons to Father le Caron as the latter's particular field of endeavour; so, in the autumn of 1615 this intrepid priest joined a party of trading Hurons and proceeded with them as far west as the village of Carhagouha on the Penetanguishene peninsula of the southern shore of Georgian Bay.   Here he persuaded the Hurons to build him a cabin apart from the village where he raised an altar "to offer God the holy sacrifice of the mass."[19]   In a short time he was visited by Champlain, which made it possible for him to celebrate mass, this being the first celebration in what is now the Province of Ontario.

Financial stringency soon compelled le Caron to leave his mission and return to Quebec to plead for greater help from the Company of One Hundred Associates, the commercial company to which had been assigned a monopoly of the fur trade in Canada and which was under charter obligation to further the conversion of the Indians.   Being largely dominated by Huguenot merchants, primarily interested in trade, this company was loathe to finance such distant missionary projects as the Récollets had in mind.[20]   For a time le Caron attempted to administer to the Indians around Tadoussac, but he was compelled to agree with his discouraged colleague, Father d'Olbeau, that the Montaignais were "incapable of Christianity." Nor had the commissary any better success with the Algonquins, whose intransigency compelled him to confine his ministry to a few white settlers at Quebec. Under these circumstances le Caron became anxious to return to Huronia, which he regarded as a far more hopeful field for the propagation of the Christian faith than the region about Quebec.

A reorganization of the Company of One Hundred Associates in 1620 and the appointment of Champlain as governor of Quebec brightened the prospects for such a return; but it was not until 1623 that the new governor sent le Caron on a second trip to Huronia.[21]   This time he was accompanied by another Récollet priest, Father Viel, and a lay brother, Gabriel Sagard, both of whom had arrived in Quebec from France the previous year. In the palisaded cabin built by the Hurons for le Caron in 1616, Brother Sagard wrote his justly famous book, *The Long Journey to the Country of the Hurons*[22] in which he gave an interesting description of the social life of the Huronian Indians.

Sagard in his book implies that the mission to the Hurons was at this time a great success, but Father le Caron's *relation* of the same year seems to contradict his colleague's optimism. In a vein of pessimism he wrote ". . . it will require more expense and toil to render them [the Hurons] men than it has required to make whole nations Christian."[23] The Récollets were ready to toil but the Company of One Hundred Associates were not ready to defray the expense; so the former felt compelled to call to their aid the financially independent Jesuits.[24] It was not without considerable trepidation that the Récollets decided to share their monopoly of missionary work in New France with the Society of Jesus. The Company of One Hundred Associates was bitterly opposed to the admission of the Order; so were the inhabitants of Quebec. Champlain himself was not very enthusiastic about their return after the episode at Saint-Sauveur.[25]

Notwithstanding this opposition, the Récollets besought the aid of the Jesuits; and in 1625 five members of the Order, including the famous Jean Brébeuf, arrived in Quebec where they received a very chilly reception. None of the inhabitants was willing to lodge them, and they would have been compelled to return to France had not the Récollets given them shelter at their convent, Our Lady of Angels, situated a mile and a half inland on the bank of the St. Charles River.[26] Such was the entrance into Quebec of the proud order that was to lay the foundations of the parochial life of New France.

Nor were they to remain long on congenial terms with the Récollets. The chief cause of dissension was their divergent policies on the relationship of the Indians and white settlers. The Récollets had reached the conclusion that the only way to convert the Indians was by first allowing them to intermingle with the French colonists, as a necessary preparation for their introduction to the Christian religion.[27] The Jesuits, on the other hand, were opposed to such social contacts and insisted on keeping their Indian converts isolated from the French, whose influence they regarded as inimical to the morals of the Indians. The Récollets represented the more liberal wing of the Roman Catholic Church, and were willing to co-operate with the Huguenot merchants in civil matters, whereas the more rigid Jesuits showed great repugnance towards any toleration of heretics.[28]

The matters at issue between the two orders were not resolved at this time, for suddenly all controversy was stilled by the English seizure of Quebec in 1629. The leader of this expedition was a French Huguenot, David Kirke, who apparently was ready to take sides in the quarrel between the Récollets and the Jesuits. According to the Récollet historian le Clercq, the Jesuits were brusquely shipped off to Tadoussac, while the Récollets would have been permitted by the English authorities on the spot to remain at Quebec "if they had not had positive orders from the King of England to carry them to France."[29] Thus was brought to an end the second attempt of the French to convert the Indians of North America to the Christian faith.

III

When Canada and Acadia were restored to the French by the Treaty of Ste. Germaine-en-Laye in 1632, the Récollets naturally expected to resume the leadership of the missionary work in New France. Much to their surprise it was the Jesuits who received this coveted honour at Quebec; what was even more humiliating, the Récollets were excluded not only from Canada, but were displaced by the Capuchins in Acadia. The source of this rebuff to the Récollets is difficult to trace and remains to this day a matter of speculation. The French Canadian historian Garneau simply says, ". . . an occult cause had prevented the Récollets from returning to Canada before 1669, though their services were greatly desired by the people. . . ."[30]

No sooner were the Jesuits re-established in Quebec than they renewed once again the mission to the Hurons. Brébeuf, who had visited the mission during his first stay in Canada, was made superior of this distant outpost, and in company with Father Antoine Daniel immediately proceeded on the long journey to Georgian Bay. On their arrival in Huronia they set up headquarters at Ihontatiria, where they built a long house which became known as St. Joseph's Mission. In the spring of 1635 Brébeuf sent his first annual report or *relation* to Paul le Jeune, the superior of the mission at Quebec. This *relation* was embodied in one which le Jeune sent to Paris the same year[31] and became the most widely read in France of all the *Jesuit Relations*, creating an unusual interest in the mission to Huronia, with the result that six more Jesuit workers were sent out to Quebec; among them was Father Jérôme Lalemant, who was to replace Brébeuf as superior of the Huronia mission.

This change of leadership came as a great surprise to Brébeuf's colleagues, who had a deep affection for their former leader. It seems, however, that the Jesuit authorities in France now placed great importance upon the strategic value of the Huronia outpost in North America and wanted someone in charge with proven executive ability. Lalemant as rector of the *Collège de Blois* had shown unusual talents and was regarded as more capable than the mystical Brébeuf of carrying out an aggressive missionary programme.

Not long after his arrival in Huronia Lalemant began to make considerable changes in his predecessor's policies. The latter had established separate mission houses at Ihontatiria, Ossossane and Teunaustayé, where he had placed individual priests, who were to attempt to identify themselves with the social life of the village in which they resided and try to introduce Christian procedures. In this policy Brébeuf seemed to be following the tactics of the Récollets rather than that of the Jesuits, who believed in creating entirely new communities of converted Indians. Consequently, Lalemant reversed Brébeuf's methods by proceeding to the erection of a permanent residence for Jesuit workers apart from all Huron villages. This became known as Ste. Marie among the Hurons, a combination of monastery and fort, the immense proportions of which have recently been revealed through modern excavations.[32] Lalemant also began to found purely Christian villages of Hurons under the direct supervision of the central house of Ste. Marie.

In order to increase the number of French workers he created a body of lay-auxiliaries known as *donnés*. These were enrolled into the Society of Jesus by a private vow, while their sustenance was guaranteed by a civil contract. Thus he was able to secure some skilled craftsmen to help in the ambitious building projects he was attempting far from the sources of building supply. Several of the *donnés* were blacksmiths and one of them, Charles Boivin, was an architect of some originality who was able to combine skilfully French and Indian architectural designs.[33]

The systematic way in which Lalemant undertook his assignment is revealed by the fact that he made a census of the Huron nation immediately upon his arrival in Huronia. This census of 1639 gave him much food for thought, as it was a portent of a coming disaster. It showed that there were thirty-two villages with seven hundred cabins, containing about twelve thousand inhabitants; whereas Champlain in 1616 had estimated a population of about thirty thousand. Although Champlain may well have made an overestimation, there can be little doubt that the Hurons were rapidly diminishing in numbers.[34] The diseases that the white man had brought to America, against which the Indians had little resistance, made their contribution to this rapid depopulation. Many of the Hurons regarded these scourges as a punishment for receiving white men into their cabins; consequently, the missionaries were in constant danger from the tomahawk of an outraged brave.

IV

A far more serious menace to the survival of the Huron nation and to Lalemant's grandiose plans was a trade war that had broken out between the French and Iroquois. The latter were incensed against the French for attempting to suppress their lucrative role as middlemen between the interior Indians and the Dutch at New Amsterdam; they also held a special enmity against the Hurons, who were not only the allies of the hated French, but were attempting to displace the Iroquois as the intermediaries between their neighbouring tribes and the coastal ports.

In this trade war a tremendous advantage had accrued to the

Iroquois when the Dutch traders began to supply them with firearms in exchange for furs. This tempted them to enter upon a career of extermination which threatened the whole French supply line from Tadoussac to Ste. Marie. The Hurons lacked any suitable organization either for defence or attack; usually they deserted their villages in time of alarm, as Brébeuf reported, leaving "only a few old people who are not able to go away but quietly await death in their cabins."[35] As the crisis deepened Montmagny, the third governor of Quebec, made a strong plea to Richelieu to send out a French regiment to retrieve the failing fortunes of the colony. The French minister responded to the extent of dispatching about forty soldiers, a hopelessly inadequate number, to police the supply line from Ste. Marie to Quebec. About all that could be attempted was to build a fort at the mouth of the Richelieu River, which the Iroquois simply by-passed in their murderous raids. Before the guns of these pitiless warriors, the Indians friendly to the French disappeared with unbelievable rapidity.

In the spring of 1642 a Jesuit *donné*, Rene Goupil, trying to return to Ste. Marie from Quebec, was captured and slain by an Iroquois band; his companion, Father Isaac Jogues, only escaped death through the friendly help of a Dutch trader at Orange (now Albany, New York) who arranged for his passage in a small sailing boat to France, a gesture of kindliness only too rare in those days when the rivalry for furs seemed to have obliterated all humane relationships among rival European traders in North America.[36]

Though Jogues had been fearfully tortured by the Indians, yet after his recovery in France he lost little time in returning to New France to volunteer his services in a most dangerous mission to his former captors. In 1645 the Iroquois offered to make peace in order to get back a captured chieftain. As a token of their good faith they invited a Jesuit missionary to come and live amongst them. Jogues readily agreed to accept the challenge, though he had a presentiment that he was going to his death. His first trip into the Iroquois country was quite uneventful, and during a visit to Quebec he reported hopefully on the prospect of a mission to France's most troublesome enemy. On his return, however, he walked straight to his death. Just as he was about to enter the cabin of a chieftain, an Indian concealed behind the doorway struck him down with a tomahawk. "Thus died," says Francis Parkman, "Isaac Jogues, one of the purest examples of Roman Catholic virtue which this Western continent has seen."[37]

The murder of Jogues was a signal that the brief peace was at an end, and the colonists of New France survived only by planting and reaping in groups with muskets hanging over their shoulders. In the meantime the fur trade almost vanished as the Indians from the west rarely had the courage to make the perilous journey down the Ottawa River to Quebec.

The result was that the mission to Huronia was, to all intents and purposes, abandoned by the French authorities to its own devices. Yet, the superior, Lalemant, refused to despair. "Do not imagine," he wrote in 1647, "that the rages of the Iroquois and the loss of many catetchumens can bring to naught the mystery of the cross of Jesus Christ, and the efficacy of his blood. We shall die, we shall be captured, burned, butchered; be it so. Those who die in their beds do not always die the best death. I see none of our company cast down. On the contrary they ask leave to go to the Hurons, and some of them protest that the fires of the Iroquois are one of their motives for the journey."[38]

But despite the brave defiance of Lalemant the mission was doomed. On July 4, 1648, the Iroquois attacked Tenanaustayé and murdered Antoine Daniel while he was saying mass. The following winter Saint-Ignace, a part of the important mission of Saint Louis, was destroyed, and in the spring of 1649 the Iroquois arrived at St. Louis itself. Here Jean Brébeuf and Gabriel Lalemant, a brother of the superior, had remained at their posts well knowing that death awaited them. The two priests were captured and taken to Saint-Ignace to be put to death by torture. The story of their long agony has been told in fearful detail by their colleague, Ragueneau. It recounts how Brébeuf was compelled to look on while Gabriel Lalemant, a young Parisian, only six months out from France, was literally roasted alive, and to listen to his unavailing shrieks to Heaven. Brébeuf himself, with a collar of red-hot hatchets around his neck and with boiling water poured over his head in mockery of baptism, never flinched nor uttered a word. And yet the robust Brébeuf only lived through this torture for about four hours, while the frail Lalemant survived for almost seventeen hours.[39]

The defeat suffered by the Huron braves at St. Louis was the end of the Huronian mission. Father Chaumonot, who was at Ossossane at the time, describes its effect on the surviving Hurons: "Two days after their defeat the news came to us that all the warriors were killed or captured. It was towards midnight it was announced to us, and at once in all the cabins were weeping, tears and pitiful cries. On every side one heard only the women bewailing their husbands, mothers weeping for their sons, and other relatives bemoaning death and captivity of their nearest ones."[40]   The Hurons were now reduced to pitiable numbers. Some of them fled westward to the land of the Petuns, the Neutrals and the Eries; others of them sought refuge in the less hospitable land of the Algonquins; only a few hundred, encamped about Ste. Marie, dared to remain in Huronia.

Finally, the Jesuits came to the bitter conclusion that Ste. Marie itself had to be abandoned. It was under the leadership of Father Paul Ragueneau that this hard decision was taken. His *relation* of 1649 expresses well the bitter frustration of giving up a project upon which so many high hopes and ambitions had been centred. "We have left our dwelling place," he wrote, ". . . rather I might call it our delight. . . . Nay more, we even applied the torch to the work of our own hands, lest the sacred house should furnish shelter to our impious enemy. In a single day and almost in a moment, we saw consumed our work of nearly ten years. . . . Desolated now is our home, desolated are our Penates. In the land of our exile, we were forced to seek a new place of exile."[41]

A new place of exile was attempted on St. Joseph's Island (now Christian Island). This also had to be abandoned, and Father Ragueneau then proceeded to lead his despairing remnant of Hurons on a thousand-mile journey to the shelter of the citadel of Quebec.

In 1651 the Jesuits built a third Ste. Marie on the Isle of Orleans in the St. Lawrence River near the city of Quebec, and attempted to resuscitate the Huron nation. Even here the Iroquois pursued this hapless remnant, and so the project had to be abandoned. Many of the Hurons in desperation sought safety through adoption into the Iroquois confederacy. About five hundred remained in the vicinity of Quebec and founded a village known as *l'Ancienne* Lorette.[42] At the opening of the eighteenth century they were transferred to *la Jeune* Lorette on the St. Charles River; but even here they failed to retain their racial identity. Those who remained around Quebec intermarried with the French; others migrated to the west and mingled with various Indian tribes.

V

The failure of the Huronian mission contributed much to the deepening animosity between the Roman Catholics and Protestants on the North American continent. It was Dutch Calvinists who had recklessly supplied European arms to untutored savages with no apparent concern for the cruel consequences. Puritan New Englanders showed little compassion while their Christian neighbours in the St. Lawrence region were being daily massacred. Yet, there were brighter episodes in the relations of Catholic and Protestant, which revealed the latent human decencies of the two cultures when not obscured by commercial covetousness or religious bigotry. In 1650 the French in desperation turned to their southern neighbours to seek help against their implacable foe. The colony of Massachusetts had indicated a willingness to make a reciprocal trade agreement with New France and Governor Montmagny conceived the idea of bargaining trade for a military alliance against the Iroquois. A Jesuit, Gabriel Druillettes, who had been conducting a mission among the Abenaki, was chosen by the French as an envoy. It was an unusual choice as Massachusetts had enacted a piece of legislation which enjoined hanging any Jesuit who ventured within her territories; nevertheless, she gave a cordial welcome to Druillettes. To quote Francis Parkman, "Massachusetts, in the person of her magistrate, became the gracious host of one of those whom, next to the Devil and an Anglican bishop, she most abhorred."[43] Druillettes was also entertained by the famous New England missionary, John Eliot, at the home of the latter in Roxbury, Massachusetts. Here Puritan and Jesuit discussed their mutual problem, the conversion of the Indians. Nothing of value was achieved by these friendly gestures; New England was only interested in a trade treaty and would not hear of an alliance against the Iroquois. Thus faded from the scene this first endeavour to bring about a peaceful co-existence between the two cultures that were both attempting in their own way to build a new and better Christian civilization in the New World.

Even if the negotiations had brought about a confederacy against the Iroquois, it would have been too late to have saved the Huronian mission. Nor would it have been possible to have renewed it, for not only the Hurons, but their neighbouring tribes were practically exterminated by the well-armed Iroquois. All that remains of that noble experiment are a few charred ruins, which modern archeologists are now piecing together, and learning with surprise what a tremendous effort was made some three hundred years ago to build a French Catholic civilization in central Canada.[44]

The results of that effort, however, were not entirely without effect upon the religious and social life of Canada. The early creation by

New France of a Canadian calendar of saints and the faithful treasuring of the relics of the Huronian martyrs contributed much to the vitality of the Roman Catholic Church in Canada and helps to explain the tenacity of French Canadian culture within a predominantly Anglo-Saxon political framework.   Huronia also made its contribution, as will be seen in the following chapter, to the formation of "a type of religious grouping to be found nowhere else perhaps but in French Canada."[45]

REFERENCES

1. *Vide* M. F. Faillon, *Histoire de la Colonie Française en Canada* (Ville Marie, 1865, 3 *tomes*), I, pp. 16-35.

2. F. X. de Charlevoix, *History and Description of New France* (trans. by J. G. Shea, New York, 1866-1872, 6 vols.), I, p. 121.

3. Samuel de Champlain, *Works* (trans. and edited under general editorship of H. P. Biggar, Champlain Society, Toronto, 1922-1936, 6 vols.), III, p. 16.

4. Charlevoix, *op. cit.*, I, p. 247.

5. Marc Lescarbot, *History of New France* (trans. by W. L. Grant, The Champlain Society, Toronto, 1907-1914, 3 vols.), III, p. 41.

6. R. G. Thwaites, ed., *The Jesuit Relations, op. cit.*, I, p. 161.

7. *Ibid.*, I, p. 81.

8. *Ibid.*

9. Charlevoix, *op. cit.*, I, p. 262.

10. Quoted by F. X. Garneau, *op. cit.*, I, p. 52.

11. R. M. Thwaites, *op. cit.*, II, p. 247.

12. Charlevoix, I, p. 280.

13. *Ibid.*, I, p. 281.

14. Champlain, *op. cit.*, III, p. 16.

15. The history of the Récollet mission to New France is told in great detail by Christian le Clercq, *First Establishment of the Faith in New France* (trans. by J. G. Shea, New York, 1881, 2 vols.).

16. A good study of the Canadian Indians is D. Jenness, *Indians of Canada* (Bulletin 65, Department of Mines, Ottawa, 1932), *vide* pp. 167-199 for religion and folklore.

17. R. G. Thwaites, II, p. 11; *vide* also W. D. Wallis and R. S. Wallis, *The Micmac Indians of Eastern Canada* (Minneapolis, 1955), pp. 142-149.

18. J. Mooney, *The Aboriginal Population of America North of Mexico* (Smith. Misc. Coll., Washington, 1928), vol. LXXX, No. 7, p. 33.

19. Le Clercq, *op. cit.*, I, p. 97.

20. Charlevoix, *op. cit.*, II, p. 31.

21. *Ibid.*, p. 35.

22. Gabriel Sagard-Théodat, *The Long Journey to the Country of the Hurons* (trans. by H. H. Langton, Champlain Society, Toronto, 1939).

23. Le Clercq, I, p. 214.

24. *Ibid.*, I, p. 225.

25. *Ibid.*, I, p. 226.

26. Charlevoix, II, p. 36.

27. Le Clercq, I, pp. 255-256.

28. Charlevoix, II, pp. 38-39.

29. Le Clercq, I, pp. 304-305.

30. F. X. Garneau, *op. cit.*, I, p. 201.

31. R. G. Thwaites, op. *cit.*, X.

32. For a good description of this residence based on archeological exploration *vide* Wilfrid and Elsie McLeod Jury, *Sainte-Marie Among the Hurons* (Toronto, 1954).

33. *Ibid.*, p. 50.

34. R. G. Thwaites, XVII, p. 227.

35. *Ibid.*, X., p. 51.

36. *Ibid.*, XXV, pp. 67-73.

37. Francis Parkman, *The Jesuits in North America* (Boston, 1878, 11th ed.), p. 301.

38. R. G. Thwaites, XXXIV.

39. *Ibid.*, XXIV, *passim.*

40. Felix Martin, ed., *Autobiography du Père Chaumonot* (Paris, 1885), p. 93.

41. R. G. Thwaites, XXXV, p. 25.

42. *Vide* Gilbert Parker and Claude E. Bryan, *Old Quebec* (Toronto, 1903), pp. 83-84.

43. Parkman, *op. cit.*, p. 326.

44. Wilfrid and Elsie McLeod Jury, *op. cit.*

45. M. Roy, *The Parish and Democracy in French Canada* (Toronto, 1950), p. 15.

IV

The Organization of Parochial Life in New France

A *relation* sent by Paul le Jeune, the Jesuit superior at Quebec, to France in 1633 voiced a need for some women workers in New France. "Is there not," he asked, "some lady in France who has enough courage to found here a seminary for girls to be under the care of some good and courageous widow, assisted by two brave young women, who would live in a house which might be built near the home of that estimable family that is here?"[1]   The home to which le Jeune referred was Madame Hébert's, the widow of Louis Hébert, the first permanent settler in New France.   It was in this home that mass had been celebrated after the restoration of Quebec to the French in 1632, and around it there began to develop a unique parochial life that is the pride of the Province of Quebec today.

I

The response to le Jeune's plea was tremendous.   Thirteen sisters at a Parisian convent signed in one day a vow to go over to New France, if they could obtain the permission of their superiors.   In a remarkably short time le Jeune was deluged with feminine volunteers who were ready to make the perilous ocean voyage to Quebec, and go, if needs be, to Huronia itself.

The next problem was to secure the money to finance the project that the superior had in mind.   Soon, it also was forthcoming.   A contract for the establishment of a hospital was signed by the Duchesse d'Aiguillon at Paris on August 16, 1637,[2] which was to be under the direction of some nuns of Dieppe, who had volunteered their nursing services.   These sisters were represented at the signing by Sebastian Cramoisy, the famous printer of the *Jesuit Relations*.

Shortly after this ceremony the three nuns who were to inaugurate the Hôtel Dieu at Quebec sailed to Canada under the protection of Father Barthélemy Vimont, who was being sent out to replace le Jeune as superior of the Jesuits in Canada. On the same ship was a group of Ursuline sisters under the guidance of two of the most remarkable women ever to have set foot on the soil of Canada, Madame de la Peltrie and Marie de l'Incarnation. To non-Roman Catholics they are unbelievable characters, but no one, Catholic or Protestant, can fail to appreciate their piety and courage. Both of them employed rather bizarre methods in order to serve God in "a wilderness church." Marie de l'Incarnation, the Madame Martin to whom reference has already been made in connection with the religious revival of seventeenth-century France,[3] had to leave behind her a son of fourteen years, whom she never saw again. Madame de la Peltrie went through a mock marriage, euphemistically called a "pious deception," in order to secure from her father an inheritance with which to endow the Ursulines of Quebec.[4] Both these women were well experienced in the ways of the world. Madame de la Peltrie had earlier been a socialite of distinction; Marie de l'Incarnation, before entering the Ursuline convent, had been a shrewd merchant. The worldly knowledge that they had acquired before embracing the religious life served them well in the New World. Both appeared equal to any circumstance and never displayed panic or fear during the most perilous days of the infant colony. The letters of Marie de l'Incarnation reveal not only an unusual mystical serenity, but also are full of practical references to the social and political life of New France.[5] Combined with her statesmanlike qualities, which made her the trusted confidant and advisor of governors and bishops, was a marvellous aptitude for learning languages. She composed several dictionaries and grammars of Indian languages for the use of the sisters in the Ursuline Convent at Quebec.[6]

The foundress of the Ursuline Convent, Madame de la Peltrie, through her wealth, contributed much to the comfort and amenities of the colony. Her glamorous personality also added a touch of colour to the social life of the community. She was not, however, as stable as Marie de l'Incarnation, and found it difficult to settle down to the routine tasks of colonization. Her somewhat inconstant spirit became evident when she temporarily deserted the Ursuline Convent at Quebec to take part in the spectacular founding of Montreal. But after an absence of eighteen months in the new colony she returned to spend the remaining years of her life at Quebec.[7]

With the establishment of a convent and a hospital, the ecclesiastical life of Quebec began to take on all the aspects of a full-blown diocesan organization. While Paul le Jeune was superior of the mission (1632-1639) he laid the foundations of a college at Quebec to which was adjoined a seminary for teaching the Indians the rudiments of the Christian religion.

Despite the difficulties the Récollets had experienced in trying to convert the primitive savages, the Jesuits continued doggedly on, and during the administration of le Jeune a habitation was designed to be occupied by converted Montaignais. It became known as the Habitation at Sillery in honour of Nöel Brulart de Sillery, commander of the Order of Malta and a member of the Company of One Hundred Associates, who had endowed the mission. A similar mission was opened at Three Rivers in 1634, to become a colony of converted Algonquins. As Three Rivers was an important fur trade centre, a number of French colonists had settled there; these began to attend the mission church. The Jesuits, however, remained firm in their policy of segregation and insisted that Europeans and Indians must worship at different hours.[8]

When Father Vimont took over the post of superior he found that the supervision of this expanding missionary work occupied so much of his time that it was necessary to assign parochial duties to two priests at Quebec. His chief enthusiasm seems to have been for the mission at Sillery, which he hoped to make a model for future missions. In this he seems to have had some success, for the "good example of the savages at Sillery encouraged those at Tadoussac to ask P. Vimont for a missionary."[9] Father Duquen was put in charge of this most difficult mission in 1641, and persuaded the Indians to erect in 1647 the beautiful chapel at Tadoussac still standing today. Vimont also initiated missions at Miscou on the Bay Chaleur and at Nesigiauit (now Chedabuctou) on the Restigouche River. The latter was under the direction of Father Richard, the pioneer missionary in what is now the Province of New Brunswick.

II

The most significant event that occurred during Father Vimont's administration was the founding of Montreal. Around the origins of the metropolitan city of Canada there has grown up a vast amount of literature, some of it so laden with the miraculous that it is difficult to evaluate. The day by day story is clearly told by Dollier de Casson,[10] who was superior of the Seminary of Saint Sulpice in Montreal from 1671 to 1701. De Casson appears to be a very careful historian, but he accepts all the supernatural events that supposedly preceded the founding of Montreal as incontrovertible.   Without some knowledge of these "passing strange" events it would probably be impossible for a student of Canadian church history to gain any true appreciation of the intrinsic nature of French Canadian Christianity.

De Casson writes after the failures of the Huronian mission, and consequently, he regards the founding of Montreal as a divine compensation for that disaster.[11]   The divine initiative first became evident at La Flèche in Anjou, where a grave citizen, Jérôme Dauversière, while at his prayers received a supernatural command to found a hospital at Montreal.   About the same time, a young priest at Paris, by the name of Jean Jacques Olier, also heard a voice during his prayers telling him to found a seminary for the training of priests in Montreal.   All contemporary accounts are to the effect that both these men were totally ignorant of Canadian geography.   It seems probable, however, that the name Montreal may have become familiar to them through the *Jesuit Relations* which the Cramoisy Press was making available to a large reading public in France.[12]

The apparently accidental meeting of Olier and Dauversière at the home of a mutual friend, and their instant recognition of one another without the aid of a third party is less susceptible of rational explanation. As a consequence of this meeting, plans were laid to establish three religious communities in the proposed colony: one for secular priests, who were to convert Indians to the Christian faith and to supervise the religious life of the colonists; one for nursing sisters; and a third for teaching sisters who would instruct children.   All came to pass as planned.   First, a company was formed, known as the Associates of Notre Dame de Montreal, to initiate the project.   This society secured from the Company of One Hundred Associates the Island of Montreal and proceeded to seek volunteers to colonize it.   Sieur de Maisonneuve[13] was persuaded to accept the post of governor; and shortly afterwards the services of Jeanne Mance, who also had received a divine message, were secured to undertake the establishment of a Hôtel Dieu at Montreal.[14]

In February, 1641, the Associates, about forty in number, met in the Church of Notre Dame in Paris and solemnly dedicated Montreal to the Holy Family. The proposed seminary was especially inscribed to Christ, the Hôtel Dieu to St. Joseph, and the proposed school for children to the Virgin Mary. The colony as a whole was to be known as Ville-Marie de Montreal.

Maisonneuve, with a party of forty men and four women, reached Quebec on August 24, 1641. Governor Montmagny and the officials of the Company of One Hundred Associates were not over-enthusiastic in their reception of these unexpected guests. The former saw in Maisonneuve a rival governor who might well overshadow the governor of Quebec; the latter feared that a settlement as far west as Montreal might endanger their monopoly of the fur trade. General opinion at Quebec was that if the colonists immediately proceeded to their proposed destination they would surely be massacred by the Iroquois. It was urged that they would be well advised to settle on the Island of Orleans in the vicinity of Quebec, where there would be far less danger from marauding Indians. But neither Maisonneuve nor his followers would be moved from their original purpose, and in the following May they proceeded to Montreal to begin their adventurous careers as the founders of a city.[15]

As yet there were no priests among the Associates, so Father Vimont assigned two Jesuits to accompany the party to Montreal. They were to remain with the colony until Father Olier, who had founded the order of Saint Sulpice in Paris, should have trained some priests to organize a similar order in Montreal. This did not come to pass until 1657 when the Jesuit, Father Pijart, who had been in charge of the parish of Ville-Marie, surrendered it to Father de Queylus, the first superior of the Sulpician Order in Montreal.

Also missing from the first arrivals was Marguerite Bourgeoys, the famous foundress of a teaching order.[16] She arrived in 1653, and immediately embarked upon her great educational career in a dilapidated house that had been abandoned by one of the settlers. From such inauspicious quarters emerged the justly renowned Congregation of the Sisters of Notre Dame which has won for its foundress the honour of sainthood. Already, Jeanne Mance had embarked on her equally famous nursing career. She soon showed herself a genius in organization, and in a short time had established a nursing tradition for the care of the sick and the unfortunate, still the inspiration of her profession in French

Canada. Both these women took a prominent part in all the affairs of the colony and displayed in the face of danger a courage and fortitude equal to that of Quebec's two famous women pioneers.

III

The arrival of the Sulpicians, who took over the administration of Montreal from the original Associates of Notre Dame, created a sharp religious tension in New France which finally eventuated in the appointment of a bishop. It was with considerable chagrin that the Jesuits agreed to such a solution to their dispute with the Sulpicians, as they feared at first that a bishop might well obstruct their plans for establishing an ultramontane church in Canada. Their general feeling had been well expressed by Marie de l'Incarnation, who wrote in 1646, "that God does not yet wish a bishop in this country which is not yet well enough established." Until the Jesuits had planted Christianity more firmly she felt it would be better "to cultivate for some time, without having a person here, who would be able to alter their designs."[17]

By 1659 the Sulpicians were busily engaged in altering the designs of the Jesuits. Because of the failure of the most daring of the Jesuit plans, the latter were rapidly losing favour both in new and old France. The loss of Huronia to the Iroquois had been a considerable set-back to their prestige, but it was still hoped that this reverse to their plan of building a French Catholic empire in central Canada might be overcome by the conversion of the Iroquois themselves.[18]

It was during an elaborate religious demonstration at Quebec in connection with the Roman Catholic jubilee of 1653 that this daring mission was seriously contemplated. Some Iroquois were present at the demonstration and were apparently so impressed with the grandeur of the spectacle that they asked for missionaries to be sent to their country. Despite all former experiences of Iroquois' treachery, the fathers at Quebec felt that they dare not let slip this opportunity to redeem their losses in Huronia. Consequently, they sent Father Simon le Moyne into the heart of the Iroquois country, where at first he received a very cordial reception. And so a new "grand design," as Marie de l'Incarnation called it, took shape.

Following upon le Moyne's negotiations, a French colony under the military leadership of M. Dupuis was established at Gannentaya on

the shore of Lake Onondago in 1656.   From this centre missionaries were
to be sent out to the various Iroquois nations.   Once again the treachery
of the Iroquois brought the second grand design of the Jesuits to an end.
The humiliation to some extent was mitigated when le Moyne and his
daring companions succeeded by a ruse in escaping the trap that had
been set for them, and found their way through the trackless forest back
to Quebec—a journey that has been compared to the "retreat of the ten
thousand."[19]   Nevertheless, the abandonment of the Iroquois mission
was another serious blow to the prestige both of the Jesuits and of Quebec.

The Sulpicians and Montreal, on the other hand, were gaining
great acclaim by their daring resistance to Iroquois raids.   Typical of the
spirit of the Montrealers to win through all adversity was the exploit of
Adam Dollard and his sixteen companions, who took the offensive
against the Iroquois after the failure of the Jesuit mission at Onondago
had left New France threatened once again with extinction.   Though
Dollard and his little band were wiped out at Long Sault (1660), yet their
bravery was such that the Iroquois became afraid to push their conquests
further.[20]

These events had their political repercussions in France and helped
to raise the prestige of the Sulpicians over that of the Jesuits.   But
Dollard's sacrifice at Long Sault came too late to win for the Sulpicians
the coveted bishopric of Quebec.   As events turned out it would probably
not have made any difference in the contest between the two orders, for
the Jesuits had direct access to the real centre of power in France, whereas
the Sulpicians always remained on the fringe.   In every other respect the
latter seemed to have had the advantage.   Having adopted the Récollet
policy of encouraging the intermingling of French and Indians, they had
gained the favour of the colonists and the commercial interests of France.[21]

Their greatest asset, however, was the patronage of the archbishop
of Rouen, who claimed the episcopal jurisdiction over New France on the
basis that most of the settlers had embarked from his diocese.[22]   The
Jesuits vigorously opposed this claim, but the archbishop had overcome
their resistance by questioning the validity of marriages and religious
vows in a country lacking episcopal oversight.   The charge was so
serious that Jérome Lalemant, who had succeeded Vimont as superior
at Quebec, sent his predecessor over to France to consult the theologians
of the Society of Jesus in Paris.   These apparently shared the archbishop's
scruples and advised Vimont to go to Rouen and persuade the archbishop
to institute Lalemant as his vicar general in Canada.   Vimont succeeded

in his mission, but on condition of a tacit acknowledgment of the juris-diction of the archbishop of Rouen over New France.   This acknowledg-ment was concealed from the colonists until 1653 when the imperious prelate compelled its revelation.

The archbishop, however, was a strong nationalist who was deter-mined that Gallican privileges which put many restrictions upon the papal administration of the Church in France should also prevail in New France.   The Jesuits, on the other hand, were above all things opposed to placing any limits upon papal power and had from the first desired to create a model ultramontane church in the New World.[23]   It was for this reason that they postponed as long as possible asking for the appoint-ment of a bishop for Canada, since such an appointment by the king of France would have automatically brought Canada under the ecclesiastical laws of France.   As long as the archbishop of Rouen appointed a Jesuit as his vicar general they were content to leave things as they were.   But the sudden rise of the Sulpicians to general favour gave Rouen the opportunity to appoint one of their number to the coveted post.   In 1659 he named the superior of Saint Sulpice, Abbé de Queylus, his vicar general, and thus created an intolerable situation for the Jesuits, compelling them to reconsider their whole attitude towards the appoint-ment of a bishop for Canada.

The Sulpicians had been agitating for such an appointment for some time, and de Queylus began to act as if he were already sure that he would become the first bishop of Quebec.   When he arrived in the city he immediately took over all the details of administration and even dared to criticize the Jesuits from the pulpit.   However, the latter were equal to the situation: they saw that a bishop for Quebec was now inevitable and they proceeded immediately to secure one of their own choosing.[24]

They still had strong support at the court of France, particularly in the person of the Queen Mother, Anne of Austria, to whom they presented their case.   This fervent admirer of the Jesuits suggested that Paul le Jeune, a former superior at Quebec, should be given the honour, but the rules of his order did not allow him to accept; consequently the Queen Mother conferred upon him the welcome task of selecting a suitable person.   The choice fell upon François de Montmorency Laval, whose sympathies with the Jesuits were so marked that one of his first acts when he reached Quebec was to ship de Queylus back to France.

The latter had no doubt severely provoked the new prelate by refusing to yield the jurisdiction which he held by the appointment of the archbishop of Rouen, being under the impression that French ecclesiastical law still prevailed in New France. He was to be greatly disillusioned when he was interdicted directly by Bishop Laval from exercising his clerical functions and found himself forcibly compelled to return to France.[25] Later he was to make his peace with Laval and return to his former position as superior of the Sulpicians at Montreal. This time he became reconciled to Jesuit dominance and co-operated loyally with the bishop in the organization of the parochial and diocesan life of Quebec.

IV

Even before Laval's arrival a rather unique parochial system was evolving at Quebec. In 1645 the parishioners of Notre Dame had elected three church wardens, introducing a representative element into the conduct of church affairs. Thus was initiated the religious and civil corporation or *fabrique* of French Canada on a rather democratic basis.[26] The new bishop did not attempt to overthrow this display of independence on the part of the *Canadiens* but wisely decided to combine it with the principle of centralized authority which had been impressed upon him by his Jesuit advisers.

Laval had been uniquely prepared for the role that he was to play in Canada.[27] He had been trained for the priesthood by a famous mystic, Sieur de Bernier, the spiritual director of a hermitage attached to the Ursuline convent at Caen, noted for its detection of disguised forms of Jansenism. It was at this hermitage that Laval had been imbued with the mystical ultramontane principles that had originally been imported into New France by both the Jesuit missionaries and the Ursuline sisters. Here he also learned to regard Gallicanism as a disguised form of Lutheranism, inimical to all sound church discipline. No sooner did he become aware of the position that was to be offered to him than he began to co-operate with his Jesuit mentors in seeking freedom as a bishop in the New World from all Gallican restrictions. It was suggested to him by le Jeune that he should seek his official appointment from the pope rather than the king of France, since a royal appointment would automatically subject him to French ecclesiastical law. Laval followed this advice and became not bishop of Quebec but rather an apostolic vicar in Canada with the title of Bishop of Petræa *in partibus infidelium*.

The implications of this arrangement had not escaped the notice of the French prelates. The archbishop of Rouen protested bitterly, as did the *parlements* of Rouen and Paris. The bishop of Bayeux whom Laval had sought as his consecrator refused to perform the ceremony. But all these protests were in vain, for the simple reason that Cardinal Mazarin who was now conducting the affairs of France was under great obligation to the Queen Mother and used his talents to overcome nationalist opposition.

There still remained the problem of consecration. But this was solved by the papal nuncio at Paris, who with the co-operation of two French bishops consecrated Laval in a church exempt from French episcopal jurisdiction. Thus was the groundwork laid to enable Laval to create in New France a church which would be a model of loyalty to the holy see.

His most unique contribution in this direction was the establishment of a seminary at Quebec in 1663 affiliated with the Paris Seminary of Foreign Missions.[28] As soon as it was completed the bishop took up residence within its walls where he was able personally to train his clergy to become a spiritual militia ready to obey his every command. Just as the Jesuits were obedient to all the commands of the general of their order, so Laval intended that his secular priests should be equally subservient to their diocesan.

The Seminary was designed to be the home not only of the bishop but of all the parochial priests as well. Rather than to think of their parish as their permanent abode the *curés* were encouraged to look upon the Seminary as their true home, where they were to stay when visiting Quebec and which would look after them in sickness and old age. In thus weaning the priests away from a permanent attachment to their parishes Laval struck a subtle blow at the foundations of Gallicanism, which laid great stress upon permanent curacies in which a parish priest receiving directly the revenue from tithes was free from any serious hierarchial interference. Laval had forestalled the possibility of any of his priests following this French example by securing from the Quebec Council a decree of revocability of curacies. The Council, also at Laval's suggestion, conferred upon the Seminary the right to collect tithes to enable it to pay the stipends of the parish priests. It was hoped to secure one-thirteenth of the produce of the land and labour of the inhabitants, but these protested so vigorously that Laval had to be content with one-twenty-sixth.[29] This was a rather meagre church revenue for all the ambitious projects that the bishop had in mind. He was able, however, to supplement the revenue from tithes with the income from three abbeys in France and also to contribute something from his own private resources.

By closely associating the authorities of the Seminary with the bishop in the administration of the diocese, Laval had thought to secure the permanency of his policy under future bishops. There was, however, one serious flaw in his scheme: it depended to a large extent upon a cordial relation between the bishop and the seminarists. This weakness revealed itself with the appointment of the second bishop of Quebec, Monseignor Saint-Vallier who, being an admirer of the French parochial system, immediately tried to overturn his predecessor's policy.[30] Thus was brought about a great tension in the Canadian church. As was to be expected, the seminarists put up fierce resistance to the new bishop; and Laval, who remained on in Quebec after his retirement from office, also felt impelled to take part in the controversy.

Saint-Vallier had the support of the French government in this contest, and he did succeed in separating the Seminary from the administrative department of the church; nevertheless, he did not fully succeed in getting his priests to settle down permanently in their parishes. "Nature," as Parkman observes, "as well as Bishop Laval threw difficulties in the way of settling him quietly over his charge."[31] This cryptic remark is amplified by pointing out that when a priest was assigned a parish which extended from Rivière du Loup to Rivière du Sud, a distance of twenty-seven leagues, with some isolated communities consisting of no more than one inhabitant, it was rather futile to suggest that he settle down forever in his parish.

A royal edict of 1692 made tenure of parishes irrevocable; but this edict was evaded by later bishops at Quebec, who reverted to Laval's policy by reserving to themselves in the letter of nomination to a parochial benefice the right of removing the priest nominated. Since the clergy as a general rule accepted this stipulation without protest, it was considered that the edict of 1692 was not violated. With the transfer of New France from French to British rule, the edict no longer applied.[32] The few endowed parishes soon disappeared, giving the bishop absolute sway in his diocese.

REFERENCES

1. R. G. Thwaites, ed., *The Jesuit Relations, op. cit.*, X, p. 145.

2. *Vide* H. R. Casgrain, *Histoire de l'Hôtel Dieu* (Quebec, 1878).

3. *Vide supra*, p. 20.

4. For an account of the origin of the early charitable organizations of New France *vide* E. M. Faillon, *Histoire de la Colonie Française en Canada, op. cit.*, I, pp. 310-328.

5. The letters of Marie de l'Incarnation were carefully collected by her son, Dom Claude Martin, and have been published under the title *Écrits Spirituels et Historiques* (Paris and Quebec, 1925, 4 vols.).

6. There are several good biographies of Marie de l'Incarnation, among them: H. R. Casgrain, *Histoire de la Mère Marie de l'Incarnation* (Quebec, 1864); P. F. Richaudeau, *Vie de Marie de l'Incarnation Ursuline* (Tournai, 1874); C. Martin, *Histoire de la Vénérable Mère Marie de l'Incarnation* (Paris, 1892, 2 vols.).

7. E. M. Faillon, *op. cit.*, I, pp. 311-323. An interesting account in English of the roles played in New France by both Madame de la Peltrie and Marie de l'Incarnation is Agnes Repplier's *Mère Marie of the Ursulines* (New York, 1951).

8. *Vide* Faillon, I, p. 336 *et seq.*

9. A. Gosselin, *La Mission du Canada* (Evereux, 1909), p. 82.

10. Dollier de Casson, *A History of Montreal* (trans. and ed. by R. Flenley, London, Toronto, and New York, 1928).

11. *Ibid.*, pp. 59-153.

12. *Vide* C. Bertrand, *Monsieur de la Dauversière* (Montreal, 1947), *passim*.

13. For a history of the founder of Montreal *vide* P. Rousseau, *Histoire de la Vie de M. Paul de Chomedey, Sieur de Maisonneuve* (Montreal, 1886).

14. The story of Jeanne Mance has been written in English by J. K. Faran, *Jean Mance* or "*The Angel of the Colony*" (Montreal, 1931).

15. E. M. Faillon, II, pp. 186-220.

16. A. Jamet, *Marguerite Bourgeoys* (Montreal, 1942, 2 tomes.)

17. P. F. Richaudeau, ed., *Lettres de la Révérende Mère Marie de l'Incarnation*, new edition (Paris and Leipzig, 1876, 2 tomes), I, p. 304.

18. E. M. Faillon, II, pp. 222-266.

19. A. Gosselin, *op. cit.*, p. 319.

20. Dollier de Casson, *op. cit.*, pp. 253-263.

21. *Vide* Henri Gauthier, *La Compagnie de Saint-Sulpice au Canada* (Montreal, 1889), p. 40.

22. Faillon, II, pp. 293-346.

23. *Vide Notice Historique sur la Compagnie de Jesus au Canada par un Collaborateur de la* "*Revue Canadienne*" (Montreal, 1889), p. 40.

24. Faillon, II, p. 313 *et seq.*

25. *Vide* Francis Parkman, *The Old Regime in Canada* (Boston, 1877), p. 98. Parkman's account of this incident is based on Belmont, *Histoire du Canada*, and on a *Memoir* by Abbé d'Allet in *Morale Practique des Jesuits*, XXXIV, 725.

26. *Vide*, M. Roy, *The Parish and Democracy in French Canada* (Toronto, 1950), p. 17.

27. For a sympathetic estimate of Laval's episcopate *vide* A. Gosselin, *François de Montmorency-Laval* (Quebec, 1901); also A. L. De Brumath, *Bishop Laval* (The Makers of Canada Series, Toronto, 1906).

28. *Mandements des Évêques de Québec publiés par Mgr. H. Têtu et l'Abbé C.-O. Gagnon* (Quebec, 1887), I, pp. 95-97.

29. *Ibid.*, pp. 160-161.   *Vide* also Faillon, III, p. 165.

30. *Ibid.*, p. 163.

31. Parkman, *op. cit.*, p. 340.

32. *Vide* F. X. Garneau, *op. cit.*, I, pp. 197-210.

V

Church and State in New France

THE COMPANY of One Hundred Associates whose governors were continually in controversy with the church was dissolved in 1663, and Canada became a royal colony. The legislative, judicial and executive power of the colony was placed in the hands of a Sovereign Council composed of the governor, the bishop, and five councillors to be named each year by the governor and bishop jointly. An attorney general and a secretary also sat in the Council, and in 1665 a new official, an intendant, was added to the membership.[1]

The first intendant was Jean Talon, and with him came to Quebec a new trading company, the West Indies, to revive all the quarrels that had brought the previous company to an end. Behind the creation of the office of intendant and also the West Indies Company can be seen the hand of Colbert, who was now conducting the affairs of France and was resolved that his country should have a commercially prosperous colony and a trading company strong enough to compete with the companies of England and Holland.[2] To this end Colbert put at the head of the West Indies Company an old soldier of noble rank, the Marquis de Tracy, who was made lieutenant-general over all the French colonies of the west. De Tracy arrived in Quebec in 1664, the year that the English seized New Amsterdam from the Dutch and renamed it New York, a momentous event in the history of North America.

Few of the fatal consequences of that momentous change of name were evident to the colonists of New France in 1664; for in that same year there also arrived at Quebec a governor of high rank, Daniel de Remy, Sieur de Courcelles, with the famous Carignan-Salières regiment, to give the colony a greater sense of security and permanency than it had ever previously enjoyed.[3] With this new sense of security and with the presence of officers and soldiers along with greater commercial activity, the social life of Canada began to take on a colouring very different from the puritanism that had been imposed upon it by the clerics. The Jesuit *Journal* of July, 1667, comments with great misgivings on the first ball held at Quebec in celebration of de Courcelles' victory over the Iroquois, and expresses the fear of the evil consequences that may follow upon this growing popularity of worldly pleasures.

I

The presiding genius behind this new social development was Jean Talon, who represented the policies of Colbert in Canada. Like his patron he was determined that the interests of the church should be subordinated to the material welfare of the state. But he was wise enough not to come into a head-on collision with Bishop Laval who had already brought about the recall of two governors. Particularly, he took great care to circumvent Laval's most trusty weapon, excommunication, with which the latter had humiliated earlier officials.

The liquor trade was the chief source of friction between the church and the civil authorities. To its credit the church had taken a strong stand against the sale of intoxicating liquors to the Indians. Twice in this controversy Laval had triumphed over the governors by means of excommunication. Talon succeeded in checkmating the Bishop by getting the Sovereign Council to issue a decree allowing the inhabitants of the colony to sell liquor to the Indians.[4] Laval refused to sign this decree, but he could hardly excommunicate the rest of the council for doing so and still expect to survive long as the bishop of Quebec.

One of the first acts of Talon as intendant was to take a census of the colony. This revealed that there were 3,215 French settlers of whom nearly two-thirds were males,[5] a very meagre number at the end of a half-century of colonization, particularly in comparison with New England which had come upon the scene later than New France.

Talon immediately proceeded to overcome this disparity of numbers between the two cultures: firstly, by encouraging Frenchmen to marry Indian women; secondly, by bringing marriageable girls out from France; and thirdly, by urging soldiers of the Carignan-Salières regiment to settle in Canada. A further step in the interests of an increased population was the imposition of penalties upon celibacy and the granting of bonuses for children. Youths were urged to marry at eighteen and girls at fourteen and fifteen.[6]

This struck a hard blow at the Jesuit policy of securing as many young men as possible for service in the church; consequently, they tried in every way to thwart Talon's policies. The Intendant retorted by giving aid and encouragement to the Sulpicians at Montreal; but an even more telling blow was struck at the Jesuits by bringing back in 1670 the Récollets to Quebec.

Under Talon's leadership there came about a great increase of industry and wealth so that a spirit of optimism began to pervade the whole colony. Officials of both church and state were hoping once more to extend the boundaries of Canada into the far west, a challenge that was taken up by explorers like la Salle and Tonty and a host of Jesuit and Sulpician missionaries, of whom Marquette is the best remembered.[7]

One of Talon's most enduring contributions to the social and political life of New France was his systematic reorganization of the rather haphazard feudalism that had sprung up under the direction of the trading companies. Sixty seigniories had been granted by the companies, but these were seldom occupied by their seigneurs. The scattered settlers on these extensive domains were left helpless victims of Iroquois raids. In 1672 the West Indies Company was compelled to surrender the right to grant lands and Talon took over the responsibility himself, with the firm resolve of making the seigneurs settle down among their tenants. He persuaded many of the officers of the Carignan-Salières regiment to become seigneurs; these with soldiers as tenants were able to defend themselves quite successfully against Iroquois raids; and so there grew up a peculiarly French Canadian seignorial way of life with its charming manor houses, communal ovens and mills and enduring customs, many of which are still evident in the countryside of the Province of Quebec.[8]

II

During the regime of Talon and de Courcelles the underlying tension between church and state never broke out into open warfare; but with their departure in 1672 there arrived as governor of Quebec Louis de Buade, Comte de Frontenac, who refused to resort to any subtleties in dealing with ecclesiastics. Though his regime has usually been regarded as a tremendous success from the materialistic standpoint, it was greatly marred by most undignified quarrels with the church and also with subordinate officials.[9]

As Laval was absent in France when Frontenac became governor there was no immediate clash with the hierarchy at Quebec, but the Governor soon became embroiled in a furious struggle with the Sulpicians at Montreal. It was a controversy reflecting little credit on either party. The Sulpicians as seigneurs of Montreal had appointed a thoroughly dishonest governor, who was engaged in illicit trade with the *coureurs de bois*, the free-lance fur traders of New France. Frontenac as governor-general, without consulting the Sulpicians, had dismissed this official from his post. Abbé Salignac de Fénelon, a half-brother of the famous French mystic of that name, preached a bitter sermon denouncing Frontenac for his high-handed act. The latter summoned the troublesome priest to Quebec for trial before the Sovereign Council. Fénelon denied the right of the council to hear his case and refused to appear before it. Frontenac then ordered his arrest and forcibly shipped him off to France.[10]

It does not appear that Fénelon was disciplined for his disobedience by the authorities in France, but he was not allowed to return to Montreal. Instead Colbert, who had retained Laval in France for a while in the interests of peace, now sent him back to Canada with the added prestige of the title, bishop of Quebec, in place of the nondescript title, bishop of Petræa. Accompanying the bishop was a newly appointed intendant, Duchesneau, who was known to be favourably disposed towards the church.[11]

It is difficult to fathom just what Colbert had in mind by thus weighing the scales against Frontenac in his struggle with the church. No doubt he had become alarmed at some of the governor's high-handed acts, and wished to place a few restraints upon him; yet if he hoped to bring internal peace to New France by creating a balance of power between contending forces, he was to be sadly disillusioned. Two such imperious personalities as Laval and Frontenac were bound to come into violent conflict. Apart from the rather ridiculous tensions over protocol, both parties were deeply suspicious of the ultimate purposes and ambitions of the other. In a particularly bitter letter to Colbert, Frontenac wrote: "Nearly all the disorders in New France spring from the ecclesiastics who want to join to their spiritual authority an absolute power over all things temporal, and who persecute all who do not submit entirely to them."[12] He accused the priests of directly or indirectly meddling in all civil affairs and even of extending their trading activities to include the English of New York. He estimated that the Jesuits, Sulpicians, the bishop and the Seminary together owned two-thirds of the good land of Canada, and that it was their intention to become complete masters in the new world.[13] Colbert does not seem to have taken these charges too seriously, for shortly afterwards he recalled Frontenac to France and appointed a new governor in his place who was quite favourable towards the church. There seems to have been general rejoicing over Frontenac's departure in 1682; but there was to be even greater rejoicing over his return seven years later.

III

After Frontenac's recall, Laval decided to resign his see and went to France in 1684 to present his resignation to the king. Louis XIV accepted the resignation but allowed Laval to choose a successor. The choice fell upon a young chaplain in personal attendance upon the king, Jean-Baptiste de Saint-Vallier who, according to one biographer, accepted the bishopric in Canada in order to avoid becoming a bishop in France.[14]

In this same year the Marquis de Denonville was made governor of Canada. When he sailed for his new post in 1685, he was accompanied, not by Saint-Vallier but by Laval, who returned to Canada to live out the remainder of his days. For some reason Saint-Vallier after a brief visit to Canada and Acadia in 1685-86 returned to France until 1688, while Laval continued to administer the affairs of the diocese; this time with a minimum of friction with state authorities, as Denonville was a very devout churchman who favoured an ecclesiastically dominated society.[15]

It was under the governorship of Denonville that Saint-Vallier began his administration, and all the portents were for a very peaceful episcopate; but as we have seen[16] friction broke out almost at once, not between church and state but within the church itself over the matter of parochial policy. That Saint-Vallier intended to be master in his own diocese was quickly made evident even to Laval, when the former set out to build a huge palace on a high cliff at Quebec where he might train priests under his own control rather than in the Seminary founded by his predecessor.[17]

On one thing both Saint-Vallier and Laval were in agreement: asceticism was the best safeguard against immorality and vice, and they co-operated in trying to impose a rigid rule of life upon the inhabitants of New France. In this they had the hearty co-operation of Governor Denonville.

When Saint-Vallier first took charge of his diocese, there was evident a general disintegration in the spiritual and moral life of the community. The settlement of the officers and soldiers of the Carignan-Salières regiment in the seigniories along the St. Lawrence River had created an entirely new social life from that which had been so carefully fostered by the Jesuits and the other religious orders of New France. The change in morals and conduct was vividly expressed by a sister at Montreal: "Our good king," she wrote, "has sent troops to defend us from the Iroquois, and the soldiers and officers have ruined the Lord's vineyard, and planted wickedness and sin and crime in our soil of Canada."[18] But not all the blame for the general breakdown of morals can be laid at the door of the king's troops. Debauchery and brawling among the fur-traders, particularly the *coureurs de bois* at Montreal, as vividly described by Dollier de Casson,[19] can be ascribed to other causes than the arrival of troops. Governor Denonville in a letter to the authorities in France blamed much of it on parents who allowed their children to be idle and vagabonds of the woods, where they had no *curés* to restrain them. He felt that the attraction of Indian life was corrupting the youth of Canada who "not only copy their way of life, but also run off with their women into the woods."[20]

Lack of moral restraint has been a persistent characteristic of frontier life, usually overcome only when the churches have found some technique for meeting the spiritual needs of the frontiersman. During the first part of Saint-Vallier's administration, the population was so thinly scattered that many of his flock only heard mass three or four times a year, and very often it was impossible to administer the last rites to the dying, or baptize infants. Separated from the admonitions of the church, the settlers soon began to retrograde into the more primitive standards of the Indians. Laval's itinerant ministry of revocable curacies was intended to meet this need, and while he had a plentiful supply of *curés* the system worked well. With the rapid increase of population during Talon's regime, it began to break down, and it was Saint-Vallier's fate to face the worst period of social disorganization since the founding of Quebec. That he succeeded in a marked degree in overcoming the extreme excesses of his parishioners and created a stable and orderly diocesan life speaks volumes for his energy and perseverance. His fierce attacks upon the immoralities of his flock and his vigilance in detecting vice hardly made him a popular bishop. But despite the disparaging remarks of a contemporary French officer, Baron de la Hontan,[21] who could not abide the snooping methods of a bishop who even dared to supervise the proper cuts of ladies' dresses, there seems little doubt that such vigilance was very necessary if the colony was to be saved from complete moral disintegration.

As an administrator of a vast diocese, including Acadia, Newfoundland, Hudson's Bay Territory and Louisiana, Saint-Vallier was continually on the move. He visited Acadia twice and Newfoundland once. During his stay in the latter colony he established Father Denis as *curé* of Plaissance with the title of vicar-general, thus laying the foundations of Roman Catholicism in that ancient colony.[22] He also contributed much to the parochial organization of the Acadians.

During his prolonged absences from Canada, Laval looked after the episcopal functions and was able to see that his former policies were not completely abandoned. Nevertheless, Saint-Vallier left some very enduring monuments of his own in Canada, particularly in the field of social welfare. Before he came to Quebec he had founded a hospital for the poor in his native town, and hospitals seem to have been one of his most serious concerns. At Three Rivers he founded one for the poor, and later he was instrumental in the construction of the General Hospital at Quebec which included a welfare department to take care of indigence and old age.[23]

IV

The sixty-six years that cover the long episcopates of Laval and Saint-Vallier (1659-1725) may well be regarded as the most formative period in the history of French Canadian society. It was a society in which there was little place for heterodox opinions. Denonville, the pious governor who succeeded Frontenac, was able to report to the authorities in France, "Praise be God, there is not a heretic here."[24] Occasionally a Jansenist found his way to Canada, but was quickly ejected when his views became known. It is said that a few Canadian clergy were impressed by Pascal's *Lettres Provinciales*, but there is little evidence to show that Pascal created much of a stir in Canada.[25]

Though both bishops were alert to combat heresy, they showed considerable tolerance towards any evidence of a supernatural intervention in the affairs of the colony. At the town of Ste. Anne de Beaupré, where Laval had established a school for the education of the poorer colonists, there early occurred a miracle; this initiated a vogue of pilgrimages which have continued to the present time.

Typical of the interest in the supernatural occurrences is the story of Jeanne le Ber.[26] Mademoiselle le Ber dwelt for twenty-three years in a cell behind the altar of a church in Montreal, sleeping on a bed of straw never disturbed lest it become too soft. The images upon which she wrote prayers achieved miracles, and according to one Sulpician admirer "equalled anything since the days of Moses." "God," says her biographer, "was the author of this design, which redounded to His glory as well as to the good of souls."[27]

The prominence given to mystical pursuits stands in sharp contrast to the educational development of the colony. Establishments for the practice of the devotional life and the furtherance of Christian charity took precedence over educational institutions. The Jesuits, it is true, sought to provide educational facilities in Quebec as early as 1626 by providing a college for Huron boys; this project was revised in 1635 to include the sons of the colonists, but the Jesuits had a difficult time to lure the youth away from the carefree life of the woods. Marguerite Bourgeoy's Congregation of Notre Dame made a brave attempt to provide for the educational needs of the daughters of the poor, but it concentrated more on handicrafts and practical lessons in good housekeeping than on intellectual pursuits. Laval's industrial school at St. Joachim was for the purpose of providing craftsmen for the colony; but in 1701 he attempted to secure a professor to teach "a beginning of humanities," which according to Abbé H. A. Scott, who deplores Garneau's low estimate of French Canadian education, was the origin of the first normal school in Canada.[28]

Nevertheless in 1714 about all the male instruction taking place in the colony, except for Laval's school at St. Joachim, was in the Seminary at Quebec, where there were seventy-five students. Considerable uneasiness was manifest among the Jesuits because of this neglect of the intellectual life of Canada, for in 1728 they asked permission to found a college at Montreal. Apparently their concern was shared by others, for in the same year the Brothers Charon suggested placing schoolmasters in all the parishes of Canada. A little later (1737) there was organized a brotherhood for the establishment of church schools. The members worked out a syllabus for the peculiar needs of French Canada, and were anxious to undertake the tasks of popular education. Very little success, however, attended these efforts and illiteracy continued to prevail throughout rural French Canada. One reason for the failure of these projects was the lack of encouragement on the part of the civil authorities who considered "the enlightenment of the population a perilous risk to the state."[29]

Such a meagre educational programme as that just depicted was hardly likely to produce men and women of intellectual eminence. The only ones that Parkman can find in the years between the founding of Quebec and the British Conquest are importations from France. Among these he lists the Jesuit missionary Lafitau, author of *Mœurs des Sauvages Americaines*; the noted physician Sarrazin; and the Comte de la Galissonière, the most enlightened of the governors of New France.[30]

V

The industrial backwardness of the Canadians in comparison with their New England neighbours is a matter of chagrin to Garneau, the famous historian of French Canada. He ascribes this lack of commercial acumen on the part of his compatriots to the French colonial administration's failure to encourage cultural pursuits among the colonists. He writes if ". . . the Gallo-Canadians, instead of being habituated to war, the chase and a roving life, had been encouraged to addict themselves to agriculture, to commerce and to the useful arts, the prosperity thence arising would have attracted increased immigration; and when the fitful border hostilities of previous years ripened into open war in 1755, the colonists would have been found rich in resources, and competent to hold their own against any amount of force likely to be brought against them."[31] The historian, however, did not forget a very important factor that contributed much to New England's commercial prosperity as well as to her intellectual pre-eminence, namely, her Calvinistic creed. If the French Calvinists, who were the first colonizers of New France, had been allowed to remain, the cultural development of the two rival communities in North America would have been strikingly similar, though greater natural resources would probably have given New England the lead in commercial prosperity. But the Huguenots, for whom Garneau shows high regard, were banished, and both Laval and Saint-Vallier were resolved that they should not return under the guise of Jansenism.

On the other hand, it can be said that Laval and Saint-Vallier laid more enduring cultural foundations than their Calvinist contemporaries in New England. The land of the Mathers and Cottons has moved far from its theocratic foundations, whereas French Canada today still remains loyal to the ideals and the theology of its founding fathers.

REFERENCES

1. An interesting account of the origin of the Sovereign Council of Quebec is to be found in an introduction by P. J. O. Chauveaux to *Jugements et Délibérations du Conseil Souverain de la Nouvelle-France publiés sous les auspices de la législature de Québec* (Quebec, 1885, 6 vols.), I, pp. i-lxi.

2. On Colbert's policy towards New France *vide* Abbé Desmagures, *Colbert et Canada* (Paris, 1879), pp. 20-38.

3. *Vide Collection de Documents relatifs a l'Histoire de la Nouvelle-France édités sous les auspices de la législature de Québec; Rolle du regiment Carignan*, pp. 172 *et seq.*

4. *Conseil Souverain, op. cit.*, I, pp. 534-536.

5. *Collection de Documents, op. cit.*, p. 166. *Vide* also G. M. Wrong, *The Rise and Fall of New France* (Toronto, 1928, 2 vols.), I, p. 384.

6. *Vide* E. M. Faillon, *Histoire de la Colonie Française en Canada, op. cit.*, III, p. 202 *et seq.*

7. The story of the French missionaries in the Great West is vividly told by Francis Parkman in *La Salle and the Discovery of the Great West* (Boston, 1869).

8. *Vide* W. B. Munro, *Documents relating to Seigniorial Tenure in Canada* (The Champlain Society, Toronto, 1916).

9. *Vide* Jean Delangley, *Frontenac and the Jesuits* (Chicago, 1939), pp. 20 *et seq.*, also Henri Lorin, *Le Comte de Frontenac* (Paris, 1895), *passim.*

10. H. Lorin, *op. cit.*, pp. 103-114.

11. *Ibid.*, pp. 118-119.

12. Quoted by Parkman from a *Mémoire addressé à Colbert, 1667, Count Frontenac and New France under Louis XIV* (Boston, 1877), p. 68.

13. *Ibid. Vide* also Jean Delangley, *op. cit.*, for a defence of the Jesuits against these accusations.

14. Sœur St. Felix, *Monseigneur de Saint-Vallier et l'Hôpital General de Québec* (Quebec, 1882), p. 39.

15. *Vide* J. B. A. Ferland, *Cours d'Histoire du Canada* (Quebec, 1865, 2 vols.), II, p. 149.

16. *Vide supra*, p. 48.

17. *Vide* A. Gosselin, *L'Église du Canada* (Québec, 1911, 4 vols.), I, p. 53 *et seq.*

18. Quoted by Francis Parkman, *The Old Régime in Canada, op. cit.*, p. 369, from *Annales de l'Hôtel Dieu, St. Joseph.*

19. Dollier de Casson, *op. cit.*, p. 375.

20. Quoted by Parkman, *op. cit.*, p. 376, from *Denonville au Ministre, Nov. 13, 1685.*

21. Baron de la Hontan, *New Voyages to North America* (trans. and ed. by R. G. Thwaites, Chicago, 1905, 2 vols.).

22. *Vide* A. Gosselin, *Monseigneur de Saint-Vallier et Son Temps* (Evereux, 1899), p. 64.

23. The works of charity of Saint-Vallier have been faithfully recorded by Sœur St. Felix, *op. cit.*, *passim*.

24. Quoted by Parkman, *op. cit.*, p. 355, from *Denonville au Ministre, Nov. 10, 1866.*

25. *Vide* Garneau, *op. cit.*, I, p. 207.

26. E. M. Faillon, *L'Heroine Chrétienne du Canada au Vie de Mlle. le Ber* (Ville-Marie, 1860).

27. *Ibid.*, p. 86.

28. H. A. Scott, *Bishop Laval* (The Makers of Canada Series, London and Toronto, 1926), pp. 261-262.

29. Garneau, I, p. 207.

30. Parkman, *op. cit.*, p. 366, footnote.

31. Garneau, I, p. 207.

VI

A Time of Troubles

A FEARFUL massacre of French settlers at Lachine by the Iroquois in 1689 was the beginning of a time of troubles for New France which finally culminated in the British Conquest.[1] The massacre was in retaliation for a treacherous act on the part of Governor Denonville, who had seized some Iroquois warriors and sent them as galley slaves to France. As matters continued to go from bad to worse under Denonville's administration, he was recalled and Count Frontenac returned once again to redeem the failing fortunes of New France. His arrival coincided with the fall of Acadia to the English, and he faced the imminent danger of the capture of Quebec by the conqueror of Acadia, Sir William Phips. This second danger was averted, but it now appeared to Frontenac that it was the English colonists who were taking the initiative in harassing the French settlers; consequently, he decided that there would be no peace for New France until the English were expelled from North America; and he felt justified in allowing his Indian allies to murder these friends of the murderous Iroquois.[2]

Both sides were now engaged in a war of frightfulness for the spoils of a continent; the spirit of co-existence which was fitfully manifest during the visit of Gabriel Druillettes to Massachusetts some forty years earlier had disappeared completely.[3] After 1690 the relations between the two cultures steadily deteriorated until nothing less than unconditional surrender would satisfy either party.

I

The evil effects of this uncompromising spirit first became evident in what is now the state of Maine. This bit of land jutting up between Canada and Acadia had become a frontier outpost of Massachusetts and was filling up with an aggressive New England population, who were severing all land connection between the two French colonies. The authorities at Quebec decided to use their Indian converts, the Abenaki, to put a stop to the New England immigration into Maine. To Sebastian Râle, a Jesuit missionary to the Abenaki, was assigned in 1691 the unchristian task of urging his converts to attack the English settlers.

When the New England colonists became aware of Râle's influence among the Indians, they attempted to gain the Abenaki over to their side by converting them to Protestantism. To this end the Massachusetts Assembly offered 150 pounds a year in depreciated currency to any of their ministers who would volunteer to go to Maine and teach the Abenaki the Protestant religion.[4] A Congregational minister by the name of Joseph Baxter accepted the offer and proceeded in 1717 to his mission field where he began to preach on the "enormities of the Roman Catholic religion."[5] Râle met this attack by threatening to excommunicate any of his flock who dared to listen to the New England "heretic." Despite this threat Baxter succeeded in gaining a following among the Abenaki, who immediately petitioned the English governor for "a small praying-house to be built for their use."[5] An amusing aspect of this rival missionary endeavour was the exchange of polemical treatises between the two missionaries in which they vigorously criticized one another's Latin.

It would have been fortunate for all concerned if the enmity between Râle and Baxter could have been confined to theological discourses and treatises, but political events began to superimpose upon the controversy a more violent aspect. The Abenaki were apparently becoming reconciled to British rule and were disinclined to continue their raids upon the New England settlements, so Râle in desperation called in Christian Indians from around Quebec for this purpose. This in turn provoked the English to send an expedition against Râle's missionary compound at Norridgewock on the Kennebec River. During the fighting the village was destroyed; the attackers collected some twenty scalps, among them Râle's. Though little defence can be offered for this murderous attack upon a missionary compound, yet it is difficult to regard Sebastian Râle a martyr in the same sense as Jean Brébeuf was a martyr to the Christian faith. The vindictive spirit of the former bears little resemblance to the pacific nature of the latter.[6]

II

What was occurring in Maine was soon to become a common feature of the struggle for supremacy in North America, a struggle that now extended from the far west frontier outposts eastward to Acadia. In the latter country the policy of frightfulness brought about one of the most tragic occurrences of the whole continental struggle, the expulsion of the Acadians.

After Champlain and de Monts had shifted their interest from this Atlantic colony to Quebec and the St. Lawrence Valley, Acadia had assumed a very secondary place in French policy. It can almost be said that the few French who remained around Port Royal became the founders of a new race of people; their homes and fortifications destroyed by the Virginians, deserted by their patrons in France and with no means of transportation across the Atlantic, they had to learn from the friendly Micmacs how to survive in the primeval forest. A few of them intermarried with the Indians, but as the Acadian historian Antoine Bernard has been able to show from church records, such intermarriages were exceptional.[7] There was a further interchange of racial stocks after some Scottish colonists, brought out from Scotland by Sir William Alexander in 1629, were in turn deserted by their patron and had to depend upon their French neighbours for food and shelter. In time these Scotch settlers became indistinguishable from their French benefactors whose language, religion and customs became their own.[8]

By various European treaties Acadia or Nova Scotia, as the Scots named it, passed back and forth from France to England for almost a hundred years.[9] During these years of uncertainty, while adventurous noblemen from Britain and France established trading posts and carried on baronial wars, the Roman Catholic Church never relinquished its oversight of the religious development of the area.

After the withdrawal of the Jesuits in 1613, the Récollets arrived in Acadia, establishing their headquarters at Port Royal with subsidiary missions at two trading stations that had been set up by Charles de la Tour, one on the opposite side of the Bay of Fundy at the head of the St. John River and the other at Cape Sable on the extreme southern tip of Nova Scotia.[10]

The seizure of Port Royal by Sir William Alexander in 1628 brought a halt to the missionary activity of the Récollets; and when Acadia was again restored to the French in 1632, they were replaced by the Capuchins. This order began its mission on the south shore of Nova Scotia, at La Have, where Isaac de Razilly had taken official possession of the country in the name of the One Hundred Associates. About three hundred additional settlers had arrived with de Razilly, and La Have became the capital of a revived Acadia. From La Have the Capuchins began to seek out the Indians in what is now the Province of New Brunswick and even ventured as far north as Bay Chaleur, where they organized a mission to the Abenaki.[11]

Acadia received its first episcopal visitation in 1686, when Bishop Saint-Vallier, accompanied by a Sulpician priest, toured the whole area from Meductec (Woodstock, New Brunswick) to Port Royal. The priest in charge of the mission at Port Royal, then known as the parish of Assumption, was Abbé Petit, who had formerly been an officer of the Carignan-Salières regiment. Ordained at Quebec in 1670, he had been sent to Acadia in 1676 with the title of vicar-general. Abbé Petit impressed upon the bishop of Quebec the good qualities of his Acadian flock who did not indulge in "swearing, debauchery or drunkenness." Their faithful attendance at church, even though they had to walk several miles through difficult wood trails, was brought to the bishop's attention, with the result that after Saint-Vallier's return to Quebec he sent an assistant to Abbé Petit, a Father Geoffrey of the Sulpician Order, who in 1687 became the first *curé* of the parish of Grand Pré.[12]

The good work of Abbé Petit was suddenly interrupted by still another capture of Port Royal in 1690 by Sir William Phips, who carried the missionary a captive to Boston. After two years' captivity he was allowed to return to his Acadian flock among whom he ministered until 1696, when he retired to live out his remaining years at the Seminary of Quebec. The dedication of this early missionary and that of his colleagues implanted in the Acadians a deep religious loyalty to the Roman Catholic Church which has never lagged to this present day.[13]

In their strict adherence to all the rites and ceremonies of their church the Acadians bear a marked resemblance to their compatriots in the Province of Quebec, but here to a large extent the resemblance ends. The greater isolation of Acadia from the outside world and the paucity of its population—at the end of the seventeenth century it did not exceed 1,500 souls—retarded its material progress. No Talon had ever stimulated the inhabitants to attempt the development of native industries in order that they might compete on better terms with their New England competitors; nor had the peaceful Micmacs required from them the same martial daring as the Iroquois had demanded of their Canadian compatriots; hence they produced no heroes or heroines of the stature of Adam Dollard or Madeleine Verchères to quicken a local nationalism of the same intensity as their Canadian cousins.[14]

In the wars between England and France in which the Acadians were not permitted to take any part in shaping their political destiny, they wished only to be left alone to their fishing, farming, and the practice of their religious obligations. Life for them was a familiar round of daily duty within a closely knit familial association, not unlike that which has been depicted in Longfellow's famous poem *Evangeline*.[15]

But it was not to be. As in Maine, so in Nova Scotia it was French policy to use Christian Indians to harass any English colonists who might attempt to settle in the province, particularly after Acadia had been ceded to Great Britain in 1713. Bishop Saint-Vallier seems to have concurred with the civil authorities at Quebec in this policy and sent missionary priests to stir up both the Micmacs and the Acadians against English rule. The Micmacs co-operated heartily, and brought upon themselves a fearful revenge from some New England fishermen who decorated the palisades of the fort they had built at Canso with Micmac heads.[16]

Abbé le Loutre, "a Breton priest with a fiery temperament,"[17] whom Saint-Vallier had made his vicar-general in Nova Scotia, was the evil genius of the Acadian tragedy. Like his colleague, Sebastian Râle in Maine, he regarded the war against the English as a holy crusade and showed little scruple in urging the Indians on to their murderous attacks. He was even accused, whether rightly or wrongly, of paying the Indians money for English scalps. There seems to be little doubt, however, that he used his Indian converts to force the Acadians to violate their promise to remain neutral in the wars between England and France.[18]

With the founding of Halifax in 1749 le Loutre redoubled his efforts to win the Acadians for the French cause, as the establishment of this strongly fortified post on the Atlantic seaboard of Nova Scotia was the first indication that the English intended seriously to colonize this much-neglected area. Only a short time before, the British government had returned Louisburg on Cape Breton Island to the French by the treaty of Aix-la-Chapelle (1748); this, after the colonists of New England under the leadership of Governor Shirley had made heroic efforts to capture it. The New Englanders had become so chagrined at the subordination of their own war efforts to European interests that the British in compensation for the loss of Louisbourg built Halifax as a token of their intention to retain the remainder of Nova Scotia at least.[19]

During New England occupation of Isle Rôyale (Cape Breton) and Isle St. Jean (Prince Edward Island) there had been constant rumours of expulsions,[20] revealing only too clearly to the Acadians of the mainland that they themselves might also expect to become the victims of mass deportation. Furthermore, it impressed even more strongly upon the Canadians themselves that they were now entering upon a final phase in the struggle for the North American continent.

III

This final phase came at a very inopportune time in the civic and church life of New France. The corruption in governmental circles, particularly during the regime of the infamous Intendant Bigot, played an overwhelming part in the disastrous fall of Quebec in 1759,[21] but the decline of the spiritual ardour of the church also made its contribution.

That something ominous and portentous was happening to the religious life of New France was made evident as early as 1727 in the unusual proceedings that followed upon the death of Bishop Saint-Vallier. Before his death the bishop had prepared a tomb for himself in the parish church of Notre Dame des Anges. As miracles were anticipated at this tomb, it was expected that there would be an unusual rush of the faithful to the parish church, prompting the canons of the cathedral to take some measures to prevent a stampede. They conceived a plan which they thought might at least lessen the rush by having the body of the dead prelate carried from church to church in Quebec and then finally brought to the cathedral for an elaborate funeral service. Their plans, however, were overruled by Archdeacon Lotbinière, who insisted that he was the acting head of the church in Quebec until the arrival of the coadjutor bishop, Duplessis de Mornay, still residing in France. With the support of the Intendant Dupuy, the archdeacon gave orders for the burial in accordance with the wishes of the late primate; the funeral then took place, precipitately at night, a weird proceeding which Saint-Vallier's biographer, Abbé Gosselin, finds difficult to explain.[22]

Whatever the explanation, the incident was indicative of the general religious apathy that was sweeping over eighteenth-century Christendom. The refusal of the third bishop of Quebec, de Mornay, to reside in his diocese because he feared to cross the ocean[23] was also indicative of a great decline from the spiritual fervour that was characteristic of the church of Laval. Nor were matters much improved with the appointment of a coadjutor, Pierre Hermann Dosquet, who continued to display the same kind of indifference to the spiritual needs of New France as his superior.

Not all of the blame, however, for the scandalous condition of the church in Canada at this time can be ascribed to lack of episcopal oversight. Even if Dosquet had been a far more vigorous leader than he proved to be, it is doubtful if he could have done much to rehabilitate the spiritual life of the diocese. When he arrived in Quebec in 1732 he discovered that out of the one hundred parishes that had been organized in Canada only twenty-three were provided with priests, and several of the incumbents were on the verge of starvation; the diocese as a whole seemed to be in a very factious mood. Dosquet soon decided that the problems of the Canadian church were beyond the competence of a mere coadjutor bishop and returned to France, thus giving Canada the unique distinction of having two non-resident bishops.

In 1733 Bishop de Mornay was persuaded to resign his see, and Dosquet proceeded again to Quebec with the enhanced prestige of full episcopal authority; but he still found the Canadian priests so disobedient and quarrelsome that he again gave up in despair, returned to France and carried on the semblance of episcopal administration from a safe retreat in Paris.[24]

IV

A good deal of the disorder that was now overwhelming the Canadian church was due to the decline of the influence of the Jesuits, who had laid the spiritual foundations of New France and had been the real power behind the throne during the episcopates of Laval and Saint-Vallier. Their decline in prestige was not unique to Canada, but was part of a world-wide revolt against the Society of Jesus, finally culminating in its dissolution by papal decree. The French government had taken the lead in forcing the pope to disavow the order; consequently, this enmity was bound to be reflected in New France, and was particularly noticeable during the latter part of Saint-Vallier's regime. It was one of the bitter griefs of the aged prelate that the Jesuits had been compelled to give up their missionary work in the western fur-trading posts of Detroit, Sault-Sainte-Marie and Michilimackinac because they were in constant danger of their lives from intoxicated Indians, and could expect little protection from those who were responsible for law and order at these stations. Behind this disguised form of persecution was la Mothe Cadillac, the founder of Detroit, whom Abbé Gosselin describes as "the inveterate enemy of the Company of Jesus."[25]

One of the most constant accusations against the Jesuits at this time was their propensity for commercial activity which they were charged with pursuing to the neglect of their spiritual duties. But the Jesuits were not the only converts to the mercantile spirit of the eighteenth century. Bishop Dosquet in one of his brief visits to Quebec had obtained a seigniory for his own personal profit and thereby set an example which, in the words of Abbé Gosselin, "started among the Canadian clergy a veritable epidemic of commercial and industrial enterprises."[26]

It is possible to offer some justification for the commercial activity of the clergy, since they were practically on the verge of destitution. Neither the government nor wealthy patrons were, as in times past, providing enough money for the upkeep of the religious establishments of New France; consequently, the clergy had to fend for themselves. The Jesuits, with their usual efficiency, were rather more successful than others in their commercial enterprises and brought upon themselves the greater condemnation.

Their general unpopularity in Canada was impressed upon them in the choice of a successor to Bishop Dosquet. The selection of a bishop had usually been under the direction of the Jesuits, but at long last this privilege was assigned to the Sulpicians.[27] The latter, fully aware that they were replacing the Jesuits as the dominant order in New France, chose a very pious and saintly priest, François-Louis de Lauberivière. But the high hopes that were raised for the future of the church in Canada by this wise choice were suddenly dashed by the death of the new bishop in 1740 from a plague he had contracted on board the ship that carried him to Quebec. The court, however, still under Sulpician influence, immediately appointed as his successor another highly regarded cleric, Abbé Henri-Marie de Pontbriand. The Jesuits were now completely out of favour and so the long-deferred Sulpician regime began.[28]

V

Unfortunately for the Sulpician order and for Bishop Pontbriand, there was to be little opportunity to bring about the reforms in church life that both had in view.   The new bishop had to begin his episcopate during the regime of the Intendant Bigot, who has been described without exaggeration as "the most unscrupulous official ever to have dishonoured the administration of New France."   Pontbriand seems to have been too deferential to the wishes of this wily politician, which resulted in several humiliations of the episcopal office.[29]

The first humiliation came in his attempt in 1749 to suppress the General Hospital at Montreal; and this only two years after he had asked a remarkable woman, Madame Marguerite d'Youville, to redeem its failing fortunes.   Though the people of Montreal had not taken kindly to Madame d'Youville at first,[30] and called her little band of followers the tipsy sisters (les sœurs grises), because of their early association with a store in which liquor had been sold, yet they had come to admire her administration of the hospital and were up in arms at the attempt to close it.   So loudly did they sing the praises of Madame d'Youville and her grey sisters, as they now translated les sœurs grises,[31] that not only were the bishop's orders countermanded by the home authorities but a patent was forthcoming which permitted Madame d'Youville to found a religious community, a rare occurrence in the religiously apathetic eighteenth century.   It is perhaps not without significance that this eighteenth-century foundation had a mercantile origin and was from the first distinguished for its financial acumen.

The humiliation of Pontbriand was perhaps a minor matter in view of the disasters that lay in store not only for the bishop, but for the whole French regime in Canada.   The last days of the old regime were beset with one calamity after another, so that it seemed that both human and supernatural forces were conspiring against the survival of New France. Besides the ever-present threat of the English who were closing in on every side, there were epidemics, storms, floods, and even earthquakes. Between the years of 1740 to 1760 there were no less than eight disastrous crop failures, leaving famine and inflation in their trail.[32]   There was the fall of Louisbourg, which might have been averted if the greedy Bigot had not deprived the unhappy defenders of the means to defend themselves.   There was the cruel expulsion of the Acadians in 1755, which filled the inhabitants of Canada with a fear that a like fate was in store for them.

The one hope of avoiding this culminating tragedy lay in the brilliant generalship of Montcalm.   But the provincial jealousy of the first Canadian-born governor-general, Vaudreuil, and the irresponsible rapacity of the Intendant Bigot made it impossible for Montcalm to save the fortress of Quebec from the British. So it came about that an equally brilliant general, James Wolfe, won the battle of the Plains of Abraham in 1759; in due course followed by the Treaty of Paris (1763), and the beginning of a new era in Canada.

Before the fall of Quebec, Pontbriand had retired to Montreal and tradition has it that he turned to Mother d'Youville and her Grey Sisters for shelter and care in the last dark days of the old regime. Nor did he survive long the fall of Quebec. On June 8, 1760, he died of a broken heart at the age of fifty-one. His bodily reserves had been exhausted by the sight of the misery of his flock, and the knowledge that three armies were closing in on Montreal.[33]

VI

The British Conquest from the point of view of church history was the frustration of the pious hope of establishing a great Catholic empire in North America. In the early days of the colony, as we have seen, this project was constantly kept in mind and very often the interests of the state were subordinated to the interests of the church. But in later days, and particularly in the second quarter of the eighteenth century, the religious motive began to take a secondary place to the growing interest in trade and commerce. It was soon revealed that in the pursuit of material rewards the *Canadien* who had formerly won so many victories while fighting for his faith was no match for the *Bostonais* who identified commercial prosperity with the favour of God.

REFERENCES

1. *Vide* G. M. Wrong, *Rise and Fall of New France* (Toronto, 1928, 2 vols.), for a sympathetic account of the fall of New France, especially vol. II.

2. W. D. Le Sueur, *Count Frontenac* (Makers of Canada Series, London and Toronto, 1926, 2 vols.), II, p. 317.

3. *Vide supra*, p. 35.

4. Francis Parkman, *A Half Century of Conflict* (Boston, 1892, 2 vols.), I, p. 220.

5. Quoted by Parkman from the petition preserved in the Massachusetts Archives, *op. cit.*, I, p. 220.

6. For conflicting views on Râle's policy *vide* A. Gosselin, *L'Église du Canada depuis Monseigneur de Laval jusqu'à la Conquête* (Québec, 1911, 3 vols.), I, pp. 379-381; and Parkman, *op. cit.*, I, p. 239; also W. I. Kip, *The Early Jesuit Missions in North America* (New York, 1847), pp. 69-78. Kip gives in full a letter from Father de la Chasse, superior general of missions in New France with a description of the death of Râle.

7. A. Bernard, *L'Acadie Vivante* (Montreal, 1954), appendix, Note A, pp. 171-174.

8. *Vide* G. P. Insh, *Scottish Colonial Schemes 1620-1686* (Glasgow, 1923), p. 89; also T. H. McGrail, *Sir William Alexander* (Edinburgh, 1940), pp. 121-123.

9. *Vide* T. B. Aikins, ed., *Selections from the Public Documents of the Province of Nova Scotia* (Halifax, N.S., 1869), for documents relating to Acadians. The impartiality of this selection has been challenged by E. Richard, in *Acadia, Missing Links of a Lost Chapter in American History* (New York and Montreal, 1895, 2 vols.), I, p. 13.

10. A. Coillard Després, *Charles de Saint-Étienne de la Tour . . . et son Temps 1593-1666* (Arthabaska, P.Q., 1930), pp. 177-179.

11. *Ibid*, pp. 279-288; *vide* also Omer le Grésley, *L'Enseignement du Français en Acadie 1604-1926* (Bathurst-Ouest, N.B., 1926), pp. 28 *et seq.*

12. *Vide* H. R. Casgrain, *Les Sulpiciens . . . en Acadie, 1676-1762* (Quebec, 1897), pp. 66-67.

13. O. Le Grésley, *op. cit.*, pp. 56-64.

14. *Vide* Lionel Groulx, *La Naissance d'une Race* (Montreal, 1919), especially p. 253.

15. *Vide* A. Bernard, *L'Acadie Vivante, op. cit.*, for a contemporary description of the Acadian people at the opening of the eighteenth century by *Sieur de Dierville*, pp. 44-60.

16. Parkman, *op. cit.*, I, p. 197.

17. Bernard, *op. cit.*, p. 66.

18. *Vide* T. B. Aikins, *op. cit.*, pp. 178-180. Also C. B. Ferguson, "The Expulsion of the Acadians," article in *The Dalhousie Review* (Halifax, 1953), vol. 35, No. 2, pp. 125-135.

19. *Vide* J. B. Brebner, *New England's Outpost* (New York, 1917), pp. 168-169.

20. D. C. Harvey, *The French Regime in Prince Edward Island* (New Haven, 1926), p. 112.

21. *Vide* Guy Fregault, *Francis Bigot* (Les Études de l'Institut d'Histoire de l'Amerique Française, 1948, 2 vols.), II, pp. 219-273.

22. A. Gosselin, *op. cit.*, I, p. 449.

23. *Ibid.*, II, p. 28.

24. *Ibid.*, II, p. 328.

25. *Ibid.*, II, p. 199.

26. *Ibid.*, II, p. 398.

27. *Ibid.*, II, p. 354.

28. *Ibid.*, III, p. 10.

29. *Ibid.*, III, pp. 164 *et seq.; vide* also Madame Jette, *Vie de la Vénérable Mère d'Youville* (Montreal, 1900).

30. *Vide* Mary Fitts, *Hands to the Needy* (New York, 1950), a recent biography of Mother d'Youville.

31. *Ibid.*, p. 95.

32. *Vide* F. X. Garneau, *op. cit.*, II, p. 163.

33. A. Gosselin, *op. cit.*, III, pp. 544-552.

VII

An Age of Transition

ONE OF THE major misfortunes of the French Canadian church at the opening of British rule in Canada was the lack of a bishop. It was ameliorated somewhat by the fact that Bishop Pontbriand before leaving Quebec for Montreal had designated the Breton-born Jean Olivier Briand as his vicar-general to negotiate with the conquerors. Briand seems to have immediately gained the confidence of General James Murray,[1] the first governor-general of British Canada, to whom he presented the need for a bishop. It was a bold request, as Roman Catholicism was not yet a tolerated religion in England or in any of her overseas possessions, and had only recently been proscribed in Nova Scotia. Furthermore, the British government had not yet seen fit to appoint a bishop of its own established church in any of its older colonies in North America, though there had long been agitation among the Anglican colonists for such an appointment.[2] Governor Murray could hardly, with good grace, give prior consideration to a proscribed religion, while ignoring the Anglican appeal. Yet Briand succeeded where the Anglicans had failed; not only that, but he himself became the governor's choice for the post, even though the canons of the cathedral of Quebec had recommended the superior of the Sulpicians at Montreal, Abbé Montgolfier. When Murray made known his own preference Montgolfier withdrew his name and the canons obediently chose Briand in his place.[3] Rome confirmed the choice and Governor Murray used his utmost persuasive powers with the English court to gain the concurrence of George III.

In 1764 Briand repaired to England where with the acquiescence of the British government he received his bulls of institution from the pope; thence, he proceeded to Paris where he secured consecration and returned to Canada with the title "Superintendant of the Romish Church," the designation given to him by the British authorities, since they were withholding the title of bishop for an Anglican incumbent at Quebec.

Thus after an interregnum of six years (1760-1766) the French Canadian church once again had a bishop upon whom was imposed the task of rebuilding a badly shattered diocese. Though the selection had been that of a British governor, it is the opinion of the church historian Gosselin that "never was made a better choice for the important and difficult work which had to be done in this critical epoch of our religious history."[4]

I

Upon assuming office Briand faced three very serious problems: the reconstruction of the physical plant of his diocese, the revival of the human agency of the evangel, and the recovery of the *morale* of his people. Along with this was the need to establish a proper relationship between the French- and the English-speaking arrivals who had immediately taken over the commercial life of Canada after the Conquest. Nor could he ever forget that in the terms of capitulation of the French to the British at Montreal in 1760, the latter had only agreed to the free exercise of the Catholic religion as far as British law would permit. It was this reservation which hung like a sword of Damocles over Briand's negotiations for the appointment of a bishop and required him to walk warily at all times in his bargaining with the ruling authorities at Quebec.[5]

In comparison with the human problems, the rebuilding of shattered churches and executive buildings was perhaps a minor matter, but it was a formidable task with many heartaches. Most of the church buildings at Quebec had been left in a shambles as a result of General Wolfe's bombardment. The cathedral church had been completely burned down. In the Quebec Seminary only the kitchen was habitable; the church in the Lower City was entirely demolished and those of the Récollets and the Jesuits were in need of extensive repairs; only in the church of the Ursulines was it possible to carry on the offices of the liturgy.[6]

Briand was determined to rebuild the cathedral at once, but in his building plans he was continually harassed by his own clergy, particularly by the canons at Quebec who had not yet divested themselves of the factious spirit that had been the despair of Dosquet. At first they opposed a cathedral as too expensive, and they long continued to haggle over details.[7] It was not until 1774 that Quebec again had a cathedral. The building of an episcopal palace provoked even more opposition among his subordinates, so that it was never completed in time for Briand's occupation, and he continued to reside until the day of his death in the Seminary at Quebec.

A far greater problem than restoration of buildings was the securing of an adequate staff to take care of the spiritual needs of the people. Though the clergy for the most part had remained in Canada after the Conquest, they were pitiably small in numbers. In 1758 there had been one hundred and eighty-one priests in Canada, but by the time Briand assumed office they were down to one hundred and thirty-eight.[8] As the British had forbidden the importation of priests from France it became almost impossible either to fill up the vacant parishes or to replace priests who became incapacitated or reached retiring age.

Also a great gap in the life of the church had been created by the suppression of the male religious orders. Though the occupying forces had permitted the religious communities of women to carry on as before the Conquest, no such leniency was shown to the Sulpicians and Récollets; the Jesuits by this time had been outlawed by the pope and their vast estates had supposedly been granted by the British government to Lord Amherst as part of the spoils of victory.[9]

For some years Briand had to leave many French Canadian parishes vacant, but he immediately proceeded to fill up the ranks of the clergy by urging young ordinands to resume their interrupted studies, and by constantly watching out for candidates for the priesthood in his diocese. During an episcopate of eighteen years he ordained no less than ninety young men.[10]

The most serious challenge that this first bishop after the Conquest had to face was the despairing mood of his people. It was some time before the *Canadiens* really grasped the significance of the Conquest or tried to make any adequate adjustment to the new era that was suddenly imposed upon them, believing that in a few years France would again, as in the past, regain her lost colonies. When the Treaty of Paris was signed by the French government in 1763, confirming the permanency of British rule in Canada, many of the more prosperous families deserted the country because they could not endure the thought of living "under subjection and perpetual inferiority."[11] There still remained, however, some sixty thousand French Canadians sadly in need of political direction and spiritual uplift. Many of them had abandoned the puritan morals of an earlier day and had followed the example of extravagant display and licentious conduct that characterized the officers and officials who

had come out to New France with Montcalm.   Nor were the native
Canadians altogether immune from the influence of those officers from
France who had been imbued with the ideas of Voltaire and the
Encyclopaedists.[12]

Signs were not wanting, however, during the last days of New
France that the colonists had not wholly succumbed to the irreligious
spirit of the times.   The establishment of the Order of Grey Nuns on the
eve of the British Conquest was one such sign; another was the continued
devotion and loyalty of local *curés* and peasantry to the *mores* and folkways
of the less sophisticated seventeenth-century New France, to which they
turned with a renewed ardour during the transition from French to
British rule.   It was this revival of a past era, perhaps more than anything
else, that saved French Canada from absorption into the dominant
Anglo-Saxon culture.[13]

Bishop Briand took the lead in encouraging this development, but
at the same time he had to avoid any serious clash between his own
people and the new-comers who had followed the British armies into
Quebec and Montreal.   It was no simple task for Briand to commend
these Calvinist traders to a flock which had been so long shielded from
all association with heretics; but he felt that there must be no outward
show of hostility lest the British officials would harden their hearts against
the Roman Church.   So in 1768 he issued a circular letter in which he
urged French Catholics "to avoid using any offensive or abusive terms
towards those subjects of the King who are of another religion."   He
also urged that "good harmony be not disturbed by making proselytes."[14]

The fruit of this co-operation with the British authorities and
particularly with Governor Murray's successor, Sir Guy Carleton, later
known as Lord Dorchester, was the Quebec Act of 1774, which was to a
large extent the work of the bishop and the governor, who were now
laying the foundations for a dual culture in Canada.   The Quebec Act
carved out a generous portion of British North America into a new
province in which the French Canadians were in a majority; these were
permitted to retain many of their old laws and customs and the church
was allowed to continue to tithe its people.   This was indeed a victory
for Briand's conciliatory policy; but he had also profited by the violence
of republican sentiment now appearing in the older English colonies
and even among the English-speaking settlers in Canada.   The Quebec
Act, in the final analysis, was an open bid for French Canadian loyalty

in the struggle that was foreseen between England and her Thirteen Colonies.[15]

When finally the American colonists to the south decided to break their ties with the mother country, they received no support from the hierarchy of Quebec. Briand's exhortations of loyalty to the British crown were re-echoed by his clergy and did much to keep the French Canadians from joining the American forces. Though the *Canadiens* showed considerable lukewarmness in defending their province, yet Briand's own exemplary conduct, along with that of most of the clergy, had given the Roman Church a favoured position in the eyes of the British officials and had acquired the gratitude of Governor Carleton. The cordial relationship that had grown up between the governor and the bishop was well expressed in one of Briand's reports to the Vatican. Writing in 1774, he said, ". . . I exercise here my ministry without restraint. The governor loves and esteems me. . . . I rejected an oath which had been proposed and the parliament of Great Britain changed it in such manner that it is possible for any Catholic to take it."[16]

II

Relations between British officialdom and the Roman hierarchy didn't always remain so harmonious, especially after the Loyalists began to enter Canada in great numbers.

Briand resigned his see in 1784 and so missed the full impact of the Loyalist invasion. Consequently it fell to later bishops, and particularly to Bishop Jean François Hubert who assumed full administrative powers in 1788, after serving for two years as coadjutor to Briand's immediate successor, d'Esglis, to consolidate the victories that had been won during the American Revolution for the retention of a French Canadian culture and language.[17] Bishop Hubert's most perplexing problem was in the field of education, since the Quebec hierarchy for the most part was opposed to any educational system in which there would be intimate association of French and English students. But this was one matter in which there developed a schism within the hierarchy itself, for Bishop Hubert had on the insistence of Lord Dorchester appointed Charles Bailly as his coadjutor. Bailly had at one time been a tutor to the Governor's children and had also during his residence at Halifax, as the vicar-general of the bishop of Quebec, learned to admire British institutions.[18]   Much to Hubert's surprise the coadjutor bishop took a strong stand for an educational system in which both Roman Catholics and Protestants should participate.

The English-speaking settlers and particularly the Loyalists soon became very impatient for greater educational facilities in Canada, and were quick to take advantage of this schism within the Roman Catholic community.   They put forth the idea that the revenue from the sequestered estates of the Jesuits should be used for a general educational programme for the whole province, which would include a "mixed" university for French- and English-speaking students, to be controlled by a board of governors consisting of the governor, chief judges, and the bishops along with sixteen to twenty leading citizens.[19]   Bishop Bailly threw himself enthusiastically behind this plan and was an active member of the committee that had been set up to consider the project.   The suggestions of this committee created considerable embarrassment for Bishop Hubert.   Not only did he have to admit a division within his own church family, but also to reveal unmistakably to the government that it was the fixed intention of the hierarchy to prevent any genuine interfusion of the two cultures that were now compelled to live together harmoniously if Canada were to survive.   Since it was the policy of the British government to bring about more cordial relationships between the two peoples over which they had the difficult task of ruling, Bishop Hubert felt he could not appear too intransigent and so he pleaded that the time was not ripe for a frontier country like Canada to have a university such as was contemplated by the committee.   Much to his dismay he found himself accused by his coadjutor of condemning the people of Canada "to vegetate in ignorance, barbarity and fanaticism."[20]

French Canadian historians are almost unanimous in their condemnation of Bishop Bailly's action at this time.   Garneau's comment is, "Happily his destiny was not to make Quebec's episcopal throne 'the seat of the scorner.'"[21]   Bailly died three years before Bishop Hubert and never had an opportunity to put his educational policy into operation; and Hubert steadfastly refused to have anything to do with a mixed university or with a combined educational system, a policy rigidly adhered to by all his successors.

When the Loyalists discovered that there was little hope of co-operation from the Roman Catholics in creating better educational opportunities in Canada they began to agitate for the annulment of the Quebec Act and to demand that English law and speech should supersede

French. As most of this agitation came from settlers in the western part of the province the British government again came to the aid of their French-speaking subjects with the Constitutional Act of 1791.[22] This act divided Canada into two parts: the upper half to be given to the Loyalists in which English law and customs should prevail; the lower half to be retained by the French where, for the most part, the feudal customs and practices of the old regime would continue as they had prevailed under the Quebec Act of 1774.

Though the Constitutional Act of 1791 seemed to have saved the hierarchy of Quebec from the worst consequences of its opposition to Loyalist demands, it still had to face severe assaults from the English-speaking commercial community that had preceded the Loyalist immigration into Canada and was now strongly entrenched in the trading centres of Quebec and Montreal. They also opposed the retention in Lower Canada of French laws and feudal practices which they found hampering to trade and commerce. At first the British authorities at Quebec showed little sympathy for this commercial class, and the English civil servants almost unanimously gave their support to the French community. While Lord Dorchester was governor there was little likelihood that the commercial community would achieve its ends. He was stoutly opposed, as was also his successor Haldimand, to convoking the popular assembly that had been promised in the Quebec Act, until some way should be found to allow Roman Catholic representation which was not permitted in British legislative assemblies. The commercial community were anxious for an assembly from which Roman Catholics were excluded, so that they might gain political control of the province. But the assembly, when it was finally convoked, had French representation by allowing Roman Catholic members to take a simple oath of loyalty to the king.[23]

Thus far the French-speaking community had had the support of the governors set over them by the British government, but there now arrived in Quebec a governor, Sir James Craig, who was thoroughly in sympathy with the aims of the commercial community and who also represented a less lenient attitude towards the Roman Church in Canada.[24] This change of policy had been foreshadowed as early as 1787 by the appointment of an Anglican bishop at Halifax, and was brought home more sternly to the French Canadians by the appointment of Jacob Mountain as bishop of Quebec in 1793.[25]

Lord Dorchester had opposed setting up an Anglican episcopate at

Quebec and hastened to reassure the French Canadians that this appointment meant no infringement upon the liberty of the Catholic Church, but no such assurance came from Sir James Craig. He and his famous secretary, Herman W. Ryland, renewed the educational issue and were sympathetic to the suppression of the French language. But what was even more startling was a demand on the part of Governor Craig to nominate Roman Catholic priests to their parishes. This right he actually compelled Bishop Denault, the successor of Hubert, to concede, inflicting upon the Roman Catholic hierarchy its greatest humiliation since the Conquest.[26]

III

At this bleak moment in the relations of church and state in Lower Canada, two events intervened to turn the tables on the commercial community and to give the church a more solid position than it had ever previously enjoyed in the history of Canada. The first of these was the ascension in 1806 of Joseph-Octave Plessis[27] to the episcopal throne of Quebec; the other was the outbreak of war between Great Britain and the United States in 1812. Of these two, the war was perhaps more decisive, but even before 1812 Plessis had proved more than a match for both Sir James Craig and Bishop Mountain. At least it is the opinion of the hierarchy itself that "Plessis was placed at the heart of the Church of Canada at a moment when it had need of a man of genius."[28]

In the same year that Jacob Mountain was appointed bishop of Quebec, Plessis had sent a *memoire* to the holy see in which he made a very candid estimate of the prospects of the Roman Catholic Church in Canada in the struggle that was then looming up between his church and the Anglican. He speaks in high praise of the Canadian priests of his own church, whose numbers had been reinforced by priests from France, who had been exiled by the French Revolution and been permitted by the British government to come to Canada. Contrasted with this happy situation of a well-staffed Catholic Church he points out that "up to the present there are few Protestant ministers in Canada, and in general they are not in good repute," an observation with which Bishop Mountain would have concurred. He also emphasized the greater steadfastness and loyalty of Catholics to their own church in comparison with the Protestants. "There are not," he said, "five Catholics who have become Protestant since the Conquest," but during this same period "two to three hundred Protestants have abjured their errors and are now in the bosom of the Church." A comparison of the relative populations of the two faiths also gave the church a sense of confidence that it would survive the present onslaught. "The diocese," he wrote, "contained about 160,000 Catholics, as many Europeans as Canadians and Indians." The large proportion of Europeans was due to the fact that Irish Catholics were arriving in Canada in considerable numbers at this time and were helping to offset the Protestant gain through Loyalist immigration. Plessis estimated that the number of Protestants in Canada in 1793 was in the vicinity of twenty thousand souls, of which ten thousand were in Upper Canada.[29]

In this very candid *memoire* Plessis concedes that literature emanating from the French Revolution may have done some harm to Catholics and he is grateful to the British government for having proscribed "systems so detrimental to the prosperity of states." He feels that the proscription has brought to an end "the tendency to accept radical ideas."[30] As one can see, Plessis, even before he took over the administration of the diocese, had been counting his resources for a final showdown with Sir James Craig. But this ultimate test of strength never took place, for with the approach of hostilities Sir James Craig was recalled by the British government and replaced by Sir George Prevost, whose immediate task was to win the active loyalty of the French Canadians for the coming war. One of the first steps in this direction was to give up all claim on the part of the governor to nominate priests into their parishes.[31]

During the war Plessis won some unusual concessions from the British government. The most surprising was the grant of a yearly stipend of one thousand pounds to the French bishop, which had been recommended by Prevost; another was the right to sit in the legislative council. This put him on an official equality with Bishop Mountain. The most pleasing of all to Plessis was the permission to discard the old invidious designation, "Superintendent of the Romish Church," and to assume the title "Catholic Bishop of Quebec." His greatest triumph came during a trip to England in 1819 when he secured permission to create four auxiliary dioceses and also received from the pope bulls for the nomination of auxiliary bishops. On his return to Quebec he appointed Jean-Jacques Lartigue to the Montreal area in quality of auxiliary, suffragan, and vicar-general of the Bishop of Quebec.[32] Joseph Provencher was made an auxiliary bishop for the territories of the Hudson Bay; Alexander Macdonnell was given the same standing in Upper

Canada; and Bernard-Angus MacEachern was made suffragan and auxiliary bishop of Prince Edward Island with a diocese that included New Brunswick, Magdalen Islands and Cape Breton Island.[33]

It was Plessis' intention to retain the supremacy of the see of Quebec over all the new dioceses that were being created in British North America, but he met a sudden rebuff to his plan in Nova Scotia from an Irish priest of unusual ability, Edmund Burke, who felt that the hierarchy at Quebec was not sufficiently alert to the spiritual and cultural needs of the Irish Catholics. Burke appealed directly to the pope over the head of Plessis for an independent Nova Scotian diocese. The pope came to his aid by creating Nova Scotia an apostolic vicariate in 1818 with Dr. Burke as its first bishop. This was an Irish revolt against French Canadian hegemony which was to have considerable repercussions throughout the Roman Catholic community in Canada. But for the most part Plessis received little opposition from the Irish, particularly in Lower Canada, as he was a humanitarian who was greatly concerned over their impoverished condition.[34] Not until the time of his successor did the Irish propensity for revolution threaten to embarrass the good relations that Plessis had established between his church and the British authorities.

IV

The grant of a popular assembly to Lower Canada in which Roman Catholic members were permitted to participate by a simple oath of loyalty to the king created an unusual challenge to the hierarchy at Quebec and led to some serious tensions with the governing authorities. This "unexpected gift of the ballot," as Garneau phrases it, required the French inhabitant "to use his personal judgment on questions of right and wrong,"[35] a task from which he had long been safeguarded by a patriarchal church which made such judgments for him. Bishop Plessis seems to have taken the assembly in his stride, recognizing it as an additional bulwark in the defence of the French language and culture. In the legislative council he opposed any curtailment of the powers of the assembly; in this he was vehemently opposed by Bishop Mountain, who feared that the religion of his sovereign would receive scant respect from a predominantly Roman Catholic assembly.

Thus in the opening phases of parliamentary government in Lower Canada, the Roman Church appeared to the British authorities as inclining towards radicalism, whereas the Anglican Church seemed to be the only religious body firm in its loyalty to the crown. On the surface, at least, there was considerable justification for British alarm over the political alignment of the Quebec hierarchy.

Hardly had the assembly been convened than the French members under the leadership of Pierre Bedard and Joseph Papineau learned the delaying tactics of British constitutional government, and were able to put up a good defence of French Canadian nationalism by appealing to Magna Carta and other British milestones in constitutional development. In this they received the hearty support of the bishop of Quebec, who aided them with his advice. But as tension in the assembly began to drive an ever-widening wedge between the English and French inhabitants of Lower Canada, which Governor Craig's open partisanship on the side of the commercial community did little to dispel, the ecclesiastics at Quebec did their best to prevent the dispute from causing serious repercussions in governmental circles. Plessis in a funeral oration at the obsequies of Bishop Briand in 1794 went out of his way to reassure the British authorities that "the recent disputes in the assembly did not mean that French Canadians were disloyal."[36] He continued, nevertheless, as late as 1822 to co-operate closely with the fiery French Canadian nationalist, Louis Papineau, and gave the latter full support in his opposition to a project for the reunion of Upper and Lower Canada. Even while Papineau was building up a personal following of extremists, the patriotes, Bishop Plessis still regarded him as a true and trusted leader of the French-speaking community.

Many of his clerical colleagues did not feel so complacent about Papineau's leadership, particularly after Lord Dalhousie became governor-general, and began to revive the policy of Sir James Craig. In 1824 Dalhousie suggested to his home government that a dissension between Bishop Plessis and the Sulpicians of Montreal was a favourable opportunity for a reassertion of the right of parochial patronage.[37] Bishop Plessis, who died in 1825, did not live long enough to see the final issue of this second attempt on the part of a British governor to control the internal administration of the diocese, so it fell to his successors, Bernard-Claude Panet and Joseph Signay, who assumed full administrative powers in 1833, to consolidate the gains that had been won for the church during the War of 1812.

Before they could come to a satisfactory accord with the British authorities they found it necessary to sever all connections with Papineau's revolutionary movement; this was not an easy task as Papineau was now firmly entrenched in the affections of the great mass of French Canadians. In the final outcome, however, the bishops were to find the abortive revolts of 1837 and 1838, precipitated by the more unruly of Papineau's followers, as useful in gaining concessions for their church from the British government as were the American Revolution and the War of 1812. When Papineau's followers put their cause to the test of the sword, the bishops roundly denounced the *patriotes* in spite of the fact that revolutionary meetings had been frequently held on Sundays after mass at the doors of the parish churches.   It was Bishop Lartigue of Montreal who took the lead in denouncing the rebellion.   His superior, Bishop Signay, immediately followed suit and warned his flock against "men blinded by a badly founded patriotism . . . inspired by doctrines that tend to favour insubordination."[38]   The stern denunciation of the *patriotes* brought about a coolness between the clergy and the bulk of the French people for a considerable period, but was offset by the more cordial relations that were achieved with the British ruling authorities, who gave up all attempt to exercise a veto over the appointment of *curés*, and allowed Signay to assume the title of archbishop, a privilege that had been withheld from Plessis.

V

The death of Mgr. Signay in 1850 may well be regarded as a date marking the end of the age of transition.   The Roman Catholic Church in Canada now had an archepiscopal see with four auxiliary bishops at Montreal, Kingston, Toronto, and Quebec.   Within its boundaries were five hundred and seventy-two priests, more than one hundred students in theology, nine hundred thousand church members, eighteen hundred pupils receiving a collegiate education in eleven ecclesiastical institutions and from religious orders occupied with the primary education of boys and girls; fifty communities of women were charged with the instruction of girls and with the care of the sick and orphans.   The Jesuits as well as the Sulpicians and Franciscans had been reinstated and there were in addition three houses of Oblates.[39]

These statistics represent a stupendous achievement in view of all the calamities and misfortunes that had befallen the French community during the years from Briand to Signay.   These have been vividly set forth by the French Canadian historian Garneau as "war, famine, devastation, alien subjugation, civil and military despotisms, the abolition of their ancient institutions and ancient laws"—a series that might well have broken the resistance of the French Canadian inhabitants to absorption into the Anglo-Saxon culture, if it had not been for the vigorous leadership of their bishops and clergy.

By the middle of the nineteenth century the hierarchy of Quebec had secured, to all intents and purposes, an impregnable position in the social and political life of Lower Canada. Though there still remained a permanent tension between the two cultures which kept the political life of Upper and Lower Canada in constant turmoil, nevertheless, the church life of Lower Canada begins to assume an unaccustomed serenity in comparison to the opening days of British administration. The *Mandements* of the bishops reflect an era of peace and progress: they deal with such matters as parochial expansion, the founding of colleges, the organization of retreats and parish revivals; they speak of zealous pastors and the piety of the faithful. There is a congratulatory note of well-attended churches, where the sacraments are "received with more fervour and less fear."[40] Particular satisfaction is expressed over the success of the Temperance Society and the phenomenal growth of missionary activity. All of which indicates that the Roman Catholic Church, like the Protestant Churches, was entering with zest into the Romantic mood of the expansive nineteenth century.

REFERENCES

1. *Vide* A. L. Burt, *The Old Province of Quebec* (Toronto and Minneapolis, 1933), p. 96; also A. Gosselin, *L'Église du Canada après la Conquête* (Quebec, 1916, 2 vols.), I, p. 19.

2. See *Report on Canadian Archives, 1888* (Ottawa, 1889), p. 153, for documentary report expressing Protestant dissatisfaction with Murray "for his discountenance of Protestant religion"; also pp. 19-23 for a testimonial to Hon. James Murray from the Seigniors of Quebec to the King.

3. *Vide Mandements Lettres Pastorales et Circulaires des Evêques de Québec publ. par Mgr. Têtu et Abbé C. O. Gagnon* (Québec, 1888, 4 vols.), II, p. 188.

4. A. Gosselin, *L'Église du Canada depuis Monseigneur de Laval, op. cit.*, III, p. 555.

5. A. Gosselin, *L'Église du Canada après la Conquête, op. cit.*, I, p. 127 *et seq.*

6. A. L. Burt, *op. cit.*, p. 7.

7. Victor Coffin, *The Province of Quebec and the Early American Revolution* (Madison, Wis., 1896), especially pp. 529-543.

8. A. Gosselin, *op. cit.*, I, p. 17.

9. A. L. Burt, *op. cit.*, pp. 460-461.

10. *Mandements, op. cit.*, II, p. 186.

11. A. Gosselin, *L'Église du Canada depuis Monseigneur de Laval*, III, p. 556.

12. *Ibid.*, III, p. 453.

13. *Vide* Mason Wade, *The French Canadian Outlook* (New York, 1946), p. 17 *et seq.*; also Georges Vattier, *Essai sur la Mentalité Canadienne-Française* (Paris, 1928), pp. 27-56.

14. *Mandements, op. cit.*, II, p. 214.

15. *Vide* A. G. Bradley, *Lord Dorchester* (Makers of Canada Series, Toronto, 1907), pp. 70-73. Also *Report on Canadian Archives, op. cit.*, Sir Guy Carleton to Lord Hillsborough, p. 890.

16. *Mandements, op. cit.*, II, p. 187.

17. *Ibid.*, pp. 341-344.

18. *Ibid.*, pp. 345-348.

19. *Report on Canadian Archives*, 1899 (Ottawa, 1900): Education in the Canadas, The Royal Institute, p. 145.

20. *Mandements, op. cit.*, II, p. 400.

21. F. X. Garneau, *op. cit.*, II, p. 194.

22. *Vide* A. G. Bradley, *op. cit.*, pp. 251-267; also V. Coffin, *op. cit.*, pp. 529-543.

23. A. L. Burt, *op. cit.*, pp. 384 *et seq.*

24. *Vide* Lt.-Col. Cruikshank, *The Administration of Sir James Craig: A Chapter in Canadian History* (Proceedings and Transactions of the Royal Society of Canada, 3rd series, Ottawa, Toronto, and London, Eng., 1909), II, pp. 61-87.

25. *Vide infra*, p. 135.

26. *Vide Mandements, op. cit.*, III, pp. 59-72.

27. *Vide* Abbé Ferland, *Joseph-Octave Plessis* (trans. by T. B. French, Quebec, 1864), p. 29.

28. *Mandements, op. cit.*, III, p. 7.

29. *Ibid.*, II, p. 485-487.

30. *Ibid.*, p. 487.

31. *Ibid.*, III, p. 79 *et seq.*

32. *Ibid.*, p. 158.

33. *Vide* Abbé Ferland, *op. cit.*, pp. 107-117.

34. *Ibid.*, pp. 158-159.

35. F. X. Garneau, *op. cit.*, II, p. 206.

36. *Mandements, op. cit.*, II, p. 532.

37. *Vide* F. X. Garneau, *op. cit.*, II, p. 368.

38. *Mandements, op. cit.*, III, p. 369.

39. *Ibid.*, pp. 313-318.

40. *Ibid.*

VIII

The Return of Protestantism

EXCEPT for a few brief years when Huguenot merchants in France were encouraged to found colonies in North America, Protestantism was a proscribed religion in Canada during the French regime. Yet, throughout the whole period of French occupation, this religion was never far from the consciousness of the *habitants* who were taught by their *curés* to regard it as an evil to be repelled at all costs. In the English colonies to the south the same spirit of intolerance prevailed, for prominently in the legislation of the Thirteen Colonies were acts prohibiting the harbouring of papists. On both sides of the ill-defined border between New England and New France it was taken for granted that triumph in battle for one side involved the suppression of the religion of the defeated party.

The first break in what had become the normal state of affairs occurred on October 10, 1710, when John Harrison celebrated an Anglican service "of thanksgiving for the success of Her Majesty's Arms in reducing Port Royal."[1] Though this service inaugurated a continuous Protestant tradition in Canada it did not involve the suppression of the worship of the defeated Acadians, for it was during this period of occupation of Nova Scotia by British garrisons that there emerged the idea of the coexistence of two cultures within British North America. On occasion even the religious barriers were disregarded as illustrated by one of the first official acts of John Harrison after his appointment as resident chaplain at Annapolis Royal—the new name given by the British to Port Royal—which was to unite in marriage Madeline Maissonat, a native Acadian, to William Winniet, an officer at the fort.[2]

The new policy of toleration adopted in the first instance by Colonel Francis Nicholson, the commander at the fort, was confirmed in the Treaty of Utrecht (1713) in which France formally surrendered Acadia to the British; the latter agreed that those Acadians who were willing to

remain and "be subjects to the kingdom of Great Britain, are to enjoy
the free exercise of their religion according to the usuage of the Church
of Rome as far as the laws of Great Britain do allow the same."[3]   Here
was a note of "live and let live" running counter to the traditional
attitude of both New England and New France, and was to be bitterly
attacked by both traditions before it was recognized as the only possible
basis upon which a Canadian nationalism could be built.   It was not,
however, until they attempted to establish a predominantly English-
speaking colony at Halifax, that the British became fully aware of the
depth of the cleavage that had developed between the English and French
colonists on the North American continent.

I

Halifax, as we have seen,[4] was founded as a strongly fortified base
in Nova Scotia in compensation to the New Englanders for the return of
Louisbourg on Cape Breton Island to the French.   The project of
colonization was put under the direction of the Commissioners of Trades
and Plantations, and this was one of the most carefully directed and
supervised of all the British schemes of colonization.   An offer was made
by the Commissioners to convey settlers to Nova Scotia and to maintain
them for twelve months after their arrival.   In 1749 there arrived in
Halifax under the leadership of Lord Cornwallis 3,760 adventurers with
their families.   Following a tradition that had been established at
Annapolis Royal and Canso the Commissioners sought the aid of the
Society for the Propagation of the Gospel in Foreign Parts to provide for
the religious needs of the settlers.   They promised the Society to set
aside in each township a site for a church to be accompanied by a grant
of land of four hundred acres to each minister and his successors as well
as two hundred acres for a schoolmaster.   The S.P.G., for its part,
promised to send out to the new colony six clergymen who were to
receive annual grants of seventy pounds, and six schoolmasters whose
stipends were to be fifteen pounds per year.[5]

The first missionaries to arrive in Halifax were William Tutty and
William Anwyl; the former conducted a service on the day of the founding
of the city (June 21, 1749) on board the ship *Beaufort* in Chebucto
Harbour.

These missionaries were accompanied by Edward Halhead, the

first schoolmaster in Halifax. He was not, however, the first English-speaking schoolmaster in Canada: that distinction belongs to Richard Watts, who in 1728 received a grant from the S.P.G. of ten pounds yearly to conduct a school at Annapolis Royal; a second schoolmaster, James Peden, had also been sent out from England to Canso in 1735, where he acted as deputy chaplain to the forces stationed there.[6]

It was an unusual flock over which the first missionaries at Halifax presided. The population for the first four years numbered about five thousand inhabitants composed of many religious traditions. There were the original adventurers who had arrived with Lord Cornwallis, a nondescript group whose religious adherence was dubious; there were the soldiers and sailors who manned the colony's fort; there were Acadians who worked on the fortifications. Most numerous of all were the New Englanders, some of whom had taken part in the siege of Louisbourg and had stopped off at Halifax on their way back to New England; others had sailed directly from Massachusetts in response to an advertisement that had been printed in a Boston newspaper. In addition to these there were a few Jews, some Sicilians from the Azores and several Irish Catholics who had come out from Ireland as servants to the more well-to-do settlers. In 1750 there arrived a group of immigrants, usually referred to as the "Foreign Protestants" from the continent of Europe. Most of them were adherents of either the Lutheran or German Reformed Churches, but among them were some French Huguenots who had been previously domiciled in Switzerland. Ever lurking outside the fortifications were the ubiquitous Micmacs who under the proddings of their French Catholic priests, notably Abbé le Loutre, made life dangerous and miserable for the non-French inhabitants.

To bring the ministrations of the Church of England into this variegated religious scene was a task to try to the utmost the patience and tactfulness of the S.P.G. missionaries. William Tutty in his first report to the Society made clear what were the realities of the situation. The French and Indians he characterized as "Bigoted Papists, and under the absolute Dominion of their Priests."[7] Nor was he much more hopeful about the immigrants from old England. "The lower sort" were "in general a sett (sic) of most abandon'd wretches . . . so deeply sunk into almost all kinds of Immorality" as to "scarce retain the shadow of religion." The settlers from New England also failed to receive his approbation. He conceded that they made "great Pretensions to religion," and were "justly scandaliz'd (sic) at the barefac'd immorality of the others"; but if they were "to be judged from their commercial dealings, the externals of religion" were "much more prevalent with them than the essence of it."[8]

Despite the bleak prospect painted by Tutty, it remained the fixed policy of the Commissioners of Trade and Plantations to win all these diverse elements to the obedience of the Church of England. This policy was outlined in a letter written by John Pownall for the Commissioners to the Secretary of the S.P.G. The writer did not at this time (April 6, 1749) despair of winning over twenty thousand French Roman Catholics —a much exaggerated estimate—to "the true Protestant religion."[9] With this hope in view he urged the S.P.G. to send out missionaries who were fluent in the French language. It was with this same purpose—the conversion of the Acadians—that the "Foreign Protestants" were brought out to Halifax in 1750. They were to be scattered among the Acadian settlements in order to permeate the original settlers of Nova Scotia with Protestant ideas and thus undermine their loyalty to the Roman Catholic Church.

II

Unfortunately, the Acadian problem was not to be so easily solved. During the final struggle between Great Britain and France for the possession of a continent, the good spirit that had prevailed at Annapolis Royal came to an end both through the ill-advised enthusiasm of Abbé Le Loutre for the French cause and the covetousness of the New Englanders who were anxious to displace the Acadians from their farm lands. The result was the tragic expulsion of the Acadians in 1755.

This expulsion, however, was not the end of the Acadian problem. It has been estimated by a Canadian historian[10] that there were about ten thousand Acadians in Nova Scotia before the expulsion, but that at the time of the death of Governor Lawrence (1760), who had given the cruel order for their deportation, there still remained some two thousand; in a short time others were surreptitiously returning from the inhospitable Thirteen Colonies. Though the government soon ceased from hounding them, the prospect of securing religious consolation seemed almost hopeless; for in 1758 the first assembly of the Province of Nova Scotia passed an act establishing the Church of England in the province. Though this act provided "that Protestants, dissenting from the Church of England, whether they be Calvinists, Lutherans, Quakers or under what denomination soever, shall have free liberty of conscience", it also affirmed "that every popish person, exercising an ecclesiastical jurisdiction, and every popish priest or person executing the function of a popish priest, shall depart out of this province on or before the twenty-fifth day of March, 1759."[11]

But even while the members of the assembly were concocting these harsh measures towards Roman priests, the British officials at Halifax became convinced of the necessity of providing some religious ministrations for the Roman Catholics in their midst, particularly for the troublesome Micmacs. Consequently, Governor Lawrence sought out Abbé Maillard, the sole surviving Roman Catholic missionary in Nova Scotia, and urged him to take up his residence in Halifax in order that he might use his good influence to conciliate the Indians to British rule. This the Abbé agreed to do, and for his services he received an annual grant from the government of two hundred pounds. Before long his ministrations included the surviving Acadians as well.

Abbé Maillard was an unusually tolerant Roman Catholic priest and soon won the goodwill of all the leading citizens of Halifax. There grew up between him and Thomas Wood, an Anglican priest at Halifax, a very cordial relationship, so that on the day before his death Maillard asked his Anglican friend to say over him in French the office for the visitation of the sick, according to the form in the Prayer Book of the Church of England. At his funeral Wood performed the office of the burial service according to the Anglican rite "in the presence of almost all the gentlemen of Halifax and a very numerous assembly of French and Indians."[12]

It was an unusually happy circumstance for the Acadians that Abbé Maillard and his successor, Charles Bailly—later to become the controversial coadjutor bishop of Quebec[13]—were able to intercede for them with the governing authorities at the capital. They succeeded in persuading the officials to relax their vigilance against returning exiles, and in 1767 one group from St. Pierre was permitted to settle on unoccupied crown land after taking an oath of allegiance to the king. Many others followed suit. In 1768 the township of Clare, bordering on St. Mary's Bay, was set aside for those Acadians who wished to settle there.

It was, however, a long time before these uprooted people again acquired social stability; they knew nothing about the township government that was being introduced into Nova Scotia by the New Englanders, and even less about the rival parochial system favoured by the officials at Halifax.   They still hankered after the old feudal customs that had prevailed before the Conquest in which the village *curé* had played the dominant role in local government.   Abbé Bailly had tried to give them some guidance during his brief visit to the St. Mary's Bay area, but without a settled priest among them, they were dispirited and confused. Affairs took a decided turn for the better with the arrival in 1799 of Jean-Mandé Sigogne, an exile from revolutionary France.[14] Before coming to Nova Scotia Sigogne had lived for a time in England, where he had learned to admire English political institutions.   This made him an admirable selection for the purpose of reconciling the Acadians to British rule.   A fellow feeling of sympathy drew him to the returning exiles who had settled along St. Mary's Bay.   Here he met a challenge of the first magnitude in the form of a seriously deteriorating social and religious situation.   His first concern was to restore the spiritual life of the people, but he also applied himself vigorously to a revival of civic virtues by prescribing a code of communal conduct which he enforced with rigorous precision.   He also gave leadership in the economic development of the community by persuading the inhabitants to combine agricultural pursuits with fishing and lumbering.   Not the least of his contributions to the future welfare of the Acadians was his insistence that they should learn to speak English, so that they might be able to play an honourable part in the social and political development of the province.   In furtherance of this object he himself began a school in his rectory at Church Point.   It was this priest's pleasure before his death to see one of his pupils take a seat in the legislative assembly at Halifax.[15]

On the site of this first Acadian school on St. Mary's Bay there now stands Ste. Anne's College, an institution which has trained a notable succession of Acadian priests, who in the great tradition of Abbé Sigogne have spread the gospel of *Acadie vivante* throughout the Maritime Provinces and even beyond.

III

For the new imperialistic policy that Great Britain had embarked upon with the founding of Halifax, the Acadians were to prove less of an embarrassment than the New Englanders.   Previously, British colonization had been very much a free enterprise project on the part of religious groups or chartered companies; now the government of England was directly involved in the welfare of the colonists and was seeking to mould both their political institutions and their religious development in the interests of a new and more vigorous imperial policy. This new policy became more explicit after the American Revolution, but it was already foreshadowed in the founding of Halifax.

As was to be expected, the New Englanders who were the heirs of a much less directed form of colonization showed considerable suspicion of the government's patriarchal interest in their welfare; they felt that their ancestors had worked out a civil administration and a church polity for the New World that was far superior to Old World forms. So almost before Nova Scotia was colonized by English-speaking residents there developed a political division in which both the Anglican and Congregational churches took a leading role; one contending for a strongly centralized administration for both church and state at Halifax, the other contending for local township responsibility with a minimum of control from the capital city.

The proponents of the former system were greatly handicapped by the promise of religious freedom that had been made by Governor Lawrence to the New Englanders in order to induce them to colonize a province that had practically been denuded of settlers by the expulsion of the Acadians. This promise, as we have seen, was embodied in the act by which the Church of England became the established religion of the province. But even this was not enough to satisfy the New Englanders, and Governor Lawrence in his anxiety to secure settlers to fill up the vacant farm lands of the Acadians issued a second proclamation on January 2, 1759, promising the establishment of the rural township system characteristic of New England—a proclamation which became known as the "Charter of Nova Scotia."[16]

Nevertheless, the government proceeded on a course that seemed to run counter to its promise of religious freedom; for in the same year that this proclamation was issued it erected in Halifax a parochial corporation with power to assess and collect rates. Pew rents also were to be collected in addition to assessments on the inhabitants of the town. This legislation which had been put forth by the predominantly Anglican legislative council was an abrupt reversal of a far more tolerant attitude that had been almost self-consciously adopted by both church and state in the first years of colonization.

In those honeymoon days the government had gone out of its way to give the dissenters every opportunity to carry on their familiar forms of

worship.   When St. Paul's Church[17] was erected at government expense
in 1750, the Congregationalists were permitted to use it on Sunday
afternoons to carry on a Congregational form of service; this had been
conducted by Aaron Cleveland, a student preacher who had accompanied
the New Englanders to Halifax.   Shortly after the erection of St. Paul's
the government also aided the Congregationalists to build a church of
their own, long known as Mather's Meeting House.   In this same mood
of tolerance and co-operation, it helped some fifteen German families to
build a Lutheran place of worship, usually referred to as the Little
Dutch Church.

But after a decade of settlement the government resolved to put
some check upon the New England township system with its defiance of
central authority, by substituting a parochial system of local government,
closely supervised by the ruling authorities at Halifax.   The dominating
spirit behind this attempt was Jonathan Belcher, who became the first
chief justice of Nova Scotia in 1754.   Belcher, the son of a former governor
of Massachusetts, had studied law in England where he had become an
intense believer in the English parochial system.   It was under his
direction that the legislative council, in drafting the bill to erect a parish
of Halifax, included a provision for poor relief.   The assembly, dominated
by the New Englanders, realizing the prestige that would accrue to the
parochial system as the dispenser of public charity, produced another bill
whereby Halifax would be managed by a president and a common
council.   A compromise was reached in 1759 by which a grand jury was
to officiate in enforcing an "Act to prevent trespass," and poor relief
was to be made voluntary by an "Act for the Relief of the Poor in the
Town of Halifax."[18]   Poor relief and its administration, however,
remained a controversial issue until 1763 when both the council and
assembly agreed to a law making town meetings responsible agencies for
deciding the amount of poor rates, thus frustrating Belcher's attempt to
give to parochial corporations the right to collect money for communal
purposes.   The only concession the assembly would make was to allow
the Church of England the legal right to assess its own membership,
giving it a sectarian rather than an official status.

It was still felt, however, that some of the realities of an establishment
might be retained by reserving to the Church of England the sole right
to perform marriages and to keep the register of births, deaths and
marriages.   In England parish registers were the responsibility of the
parochial clergy, and this gave them a civil status not enjoyed by dissent-

ing clergymen. The paucity of the Anglican clergy in Nova Scotia soon made the English system unworkable, and in 1761 civil registers were permitted where there was no parish; this was confirmed by a law in 1782, whereby town clerks were made responsible for keeping registers, and clergymen who solemnized marriages were required to send in returns to the nearest town clerk,[19] a decided victory for the New England township system.

The right to perform marriages was the most bitterly contested of all the privileges that had been conferred by the government upon the Anglican clergy, and brought more opprobrium upon the Church of England than any of the other matters in dispute. The proponents of establishment, being compelled to yield on one privilege after another, made a last ditch stand on this particular one, but in 1795 even it was partially abandoned by an act authorizing the governor, lieutenant-governor, or commander in chief for the time being "to appoint persons to solemnize marriages in places wherein no established Clergyman resides."[20]

IV

During this long drawn out struggle between Anglicanism and Congregationalism, with their respective forms of local government, various other denominations were moving into Nova Scotia,[21] and were almost immediately called upon to take sides in the controversy. For the most part the Congregationalists found ready allies among the newcomers.

The Ulster Irish from New Hampshire, mostly Presbyterian, who arrived in Nova Scotia during a land boom era between 1763 and 1768, and had settled around Amherst in Cumberland County, soon showed their preference for the New England township system. Later (1772) they had as neighbours more than a thousand Yorkshire farmers, mostly Methodists, who settled on the Isthmus of Chignecto. These also fitted comfortably into the township system and soon developed communal ties with the New Englanders. The Highland Scots began settling in the Pictou area in 1773; with their close clan association they were less easily assimilated into the New England social system, but they had been preceded by some Pennsylvania Presbyterians who helped to mediate between them and their Congregational neighbours. The Ulster Presbyterians who were brought out in 1764 by the famous land speculator, "Colonel" Alexander MacNutt, and settled in various parts of the province, were enthusiastically at one with the Congregationalists in their opposition to any patriarchal supervision from Halifax; nor did their enthusiasm wane even after the outbreak of the American Revolution.

Sometimes confused with the Congregationalists were several Baptist communities, who because of the persecution they had endured from the established churches of New England might have been expected to have sided with the Anglicans against their former persecutors; but after their arrival in Nova Scotia they also preferred the more familiar township system to Anglican parochialism.

The only group of dissenters who showed any inclination to follow Anglican forms were the so-called "Foreign Protestants" from Germany and Switzerland. At the Little Dutch Church in Halifax they allowed an Anglican clergyman to conduct their services according to Lutheran forms. Later they accepted the Anglican Prayer Book and the congregation ultimately became embraced in the Anglican parish of St. George in Halifax.[22]

Most of the German- and French-speaking Protestants had early removed from Halifax to Lunenburg when it was found impossible to scatter them among the Acadians. Here the government built for them a church in 1754 (St. John's) and provided them with a French-speaking missionary, Jean-Baptiste Moreau, who endeavoured to conduct services in both German and French, following as closely as possible the Anglican Book of Common Prayer. There was some complaint from the Germans that their language was being neglected, but these for the most part were appeased when in 1766 Paulus Bryzelius (formerly a Lutheran minister but later ordained by the Bishop of London) was sent to Lunenburg where he conducted services acceptably until his death in 1773. In 1771 Peter de la Roche replaced Jean Moreau as a minister to the French-speaking residents and on the death of Bryzelius he continued to conduct services at St. John's in French, English and German to the satisfaction of all concerned.[23] As English in time replaced the other two languages the congregation at St. John's became thoroughly Anglicized.

Not all the Germans who removed to Lunenburg were willing to accept Anglican leadership. Adherents of the German Reformed Church finally chose one of their own compatriots, a devout fisherman, Bruin Romcas Comingoe (commonly known as Mr. Brown), as their minister, and asked two Presbyterians and two Congregational ministers to constitute themselves into a special presbytery for the purpose of ordaining him.   The ordination took place at Mather's Meeting House in Halifax (July 3, 1770), in the presence of the governor, members of His Majesty's Council, and other distinguished guests.[24]

The formation of a united presbytery of Congregationalists and Presbyterians in the opening days of Canadian Protestantism was prophetic of the religious development of Canada, though many years were to elapse before Protestantism would again display such unity. In these first days of settlement in Nova Scotia the Congregationalists, Presbyterians and to a lesser extent the Baptists quickly realized that they had more in common with one another than the bitter enmities in their homelands had seemed to indicate.   At Mather's Meeting House in Halifax, Congregationalists and Presbyterians worshipped together with either a Presbyterian or a Congregational minister conducting the services.   When the Congregational cause began to decline in Nova Scotia, the Presbyterians fell heir to the church.   There were several Baptist ministers among the early settlers who ministered to Congregational Churches and open communion was quite general for a time.[25] All this harmony was soon to disappear during a great religious awakening in Nova Scotia—the subject of a later chapter in this history.   Nevertheless, a tradition of ecumenicity was laid in the founding days of British Canada which lingered on and kept alive the ideal of a united Protestant church for Canada.

In spite of this show of unity among the dissenting congregations, all was not well within their ranks.   The leadership in the struggle against the encroachments of the Church of England fell upon the Congregationalists, being the most numerous of the dissenters.   There were, however, some serious weaknesses in the Congregational system of church government, when transplanted from the New England scene; and these weaknesses provided the Anglican Church with a real opportunity to become the dominant religion in Nova Scotia.   Congregationalism as a loose federation of sovereign congregations had been held together in New England by the co-operation of the civil government and through pious and orthodox magistrates whose duty it was to support the true faith and to suppress all other denominations.[26]   But even more serious was the difficulty of securing clergymen for the Nova Scotian townships. The Cambridge Platform of 1648 which laid down the procedure for the ordination and induction of Congregational ministers asserted that a pastor must not only be chosen by the local church but he must also be ordained by the same church, even though he had been previously ordained to another pastorate. When elders were lacking for this purpose the service could be performed with the assistance of neighbouring elders. Neighbouring elders in Nova Scotia were few and far between and so it was almost impossible for a township to secure a directly settled pastor. This difficulty was got over to some extent by having a minister ordained in New England for a designated community in Nova Scotia, but few New England pastors were willing to settle down in this remote province. Because of the strict rules on ordination the Congregational Church was unable to utilize local talent which might have been forthcoming in Nova Scotia itself. The Presbyterians also suffered from a similar handicap, involved in a call to a settled pastorate which was hardly feasible in a country that required an itinerant missionary serving among many scattered families.

It wasn't long before serious impatience began to manifest itself against ecclesiastical restrictions which deprived the settlers of spiritual ministrations. The first significant revolt broke out in Chebogue, Yarmouth County,[27] where a Congregational community chose one of its own members to be a pastor without reference to the Cambridge Platform, a move in the direction of Baptist polity with ominous overtones for the future of New England Congregationalism in Nova Scotia. Other congregations tried to solve the problem of vacant pastorates by enlarging the function of ruling elders to include that of preaching; the ruling elders then began to read "dry as dust sermons" which developed a spirit of religious indifference among the long-suffering congregations, and the churches became centres of much quarrelling and factiousness.

Within this loose alliance of Congregational, Baptist and Presbyterian polity there was brewing a spirit of social revolt[28] and disruption, partly inherited from New England, and destined to explode into a most unusual religious awakening which would practically destroy Congregationalism in Nova Scotia, and leave an enduring impress upon all the other denominations. It was also to react with devastating consequences upon the Church of England. This, however, is an involved story so closely tied up with the American Revolution and the Loyalist immigration into Nova Scotia that it must be postponed for a later chapter.

V

At first the Church of England was not adversely affected by this incipient revolt within the ranks of the dissenters, but regarded it as a favourable opportunity to strengthen its own position as an established church.   Consequently, a vigorous missionary campaign was undertaken in the dissenting townships under the direction of Dr. John Breynton, the rector of St. Paul's parish, Halifax.   The campaign proved to be a great success and many encouraging reports were being sent by the missionaries to the S.P.G. relating the favourable reception they received from dissenting congregations.

The ablest and most dedicated of these early missionaries was Thomas Wood, who also endeavoured to include the Micmac Indians in his ministrations.   He had learned the Micmac language with the help of his friend Abbé Maillard, and was able to officiate in Micmac publicly in 1767 in St. Paul's, Halifax, "in the presence of the Governor, most of the army and navy officers, and inhabitants."[29]   During a missionary journey from Halifax through the Annapolis Valley and across the Bay of Fundy into the St. John area he received a cordial reception on all sides, particularly from the Micmacs along the St. John River valley.

A remarkable testimony to the persuasive powers of this missionary was given by the inhabitants of Annapolis and Granville.   In an appeal for a clergyman, addressed to their former Congregational pastor who had conformed to the Church of England and was at the time (1770) serving as a missionary at Dedham, Massachusetts, they pointed out that they had been educated and brought up in the Congregational way of worship before they had come to Nova Scotia and therefore would have chosen to have had a Congregational minister settled amongst them; "but," they go on to say, "the Rev. Mr. Wood by his preaching and performing of other offices of his Holy function occasionally amongst us in the several districts of this county hath removed our former prejudices that we had against the forms of Worship of the Church of England as by Law established, and hath won us into a good opinion thereof; (sic) inasmuch as he hath removed all our scruples of receiving of the Lord's Supper in that form of administering it, at least many of us are communicants with him and we trust and believe many more will soon be added."[30]

Though Thomas Wood was an unusual Anglican priest who seems to have adapted the Anglican liturgy to meet the peculiar needs of his congregation, yet he was not the only missionary welcomed by non-Anglicans at this time.   Joseph Bennet, who had been sent as an S.P.G. missionary to King's County, also met with considerable success, as did W. Ellis in Hants County.[31]   John Eagleson also reported a very hopeful

prospect from the Cumberland district.   In 1773 Eagleson made a trip
to the Island of St. John (Prince Edward Island) now filling up with
Scotch settlers and a scattering of New Englanders.   He reported from
the Island that he had met "a number of well disposed persons" rejoicing
"in the opportunity of hearing a Protestant clergyman . . . for the first
time since St. John's was made a separate government."[32]

Unfortunately, Eagleson's good work was cut short when he was
taken prisoner in November, 1776, by some New England privateers
who regarded Church of England clergymen as the bitterest opponents
of their revolution.   The outbreak of the American Revolution brought
an end for the time being to the Anglican mission among dissenters who,
for the most part, were favourably disposed toward the revolutionary
cause.   When Eagleson finally escaped from his captors and arrived in
Halifax he found the city full of Loyalist refugees from the Thirteen
Colonies.[33]

The coming of the Loyalists and the profound influence they had
upon the social and religious development of British North America
carries us into a new phase in the religious history of Protestant Canada.

REFERENCES

1. *Journal of Colonel Nicholson at the Capture of Annapolis* in *Report and Collections of the
   Nova Scotia Historical Society for the year 1878* (Halifax, 1879), I, p. 86.

2. W. A. Calnek and A. W. Savary, *History of the County of Annapolis* (Toronto and
   London, 1897), p. 631.

3. Quoted by Edouard Richard, *Acadia, Missing Links of a Lost Chapter in American
   History* (New York and Montreal, 1895), I, p. 74; *vide* also J. B. Brebner, *Acadia,
   New England's Outpost* (New York, 1927), *passim.*

4. *Vide supra*, p. 67.

5. *Nova Scotia in S.P.G. Reports, 1749-1783* (Public Archives of Nova Scotia), p. 1.

6. Original sources for this period are the S.P.G. *Records and Reports;* a good digest
   of these Reports is C. F. Pascoe's *Two Hundred Years of the S.P.G.* (London, 1901,
   2 vols.), especially I, pp. 107-108.

7. *Ibid.*, I, p. 110.

8. *Ibid.*

9. *Ibid.*, I, p. 108.

10. J. B. Brebner, *The Neutral Yankees of Nova Scotia* (New York, 1937), p. 6.

11. *The Statutes at Large passed in the Several General Assemblies held in His Majesty's
    Province of Nova Scotia . . . 1758-1804* (Halifax, 1805), pp. 7-8.

12. C. F. Pascoe, *op. cit.*, I, p. 112.

13. *Vide supra*, pp. 77-78.

46362

14. Isaiah W. Wilson, *A Geography and History of the County of Digby, Nova Scotia* (Halifax, 1900), pp. 311-312. A laudatory account of the ministry of Jean-Mandé Sigogne is to be found in *Centenaire de la Mort du Père Jean-Mandé Sigogne: 1844-1944* (Yarmouth, N.S., 1944).

15. I. W. Wilson, *op. cit.*, p. 174.

16. So called by Thomas C. Haliburton in *An Historical and Statistical Account of Nova Scotia* (Halifax, 1829, 2 vols.), I, p. 220.

17. *Vide* R. V. Harris, *The Church of Saint Paul in Halifax, Nova Scotia: 1749-1949* (Toronto, 1949), p. 119.

18. *The Statutes at Large, etc., op. cit.*, pp. 53-54.

19. *Ibid.*, pp. 126-127.

20. *Ibid.*, p. 348.

21. A good account of these early religious settlements is to be found in I. F. Mackinnon, *Settlements and Churches in Nova Scotia* (Montreal and Halifax, 1930), pp. 10-36.

22. Canon Partridge, *The Early History of the Parish of St. George, Halifax.* Found in *Report and Collections of the Nova Scotia Historical Society for the years 1889-91* (Halifax, 1891), VII, p. 8.

23. M. B. DesBrisay, *History of the County of Lunenburg* (Toronto, 1895, 2nd ed.), p. 84.

24. I. F. Mackinnon, *op. cit.*, p. 91.

25. *Vide* E. M. Saunders, *History of the Baptists of the Maritime Provinces* (Halifax, 1902), p. 11.

26. *Vide* T. J. Wertenbaker, *The Puritan Oligarchy* (New York and London, 1947), pp. 75-76.

27. E. M. Saunders, *op. cit.*, p. 12.

28. *Vide* S. D. Clark, *Church and Sect in Canada* (Toronto, 1948), pp. 17-18.

29. C. F. Pascoe, *op. cit.*, I, p. 113.

30. For a good estimate of Wood as a missionary *vide* C. W. Vernon, *Bicentenary Sketches and Early Days of the Church in Nova Scotia* (Halifax, 1910), pp. 71-84.

31. A. W. H. Eaton, *The History of Hants County, Nova Scotia* (Salem, Mass., 1910), pp. 242-243.

32. C. F. Pascoe, *op. cit.*, I, p. 114.

33. *Vide* C. W. Vernon, *op. cit.*, pp. 95-111; deal with the arrival of the Loyalists in Halifax.

IX

The Loyalist Era

IN THE OLD Province of Quebec there were at the beginning of the
American Revolution some two thousand English-speaking Canadians
and one hundred thousand French. The population of the Maritime
Provinces did not exceed seventeen thousand, of which considerably
more than two thousand were French-speaking Acadians. Authorities
differ as to the actual number of Loyalists who settled in Canada as a
result of the American Revolution, but they are pretty well agreed that
between the years 1776 and 1784 some thirty or forty thousand refugees
from the south moved into the former French colonies of North America.[1]
This sudden increase of English-speaking inhabitants reduced drastically
the disproportion between the French and English and made certain that
Canada would now become an integral part of the British Empire. In
other words, modern Canada, with its predominantly Anglo-Saxon
culture and institutions, is as much a creation of the American Revolution
as the United States itself.

What is even more significant, from the point of view of Church
history, is the importation into Canada at this time of a distinctive way of
life that gave the northern colonies, even before the Confederation pact
of 1867, a sense of fellowship and unity; if it were possible to express this
peculiarly Canadian outlook in one word, the word would be "Loyalism."

I

Loyalism had behind it a long history of struggle and development
before it became the dominant theme in Canadian national development.
In the home of its birth it was derisively known as Toryism, but it was a
quite different kind of Toryism from that upheld by the followers of
George III in England. It first appears in the old Province of New
York as a political philosophy as early as 1689, when an aristocratic party

insisted that any transference of the government of New York from the authority of James II to William and Mary must be done in a strictly legal way, and it denounced any hasty and unwarranted break with the past.[2]

It was, however, in reaction to the covenant theory of government (later expanded into a compact theory) as expounded by the early New England divines, that Loyalism received its peculiarly American expression. The exponents of the compact theory of government had claimed as early as 1750 the right of revolution[3]; Loyalism on the contrary "stood for the recognition of law as against rebellion in any form, for the unity of empire as against a separate, independent existence of the colonies, and for monarchy instead of republicanism."[4] The Loyalists, as the adherents of this political philosophy became known, also held firmly to the idea of a hierarchical society in which rights and privileges adhered to certain classes by virtue of their wealth or birth; and the dutiful recognition of such rights and privileges by all classes, they considered the best assurance of a well-ordered and well-mannered society.

Loyalism, however, had a religious as well as a political content. This was based upon the fundamental teachings of Anglicanism which made loyalty to the ruler and obedience to law religious duties; consequently Anglican clergy were frequently called upon to formulate the political platform of the Loyalist party. During the meetings of the Continental congresses prominent Anglican clergymen like Dr. Myles Cooper, the president of King's College, New York; Dr. Samuel Seabury, who was later to become the first Protestant Episcopal Bishop of the United States; and Dr. Charles Inglis, the rector of Trinity Church and later the first bishop of Nova Scotia, all took part in writing political pamphlets to be used for the purpose of winning elections.

Though the Loyalist party was pretty well under the dominance of Anglican leadership, it was by no means co-extensive with membership in the Church of England; nor was it a well-integrated group, for it had an extreme right wing for whom the king could do no wrong, and a moderate group who stood with the Whigs in opposition to the Stamp Act. Not until after the proclamation of the Declaration of Independence by the Continental Congress on July 4, 1776, did the moderate party make common cause with the extreme Tories in opposition to the new doctrine of nationhood as expounded by Thomas Jefferson and his Whig followers. From now on the party contained not only Anglicans but also Roman Catholics, Methodists, Presbyterians, Quakers and even members of an unusually liberal sect, the Sandemanians. Likewise, its racial composition was extended to include not only Englishmen, but also Irish, Scots, Germans, Dutch, French, Indians, and Negroes.[5] No doubt some of these had blindly followed a strong leader or a former master with no serious convictions of their own. When the British finally conceded the independence of the Thirteen Colonies, almost every religion and racial group were represented in the great trek northwards.

Even before the exodus was well under way the Anglican clergy in the Thirteen Colonies began to make careful preparation for the future of Loyalism in the remaining colonies of British North America; this they felt could best be done by setting up Anglican episcopates in the former French colonies. On March 21, 1783, eighteen Anglican clergymen met in New York to discuss and adopt a plan for the establishment of an episcopate in Nova Scotia, where thousands of Loyalists had already gone. They presented their plan to Sir Guy Carleton, the governor of New York, urging that "the fixing of a bishop in Nova Scotia and the consequent supply of clergymen, will strengthen the attachment and confirm the loyalty of the inhabitants and promote the settlement of the province."[6] Included in their plan was the suggestion that Dr. Thomas B. Chandler, who was then in England, should be consecrated for the proposed bishopric.

It is interesting to recall that this same convention also suggested to Sir Guy Carleton that he intercede at London for the consecration of Dr. Samuel Seabury to become an episcopal head of what might survive of the Anglican Church in the newly constituted nation of United States.[7] At the time this seemed a rather despairing hope as it was expected that all Anglican clergymen would be expelled from the United States and the establishment of an episcopate in Nova Scotia would serve as a rallying point for clerical refugees. As it turned out, however, many of the Anglican clergy were able to make their peace with the new government, and Dr. Seabury by going to Scotland for consecration was able to create an episcopate in the United States (1784), three years before the British authorities got around to providing one for British North America. When finally they did take up the plan of the New York convention and offered the post of bishop of Nova Scotia to Dr. Chandler, he was too ill to accept the appointment.[8] In his place he suggested Dr. Charles Inglis, who was duly consecrated at Lambeth Palace on Sunday, August 12, 1787.

II

It was a man strong in the old faith as he had learned it in his father's rectory at Glencolumbkille, Donegal, Ireland, who became the first colonial bishop in the British overseas dominions. He was also equally strong in the principles of Loyalism as they had been worked out by himself and his colleagues in the old Province of New York. Upon assuming office in Nova Scotia he immediately proceeded to shape the polity of Anglicanism in British North America as the trusty guardian of the cultural values of eighteenth-century England. He had early expressed himself on the rebellion in the Thirteen Colonies as "one of the most causeless unprovoked and unnatural that ever disgraced any country"[9] and he had come to Nova Scotia with one dominant purpose in mind: to establish a strong Anglican Church to serve as a defence against "levelling Republican principles" which he said were "calculated to produce and have actually produced the greatest evils to Society."[10]

It was also with this same purpose in view that the British authorities had established the Church of England in the various provinces of Canada, and it wasn't long before the lieutenant-governor of Nova Scotia, Sir John Wentworth, was able to report very favourably on Bishop Inglis' general policy. The Bishop of Nova Scotia, he wrote to the secretary of state, "fully concurs with me, in opinion that every exertion should be made to provide for constant performance of public worship according to the Church of England, both in Halifax, and in other parts of this Province, where it is certain missionarys (sic) are most seriously wanted to preserve the poor dispersed settlers from the dangerous fanatical assiduity of mendicant, migratory new light teachers, who are generally as badly disposed to the duty's of loyalty as they are to our religious establishment."[11]

Thus did Wentworth reiterate the hope of the British government in setting up an episcopate in British North America. But its influence was not to be confined only to Nova Scotia, for Bishop Inglis' diocese also included Upper and Lower Canada (now Ontario and Quebec); St. John's Island (now Prince Edward Island); New Brunswick and Cape Breton, both set up in 1784 as separate provinces; the ancient colony of Newfoundland; and for good measure Bermuda. Into nearly all these colonies men and women who had suffered much for their loyalty to the king were settling down to the hard task of creating a new social life. Great Britain now foresaw an opportunity to redeem the loss of its first American empire by building a second empire in which the United Empire Loyalists would be the chief architects of a society free from the democratic and egalitarian ideas that had wrecked the first. An imperial church was now considered a most important arm in the building of a stable and well-ordered empire.

In their zeal to keep the new arrivals faithful to the ideals for which they had been driven out of the United States, both the government and Bishop Inglis overlooked the primary need of all uprooted peoples on the frontier, namely, social reorganization and unification. Especially was the need for social reorganization acute among the Loyalist settlers, some of whom had spent a long time in army camps, where they had developed intemperate habits which cut across the established *mores* of the earlier settlements. The result was that the Loyalist migration, particularly into the Maritime Provinces, had a disintegrating effect upon community life. In view of these circumstances the first concern of an established church ought to have been to bring about a reorganization of social life by an emphasis upon the spiritual values of religious associa-tion.[12] But the extreme importance which Bishop Inglis and his colleagues placed upon a graded hierarchical society with its class distinctions and party spirit militated against the creation of a social solidarity which alone might have saved Governor Wentworth's "poor dispersed settlers from the dangerous fanatical assiduity of mendicant, migratory new light teachers." Bishop Inglis, himself, opposed free seats in the churches because they made it possible for men of the worst character to sit down beside "the most religious and respectable characters of the parish."[13] The Church of England's concern to preserve tradi-tional loyalties and cultural values of European society prevented it from developing new loyalties appropriate to frontier conditions, thus reducing its effective work to a colonial upper class society.

But even if Bishop Inglis had recognized the real challenge of pioneer communities to the church, and had been prepared to develop a new sense of group solidarity to take the place of disintegrating loyalties, it is extremely doubtful if he could have stemmed the tide of sectarianism that finally overthrew the church establishment, for the simple reason that the Anglican communion was so lacking in missionary zeal at this time, that it was impossible to find sufficient clergy to man the colonial parishes, much less to secure men who would identify themselves with the needs and aspirations of a frontier people, a prime necessity for rural leadership. A few such men were available who did create live centres of Anglicanism, but such priests, as Bishop Inglis soon discovered, were few and far between. Writing to the archbishop of Canterbury in 1788, the first year of his episcopate, he gave a rather gloomy description of the eleven missionaries then working in Nova Scotia and Cape Breton. "Of these," he wrote, "four are diligent useful clergymen, three are indifferent, neither doing much good or harm, and as for the remaining four, it would be happy for the church, if they were not in their orders."[14]

The lack of qualified clergy was to be a constant theme in the Bishop's reports; nevertheless, he did not allow this serious handicap unduly to depress him. With an apostolic zeal unusual to an eighteenth-century prelate, he set himself to the task of organizing his tremendous diocese and visited, with the exception of Newfoundland and the West Indies, all the various provinces included in his royal patent. His diaries in which he faithfully recorded his experiences and thoughts along the way "have all the charm of a romance . . . and throw a flood of light upon conditions in at least four of our Canadian provinces in which the Bishop laboured."[15]

III

Dr. Inglis' first tour in 1788 took him into the newly created province of New Brunswick, which up to 1784 had formed a part of Nova Scotia. Since the population of the province was largely Loyalist, the Bishop found church life there far more congenial and familiar to him than in Nova Scotia.

Before the arrival of the Loyalists there had been no serious attempt to carry on Anglican services in this area. Thomas Wood and John Eagleson had made occasional visits, but they were barren of any permanent results; so the beginnings of the Church of England in New Brunswick may be said to coincide with the Loyalist migration of 1783. Among the first arrivals was an Anglican clergyman, John Sayre, who ministered to his fellow refugees in the Congregational church at Mauger-ville, a village not far from Fredericton. His ministry was brief, as he died in 1784, but the mission in this Congregational stronghold was continued under the direction of John Beardsley, who was still in charge when Bishop Inglis arrived in 1788.[16]

The government officials in New Brunswick were for the most part enthusiastically Anglican[17] and they co-operated in securing clergy from the United States to look after the spiritual needs of the settlers in the new communities that were springing up all over the province. Parrtown (St. John), Gagetown, Kingston, Fredericton, and other Loyalist centres all were provided with priests who immediately proceeded to make collections among the people for the erection of churches, showing an initiative in this respect that was sadly lacking among Anglicans in the other provinces of Canada. One of the most energetic of these priests was Samuel Cooke, a Cambridge graduate, who had held several charges in New Jersey before coming to New Brunswick. After a brief ministry in Parrtown (1785) he moved on to Fredericton where he became in 1788 the Bishop's commissary, which virtually made him the archdeacon of the province of New Brunswick. Two years after his appointment he held a convocation of all the clergy at Fredericton, where plans were made for greater expansion. New Brunswick seemed to be blessed in its foundations with unusually devoted Anglican priests, a fact which Bishop Inglis remarks upon constantly in his reports. After a visit to this province in 1798 he writes in his *Journal* that the clergy "are a worthy respectable body of men—of good moral and exemplary lives, diligent in the discharge of their clerical Duty and beloved and respected by their congregations. The number of New Lights and Methodists is diminished."[18] But even New Brunswick, despite its predominantly Anglican foundation, was not immune to the propensity of pioneer communities for enthusiasm. Only two years after Bishop Inglis' remarks on its decline, he has to revise his opinion, reporting that "all the Missionaries and some of the laity also lamented in strong terms the fanaticism that abounded and the many strolling teachers who ran about the country bringing by their preaching and conduct the greatest disgrace both on religion and morals and exciting a spirit of enmity to the Established Government."[19] New Brunswick, however, was to continue during the Bishop's lifetime a source of encouragement and good cheer; at least, when placed in contrast to the other provinces of his diocese.

IV

A visit to St. John's Island and the old province of Quebec in 1789 revealed forcibly the full proportions of the task that faced the Bishop in creating an established church for British North America. Because of the difficulty of settlers in securing clear titles to lands granted to absentee landlords, the population of the Island of St. John had not been greatly increased by Loyalist migration; consequently, the Anglican church had not received any new infusion of life as had been the case in the other Maritime Provinces. As a matter of fact, the religious history of the province up to 1789 reflected the low estate of eighteenth-century Anglicanism in its most acute form. When in 1769 the Island had been given a separate government from Nova Scotia, King George III had ordered that one hundred pounds per annum be set aside for a minister. In due course John Caulfield was appointed the rector of the parish of Charlotte; but this first Island rector never left his native land though he collected his stipend for four years.[20]

The situation was hardly improved when it was decided by the authorities in charge to secure the ordination of a mere youth of twenty, Theophilus Des Brisay, the son of a prospective governor of the Island, and to send him off to his parish without making any provision for his stipend. Des Brisay arrived in Charlottetown in 1775 and remained on the Island until his death some fifty years later, having won the respect and esteem of all who knew him; nevertheless, the administration of his parish seems to have been less than half-hearted. Discovering that there was no provision for a stipend he immediately took duty as an army chaplain with a regiment stationed on the Island; at the same time he provided a few intermittent church services for his parish of Charlotte. Later the government set aside one hundred and fifty pounds as a stipend and so Des Brisay undertook to provide regular services, but refused to reside in Charlottetown, preferring the rural quiet of Cove Head on the north side of the Island, only visiting his parish on Sundays. At the time of Bishop Inglis' visit, there was no church building on the Island of any denomination, "although," as he wrote, "it (St. John's) has been in our possession upwards of twenty years, and the inhabitants are computed to be between five and six thousand."[21]

One-third of these were French Roman Catholics who had survived the Acadian expulsion. For the first twelve years after the Conquest the Roman Catholics had been without religious services until the arrival in 1772 of a Scottish priest, James MacDonald, who had accompanied some Highland settlers. After his death in 1785 the Roman Catholic communion was again without spiritual care until the arrival in 1790 from Scotland of Bernard MacEachern, who ultimately became the first Roman Catholic bishop of Prince Edward Island. The Scotch Presbyterians who began to arrive on the Island as early as 1770 were equally destitute of religious services, as no Presbyterian minister made an appearance until James McGregor came over from Pictou in 1791 for a brief visit.[22]

On the occasion of the Bishop's visit, Theophilus Des Brisay was the only clergyman on the Island; consequently, it was a matter of chagrin to the Bishop that neither the incumbent at Charlottetown nor the leading officials in the government had attempted to give reality to the Anglican claim of establishment when the field was so clear of rival denominations. Calling the rector and vestry together, he expressed his astonishment at their neglect in failing to build a church and he mentioned "the pain he felt at not finding this mark of even their belief in the existence of a Supreme Being." When the wardens inquired as to how a church might be obtained, the Bishop drew up a subscription paper with his own hand and presented it to them with the suggestion they "carry it about and solicit subscriptions from the Inhabitants."[23]

These very practical suggestions did not produce any immediate results. The subscription paper was circulated for a decade before enough money was raised to begin building operations. And when St. Paul's, Charlottetown, was finally completed in 1801, it was only with the help of a grant from the legislative council with the stipulation that the church was to be "for the use of the Established churches of England and Scotland."[24] This stipulation was fulfilled by allowing the Presbyterians to conduct the services on one Sunday and the Anglicans on the following, an arrangement which persisted until 1835, when a new St. Paul's was erected free from any entanglement with the Scottish establishment.

V

If Bishop Inglis was to be astonished at the failure of the Church of England to seize the opportunity that was presented to it on the Island of St. John, he was to be even more astonished at lost opportunities in the old Province of Quebec. It is true that before the arrival of the Loyalists the English-speaking community belonged for the most part to the Presbyterian or Congregational churches, but these seemed quite prepared to accept Anglican leadership and services. Anglicanism, however, could hardly have been presented to them in a less attractive form, for the British authorities in the hope of winning the French Canadians into the Anglican fold had in 1766 appointed three French-speaking rectors to the parishes of Quebec, Montreal and Three Rivers. Very few of the

French came to hear them, and so their services were confined chiefly to the English-speaking residents, who complained bitterly because of the linguistic difficulties of the preachers.

Before the arrival of the French-speaking rectors the religious needs of the Protestants had been provided by the usual haphazard eighteenth-century formula of depending upon army chaplains. In 1760 we find a John Brooke serving in a double capacity as chaplain and incumbent at Quebec.[25] In Montreal Dr. John Ogilvie held a similar position during the winter of 1760, but shortly after organizing a congregation he had to follow his regiment to Quebec. Four years later his regiment returned to Montreal and he once again officiated in the double capacity of chaplain to a regiment and incumbent of the parish of Montreal.

Dr. Ogilvie was succeeded by Samuel Bennett, who began to agitate strenuously for better supervision of Protestant development in Canada. In a letter to the S.P.G. (November 19, 1764) he points out that there are but two Protestant clergymen in Canada and that "this unhappy neglect of the mother country to form a religious establishment, was so improved by the Friars and Jesuits as to induce the French inhabitants to look upon their conquerors in an odious light, and to become more impatient of the English yoke."[26] Because of this neglect, both the Presbyterians and the Congregationalists in Quebec tried to provide services for themselves but not with any great success. In 1765 George Henry, a Kirk minister, organized the Congregation of St. Andrew's in Quebec, but the bitter divisions within Scottish Presbyterianism militated against building up a strong church community at this time. During the incumbency of Henry Sparks there was a disruption which led to a plea on the part of the dissatisfied members to the London Missionary Society for a Congregational minister.[27] This plea, which coincided with Bishop Inglis' visit, indicated a division at St. Andrew's between the Presbyterians and Congregationalists.

In Montreal, also, the Presbyterians made some half-hearted efforts to secure their own type of service, but with less success than at Quebec. John Bethune, whose sons were to play very prominent rôles in the Anglican Church, began to collect together a congregation in 1786, but his ministry lasted less than a year as he moved on to take care of a more flourishing congregation of Scotsmen at Glengarry; so that when Bishop Inglis arrived in Montreal in 1789, there was only one Protestant clergyman there who, like Theophilus Des Brisay on the Island of St. John, had the whole field to himself. This clergyman was David Chabrand

Delisle, French by birth, and one of the three French-speaking clergymen that the British had sent out to Canada in 1766 to replace the army chaplains. He seems to have made little effort to take advantage of his unique opportunity. When he first arrived he immediately wrote to the S.P.G. "on the sad and neglected state of the Church of England about Montreal," pointing out that "the English residents were destitute of a place of worship."[28] When Bishop Inglis arrived twenty-two years later the English residents were still destitute of a place of worship, hardly indicative of vigorous leadership on the part of Delisle.

Nor were there any more signs of vigour in Quebec, where Francis de Montmollin, a former Huguenot minister from Neuchâtel, Switzerland, preached in the Church of the Récollets in poor English to a very impatient congregation. In 1785 he had been provided with an unwelcome assistant, Philip Toosey, to look after the English-speaking portion of the congregation. As there were practically no French-speaking members, the appointment looked almost like a dismissal of Montmollin, and there had developed unusually bad feeling between the two clergymen, which Dr. Inglis tried to moderate during his visit but with very little success.[29]

The most criticized of these French-speaking clergymen was Legere J. B. N. Veyssière, a former member of the Récollets who had abjured his order in 1766 and sought entrance into the Church of England. Sir Guy Carleton did not think very favourably of this former Récollet, but after the latter had secured a licence from the bishop of London he was placed in charge of a congregation at Three Rivers, where, according to Canon Hawkins, the secretary of the S.P.G., he "seems to have done no more credit to the Church of England than he had done to the Church of Rome."[30]

After the appointment of Veyssière to Three Rivers, no other Anglican mission was undertaken until eleven years later, when services were begun at William Henry (Sorel) by the chaplain of a regiment stationed there. Services, however, were irregular until the arrival in 1784 of John Doty, one of the first of the United Empire Loyalist clergy to enter Canada. Shortly before Bishop Inglis' visit James Tunstall from England, who had been assisting the rector at Montreal, started a mission among some Protestants settling at St. Armand.

Apart from the promising missions at William Henry and St. Armand the Bishop found matters in a sorry state in the valley of the St. Lawrence.[31] Thirty years had elapsed since the Conquest and both

Montreal and Quebec were without Anglican churches, eloquent testimony to the religious lethargy of the Church of England in Canada during those critical years of transition from French to British rule.

There was, however, a brighter side to the picture; the Loyalists who were flocking into the new settlements to the west, soon to become a separate province, were showing more spiritual vitality, particularly under the leadership of John Stuart, who had first arrived in Canada as chaplain to the Six Nations during their pilgrimage from the United States to the Niagara district. Stuart, a former Presbyterian, displayed all the zeal characteristic of converts, in the extension of Anglicanism, and gained for himself the title of "the father of the church of England in Upper Canada."[32] After guiding the expelled Mohawks to their new home in Canada he settled at Cataraqui (Kingston) in 1785, from where he continued to oversee the religious development of both Indian and English speaking Loyalist settlements. Since it was impossible for him to provide regular services in all the new villages that were springing up, he made the best use he could of the laity. At Fredericksburg, where the people had purchased a house to serve both as a school and chapel, he set aside "a serious and discreet man to read prayers every Sunday," a practice continued until the appointment of John Langhorne as a resident missionary in 1787.

In a Mohawk settlement, Stuart chose a young Indian to act both as a catechist and a schoolmaster, enabling the Indians to become more self-reliant in their religious development. In thus using every human means at his disposal this pioneer clergyman was demonstrating the possibility of making the Anglican Church a church for all classes and tastes even on the frontier.

Unfortunately for the Church of England in Canada it had few men of the versatility and enthusiasm of John Stuart. It was also unfortunate for the plans of Charles Inglis that this was so, since apart from the few Loyalist clergy that had recently arrived, there seemed little hope of providing for the spiritual needs of the English-speaking people now flocking into Canada.

At one point in his tour the Bishop called together his clergy, eight in all, for a visitation and endeavoured to impress upon them the serious challenge that was now presented to the Church of England in Canada by the increasing growth of the non-Roman Catholic population, which he felt only his own Church could keep loyal to the British connection. The western settlements were particularly on the Bishop's mind since they were attracting not only Loyalists but Americans whose sole interest was to secure new lands. He knew that they were already demanding separation from French-speaking Quebec and so he appointed John Stuart as his commissary in this area[33]; for the older section of the province he chose as his commissary Philip Toosey, whom he had made rector of Quebec in place of Montmollin. It seems questionable, however, whether these administrative changes brought about any improvement in the church life of the Canadas, for when Jacob Mountain arrived in Quebec in 1793 to assume episcopal jurisdiction, the eight clergy of Bishop Inglis' visitation had dwindled to six.

VI

On his return to Halifax the Bishop found himself confronted with what appeared to him a revolt against the principles of Loyalism within his own church family. St. Paul's Church, which he had designated his cathedral, early evinced a desire to select its own rectors free from episcopal interference. Before the Bishop's arrival the vestry had in 1785 granted its rector, Dr. John Breynton, a year's leave of absence and later extended it to June 30, 1788, but also informed him that if he failed to return to his parish by that date it would be declared vacant, and that the archbishop of Canterbury would be asked to suggest a successor. Both the bishop and the governor of Nova Scotia had been ignored in these later communications and they felt slighted. But what troubled the Bishop most of all was the upsurge of "Congregationalism" within the cathedral church of the diocese. The vestry, however, remained obdurate and insisted upon the right of the congregation to choose its own rector. When finally in 1791 the archbishop of Canterbury recommended Robert Stanser as rector, he was accepted by the vestry only after it was officially placed on record that the right to present a rector for induction was vested in the parishioners.[34]

It was now becoming painfully evident to the Bishop that something was stirring in the New World even within the ranks of Anglicanism, that was going to make it impossible to transfer in its entirety the Elizabethan church settlement to Nova Scotia. The long years that the church in the colonies had been without a bishop accustomed the laity to a commanding voice in parochial affairs, nor was the day far distant when the laity would also insist upon representation in diocesan affairs as well.

To yield to such demands Bishop Inglis felt was an encouragement to social disorder and revolt. Nevertheless, at St. Paul's he had to yield with as good a grace as possible to the frontier impatience with direction and control, as he would be compelled to yield on many other occasions to the democratic spirit of the New World.[35]

The uprising within the parish of St. Paul's, though it was symptomatic of much to come, was mild compared to the discontent within the ranks of the powerful Congregational Church. Beyond the city of Halifax, in the outlying sections of the population, farmers' sons were turning to theology and organizing their own congregations with no regard for the niceties of the *Cambridge Platform*. This theological revolt ascribed by Bishop Inglis to "a spirit of fanaticism" was a genuine religious awakening that was to have a decisive effect upon the social development of Canada. Though it was far less of a revolt against the political aspects of Loyalism than the authorities suspected, it was certainly destined to frustrate all attempts to create an established church in Canada.

REFERENCES

1. According to Egerton Ryerson, *The Loyalists of America and their Times* (Toronto and Montreal, 1880, 2 vols.), "30,000 of them were driven from the homes of their birth." II, p. 184 *et seq.*
   Vide also J. G. Bourinot, *Canada Under British Rule* (Toronto, 1901), p. 81; and A. R. M. Lower, *From Colony to Nation* (Toronto, London, and New York, 1946), p. 118.

2. *Vide* A. G. Flick, *Loyalism in New York During the American Revolution* (New York, 1901), p. 16.

3. *Vide* P. Miller and Thomas H. Johnson, *The Puritans* (New York, 1938), p. 277.

4. A. G. Flick, *op. cit.*, p. 11.

5. *Ibid.*, pp. 31-36.

6. Quoted by R. V. Harris, *Charles Inglis* (Toronto, 1937), p. 59.

7. For the attitude of the Archbishop of Canterbury towards Bishop Seabury's consecration *vide* Charles Inglis, *Journal of Occurrences 1785-6* (Copy in the Public Archives of Nova Scotia), p. 3.

8. *Ibid.*, p. 1.

9. Charles Inglis, "State of the Anglo-American Church," found in *The Documentary History of the State of New York* (ed. by E. B. O'Callaghan, Albany, 1850), III, p. 1052.

10. Bishop Charles Inglis, *Letters etc.*, *1799-1811* (Copies in P.A.N.S.), p. 49.

11. *Nova Scotia in State Papers*, vol. A, 133, July 27, 1801, Wentworth to the Secretary of State.

12. On the need for social reorganization *vide* S. D. Clark, *Church and Sect in Canada*, *op. cit.*, pp. 81 *et seq.*

13. Quoted by R. V. Harris, *op. cit.*, p. 126.

14. Bishop Charles Inglis, *Letters, 1789-1791* (Copies in P.A.N.S.), p. 123.

15. R. V. Harris, *op. cit.*, p. 139.

16. C. F. Pascoe, *Two Hundred Years of the S.P.G.* (London, 1901, 2 vols.), I, p. 12.

17. Inglis, *Letters*, *op. cit.*, p. 100.

18. Bishop Charles Inglis, *Journal* (Copy in P.A., N.S.), Book 9, p. 5.

19. C. F. Pascoe, *op. cit.*, I, p. 130.

20. A. B. Warburton, *A History of Prince Edward Island* (Saint John, N.B., 1923), p. 385.

21. Inglis' *Journal*, *op. cit.*, Book 3, p. 2.

22. A. B. Warburton, *op. cit.*, pp. 393-411.

23. Inglis' *Journal*, *op. cit.*, Book 3, p. 2.

24. A. B. Warburton, *op. cit.*, p. 390.

25. H. C. Stuart, *The Church of England in Canada, 1759-1793* (Montreal, 1893), p. 17.

26. *Ibid.*, p. 24.

27. W. S. Reid, *The Church of Scotland in Lower Canada* (Toronto, 1936), pp. 24-25.

28. H. C. Stuart, *op. cit.*, p. 25.

29. *Vide Lettre de David François de Montmollin du 8 Fevrier à sa cousine à la cour du roi* (*Archives Roy de la Tour, No. 3752 aux AEN, Neuchâtel*).   A copy of this letter in which de Montmollin expresses his resentment towards Toosey is to be found in Divinity Hall Library, McGill University.

30. H. C. Stuart, *op. cit.*, p. 80.

31. Inglis' *Journal*, *op. cit.*, Book 3, p. 9.

32. *Memoirs of the Reverend John Stuart, D.D., Father of the Upper Canada Church* (Copy in Divinity Hall Library, McGill University).

33. Inglis' *Journal*, *op. cit.*, Book 3, No. 2, p. 4.

34. A good analysis of this controversy is to be found in N. Storey, *Church and State in Nova Scotia* (an unpublished MSS.), Chap. III, p. 9.

35. *Bishop Charles Inglis' Letters, 1787-91* (Copies in P.A.N.S.), pp. 249-250.

X

Church and Sect in the Maritime Provinces

THE RELIGIOUS REVOLT that occurred in Nova Scotia during the height of the American Revolution was known as Newlightism, and was characterized by an unusual amount of enthusiasm for things of the spirit. Such an outburst of religious ecstasy is, as Ronald Knox has pointed out in his distinguished study of the subject, a "recurrent phenomenon in Christianity and manifests itself in periods of extraordinary emotional activity when immense energies are unleashed." The Nova Scotian outburst does not seem to fit completely into this pattern since the enthusiasts were for the most part "neutral Yankees" by circumstance and were compensating themselves for their enforced political inactivity by finding self-expression in a religious revival.

This Nova Scotian awakening, as it has been called, however, is a good illustration of Knox's distinction between two kinds of enthusiasm: mystical and evangelical. The former, he says, "consults only the light within and may be guilty of the most outstanding profligacies"; the latter regards the *Bible* as the ultimate source of theological certainty and is able to keep its adherents within prescribed bounds.[1] It was mystical enthusiasm that brought about a very necessary awakening in Nova Scotia, but because of its lack of objective standards it degenerated into the most unseemly antinomianism. Before it had run its course, however, evangelical enthusiasm had taken over and used the revivalistic techniques developed by the Newlights, as an instrument of social reorganization on the ever-turbulent frontier.

I

Since Nova Scotian Newlightism comes out of New England Puritanism, against which it was to some extent in revolt, it is difficult to understand it fully without some knowledge of New England's peculiar form of church membership. The early Puritans of New England had based church membership upon the inner working of God in the soul; but in succeeding generations there was a considerable let down in religious zeal, and a failure of the recognizable signs of grace whereby individuals were admitted into covenantal membership. The civic life of New England was closely bound up with the Congregational Church, so it was found necessary to devise a half-way covenant which allowed unawakened persons to become half-way church members, thus making them eligible for civic responsibilities. There was among the more rigid Calvinists considerable discontent with this compromise and some talk of the half-way members as belonging to the reprobate; these in turn took up a very defiant attitude towards such terms as "elect" and "reprobate" and created a religious foundation for a bitter class struggle that arose out of the recurring depressions that were a constant feature of New England economy.[2]

A good deal of the economic discontent found an outlet in religious revivals, occurring first in a Congregational church in Northampton, Massachusetts, where Solomon Stoddard was pastor. Stoddard in defiance of Calvinistic polity had opened his church to all and sundry, and had collected a congregation that was inclined to excitable outbreaks of religious fervour. These took on more serious proportions during the pastorate of Jonathan Edwards, who in 1735 had succeeded Stoddard at Northampton. Edwards' revival was greatly stimulated by the appearance upon the scene of George Whitefield who began to preach at Philadelphia in 1740, thus bringing together the Methodist revival of old England with the Newlight revival of New England.

The Awakening, however, touched off a great religious controversy, since many people were shocked by the emotional extravagance it engendered: "screamings, convulsions, falling down exercises and prolonged meetings far into the night." Repressive laws were passed in some states with the hope of bringing the disorders to an end. For a time the jails were unable to accommodate the large number of separatists sentenced to prison by this attempt to "blow out the New Light."[3] In 1750 Edwards was dismissed from Northampton "amidst bitterness and slander"; the enthusiasm then began to wane and the fifty years that followed have been characterized by W. W. Sweet as a "period of religious and moral indifference throughout New England."[4]

It was towards the end of this religious awakening that the immigration of New Englanders into Nova Scotia began; the immigrants carried over into their new settlements many of the bitter feelings that had been engendered both by the class struggle and the religious persecutions of their home states. The religious indifference of New England itself is vividly reflected in the neglected condition of the church life of this outpost colony.

At the outbreak of the Revolution there were ten Congregational churches in Nova Scotia and closely allied to them were four Baptist and four Presbyterian. Most of them were without regular ministers, or indifferently served by student pastors from New England. The war greatly intensified the problem of pastoral care since most of the Congregational ministers were in favour of the Revolution. Benaiah Phelps, the pastor of Cornwallis Church, after being accused of sedition, left the province; Seth Noble, the pastor of Maugerville, fled to Machias, Maine, after taking part in an abortive uprising in the St. John River area. All the Baptist ministers left their congregations, as well as one Presbyterian. Only Israel Cheever of Liverpool, "a hard drinker," and Jonathan Scott of Chebogue managed to survive governmental vigilance and continued "to preserve the New England way in Nova Scotia."[5] One result of this lack of pastoral care was the development of a great deal of quarrelsomeness among the congregations; severe economic hardship also deepened the bitterness and discontent.

Since it was impossible during the war to find any redress by political means, and as all revolutionary movements had been quickly suppressed, there was only one outlet for pent-up emotions and that was in the realm of the interior life. The result was an outburst of mystical enthusiasm in Nova Scotia that almost duplicated the events that followed upon the revival in Northampton, Massachusetts, some fifty years earlier.[6]

II

At the centre of this religious movement was a rather boisterous farm boy, Henry Alline. Born in Newport, Rhode Island, in 1748, he had at the age of twelve moved with his parents to Falmouth, Nova Scotia. Though he had never gone to school after his arrival in Nova Scotia, he seems to have read a great many religious books, including the works of William Law, John Fletcher and Isaac Watts. William Law's writings apparently influenced him more than any of the others and so coloured his preaching as to bring against him the charge of *Boehmism*.

The spiritual and mental turmoil that preceded his determination to become a preacher of a new doctrine is told in vivid detail in his *Journal*,[7] and was probably typical of the religious experience of many young men and women of New England Puritan background living in the out settlements of Nova Scotia during the American Revolution. Since they were debarred from the excitement of taking active part in the Revolution they at first sought diversion in "frolics"; but these, because of a Puritan conscience, were not unalloyed pleasures. Henry Alline seems to have been a leader in organizing "frolics," but was never too happy at such gatherings because of the guilt feeling that accompanied outbursts of exuberant spirits; suddenly he would find himself in a state of melancholy, being convinced that an angry God would condemn him to hell.   The fear of hell had begun to haunt him as a child, for he has recorded that at the age of eight he was crying in bed at the awful prospect of eternal damnation.[8] The unusual visions that this fear brought to his mind are recorded in his *Journal* and have found a place in William James' *Varieties of Religious Experience*.   James regards Alline as a typical example of a sick soul whose divided mind finally became unified on a particular day in March, 1775.[9]

Once he found peace, or partial peace at least, Alline felt impelled to publicize his good news as widely as possible.   His gospel was a strange mixture of various systems of theology, based largely upon William Law's *Spirit of Prayer*, but even included Origen's seminal theory of the origin of souls.   Whatever its defects, and there were many, it did allow Alline to proclaim a new hope to a depressed people who in the harsh conditions of eighteenth-century Nova Scotia were beginning to despair of the goodness of God.   Alline's sympathy with the sad mien of his compatriots in the Maritime Provinces would never allow him to rest or settle down in one place.   During a brief ministry of seven years he visited all the chief settlements of the Maritime Provinces.   By horseback, snowshoes and coastal schooners he was transported from one scene to another, refusing all offers to become a permanent pastor in any one community.

On his way to Boston in 1784 he took ill at the home of a Congregational clergyman at Northampton, New Hampshire, where he was compelled to break his journey.   Here he died literally worn out from his constant labours at the early age of thirty-five, fulfilling the words of his own hymn:

> Lord, I am young, but soon may go
> Down to the silent tomb,
> When endless joys or endless woe
> Must be my lasting home.[10]

He was carried to his grave in the Northampton churchyard by six ministers; over his tomb was raised a monument with the following inscription: "The Reverend Henry Alline of Falmouth, Nova Scotia, in the midst of his zealous travels in the cause of Christ languished on the way, and cheerfully resigned his life at North Hampton, 2. Feb., 1784, in the 35 year of his age, whose remains are here interred. He was a burning and a shining light and justly esteemed the Apostle of Nova Scotia."[11]

The mystical religion which he preached with such vehemence did not long survive his death, but his demand to bring religion to the test of feeling and experience was taken up by other sects and became a determining influence in the social and political development of Canada. Nor did the churches which he had organized in the Maritimes continue long an independent existence after the death of their founder, as the blight of antinomianism was upon them. Furthermore, the Newlight itinerant ministers who attempted to expound Alline's doctrine became almost unintelligible in their preaching. A British officer who looked into a meeting at Maugerville in 1791 was struck "with amazement at the hideous noise" and stood with his "hair almost standing on end at the horror of the scene these miserable people exhibited," making noises "more horrible than any Indian war hoop."[12]

Before Newlightism disappeared it had practically destroyed the Congregational church in the Maritimes; the latter's doughty defender, Jonathan Scott, finally gave up the struggle and withdrew to Maine in 1792, "leaving Yarmouth to the mercy of the enthusiasts."[13]

III

The chief beneficiary from the disintegration of the Congregational system was the Baptist church of the Maritimes, and this despite the fact that all the Baptist ministers had disappeared from Nova Scotia before the outbreak of the Revolutionary War. Renewed interest in Baptist principles seems to have appeared almost simultaneously with the Newlight movement. This became evident when ten persons got together at Horton in 1778 to organize a Baptist church and to choose one of their own number as a pastor. The choice fell upon Nicolas Pierson, who was immediately ordained by his fellow Baptists.[14]   At his ordination there was present a delegation from the Newlight Congregational church at Falmouth; Henry Alline accompanied the delegation and was asked to preach a sermon, but was not allowed to take part in the ordination nor to share in the communion service.   Later, when he himself decided to be ordained by some of his followers, the Baptist church at Horton sent delegates to Falmouth as a friendly gesture towards the Newlight churches—thus establishing an early bond of friendship between the revived Baptist church and the emerging Newlight organization.   When the latter began to disintegrate after the death of its founder, it was natural that the members should turn to the Baptists for shelter and guidance.

An attack by Anglican officialdom, impugning the loyalty of the Newlights, probably hastened this transference to the Baptist discipline. In a letter to the S.P.G. in 1799, Bishop Inglis denounced the leaders of the Newlights as "engaged in a general plan of total revolution in religion and civil government."[15]   Charges of this nature persuaded the Newlights to find a name less suspect to the ruling authorities for their organization. At a conference in Cornwallis, called together the same year that the Bishop was hurling his charges of treason, the Newlights began to style themselves the Baptist and Congregational Association of Nova Scotia. The following year the name Congregational was dropped and their annual gatherings were henceforth designated as the Nova Scotian Baptist Association.   One of their members, Edward Manning, who had sought adult baptism from a Baptist minister at Halifax, was asked to draw up a body of rules for the renamed organization in accordance with Baptist practices; a correspondence was initiated with the Baptist associations of the United States and England, and a statement was given out declaring that the Baptist Association in Nova Scotia adhered to the same faith "as set forth by upwards one hundred congregations in Great Britain in the year 1687, and adopted by the Association of Philadelphia in 1742."[16]

The acceptance of the creedal statements of the English and American Calvinistic Baptist associations was a serious breach with the Newlight tradition, in which the guidance of the inner light over any dogmatic formulations had long been given pre-eminence. Just as startling a breach was made when adult baptism was accepted as a test of full fellowship. There was strong opposition to this latter move and for some years there was prolonged and bitter debate over the question of "close" or "open" communion. When the adherents of "close" communion won their case in 1809 by the adoption of a resolution calling for a withdrawal of "fellowship from all the churches who admit unbaptized persons to what is called occasional communion,"[17] John Payzant, a brother-in-law of Henry Alline, and four other ministers withdrew from the Association, taking their congregations with them.

This loss of membership was compensated to some extent by the fact that the resolution for exclusion brought into the Association as a full participating member John Burton, who with his wife had organized in 1795 in Halifax a Baptist church on "close" communion principles. His congregation consisted chiefly of the Negroes who had arrived in Halifax at the close of the American Revolution. Over these members of a depressed and alien race Father Burton, as he was affectionately called, had gained an influence so complete that "several Governors of the Province were much disposed to give the general management of these people principally into his hands."[18]

With the accession of Burton and his following, the Baptist Association gained a more established status in the province, especially among the official classes who had feared the antinomianism of the early Newlight preachers; but at the same time it seems to have lost much of its appeal to the individualistic and undogmatic frontiersman. As a matter of fact, the Baptists of the Maritimes by their adherence to a formalized creed had taken themselves out of the running as a missionary church on the more distant frontiers of western Canada. The leadership passed to the Methodists, who as it were took up the torch for a more liberalized Christianity when the Newlights in their search for status and security had reverted to an even more rigid Calvinism than that which they had first repudiated.

IV

Methodism has long been recognized as one of the determining influences in shaping the national character of English-speaking Canada. Though it had close affiliations with the pietistic movements on the continent of Europe and with Newlightism in America, there were in its early development certain historical factors which gave it a decided advantage over its rivals as a frontier religion both in the United States and Canada. The first of these was the class meeting, which was organized by Wesley as a means of keeping his followers true to their conversion experiences and to serve as a check upon the extravagances of religious enthusiasm. These class meetings, however, met an even more pressing need both in the wilderness of industrial England and frontier America, a need, as has been said, for "a change from dependence and self-distrust to independence and self-confidence."[19] The class meetings by providing a medium of self-expression in the socially dis-organized but mentally alert industrial areas of England and the out-settlements of America were the secret strength of Methodism. A second factor in its favour when it reached America was the circuit system with its itinerant ministry. Though this had been devised by Wesley to supervise his scattered societies in industrial England, it was found to be suited ideally for the supervision of the isolated settlements on the frontiers of America.

Other denominations soon learned the value of an itinerant ministry, but the Methodist ministers had an advantage over all the other itinerants in that they carried along with them less baggage in the form of doctrinal tests. Wesley refused to allow his colleague Whitefield to confuse class meetings with the problem of predestination and election; he boldly accepted the accusation of being an Arminian, and it was an Arminian type of Methodism that predominated on the American continent; consequently, activism rather than pietism has long been a characteristic of American theology.

It is difficult to fix the exact date for the beginnings of Methodism in Canada. Its historians usually begin with the preaching of Lawrence Coughlan in Newfoundland in 1765[20]; moving on to Nova Scotia where Yorkshire Methodists arrived in 1772; in Lower Canada, its history begins with the preaching of James Tuffy, an Irishman and a local preacher, who with his regiment was stationed in Quebec in 1780; and in Upper Canada with the arrival of the Hecks and Emburys in the Bay of Quinte district in 1785. Several years passed, however, after these first arrivals before there were any regularly appointed ministers or authorized circuit riders.

The first initiative in this direction was taken by William Black, who with his parents had emigrated as a boy of fifteen from Yorkshire to the Cumberland area of Nova Scotia. It was during the Newlight revival in Cumberland in 1779 that he had a religious experience which led to his preaching within his family circle.[21]   After he attained the age of twenty-one he began to travel extensively throughout the Maritime Provinces and soon had a following beyond his capacity to shepherd. He wrote to John Wesley seeking for missionaries from England, but when none were forthcoming he proceeded in 1784 to a Methodist conference at Baltimore, to which he presented the needs of the Maritime Provinces. In answer to his plea, Freeborn Garretson was assigned to a circuit in Nova Scotia and James O. Cromwell to one in New Brunswick[22]; from this date on Methodism was firmly established in the Maritimes.

Though William Black's conversion was due to the religious awakening that Henry Alline had stimulated in the Cumberland area, the two evangelists did not get along well together.   Black could not comprehend nor endure Alline's mystical theology; also he became much incensed when the latter dared to criticize the teachings of John Wesley. He expressed his feelings about Alline's theology openly and brought down upon his head a volley of abuse from the Newlights, who declared that Mr. Black was "no minister of Christ" but "a minister of Antichrist."[23]

In contrast with the strained relations between the Methodists and Newlights, there was at first comparatively good feeling between Black and the representatives of the Anglican church.   Black himself had been in the habit of attending the Anglican services conducted by John Eagleson in Cumberland County; a Methodist group in Halifax continued to receive Holy Communion in St. Paul's Anglican Church even as late as 1809.   It is reported that when Freeborn Garretson first arrived in Halifax he called upon the rector of St. Paul's, Dr. Breynton, and was greeted in the following words, "You are on a blessed errand and I will do what I can to assist you. I desire to see the Gospel spread."[24] William Black himself received an almost identical welcome from the rector of St. Paul's, Charlottetown, Theophilus Des Brisay, when he first visited the Island of St. John in 1783; Governor Fanning also spoke to him in appreciative terms of Wesley and his people and "offered him the use of the unfinished church"[25] in Charlottetown.

Dr. Breynton and Theophilus Des Brisay represented a more tolerant Anglicanism than that which came to power after the arrival of the Loyalists. Bishop Inglis was unable to distinguish between Methodists and Newlights, a confusion which infuriated the former and led Black to take a far more aggressive attitude towards the established

church. The ruling authorities in the new Loyalist Province of New
Brunswick were unduly suspicious of the Methodist itinerants and put
every obstacle they could devise in the way of·their preaching. Such
petty persecution only widened the breach between the Methodists and
the Church of England and finally led Black to seek ordination at the
hands of Bishops Coke and Asbury while attending a Methodist conference at Philadelphia.[26] By this same Conference (1789) he was
appointed superintendent of the Maritime circuits, which at this time
embraced both Newfoundland and the West Indies.

The close association of American conferences with the Maritime
circuits implied in this appointment did not long survive the arrival of
Methodist Loyalists in Nova Scotia. These had been regarded by the
American authorities as adherents of the Church of England and had
received very harsh treatment from the triumphant Whigs before they
reached the safety of Canada; consequently, they resented very much
the direction of their church life by American conferences. The dissatisfaction became so vocal that the American Conference of 1799
decided it would be wise to withdraw their preachers from the Maritimes.
In that same year William Black proceeded to England to the English
Wesleyan Conference and secured from it four itinerants for work in the
new world. Two of these found life on their circuits too strenuous and
gave up in despair; two others, William Bennett and Joshua Marsden,
fulfilled long and arduous ministries in their adopted country.[27]

But the real strength of the Methodist movement on the frontiers
depended not upon the importation of old country ministers, but rather
upon the spontaneous response of pioneer laymen to the religious needs
of their own communities. Duncan McColl, an ex-soldier and a Loyalist
who had settled at St. Stephen, New Brunswick, provides a typical
example of the emergence of a lay preacher in the frontier colony to meet
the challenge of spiritual destitution. During his army service McColl
had come in contact with a Methodist class group; after his discharge
and settlement in New Brunswick he found himself in a community where
there were no religious services, so he invited a few neighbours to his
house to read the Bible and pray with him and his wife. It was not long
before his house became crowded with worshippers, until finally he
decided to organize the believers into a society as near as he knew to the
Methodist plan, after which he gave up "all worldly business, took to
the study of the word, to preach and exhort on all occasions."[28] Ulti-

mately, he sought ordination from an American conference, and was ordained in 1795 by Bishop Asbury.

Newfoundland also furnishes examples of the value of local volunteers when missionaries from the English Conference failed to stand up to the rigours of a harsh climate and a deteriorating social situation. As has been intimated earlier, a religious revival in 1765 under the leadership of a S.P.G. missionary, Laurence Coughlan, gave Newfoundland the distinction of hearing the Methodist message before its introduction into the provinces of Canada or even into the United States itself. Opposition, however, soon developed to Coughlan's unorthodox methods, and he was recalled by the S.P.G. in 1773 to be replaced by a more conventional preacher who was to have nothing to do with Methodist class meetings.[29] The meetings continued, however, under the leadership of two merchants at Harbour Grace, John Stretton and Arthur Thomey, and with the help of a school teacher, John Hoskins, at Old Perlican. The emergence of local preachers at this time was necessary as the S.P.G. had not been able to find any suitable missionaries for Newfoundland, and the old Roman Catholic mission under the supervision of the bishop of Quebec had been brought to an end by the Conquest. All reports on the population of Newfoundland (varying between 17,000 in the summer and 7,000 in the winter) were to the effect that the people were slipping into barbarism.[30] The first gleam of light breaking into this darkening situation was the preaching of Laurence Coughlan, which Stretton and his colleagues made valiant attempts to keep alive after Coughlan's recall. Despite their best efforts, the work began to decline, as considerable dissension seems to have broken out among the organized classes. An appeal was made to Wesley to send out a duly ordained Methodist preacher who might with sufficient authority establish peace among the discontented societies. In answer to this plea John McGeary was sent to Newfoundland by the English Conference of 1785, but he succeeded no better than the local preachers in dispelling the prevailing animosities. It was then that John Wesley turned to William Black and asked him to go to Newfoundland and attempt to organize the societies on a more secure basis. The latter landed at St. John's on August 10, 1791, and immediately proceeded to Carbonear, where he found McGeary on the point of abandoning his field. "I have been weeping before the Lord," he said to Black as they met, "over my lonely situation and the darkness of the people, but your coming is like life from the dead."[31] Under the influence of Black's preaching the old animosities were quickly dispelled and with the proper organization of the classes the permanence of Methodism in Newfoundland was secured. McGeary, however, remained only a few months after Black's departure, but local preachers now found their work less hampered by factions, and Methodism soon became a great disciplinary force in the social development of Newfoundland. One of the by-products of this first visit of Black's was to create a bond of unity between Newfoundland and the mainland of British North America which helped to draw this colony within the cultural orbit of what was to become the nation of Canada.

William Black's ministry was a series of triumphs as he moved from one Maritime province to another, not only in the number of converts he gained for Methodism but also for the men of eminence and rank in Maritime society that he brought into the new movement. Among these was Simeon Perkins,[32] a judge of the probate court at Liverpool, and Lieutenant-Colonel Samuel Vetch Bayard of Wilmot. The latter's desertion of Anglicanism was a severe blow to Nova Scotian aristocracy; the Bishop, whose summer home was close by Bayard's in Wilmot, gave his converted neighbour to understand that he could no longer visit him in view of the "low company kept by him." The Duke of Kent, the governor, expressed himself more charitably in severing relations with a former boon companion, saying in a letter that he thought it was probable they would no longer meet "in the field or in the ball room," nevertheless, he hoped he would be remembered in Colonel Bayard's prayers.[33] Within the Methodist community Bayard became a great religious hero, being affectionately known as "the Fletcher of Nova Scotia."[34]

Notwithstanding these eminent conversions, Methodism never became as influential a factor in the social development of the Maritimes as in the other provinces of Canada. This may have been due to its rather rapid rise to a respectable middle class status, thus losing touch with the socially depressed from which it first drew its membership; or it may have been that immigration favoured other churches more than the Methodist Church.

V

Be that as it may, when the great religious upheavals of the late eighteenth century began to subside in the Maritimes, it was neither the Baptists nor the Methodists that presented the strongest front of opposition to the exclusive claims of the established church, but the Presbyterians.[35]

One reason for this was the survival in the new world of the spirit of the clan among the Scotch Presbyterians which proved to be an effective defence against proselytism; another was the fact that Presbyterianism in the Maritimes was represented by both the sect and church type of religion: the former were able to hold their own in emotional enthusiasm with the Newlights and Methodists; the latter were able to enroll in their membership the more conservative Congregationalists who were looking for some alternative to "Newlight madness."   Furthermore, in pre-revolutionary Nova Scotia the Presbyterians and Congregationalists had been very closely associated, with semi-official approval, in meeting the spiritual needs of the dissenters from the established church.   The pulpit at Mather's Meeting House in Halifax was successively occupied by Congregationalist and Presbyterian ministers.   With the general disintegration of Congregationalism, Mather's Meeting House naturally fell to the Presbyterians, who renamed it St. Matthew's Church.   The close association of Presbyterians and Congregationalists was also evident as we have seen in the first Presbytery set up in Nova Scotia for the purpose of ordaining Bruin Comingoe for the Reformed Church in Lunenburg.[36]

With the outbreak of the American Revolution the Presbyterians were under the same suspicion as the Congregationalists with regard to their loyalty; and to some extent this suspicion was justified, as one of their ministers, James Lyon, who had been a member of the first Presby-terian-Congregational Presbytery in Nova Scotia, openly expressed himself in sympathy with the rebel cause and had to flee from the province. The other Presbyterian member of this Presbytery, James Murdoch, an Anti-Burgher from Scotland, was able to convince the authorities of his loyalty to the British Crown and was allowed to complete a thirty-three years' ministry (1766-1799) in the Annapolis and Musquodoboit valleys unmolested until his untimely death by drowning.[37]

In 1786 there was organized a second Presbytery at Truro, consisting of three ministers of the Associate or Burgher Synod of Scotland: Daniel Cock, David Smith and Hugh Graham.   There was also present at the formation of this second Presbytery a member of the General Associate or Anti-Burgher Synod, James MacGregor, who had just arrived from Scotland, and a member of the United Church of Scotland, George Gilmour.   Neither of these men could forget their old country religious differences enough to become members of a mixed presbytery, though vehemently pressed to do so by the Burghers.   Absent from the meeting were James Murdoch and Thomas Russel, the latter a member of the

Church of Scotland who had taken over the pastorate of St. Matthew's Church in Halifax at the close of the American Revolution.[38]

Daniel Cock, the first moderator of the Truro Presbytery, had been in Nova Scotia for nine years previous to its formation and had become convinced that the divisions among the Presbyterians had little relevance to the Nova Scotian situation. He was anxious to create a united front of Presbyterianism in meeting the Newlight peril. His colleague, Hugh Graham, stationed at Cornwallis—a hotbed of Newlightism—was equally anxious to bring about a consolidation. But James MacGregor, fresh from the controversial atmosphere of Scotland, was deaf to all entreaties.

His arrival in the province was a great disappointment to Daniel Cock, since at this time MacGregor gave little evidence of the big-hearted charity which has made his name one of the most revered in the annals of Canadian Presbyterianism. A letter to a friend in Scotland reveals a rather mischievous pleasure in Cock's discomfiture. The latter, he writes, "was disappointed, and a little chagrined at my refusal to unite as a member of the same presbytery . . . . He was the more disappointed as he was the writer of the petition which the Pictou people sent home, and never had doubted but that the person it would bring out would sit in presbytery with him; besides he had given most supply of sermon and other ordinances to the Pictou people previous to my arrival."[39] Having rebuffed the Truro Presbytery, MacGregor proceeded to Pictou where he soon began to divest himself of his churlish manner towards fellow-missionaries when he realized the full proportions of the challenge before him; particularly was he sobered as he became aware after only a brief residence in Nova Scotia of the rapid deterioration in the moral and cultural life of the Scottish communities.[40] It soon became his conviction that the fundamental cause for this decline of morals was the lack of church teaching and spiritual oversight; and so he strove with might and main to see that all the various Scottish communities were supplied with pastors, while at the same time he kept on the lookout for some suitable person to start an academy in Pictou. His pleas for help from the churches in Scotland produced hardly any better response than had the pleas of Bishop Inglis to the churches in England. The Scottish clergy at this time were no more missionary-minded than were their colleagues in England.

Because of his failure to secure helpers from the old country, Dr. MacGregor felt compelled to become a part-time itinerant; it was he who brought the gospel of Presbyterianism for the first time to New Brunswick and the Island of St. John; in 1790 he spent six weeks in the latter province, where he became a fast friend of Theophilus Des Brisay, the rector of St. Paul's, who on one occasion acted as his guide to some of his flock at Cove Head. Dr. MacGregor, like Bishop Inglis, was greatly shocked at the spiritual destitution he found on the Island; in a report to the General Associate Synod of Scotland he wrote that there were only two clergymen on the Island, a Mr. Des Brisay, who seldom preached except in Charlottetown, and a Roman Catholic priest, and that the most Gospel the people got was from the Methodists.[41] The report closed with a strong plea for four young ministers to come over from Scotland to minister to congregations on the Island—"perishing for lack of knowledge." It took the General Associate Synod five years to find two young men, Duncan Ross and John Brown, who were ready to accept the MacGregor challenge. With their arrival there was immediately constituted an Anti-Burgher Presbytery at Pictou, which turned out to be less interested in the Island of St. John (or Prince Edward Island, as it is now called) than Dr. MacGregor; for it decided that both Ross and Brown should accept calls in Nova Scotia. In 1803 Dr. Thomas Mc-Culloch was sent out from Scotland to assume duties on the Island, but while waiting at Pictou for the ice to melt in the Gulf of St. Lawrence so that he might cross the straits to the Island, he became involved in an educational project at Pictou which brought about a decision not to leave Nova Scotia.[42] Once again the needs of Prince Edward Island were postponed, and it was not until 1806, when Peter Gordon was added to the Pictou Presbytery, that the Island received its first Presbyterian clergyman, who took up his residence at Cove Head.[43]

VI

The arrival of Dr. Thomas McCulloch in Nova Scotia was a momentous event not only in the history of Canadian Presbyterianism but in the social and cultural development of the Maritime Provinces. MacGregor soon recognized in him a great educator, and was quick to take the opportunity to bring to fruition a plan that had long been brewing in his mind—to found an academy from which it would be possible to recruit young men for the ministry.[44] He saw that the Baptists and Methodists were meeting the challenge of the spiritual needs of the frontier by raising up and ordaining local preachers who showed an aptitude for preaching; but such a simple method of recruitment was not possible for either the Presbyterians or the Anglicans, who continued to impose intellectual tests upon their ordinands. Without educational centres it was going to be impossible for these two churches to secure clergymen suitable for work on the ever-advancing frontier. There was, however, little money available in pioneer settlements for building denominational schools or colleges; consequently the Presbyterians demanded a share of the subsidy the government was providing the established church for its educational activities. This demand was a direct challenge to the whole idea of an established religion, one of whose functions was the supervision of education. The Baptists and Methodists were not slow in following the Presbyterian lead and thus was set in motion a great religious controversy, destined to leave a permanent impress upon the political and cultural life of Canada.

REFERENCES

1. *Vide* R. A. Knox, *Enthusiasm, A Chapter in the History of Religion* (New York and Oxford, 1950), pp. 578-591.
2. *Vide* M. W. Armstrong, *The Great Awakening in Nova Scotia* (Hartford, Conn., 1948), p. 4.
3. *Ibid.*, p. 12.
4. W. W. Sweet, *The Story of Religion in America* (New York, 2nd revised ed., 1950), p. 137.
5. M. W. Armstrong, *op. cit.*, p. 6.
6. *Vide* K. S. Sulman, *New England Puritanism in Nova Scotia* (M.A. thesis, 1943, deposited in P.A.N.S.), pp. 76-95: an interesting comparison of Edwards and Alline.
7. Henry Alline, *Life and Journal* (Boston, 1836).
8. *Ibid.*, p. 4.
9. William James, *Varieties of Religious Experience* (London, 1920), pp. 173-175, 217-220.
10. Henry Alline, *Hymns and Spiritual Songs* (Dover, Mass., 3rd ed., 1797), p. 6.
11. M. W. Armstrong, *op. cit.*, p. 86.
12. Patrick Campbell, *Travels in North America* (Champlain Society, Toronto, 1937), pp. 255-256.
13. M. W. Armstrong, *op. cit.*, p. 126; *vide* also *Records of the Church of Chebogue* (Copy in P.A.N.S.), pp. 191-264: a vivid account of the disruption of a Congregational church.
14. E. M. Saunders, *History of the Baptists of the Maritime Provinces* (Halifax, N.S., 1902), p. 69.
15. Quoted from the *S.P.G. Records* of 1800 by E. M. Saunders, *op. cit.*, p. 115.
16. M. W. Armstrong, *op. cit.*, p. 136.

17. G. E. Levy, *The Baptists of the Maritime Provinces* (St. John, N.B., 1946), p. 78.

18. *Ibid.*, p. 48.

19. S. G. Diamond, *The Psychology of the Methodist Revival* (Oxford and London, 1926), p. 38.

20. T. W. Smith, *Methodism in Eastern British America* (Halifax, 1877, 2 vols.), I, p. 45.

21. M. Richey, *A Memoir of the Late Rev. William Black* (Halifax, 1839), pp. 33-37.

22. *Ibid.*, p. 137.

23. *Ibid.*, p. 67.

24. Nathan Bangs, *The Life of the Rev. Freeborn Garretson* (New York, 1829), p. 155.

25. T. W. Smith, *op. cit.*, I, p. 302.

26. M. Richey, *op. cit.*, p. 243.

27. T. W. Smith, *op. cit.*, I, p. 369 *et seq.; vide* also Joshua Marsden, *The Narrative of a Mission in Nova Scotia, New Brunswick and Somers Island* (Plymouth-Dock, 1816), *passim.*

28. Quoted by S. D. Clark, *Church and Sect in Canada, op. cit.*, p. 58, from "Memoirs of the Rev. Duncan McColl" (*British North American Wesleyan Magazine* for the year 1841, Saint John), I, pp. 299-300.

29. *Vide* T. W. Smith, *op. cit.*, I, p. 62 *et seq.*

30. On the state of public morals in Newfoundland in the middle of the eighteenth century see Charles Pedley, *The History of Newfoundland from the Earliest Times to the Year 1860* (London, 1863), pp. 87-98.

31. T. W. Smith, *op. cit.*, I, p. 281.

32. *Diary of Simeon Perkins* (Copy in P.A.N.S.), pp. 478-595; *vide* also J. F. More, *The History of Queen's County, N.S.* (Halifax, 1873), pp. 149-153.

33. T. W. Smith, *op. cit.*, p. 302.

34. M. Richey, *op. cit.*, p. 323.

35. W. Gregg, *History of the Presbyterian Church in the Dominion of Canada* (Toronto, 1885): Gregg estimated that there were 90,000 Presbyterians in the Eastern Provinces in 1834, being equal in number to the Roman Catholics; 70,000 members for the Church of England; 60,000 Baptists; 30,000 Methodists; other denominations, 10,000.

36. *Vide supra*, p. 152.

37. W. Gregg, *op. cit.*, p. 61.

38. R. M. Hattie, *Looking Backward over Two Centuries: An historical paper dealing with certain phases of the history of St. Matthew's Church, Halifax, N.S.* (Copy in P.A., N.S.), p. 13.

39. George Patterson, *Memoir of the Rev. James MacGregor, D.D.* (Philadelphia, 1859), p. 93.

40. George Patterson, *A History of the County of Pictou, Nova Scotia* (Montreal, 1877), pp. 140 *et seq.*

41. G. Patterson, *Memoir of the Rev. James MacGregor, D.D., op. cit.*, p. 220.

42. G. Patterson, *A History of the County of Pictou, op. cit.*, p. 267.

43. W. Gregg, *op. cit.*, p. 112.

44. William McCulloch, *Life of Thomas McCulloch, D.D., Pictou* (Truro, 1920), pp. 26-27.

XI

Church and Sect in the Canadas

IN THE OPENING YEARS of the nineteenth century there occurred a great religious revival in the Canadas. This revival, except indirectly, had very little connection with the earlier one in the Maritimes, as the forest divide between these two areas of British North America was until the building of the railroads an effective barrier against any intimate interchange of religious ideas. The direct stimulus in the western provinces came from the United States during a second awakening on the American frontier. It was an awakening which produced an unusual crop of schisms and "was attended by such excitement and by such strange manifestations as were never before seen in America."[1] Western Canada felt the full force of this unusual outburst of religious enthusiasm, in which the camp meeting with its week-long services attracting people of all denominations, including "rowdies and roughs,"[2] played a conspicuous role. As in the United States, so also in Upper Canada this revival made an important contribution to the social and political development of the new province, largely peopled by American immigrants; and yet when it had run its course and a period of consolidation followed, the social and cultural institutions of Upper Canada resembled more closely those of the Maritime Provinces than any of the neighbouring American states.

One obvious explanation for the resemblance was the influence of Loyalism in the original four provinces of Canada; another lies in the fact that the cultural values of an older society as represented by New England Congregationalism in the Maritimes and by Roman Catholicism in the Canadas had been too firmly established to be overwhelmed completely by the new cultural institutions thrown up by frontier revivalism. But what may have contributed even more than anything else to the variation in American and Canadian religious and social development was the long struggle that occurred in all the provinces of British North America between free and established churches.   This struggle was preceded by an earlier one, the clash of church and sect, which is the immediate interest of this chapter.   Both issues, however, were constantly to the fore during the episcopate of Jacob Mountain, who in 1793 became the first Anglican bishop of Quebec.   The purpose of his appointment may not have been as ambitious as was the establishment of an earlier episcopate at Halifax, but it was still the hope of the British government that an established church in the Canadas would help to protect the new citizens flocking into the western provinces from the levelling ideas associated with sectarian Protestantism; it was also intended to remind the French Canadians that their Roman Church was merely tolerated by a government now showing its own religious preference.

I

The government, however, failed to make crystal clear that it actually intended to set up a fully established church.   The Constitutional Act of 1791 did not definitely indicate the Church of England as the established religion.   What it did do was to set apart one-seventh of all future land grants for the support of a Protestant clergy; but there seems little doubt that the framers of the Constitutional Act intended by this endowment to give the Anglican Church the prestige of establishment, but at the same time they wished to permit the Roman Church, which was still allowed to tithe its people in Lower Canada, a semi-official status.

The hesitancy of the government to go the full way in establishment made Bishop Mountain's episcopate a very disturbed and frustrating one. He had come out from England to the Canadas with the understanding that he was to be the bishop of an established church and he immediately proceeded to put the other churches in what he conceived to be their proper places.   As we have seen, he failed lamentably in his attempt to discipline the Church of Rome, whose prestige was greatly enhanced during the War of 1812.[3]

What was even more disastrous to an Anglican establishment than the exaltation of the Roman Catholic hierarchy was the claim of the Church of Scotland to be regarded also as an established church and thus eligible for a share of the clergy reserves.   This claim was based on the Act of Union between England and Scotland (1706), in which the Church of Scotland was given a position of equality with the Church of England.[4]

A recognition of the claim might not have been so disastrous to the Church of England, if it had not been that in the debate over the matter, the representatives of the Church of Scotland contended that "Protestant clergy" in the Constitutional Act of 1791 meant the clergy of the Church of Scotland as well as the Church of England.   By thus emphasizing the ambiguity of the word "Protestant" in the Constitutional Act, the Presbyterians had opened the way for all Protestant denominations to put in a claim for a share of the reserves, creating one of the most thorny issues in the political life of the infant province of Upper Canada.

Apart from the constitutional issues created by the indefiniteness of the law, the personality of the Bishop himself also contributed some of the ill-feeling that undermined any attempt to build up a united Protestant front as over against the Roman Catholic Church.   Though not without many gifts, one being a firm character which even his most bitter critics had to concede, Jacob Mountain was, nevertheless, a "haughty eighteenth century cleric" who little understood the work of a missionary bishop on the Canadian frontier.   He early created a bad impression among his Protestant colleagues by the prominent part he played in securing the imprisonment of a Congregational minister, Clark Bentom, who had been sent out to Quebec as a preacher of the gospel by the London Missionary Society.   Bentom had been refused by the government a register in which to record marriages and other civil acts usually performed by a clergyman; when he protested bitterly in a pamphlet, he was tried for libel, convicted and confined to jail for some considerable time.   The Bishop's opinion of the imprisoned cleric was expressed in a letter to the Archbishop of Canterbury: "Bentom is a very young man, but remarkably confident, and possessing that noisy & random eloquence which captivates weak & enthusiastic people."[5] Unfortunately for the Bishop, he was soon to be assailed from all sides by young men equally eloquent and whose preaching was far more acceptable to the early settlers of the Canadas than were the manuscript sermons of the Anglican missionaries on the frontier.

But whatever were the merits or the demerits in Bishop Mountain's personality, the fact remains that he was given an impossible task which would have broken the spirit of a man of less stable character.   The magnitude of his task was vividly brought home to him during his first visit to Upper Canada in 1794.   He immediately communicated his impressions to Lord Dundas: "From Montreal to Kingston," he wrote, "a distance of 200 miles, there is not one Clergyman of the Church of

England, nor any house of Religious Worship, except one small Chapel belong'g to the Lutherans, & one or two belong'g to the Presbyterians." He had overlooked two Roman Catholic chapels, an omission corrected in a later letter.   He conceded that the Presbyterian and Lutheran clergy were probably "men of good character but their influence is necessarily limited to their own little congregations."   "The great bulk of the people," he continues, "have and can have no instruction but such as they receive occasionally from itinerant & mendicant Methodists." These the Bishop characterized as "a set of ignorant Enthusiasts whose preaching is calculated only to perplex the understanding & corrupt the morals, to relax the nerves of industry, and dissolve the bands of Society."[6]

It was during this visitation that the Bishop met at Niagara (a small village then serving as the seat of government of Upper Canada) for the first time one of his most enthusiastic supporters, John Graves Simcoe, the lieutenant-governor of Upper Canada.   Simcoe had been an officer in a Loyalist regiment during the American Revolution and came to feel a profound dislike for the democratic principles of the United States, which he believed were furthered by the sectarian movement in the Canadas.   It was to combat the republican spirit of the sects that he wanted an established church.   Writing to the Archbishop of Canterbury in 1790, he said, "I am decisively of opinion that a Regular Episcopal Establishment, subordinate to the primacy of Great Britain, is absolutely necessary in any extensive colony which this country means to preserve."[7] When he finally realized that the Anglican Church was too poorly staffed to serve the purposes he had in view, he became willing to make grants to any of the more conservative churches, including the Roman Catholic, in the hope that they might help to stem the onslaught of the evangelical sects in Upper Canada.

II

All was in vain.   The second great American frontier revival with its "falling exercises," "jerks," camp meetings, noise and confusion spilled across the border, creating as much excitement and almost as many schisms as in the United States.   Most numerous of the American itinerants who crossed over to the Canadian side were the Methodists. The first of these was William Losee, who while serving the New York Conference on the Lake Champlain circuit visited some of his relatives in the Bay of Quinte district of Upper Canada.   During his stay he preached a few sermons at Adolphustown and so impressed the people there that they urged him to become their minister. Losee carried a petition to this effect to the New York Methodist Conference in 1790 and received authority from Bishop Asbury to form a Canadian circuit. On his return to Canada Losee established his headquarters at the house of Paul Huff, on whose farm at Hay Bay was erected in 1791 the first Methodist chapel in Upper Canada. As has been pointed out by one of the early historians of Methodism, the "year of the first Parliament of Upper Canada, was the year for the commencement of the first Methodist chapel or church"[8]; so it might be said that Methodism and the future Province of Ontario began their careers together.

One of Losee's first converts, John Roblin, became a local preacher and was elected to a subsequent parliament of Upper Canada, though "he rather served by constraint than willingly."[9] Thus early did the Methodists begin to make their influence felt in the political life of the new province.

After Losee, the next most notable of the early preachers from the United States was Nathan Bangs, who specialized in opening up circuits in the more remote and sparsely settled areas of the west. In doing so it was his custom to go from house to house and greet whomever he met at the door as follows: "I have come to talk with you about religion, and to pray with you. If you are willing to receive me for this purpose I will stop; if not I will go on."[10] The majority of the people in these isolated sections heard him gladly—"except a stout High Churchman" who "vociferously threatened to 'pitch him, neck and heels' out of the cabin, and would probably have done so had it not been for the interference of his daughter."[11]

More famous American itinerants than either Losee or Bangs were William Case and Henry Ryan. They were designated by the New York Conference of 1805 to serve jointly on the Bay of Quinte circuit. Though both these men were citizens of the now quarter-of-a-century-old republic of the United States, they somehow managed to identify them-selves completely with Canadian interests and Henry Ryan during the War of 1812 was vociferously on the side of the British.

Few of these early missionaries made any pretence to scholarship; nevertheless, they were "in advance of the great bulk of the people in intelligence" and "their lively and instructive talk at the fireside made their coming anticipated and greeted with the liveliest interest." More-over, "they were indefatigable salesmen of good books, which they carried about with them in their saddle bags," and sold to their people both to improve the religious education of their congregations and "to supplement their very small allowances."[12]   Thus they stimulated the desire for greater educational facilities wherever they went.   It was in keeping with this tradition that a Methodist minister became the architect of the public school system of Upper Canada and assured its success by himself becoming its first superintendent.

The close surveillance of the Canadian circuits by American conferences was a distinct advantage to the Methodist cause in the early period of settlement in the west; no other religious grouping had behind it an ecclesiastical organization so well equipped to cope with the mass movement of peoples on the frontier; but this advantage suddenly became a liability during the War of 1812 and for some years after.   While actual fighting was going on a good many American itinerants were compelled to abandon their circuits, leaving their converts in a rather confused state of mind.   The importation of some Methodist ministers from Ireland, though it saved the situation for the time being, was to create a rather tense situation within the Methodist family for many years to come; nor was harmony restored with the advent of missionaries from the Wesleyan Missionary Society of England.   At first, these latter confined themselves to the vacant circuits in Lower Canada; but as the volunteers from England became plentiful it was decided to send some Wesleyan missionaries into Upper Canada as well.   Henry Pope accompanied by a few colleagues led the way in 1816; but he adopted such an arrogant attitude towards the American-trained Canadian itinerants as to produce a sectarian war on the circuits.

The rivalry between the British and Canadian ministers became so unseemly that it compelled the English and American conferences to attempt to negotiate a truce.   In 1820 it was agreed by both conferences that the American-sponsored societies of Lower Canada should be placed under the care of the British brethren while British societies in Upper Canada were to come under the care of the American or Canadian brethren.[13]   Though there seemed to be a sincere desire at these conferences to bring to an end the "setting up altar against altar," it was next to impossible to bring peace into the circuits.   In the Montreal area, where there was a persistent admiration of things American, the feeling against the Wesleyan ministers was so intense as to cause some dissidents to throw in their lot with the Presbyterians who were breaking away from Scottish dominance to form the American Presbyterian Church in Montreal.[14]

In Upper Canada the discontent moved in an opposite direction: pro-British congregations refused to accept the services of Canadian or American ministers and were insistent on the return of the Wesleyans. Because of these persistent rivalries and in deference to the growth of Canadian national feeling, following upon the War of 1812, the leaders of the American General Conference arrived at the conclusion that it was now necessary to organize a Canadian conference independent of any of the American conferences. The first tentative move in this direction was taken at a meeting of the Canadian itinerants held at Hallowell (now Picton) in August, 1824. It was a small gathering consisting of about thirty-three preachers presided over by two American bishops, George and Hedding. The bishops gave assurance that the complete independence of this group which was now constituted the Canada Conference would be proclaimed at the next General Conference in the United States.

In due course the General Conference convened in the city of Pittsburgh (May 1, 1828) and proclaimed the independence of the Methodist Episcopal Church of Canada[15]; but not before the impatient Henry Ryan, who had long been agitating against the American connection, had created a schism in the Canada Conference. Putting himself at the head of the Irish preachers, who had also been chafing under the American Conference, he proceeded to form a new body called the Canadian Wesleyan Church. As one Methodist historian has put it, ". . . there was an apparent argument and sentiment in the proposition, and the great loyalists with some Government officers, therefore aided Ryan."[16] Among the contributors to his cause was the Archdeacon of York, Dr. Strachan, who sent Ryan a present of fifty pounds.

To add still further to the cup of woe of the Canada Conference, the English Conference decided that the truce entered into with the General American Conference in 1820 did not apply to the Methodist Episcopal Church of Canada; consequently, it was decided to renew their interrupted missionary work in the upper province. So the Wesleyan missionaries returned under the leadership of Robert Adler, long a thorn in the side of the Canada Conference, to create an unusually tense situation in the Methodist family of Upper Canada. Since the return of the Wesleyans meant nothing but quarrels and disruptions on the circuits, with both the Wesleyans and Ryanites pleading greater loyalty to British institutions than their Canadian brethren, the leaders of the Canada

Conference decided to seek peace and respectability by a corporate union with the English Conference.   The story of this union and its aftermath is so closely bound up with the careers of a great Methodist family, the Ryersons, and with the emergence of Methodism as a political force in Upper Canada, that it is better postponed to a later chapter in this study on the relations of church and state in Upper Canada.[17]

III

The Methodists were not the only ones embarrassed by their connection with American churches—the Presbyterians and the Baptists were open to similar accusations of "guilt by association."   As early as 1793 two American Presbyterian ministers, Jabez Collver and Daniel Ward Eastman, entered the Niagara area and without waiting for a call began to preach to widely scattered settlers where there was little possibility of a presbytery being organized.[18]   Their method of preaching resembled very much the emotional appeal of the Cumberland Presbyterians of the United States and was somewhat startling to their Scottish colleagues, who considered it "Anti-Burgher madness."   American immigrants, particularly in the Montreal area, did not agree with this estimate and united as we have seen with some Methodist dissidents to found a Presbyterian Church which remained for some decades closely associated with American presbyteries.[19]

It was, however, by a strange series of schisms from the original Presbyterian congregation that had been organized by John Bethune in Montreal that the American Presbyterian Church emerged.   This congregation, under the leadership of John Young who had succeeded in getting a church erected (1792) on St. Gabriel Street, had become connected with the Presbytery of Albany.[20]   In 1793, Young joined with John Bethune and Dr. Alexander Spark of St. Andrew's Church, Quebec, to form the first presbytery in the Canadas which leaned towards the established Church of Scotland.   This move by the St. Gabriel Street Church so incensed former Secession and American membership that during the pastorate of James Somerville they withdrew (1804) and built themselves a new church on St. Peter's Street and chose Robert Easton as their first pastor.   But even in this second church, which became known as St. Andrew's, the Scottish element began to predominate, so that by 1822 it also decided to affiliate with the Church of Scotland, and as a consequence called John Burns, a Kirk man, to be their pastor. Once more the American element withdrew and this time they definitely named their new church the American Presbyterian Church of Montreal and chose for their pastor Joseph Stibbs Christmas, a graduate of Princeton Seminary, who was inducted into his office by the New York Presbytery.[21]

The War of 1812 was almost as serious a setback to the progress of Presbyterianism in Canada as it had been to Methodism. Apart from Joseph Stibbs Christmas few American preachers dared to cross the border into Canada until 1830, when a renewed revival in the United States led to a return of the American preachers.

In the meantime there had been a serious attempt by the Scottish clergy to meet the pressing need for pastors by uniting forces under one comprehensive presbytery, which would allow a more equable distribution of manpower. One such attempt was initiated by a meeting of some ministers, formerly of the Associate Synod, at Cornwall in 1818, when it was decided to form a presbytery without any connection with the synods of Scotland. In this way it was hoped to bring into one organization not only the various branches of Scottish Presbyterianism in the Canadas but also adherents of the Dutch Reformed and Congregational Churches as well, both of which had representatives on the western frontier. A second meeting was arranged to take place in July of the same year at Montreal to which were invited all the Presbyterian brethren in the Upper and Lower Canadas "whose character and academical education entitled them to respect . . ."[22] Though the invitation was ignored by members of the Church of Scotland, yet the Presbytery of the Canadas, as it was called, did prepare the way for a unified Presbyterian Church of Canada. This Presbytery and others fostered by it were greatly strengthened by acquisitions from the Dutch Reformed and Congregational settlers in Upper Canada.

The Dutch Reformed Church had at first its own pastors, John Ludwig Broeffle and Robert McDowall, who between the years 1795 and 1798 had been sent into Upper Canada by the Albany Classis to look after the spiritual needs of their compatriots in Canada.[23] Shortly after the formation of the Presbytery of the Canadas McDowall withdrew from the Albany Classis to throw in his lot with the native Presbytery. Broeffle had died in 1815, three years before the formation of the new Presbytery, but his congregations with the exception of some Lutherans followed

McDowall into the Presbyterian Church. The Lutherans, following the example of two of their ministers in Upper Canada, Weagant and Myers, attached themselves to the Church of England.

Organizing presbyteries, however, was no real solution to the shortage of ministers in the fast-growing Scottish settlements; consequently, the return of the American preachers, despite their unconventional ways, helped to sustain the Presbyterian cause in Canada during a period when missionary zeal burned low in Scotland. With the help of the Americans and with increased Scottish immigration it looked as if Presbyterianism was destined to become the largest Protestant group in the Canadas as well as in the Maritimes. According to their historian, Gregg,[24] they numbered in 1834 about 102,000 souls. The leading religious group was still the Roman Catholic with a membership of about 483,000; the Church of England exceeded the Presbyterians with a nominal membership of 119,000 but was soon destined to fall behind. The Methodists at this time were only about 70,000, but they were rapidly winning members from the traditional churches, and before many decades had passed they were out in front with the Anglicans occupying third place.[25]

<h1 style="text-align:center">IV</h1>

The Baptists, at this time, with a membership of approximately 15,000, occupied fourth place—a rather surprising showing in comparison with Baptist progress in the Maritimes during the first great awakening. One reason for this slow start on the western frontier was the division that had occurred within the Baptist community during the first New England awakening. At this time the Baptists divided into Regulars and Separates; the former opposed revivalistic meetings, while the latter favoured them. This division was imposed upon an earlier one, the General or Arminian Baptists as over against the Particular or Calvinistic. Just at the time that the Baptists should have been closing their ranks to meet the challenge of the western frontier there emerged a still further division or schism which became known as the Primitive or Hardshell Baptist Church, which set its face against all missionary endeavour and actually considered it sinful.[26]

Individual Baptist ministers, however, took up the challenge of the frontier and roamed far and wide throughout the settlements, identifying themselves with reform movements, such as the abolition of slavery and the suppression of the liquor traffic. Some of these ministers began to cross the border from Vermont into the Canadas in the second decade of the nineteenth century, where they made contact with a few Baptist congregations in widely scattered areas. One of these communities, Beamsville in Lincoln County, Upper Canada, is said to have a continuous history going back to the eventful year of 1776. It is known that a church was constructed there in 1796 with William Holmes as its first pastor.[27] About the same time a young shoemaker and farmer, William Marsh, began preaching in the Eastern Townships, and carried on a combined ministry and secular occupation until he removed to Whitby, Upper Canada, in 1825.[28]

One of the first of the American ministers to arrive in the Canadas to give a renewed urgency to the Baptist cause was a "young evangelist," Reuben Crandall, who laid the foundations for a society in the Haldimand township in 1785; but it was over a decade before this congregation was finally organized and built a church (1798), and it does not seem to have secured a regular pastor until 1818 when Peleg Card began to conduct services in the townships. Another American itinerant, Abel Stevens, organized a church at Harlem in the county of Leeds in 1803 and was ordained its pastor the following year. About this same time there arrived in the valley of the Ottawa a colony of Scottish Baptist immigrants who named their new home Breadalbane, after the district in Scotland from whence they had come. Their first concern was to secure a pastor for the new settlement. Here they experienced difficulty as they were badly divided on doctrinal matters even before their arrival in Canada; they did succeed, however, in issuing a unanimous call to William Fraser to come out to Canada from Inverness in 1829. After a ministry of some nineteen years he was able to declare that he had never "heard an oath nor seen a glass of liquor drunk in Breadalbane."[29]

One of the most notable of the Scottish Baptist preachers in these pioneer days was John Edwards, a former member of the Haldane mission in Scotland. In Canada he became quite famous for his eloquent sermons, but he is chiefly remembered for having induced John Gilmour of Aberdeen to come out to Lower Canada to organize a Baptist society in Montreal. Through his initiative the first Baptist church of Montreal was opened for worship on St. Helen Street in 1831.[30] Under Gilmour's leadership a certain amount of co-operation was brought about between the Baptists of the Eastern Townships and the Ottawa Valley, which ultimately led to an organized effort to make Baptist principles more generally known throughout the Canadas.[31]

V

There remains to record the establishment, or rather the re-establishment, of still another major communion—the Roman Catholic—on the western frontier from which it had been so cruelly repulsed in the seventeenth century. It had not been wholly eliminated during the old regime, as Roman priests constantly accompanied French explorers and fur traders to their stations in the west long after the failure of the Huronian mission, but most of these were situated south of the present Canadian border. There were also a few scattered settlers north of the border who were soon to be reinforced by Roman Catholic Scots from the Highlands.[32] Though these Catholics were not completely immune from the depredations of the sects, they seemed to have put up a firmer resistance to the sectarian movement than the members of any of the other traditional churches; and this despite the faltering leadership of the Quebec hierarchy during the first waves of mass immigration into Upper Canada. The confusion of those early days is well told by a Roman Catholic missionary, Edmund Burke, in a letter he wrote in 1795 to the Bishop of Dublin. He says that he was called upon to administer a large territory "with every episcopal power except what requires the episcopal order, yet he found a very great want of power since the limits of his jurisdiction were uncertain and unsettled." "The very parish in which I live," he wrote, "may be a subject of dispute between the Bishops of Quebec and Baltimore, though it may be distant 400 or 500 leagues from either."[33]

The following year the boundary line was settled and Burke found his headquarters on the American side, which left unshepherded a colony of Roman Catholic Highland Scots, mostly United Empire Loyalists, in Glengarry. Consequently, Burke returned to Quebec to rearrange his affairs and to transfer his mission into Upper Canada. While there he pleaded that the western missions in the interest of efficiency be placed under the direction of the Sulpicians of Montreal. He also urged that the needs of the new immigrants would be better served by the erection of dioceses closer to the scene of action; in other words, a diocese at Montreal and another at Kingston.   As he received little encouragement for his expansive ideas from either the bishop of Quebec or his coadjutor, he finally betook himself to Nova Scotia where, as we have seen, with the help of the papal see, he established a diocese independent of the Quebec hierarchy.[34]

In the meantime, it appeared as if the Roman Catholics in the new province were to be abandoned to the sects; the situation was redeemed, however, with the arrival in Glengarry in 1803 of Alexander Macdonnell, who was destined to become the first Roman Catholic bishop of Upper Canada.   It was a most fortunate turn of events that Father Macdonnell, a tactful Scotsman, rather than the fiery Edmund Burke became the leading missioner in Upper Canada, as the province had become predominantly populated with Protestants from the United States, nourished in fearful anti-papal prejudices, "Hating Pope and Popery with an honesty and sincerity that there was no disputing."[35]   Macdonnell proved himself adept at turning away wrath with a soft word and he soon taught his following how to live on tolerable terms with their anti-Catholic neighbours.   The secret of his success was his sincere endeavour to understand sympathetically the inner meaning of the religious enthusiasm that was producing such unusual behaviour among his Protestant neighbours, for he insisted even when the din of revivalistic meetings outside his rectory window was almost deafening that "perhaps these people have some merit."[36]

Very early in his ministry Bishop Macdonnell won the goodwill of the government of Upper Canada by his insistence upon obedience to the higher powers and in his scathing denunciation of all revolutionary ideas. For this service the government subsidized the building of Roman Catholic churches and also contributed to the Bishop's educational projects.   At the invitation of the governor, Sir John Colborne, he became a member of the legislative council of Upper Canada.

The measure of the success of his missionary activities can be seen in the fact that at the time of his arrival in Upper Canada, there were only three Roman Catholic churches in the whole province and only one priest who could speak English.   At the end of a ministry of thirty years, during ten of which he was for all intents and purposes alone, he had secured the erection of thirty-five churches and there were twenty-two priests in his diocese, ministering to widely scattered flocks.[37]

VI

The invitation to Bishop Macdonnell to take a seat in the legislative council and an unofficial acceptance by the government of the Church of Scotland of equality with the Church of England was an implicit acknowledgment by those in authority that an exclusively established church was an impossible ideal for the Canadas. But Bishop Mountain, because of his conviction that the Church of England had a secure legal right to the income of the clergy reserves, would not concede the Church of Scotland's claim to equality, even when the government was urging that such an acknowledgment might well help to hold back the rising tide of sectarianism.[38]

More annoying to Bishop Mountain than the government's attempt to appease the Presbyterians was its tendency to grant special favours to the Roman Catholics. It was with considerable chagrin that he learned that Alexander Macdonnell after a trip to England in 1817 had returned to his diocese with a promise that the salaries of several Roman Catholic priests would be provided out of governmental grants. All through his episcopate Bishop Mountain was constantly warning the British government of the danger of making concessions to the Roman Catholic hierarchy. His final communication to the Home Secretary, Lord Bathurst, underlined with wearying importunity "the importance of continuing to maintain the establishment, & ascendancy of the Church of England, in these Provinces."[39]

With the accession of Charles James Stewart, the fifth son of the Earl of Galloway, to the see of Quebec in 1826, a more flexible note was introduced into the polity of the Church of England in Lower Canada. It was now tacitly recognized that an Anglican establishment was an impossible objective; by 1828 the new bishop was ready to concede that some compromise on the clergy reserves might be worked out with other churches.

Bishop Stewart before coming to Canada had been deeply influenced by the evangelical movement within the Church of England, which gave him a more sympathetic understanding of the strange revivals on the frontier; he had also shown some of the evangelistic fervour of the sects during his ministry in the Eastern Townships both as minister at St. Armand and as a travelling missionary.[40] Under the leadership of such a bishop, whose piety and largeness of spirit were proclaimed by Anglicans and non-Anglicans alike, much of the earlier asperity disappeared from the religious life of Lower Canada. From now on the Anglican Church and the Protestant denominations generally began to lay their emphasis upon an autonomous development, thus effecting a discreet withdrawal from the political life of a predominantly French-speaking province. A circular sent out by Bishop Stewart in 1834, making a plea to congregations to begin to support their own clergy, "was the first call ever made upon Canadian Anglicans to pay for the support of their Church."[41] This was a triumph for the voluntary system, long the distinguishing mark and boast of the sectarian churches. Toward the end of his episcopate the Bishop began to urge the formation of church societies "for mutual conference, support and counsel" among the clergy. These in turn paved the way for synodical government, a long step towards democratic self-rule, another sectarian emphasis. All of which seemed to indicate that the bitter struggle between church and sect had ended with the capitulation of Anglicanism to sectarian principles. But this was true only of the lower half of Bishop Stewart's diocese; in Upper Canada the archdeacon of York, John Strachan, continued the struggle long after the death of Charles James Stewart (1836) for a fully endowed and established Church.

When Strachan was finally compelled to admit defeat he gave vigorous leadership in creating an autonomous and synodically-governed Church, dependent upon the goodwill and voluntary contributions of its members; the sects, on the other hand, and particularly the Methodists during their long and arduous struggle with the doughty Archdeacon, began to abandon their own voluntary principles and to take on many of the characteristics of the church type of religion. This spectacular reversal of roles in which an outstanding leader of Methodism becomes a dominant political influence in Upper Canada, while the architect of the Family Compact begins to fade into sectarian obscurity, is one of the surprising turns in Canadian church history which must be reserved for a later chapter in this study.

REFERENCES

1. W. W. Sweet, *The Story of Religion in America, op. cit.*, p. 227.
2. W. W. Sweet, *The American Churches* (New York and Nashville, 1948), p. 53.
3. On the question of rival establishments *vide* T. R. Millman, *Jacob Mountain, First Lord Bishop of Quebec* (Toronto, 1947), pp. 60-79.
4. For a full account of the Presbyterian claim to establishment *vide* W. S. Reid, *The Church of Scotland in Lower Canada: Its Struggle for Establishment* (Toronto, 1936).

5. T. R. Millman, *op. cit.*, p. 47.

6. *Ibid.*, p. 57.

7. *Ibid.*, p. 13. For an estimate of the character of Simcoe *vide* A. R. M. Lower, *Colony to Nation* (Toronto, London and New York, 1946), pp. 162-163.

8. George F. Playter, *The History of Methodism in Canada* (Toronto, 1862, 2 vols.), I, p. 30.

9. *Ibid.*, I, p. 25.

10. Abel Stevens, *Life and Times of Nathan Bangs* (New York, 1863), p. 100.

11. *Ibid.*, p. 101.

12. John Carroll, *Case and His Cotemporaries* (Toronto, 1867, 5 vols.), I, p. 257.

13. G. F. Playter, *op. cit.*, I, p. 187.

14. John Carroll, *op. cit.*, II, p. 335.

15. G. F. Playter, *op. cit.*, I, p. 315.

16. *Ibid.*, p. 298.

17. *Vide infra*, p. 278.

18. William Gregg, *History of the Presbyterian Church in the Dominion of Canada* (Toronto, 1885), pp. 182-189.

19. G. R. Lighthall, compiler, *A Short History of the American Presbyterian Church of Montreal, 1823-1923* (Montreal, 1923), *passim*.

20. Robert Campbell, *A History of the Scotch Presbyterian Church, St. Gabriel Street, Montreal* (Montreal, 1887), pp. 176-182.

21. G. R. Lighthall, *op. cit.*, p. 7.

22. W. Gregg, *op. cit.*, p. 207.

23. *Ibid.*, pp. 172-182.

24. *Ibid.*, pp. 550-562.

25. The census of 1842 found in *Census of Canada 1870-71* (Ottawa, 1876) gives Church populations as follows: Roman Catholics, 637,742; Anglicans, 151,318; Presbyterians, 129,076; Methodists, 98,747; Baptists, 20,474; Congregationalists, 8,159; Lutherans, 4,625; and Quakers, 5,200.

26. W. W. Sweet, *Religion on the American Frontier, The Baptists, 1738-1830* (Chicago, 1931), pp. 43-44.

27. James Croil, *Genesis of Churches in the United States of America, in Newfoundland and the Dominion of Canada* (Montreal, 1907), p. 273.

28. *Ibid.*

29. *Vide* article, "The Baptists in Canada," by J. L. Gilmour, in *Canada and Its Provinces*, editors A. Shortt and A. G. Doughty (Toronto, 1914-1917, 23 vols.), vol. XI, p. 362.

30. Newton Bosworth, ed., *Hochelaga Depicta* (Montreal, 1839), pp. 120-121.

31. J. L. Gilmour, *op. cit.*, p. 364.

32. W. R. Harris, *The Catholic Church in the Niagara Peninsula* (Toronto, 1895), p. 166 *et seq.*

33. C. O'Brien, *Memoirs of Rt. Rev. Edmund Burke* (Ottawa, 1814), pp. 15-16.

34. *Vide supra*, p. 82.

35. W. R. Harris, *op. cit.*, p. 183.

36. W. J. Macdonnell, *Reminiscences of the Late Hon. and Right Rev. Alexander Macdonnell, First Catholic Bishop of Upper Canada* (Toronto, 1888), p. 27.

37. *Vide* H. A. Scott, "The Roman Catholic Church East of the Great Lakes" in *Canada and Its Provinces, op. cit.,* vol. XI, p. 362.

38. *Vide* E. R. Stimson, ed., *History of the Separation of Church and State in Canada* (Toronto, 1888, 3rd ed.), p. 90 *et seq.*

39. *Vide* T. R. Millman, *op. cit.,* p. 79.

40. *Vide* T. R. Millman, *The Life of the Right Reverend the Honourable Charles James Stewart* (London, Ont., 1953), pp. 13-23.

41. *Ibid.,* p. 122.

XII

An Era of Ill Feeling in the Maritime Provinces

BEGINNING with the founding of King's College at Windsor, Nova Scotia, in 1789, there developed an era of ill feeling in the relations of the churches that has left significant scars in the social and political life of Canada. A good deal of the animosity was due to a firm conviction on the part of the ruling classes that if the colonies were to remain loyal to the British Empire, then the education of youth must be reserved to the established church. Before all the Loyalists had left New York state for Nova Scotia, a plan was submitted by some Anglican clergymen to Sir Guy Carleton for the founding of a seminary at Windsor to make it possible for the inhabitants to educate their sons at home rather than sending them to the independent states to the south where they would be sure to imbibe principles unfriendly to the British constitution.[1] Equally keen was John Graves Simcoe to provide a satisfactory educational system for the new Loyalist province of Upper Canada. From his little capital on the edge of the forest he issued plans for the immediate establishment of grammar schools and a university to be under the direction of clergymen of the Church of England. It was taken for granted that these clergymen would warn their students away from revolutionary ideas.

The emphasis put by leading Loyalists upon grammar or secondary schools was one of the first causes for a division into political parties in nearly all the provinces of British North America. These grammar schools, as was quickly recognized, "did fine service for the Family Compact, training a select few for Law and Divinity, in an education which bound them together but separated them from the common people."[2] The common people were more interested in state-supported elementary schools to save their children from the blight of illiteracy that spread so rapidly over pioneer communities. But the progress of education in all the provinces proceeded on identical lines: "The members of the governing class felt first the need for their own children and provided for them; the common people came afterwards."[3]

I

One of the first matters to which Bishop Charles Inglis gave his attention after his arrival in Nova Scotia was the establishment of an academy at Windsor. When it was first opened in 1789 it was quite largely attended and was soon expanded into a chartered college; then came what its most recent historian has described as "the almost fatal blow, from which the College never fully recovered."[4] This was the adoption in 1803 of a set of statutes, including the requirement that every student at matriculation must sign the Thirty-Nine Articles of religion as set forth in *The Book of Common Prayer* and to promise to attend no place of worship other than the Church of England. These two crippling requirements were insisted upon by Sir Alexander Croke, judge of the court of vice-admiralty, in spite of the vehement protest of Bishop Inglis. The majority of the board of governors under the leadership of Judge Croke, who played upon their fears of American democracy, were now intent on creating a class-conscious society by providing secondary education for a small minority of the population and allowing the majority to sink into ignorance or virtual illiteracy. Such action was indicative of a narrowing of Anglican and upper class interest regarding the general welfare of the colonies. In the first days of settlement the government through land grants for schools attempted to provide a general education for all; this wider purpose was still evident in the opening years of Charles Inglis' episcopate, when it was hoped that the established church might embrace people of widely divergent religious views. There was also a willingness on the part of the first bishop of Nova Scotia to overlook variations in the interpretation of doctrine and ecclesiastical government. Dr. Thomas McCulloch, in a book he wrote at Bishop Inglis' suggestion and to whom he dedicated it, was able to say of Charles Inglis: he is "superior to those narrow and selfish principles which restrict the benevolence of religion to membership of a party,"[5] something he never ventured to say of Charles Inglis' son, John Inglis, one of the first graduates of King's College, who became the third bishop of Nova Scotia in 1825. According to McCulloch it was the son who created the bitter antagonism that was felt by dissenters toward "Windsor Episcopacy."[6]

Changed circumstances probably made the difference. It was inevitable that an established church would be influenced decisively by the prevailing mood of the dominant party in the government; as the governing class in its warfare against the rising tide of liberalism and democracy hardened its heart and narrowed its interest so did the Anglican Church. The increasing rigidity becomes particularly evident in the first official act of John Inglis after his elevation to the episcopate; this was a refusal to accept the nomination of John Thomas Twining by the parishioners of St. Paul's, Halifax, to succeed himself as rector of the church. Rather he threw his influence behind Robert Willis, the nominee of the provincial administrator, thus "hopelessly and disastrously dividing the parish."[7]

The chief reason for the Bishop's objection to Twining, who had been his curate at St. Paul's, was the latter's identification with the evangelical movement within the Church of England. The emergence of this movement in the diocese of Nova Scotia is usually ascribed to Isaac Temple, who arrived in Halifax in 1819 as the private chaplain to Lord Dalhousie, the lieutenant-governor. But even before Temple appeared upon the scene there had been a spontaneous outburst of evangelical fervour in the Church of England in the Maritimes, particularly among the students of King's College. Prominent in this movement at King's was Hibbert Binney, who, while acting as a lay reader at Liverpool, had been persuaded to attend a Methodist revival meeting, with the result that he had a conversion experience and became "an earnest preacher of evangelical truth."[8] After his graduation he proceeded to Halifax, where he met Temple and together they exerted a marked influence upon the younger generation at St. Paul's. Among their converts was the popular young curate, Twining, whose nomination as rector so greatly provoked Bishop Inglis, who apparently associated the evangelical movement with the same levelling ideas he found in Protestant dissent and was determined to discourage its continued growth at St. Paul's by refusing to allow Twining to become the rector. But he paid a very high price for his rough handling of the situation, for a majority of the congregation left the church,[9] some of them to join the Baptist communion, where they became the leaders in an educational movement at Horton which soon dwarfed King's College in size and significance.

Few dissenters had a kind word to say of a bishop who so summarily disposed of any liberal movements either within or outside his church, and turned a deaf ear to all pleas for a more tolerant policy towards nonconformists. Yet there seems to have been another side to the personality of this much berated bishop. He was unsparing of himself in carrying out his duties to a huge diocese over which he ruled to all intents and purposes for forty years, as he was virtually in charge during the later years of his father's episcopate and also during the seven years (1816-1824) the see was held by the ailing and absent Robert Stanser. His visitations were frequent even to the most remote sections of the diocese,[10] and it was during his regime that Newfoundland saw an Anglican bishop for the first time (1827). It was he who urged upon the S.P.G. the need for closer episcopal supervision of Newfoundland, resulting in the appointment of A. G. Spencer as bishop in 1839. Because of his faithful discharge of duty which made him a familiar figure to little groups of Anglicans scattered throughout the Maritimes, very much conscious of their minority status, it is probably not untrue to say, as one church historian does, that he was "venerated and beloved by the people amongst whom he had lived and laboured so long."[11]

II

About two years after John Inglis' accession to the see of Nova Scotia there occurred at Windsor a united meeting of representatives of the Presbyterian, Baptist and Methodist churches to plan a campaign to bring about the extension of full religious liberty to all Protestant denominations. Among the matters discussed were "the right of dissenting ministers to marry by license" and "the right of religious congregations to hold real estate,"[12] both being denied by an Anglican dominated legislative council. These were old longstanding grievances; a more recent one was a denial to the dissenting churches of "a proportionate share of whatever money was granted by the British government for the support of the gospel in the province."[13] In other words, the meeting was demanding that non-Anglican educational institutions should receive the same treatment as King's College at Windsor, at that time endowed by British funds and also receiving grants from the provincial government. A non-Anglican school that came in for considerable commendation at this meeting was the Pictou Academy founded by Dr. Thomas McCulloch in 1808. On the basis of a law passed by the provincial legislature in 1811 the people of Pictou had made an application for a government grant of four hundred pounds annually; this they secured in 1816, but subject to review each year, and continually challenged by the legislative council.   One of the strongest arguments put forward for public support of the Academy was that it provided secondary education for those who were prevented on religious grounds from attending the institution at Windsor.   It was this feature of the Academy that Dr. McCulloch presented at the Windsor meeting, not only to secure support in his struggle against the legislative council, but also to receive letters of commendation to take to Scotland and England, where he was going to seek private subscriptions for the Pictou venture in higher education.

Not much was achieved at the conference so far as support for the Academy was concerned.   The Baptists found Pictou too far away from their chief centres of population and began an institution of their own at Horton; the Methodists at this time were under the close surveillance of the conservative Wesleyan Conference in England and did not dare to become involved in a controversy with the authorities of the established church.

Another complicating factor was the fact that the real motive behind the founding of the Pictou Academy was the need of training native Nova Scotians for the ministry of the Secession Presbyterian churches.   It was well known that Dr. McCulloch was preparing some young men at the Academy for the ministry.   Other church groups found it difficult to regard the Academy as anything but a Presbyterian school. Consequently it soon became evident that if the Academy were to survive it would need strong united Presbyterian support.   This need did actually bring about the union in 1817 of the Associate Presbytery of Pictou with the General Associate Presbytery of Truro to form the Presbyterian Church of Nova Scotia with Dr. James MacGregor as its first moderator.[14] Dr. MacGregor had modified his opinion considerably from those early days when he had refused to become associated with the newly organized Truro Presbytery.   The passing years in the hard environment of Pictou county and the pressing need for a faculty of divinity had brought great changes in this once uncompromising Anti-Burgher.

One of the first acts of the fledgling Synod was to request Dr. McCulloch "to give instruction in theology to young men who had completed their classical and philosophical course under his care."[15] This gave the Academy, as it were, the official approval of the Synod, but at the same time made it appear as a sectarian institution, thus undermining a good deal of public support for a grant from the government. What was to be an even greater menace to the grant was the absence from the new Synod of any representation from the Church of Scotland, just beginning to take seriously its missionary responsibility to the colonies. In the year of the formation of the Nova Scotian Secession Synod there arrived in the Maritimes Dr. George Burns and Donald F. A. Fraser, both Kirk men. The former began a missionary campaign in New Brunswick, while the latter entered boldly into the Pictou area and organized a Gaelic Kirk congregation, much to the disgust of Dr. MacGregor. Later Fraser moved on to Shelburne, Lunenburg County, and then to St. John's, Newfoundland, where in 1842 he organized a Church of Scotland congregation, gaining the distinction of being the first Presbyterian minister to have a settled charge in Newfoundland.[16]

While at Pictou Fraser gave his support to the Academy, but his successor, Kenneth John MacKenzie, immediately upon his arrival (1824) put himself in opposition to Dr. McCulloch on every political issue and also persuaded Fraser (now at Shelburne) to join in protesting any grant from the government to the Pictou Academy. Shortly after coming to Nova Scotia, MacKenzie was appointed the corresponding secretary of the Glasgow Colonial Society, established in 1825 in connection with the Church of Scotland "for promoting the moral and religious interests of the Scottish settlers in British North America."[17] The appointment gave him considerable prestige in the eyes of the increasing number of missionaries the Church of Scotland was sending into the Maritimes. These, for the most part, were easily persuaded by MacKenzie to give their support to the conservative element in the colonies.

When the Church of Scotland under MacKenzie's leadership combined with the Church of England and other reactionary forces in the province to change the character and purpose of the Pictou Academy, Dr. McCulloch finally abandoned his project in despair, but not before he had become deeply involved in the political struggles of the day. His contributions to the *Colonial Patriot* (a weekly journal, founded in Pictou in 1824) gave a new vigour to a rather inchoate Liberal party, but they also brought down upon him the bitter enmity of the powerful Michael Wallace, a Tory Presbyterian who often acted as the administrator of the province. What was perhaps even more serious, they alienated many of the clergy of the Presbyterian Synod of Nova Scotia, who began to regard the struggle over the Academy as "something personal to him

[McCulloch], or as a contest between Pictou and Windsor, with which they had nothing to do."[18]

Sensing this alienation from his own Synod, McCulloch grew weary of his controversial life at Pictou and turned his attention to an educational scheme being set forth very eloquently by the great Nova Scotian Liberal, Joseph Howe; this was to create one good university at Halifax to which the provincial government would give a subsidy. The university in view was the one founded by Lord Dalhousie in 1818 out of a portion of the customs that had been collected at Castine, Maine, while this port had been held by the British during the War of 1812. The college building had been completed in 1823, but the project had languished because many of the trustees were Anglicans who did not wish to see Dalhousie College, as it became known, competing with King's at Windsor. By 1836, however, there was a persistent demand that Dalhousie College should be made available to those who were excluded from King's, and it was generally agreed that Thomas McCulloch was the man best fitted to guide the destinies of the much-neglected institution. His unusual talents as a teacher were firmly established by the success of his students, whose fame even then was being noised abroad. Seven of McCulloch's students at Pictou Academy were in time honoured with the degree of Doctor of Divinity and six of them obtained knighthood.[19]

By an act of the assembly (1838) McCulloch was made president of Dalhousie College, but no sooner did he take over his new duties than he found himself once more in the midst of sectarian and political warfare which saddened the remaining years of his life.

Joseph Howe's plan to create "one good college, free from sectarian control, and open to all denominations, maintained by a common fund, and rallying around it the affections of the whole people,"[20] also envisaged representation on the teaching staff of various denominations. Two candidates Howe had particularly in mind were Dr. E. A. Crawley, a graduate of King's College who had gone over to the Baptists after Bishop Inglis' refusal to accept J. T. Twining as rector of St. Paul's, and Cornelius O'Brien, a Roman Catholic priest and biographer of Bishop Burke. Much to the amazement of both Howe and McCulloch, Crawley's application was turned down by the board of governors, on the specious plea that Lord Dalhousie intended the College for the Kirk of Scotland, and two members of that Church were ultimately appointed as the sole colleagues of Dr. McCulloch.[21]

The Roman Catholic candidate also failed of approval, but in his case the objection came from the president himself. Though Howe admitted to having learned his liberalism from Pictou and "was known to say that personally he owed to the Anti-Burghers all that he was," he had now far outstripped his chief mentor, Dr. McCulloch, whose liberalism did not include allowing Roman Catholics to give instruction to Protestants. It was probably expecting too much of the author of a book, *Popery Condemned*, to share his classroom with a Roman priest, and Howe hesitated to make the request himself, but got a mutual friend to sound out McCulloch on the proposition. The answer was: "Please say to the Governors that the College is theirs, to do with as they deem best, but that when Mr. O'Brien comes in at one door, I go out at the other."[22]

III

One of the surprising results of the sudden turn of events at Dalhousie University was the conversion of the Baptists to sectarian education and conservative politics. When Joseph Howe first put forward his plan for one good college the Baptists were his most enthusiastic supporters, as they were of most of his liberal policies. Dr. Crawley had written persuasively on the advantages of one provincial university, but when his application to become a member of the faculty was turned down he immediately proceeded to take the lead in building a Baptist college at Horton, where the Baptist Education Society had opened an academy in 1829.

It would be unfair to attribute Dr. Crawley's change of heart merely to personal pique; the Baptists were now engaged in raising the intellectual standards of their clergy, a venture in which Dr. Crawley was participating wholeheartedly. "Ignorance and lack of culture in the ministry," writes their historian, Saunders, "became more and more a stigma and a reproach," which they were determined to remove, or at least some of their more discerning leaders were convinced of the necessity of an academically trained clergy. It is to Edward Manning that Saunders gives the credit of discerning the signs of the times and of realizing that "in the onward march of the denominations, the Baptists, without an educated ministry, would be left in the rear, and would lose the power and influence they had already obtained."[23] The converts from St. Paul's congregation as well as the Congregational tradition within the Maritime Baptist Association favoured an educated clergy, and they found a strong leader in J. W. Johnstone in the political field. A former member of St. Paul's congregation at Halifax, Johnstone was determined that the church of his choice should have equal educational opportunities with the denomination he had abandoned; he reasoned that if the Anglicans and Presbyterians were to receive aid from the government for their universities, then the Baptists had a right in equity to a grant from the government for the construction of a college building. Howe saw the erection of such a building as fastening forever upon the Maritimes a sectarian system of education.

The issue broke up a coalition government of which both Howe and Johnstone were members, and brought about a general election.   During the campaign (1843) Baptist ministers, including the veteran Edward Manning and a fiery young minister from Nictaux, I. E. Bill, entered the fray and helped to win an electoral victory for the Tory party.   Two surprising results emerged from this election which were to have rather permanent effects on the educational and political development of the Maritimes.   One was that the Baptists who had enthusiastically supported a non-sectarian college for the province when first put forward by Howe became, through the heat of this and later campaigns, so wedded to their denominational college (now Acadia University) that Saunders, commenting in 1902 on the election of 1843, could complacently say: "The one college scheme then vanished, and has since been flitting about in the dreams of enthusiasts, like some weird ghost that has no certain dwelling place."[24]

The second surprising outcome of the election was the creation of a more liberalized Tory party.   Howe by his intemperate language towards the Baptist pastors contributed much to this unexpected transformation, for he lost from the Liberal party some of its most convinced reformers, who made an alliance with the Tories in order to obtain the educational facilities that alone could help to raise their social status in the community.   This breakup of the Liberal party gave Johnstone with his Baptist following a commanding voice in shaping the policy of the Conservative party, which became far more enlightened than formerly.   As Saunders put it, "Johnstone did not profess to be opposed to the principles of reform advocated by Mr. Howe; but he counselled delay and care in their application, lest by changes too sudden, for which the people were not prepared, there might come evil instead of good."[25] The most concrete evidence of the new spirit the Baptists contributed to the Conservative party came when it put into effect, under the leadership of Charles Tupper, the son of a Baptist minister and the most famous of Acadia's graduates, the Free School Act of Nova Scotia (1864).

In New Brunswick also the Baptists sought to raise the cultural level of their membership through the establishment of a seminary at Fredericton. As in Nova Scotia so in New Brunswick, it was Anglicans turned Baptist who gave the lead. Two of the most prominent of these were the Hon. W. B. Kinnear of St. John and F. W. Miles. The former, of Irish parentage and Anglican background, had been influenced by Baptist converts from St. Paul's in Halifax; the latter during his student days at King's had experienced "an evangelical form of religious experience"[26] which led him to unite with the Baptist church at St. John (1828), and later to proceed to Newton Theological Institution, to train for the Baptist ministry. Kinnear headed the list of contributors to the Fredericton Seminary, while Miles became its first principal, with his wife conducting a young ladies' department.

Keeping the Seminary functioning was a serious burden upon the small Baptist community of New Brunswick and it was not long before this pioneer experiment in co-education came to an end with the closing of the female department in 1843. At a great sacrifice the male section was kept going for many years, indicating how intensely the Baptists were resolved that their children were to have equal educational opportunities with their Anglican neighbours.

IV

Though the board of governors of Dalhousie University had excluded the Baptist candidate from the faculty they seemed ready to accept the Roman Catholic applicant, so vigorously supported by Joseph Howe. Some of his contemporaries were unkind enough to say that for Howe it was a question "to bait the political hook," since "the position of the Roman Catholics in relation to the different parties was becoming a matter of importance and much scheming."[27] Be that as it may, the serious consideration of a Roman Catholic applicant was indicative of a tremendous change of social climate from the days when it was decreed by legislation that every Romish priest should be hounded out of the province. This law against Roman priests had been repealed in 1783, but test acts remained part of the Nova Scotian legislation until the era of emancipation towards the end of the second decade of the nineteenth century. And here the initiative was taken by Anglicans rather than the dissenters, for toleration of Roman Catholics was a more difficult matter for extreme Protestants than for members of the established church. It was the liberal Anti-Burgher McCulloch who blocked O'Brien's teaching at Dalhousie College, and even Joseph Howe at a later date (1851) took the lead in organizing a Protestant Alliance to combat so-called Roman Catholic "subversive influence" during the Crimean War.[28]

The victory for emancipation in the Nova Scotian legislature seems to have been due to the good opinion won by the Acadians under the leadership of their "venerable and respectable pastor, Abbé Sigogne." The Abbé "had been in habits of intimacy for many years" with Thomas Chandler Haliburton, who with Richard John Uniacke (both members of the Anglican Church) took the lead in expunging the test acts from Nova Scotian legislation.   Haliburton's speech in favour of emancipation was described by the historian Beamish Murdoch as "the most splendid piece of declamation, that it has ever been my fortune to listen to."[29]

Some of the good feeling that had been won for the Roman Catholics by Sigogne was lost by Edmund Burke, who was made vicar-general and supervisor of the mission of Nova Scotia by the bishop of Quebec in 1801, a position as we have already observed he converted into an apostolic vicariate in 1818. A steady influx of Irish priests into Nova Scotia, beginning with William Phelan (1786) with headquarters at Arichat, had prepared the way for Father Burke's declaration of independence from the see of Quebec.

Like the other religious leaders of the province, he also recognized the need for educational facilities if he was going to secure enough priests to look after a fast-increasing Roman Catholic population; but like the others he soon found his way blocked by the bishops of the established church.   He wrote bitterly to a friend in Ireland that "Bishop Inglis, aided by his clergy and some other anti-Catholics, have succeeded in inducing the Lieutenant-Governor to refuse me a licence to open our school, although the law of the Province permits it."[30]   Being Irish, Burke retorted to Bishop Inglis' opposition by starting a violent theological controversy with the leaders of the Anglican Church, attacking some of the views of Robert Stanser, the rector of St. Paul's, in a newspaper article and writing a pamphlet of some two hundred pages criticizing strongly the anti-Catholic writings of William Cochran, the president of King's College.   It was during this era of controversy in which the

Anglicans seemed to be getting the worst of the argument that Bishop Inglis called upon Thomas McCulloch to write a refutation of Dr. Burke's pamphlet. The result was that McCulloch wrote two rather notable volumes, *Popery Condemned* and *Popery Again Condemned*, which were published in Edinburgh.[31]

The hard-hitting tactics of Dr. Burke seem in time to have won the admiration of officialdom in Halifax, particularly after he had secured the independence of the Nova Scotian Roman Catholic Church from Quebec, with himself as its first bishop. This admiration became evident on the occasion of a great dinner given to Lord Dalhousie by the St. Andrew's Society (1818) to which Bishop Burke was invited as an honoured guest.

As soon as Burke secured the prestige of the episcopal office he renewed with vigour his educational programme, being fully persuaded that the members of his church would never attain equality with the Protestants unless they overcame the handicap of illiteracy. In this he was ably seconded by his colleague on Prince Edward Island, Bishop MacEachern, who from the time of his arrival in 1790 had been beseeching the hierarchy of Quebec to persuade the Canadian seminaries to begin to train priests proficient in the Gaelic language. MacEachern's need for a local seminary was even greater than Dr. Burke's, since he was expected to provide services for the Gaelic population not only on Prince Edward Island but in Cape Breton and New Brunswick as well. When he arrived on the Island there were 1,500 Roman Catholics, both Gaelic and French speaking, who had been without a priest since the death of James MacDonald (1785). It was soon possible for the new administrator to secure French priests for the Acadians from among the clerical refugees from the French Revolution, but it was not until 1820 that the first trained Gaelic priest came to share the labours of this much-overworked bishop.

After his consecration as an independent bishop of Charlottetown (1829) he, like Burke, determined to do something effective about the shortage of priests in his diocese, which still included New Brunswick and Cape Breton. His most serious problem was to find a teacher for the college he had in view. On a visit to Halifax, he met Edward Walsh, a cultivated priest who had taught in an Irish college, and persuaded him to accept the rectorship of St. Andrew's College, opened in 1831. Later (1855) the name was changed to St. Dunstan's.[32] The founding of St. Andrew's College gave the Roman Catholics of Prince Edward Island an institution of higher learning before their co-religionists in Nova Scotia; for Bishop Burke, though he fitted up an abandoned presbytery as a school for girls and taught boys in his own residence, never did succeed in obtaining a degree-conferring college; nor did he live to see complete emancipation for Roman Catholics in the Maritimes.

He died in 1820 and it was left to his successor, Bishop Fraser, to secure "An Act for Incorporating the Trustees of Saint Mary's College at Halifax" (1841),[33] after his offer to co-operate with the dissenters in making Dalhousie College a provincial university had been rebuffed by President McCulloch in 1839. And so the Roman Catholics, simultaneously with the Baptists, embarked upon building up their own educational centres and became as wedded to sectarian higher education as the other Maritime churches.

V

The last church to fall in line with the sectarian educational policy was the Methodist. At the famous gathering of dissenters in Windsor in 1826, the Methodists because of their subordination to the English Wesleyan Conference did not feel free to take part in the controversy then raging over the Pictou Academy. Furthermore, like the Baptists, they had been emphasizing the voluntary method of supporting religious institutions and they hesitated to ask the government to make a grant to a sectarian college. But when they finally decided to erect in 1839 a college of their own at Sackville, New Brunswick, governmental grants had become so much the pattern in the Maritimes that the Methodists immediately received two thousand dollars from the New Brunswick legislature; and when a deputation went to the Nova Scotian assembly seeking aid, it obtained the able advocacy of Joseph Howe himself, "who claimed that the location of the college on the Provincial border was at once a proof of the wise judgment of its promotors and a guarantee of its greater efficiency."[34]

The college at Sackville (Mount Allison) was not the first venture of the Methodists into the educational field in the Maritime Provinces. In Newfoundland an appalling illiteracy became a challenge to the Methodist preachers to provide at least enough education to enable their classes to read the Bible and to take part in hymn singing. As early as 1814 they began Sunday schools in Newfoundland in which adults as well as children were given instruction in reading and writing.[35] The

English Wesleyan Missionary Society also made small grants toward three day schools; thirteen others were conducted under the auspices of the S.P.G.; these, however, served a very tiny minority of the seventy thousand persons scattered around the coasts of the Island. Nevertheless the tradition of church schools became so firmly established in Newfoundland that when the provincial government began to assume educational responsibilities it did so by making grants to Protestant and Roman Catholic school boards, a policy still prevailing at the present time.

Methodist interest in primary education, as has been observed, was to further their warm-hearted gospel, which required a certain amount of literacy. In Nova Scotia a Methodist teacher, Andrew Henderson, conducted a very successful school (Albion Vale) at Annapolis Royal.[36] He also used his school building as a Methodist meeting house to which he often welcomed itinerant ministers; nevertheless, he received a generous grant from the government with little opposition from the legislative council, due to the fact that Methodist ambition did not go beyond elementary education. There was, apparently, a genuine reluctance to proceed further, due to a belief on the part of the older members that the Methodist mission was to the lowly rather than to university graduates. Some of the younger ministers who had gone to the United States for training felt differently; while there they came under the influence of a great Methodist teacher, Wilbur Fisk, who had long been crusading against the "old Methodist Theological Seminary"— a system whereby "young men while on trial and still deacons were placed with experienced fathers who taught them."[37] He finally persuaded his American colleagues that the time had come for an academically trained Methodist ministry and he himself became the first president of Wesleyan University, founded at Middleton, Connecticut, in 1830.

One Maritime minister who studied and absorbed all that Fisk had to say on education was Humphrey Pickard, a native of New Brunswick. When Charles Frederick Allison, a wealthy merchant retired in Sackville, New Brunswick, decided that the Methodists, like the other denominations, must have their own university, he turned to Pickard for advice and guidance in his project.[38] With the concurrence of the London Committee of the Methodist Missionary Society he proceeded to erect two suitable buildings for both men and women at Sackville, and when they were ready for occupancy in 1842, Humphrey Pickard was chosen to become principal of a new venture in university education.

Though the Methodists were the last of the denominations to enter the competition for the education of the youth of the Maritimes, yet their university, Mount Allison, flourished from the beginning. One reason for its success was due to its strategic position on the border of New Brunswick and Nova Scotia; another was its easy access from Prince Edward Island, lacking a Protestant college of its own. Still another was the adoption by Pickard of the Fisk philosophy of education which, in deference to the semi-frontier conditions still prevailing in mid-nineteenth-century America, combined a professional training with a general course, thus helping to shorten the time of the withdrawal of much-needed man power from the exploitation of a continent.

VI

As Mount Allison University now took care of the educational needs of the last major religious group in the Maritimes, little more was heard in Nova Scotia about one good provincial university. With this issue out of the way the churches became less actively involved in political campaigns. But a habit had been formed which was hard to break, and new issues like temperance, Sabbath observance and a renewed tension between Catholic and Protestant, due to a large influx of Irish labourers, never allowed Protestant leaders to get far away from legislative halls. After the controversy over education began to subside, temperance or the control of the liquor traffic began to engage the interests of the churches to the exclusion of many other things. This was due in part from a failure of education to do all that was expected of it. Schools and colleges had been urged by liberal politicians and clergy alike as one way of meeting the challenge of a deteriorating social situation. When they failed, other alternatives were sought to raise a rather boisterous com-munal life to a higher cultural level. One obvious alternative was to make an attack upon the intemperate use of alcoholic beverages, a serious moral and economic blight that immediately descended upon most pioneer communities. Taverns were unusually numerous throughout the Maritime Provinces and drunken brawls at "frolics" were a common feature of both urban and rural life. These "frolics" were as shocking to Bishop Burke as they were to the Puritan pastors, and he made valiant efforts to regulate them[39]; the more extreme Protestant reaction was to abolish them altogether along with their chief attractions, dancing and card playing.

It was agreed, however, that the real source of rowdiness in Maritime society was drunkenness and as a consequence there emerged temperance societies put forward as a substitute for frolics. A few concerned Methodists organized the first one at Beaver River in the county of Yarmouth in 1828; a second followed shortly afterwards at Wilmot through the combined efforts of a "godly Methodist,"[40] Samuel Bayard, and a Baptist minister, I. E. Bill. Temperance societies caught on as a respectable alternative to "frolics." When they were organized into chapters they became unusually powerful in their influence upon public opinion: ultimately in their organized crusade against the liquor traffic they involved the churches in political campaigns almost as deeply as did the educational issue.

REFERENCES

1. C. W. Vernon, *The Old Church in the New Dominion* (London, 1929), p. 77.

2. W. H. Elgee, *The Social Teachings of Canadian Churches, Protestant* (Published by The Ryerson Press, Toronto, 1964), p. 76; *vide* also C. B. Sissons, *Egerton Ryerson, His Life and Letters* (Toronto, 1937-1947, 2 vols.), I, p. 80.

3. *The Cambridge History of the British Empire* (Cambridge, 1930, 8 vols.), VI, p. 791.

4. F. W. Vroom, *King's College: A Chronicle 1789-1939* (Halifax, 1941), p. xi.

5. Thomas McCulloch, *Popery Again Condemned by Scripture and the Fathers* (Edinburgh, 1810), p. vii.

6. William McCulloch, *Life of Thomas McCulloch, D.D., Pictou* (Truro, 1920), p. 112.

7. *Bishop John Inglis Letters 1825-1849* (Copies in P.A.N.S.), pp. 8-9.

8. E. M. Saunders, *History of the Baptists of the Maritime Provinces* (Halifax, N.S., 1902), p. 186.

9. R. V. Harris, *The Church of Saint Paul in Halifax, Nova Scotia, 1749-1949* (Toronto, 1949), p. 171.

10. *Vide* John Inglis, *A Journal of Visitation in Nova Scotia, Cape Breton and along the Eastern Shore of New Brunswick 1843-1848* (The Church in the Colonies Series, S.P.G.), *passim.*

11. J. Langtry, *History of the Church in Eastern Canada and Newfoundland* (London and New York, 1892), p. 32.

12. E. M. Saunders, *op. cit.*, p. 175.

13. *Ibid.*

14. William Gregg, *History of the Presbyterian Church in the Dominion of Canada* (Toronto, 1885), p. 136.

15. *Ibid.*, p. 231.

16. George Patterson, *History of Pictou County* (Montreal, 1877), p. 362.

17. W. Gregg, *op. cit.*, pp. 278-284.

18. W. McCulloch, *op. cit.*, p. 140.

19. J. W. Falconer and W. G. Watson, *A Brief History of Pine Hill Divinity Hall and the Theological Department of Mount Allison University* (Halifax, 1846), p. 6.

20. *The Speeches and Public Letters of Joseph Howe Based upon Mr. Annand's edition of 1858*, revised and ed. by J. A. Chisholm (Halifax, 1909, 2 vols.), I, p. 418.

21. For the Baptist point of view *vide* I. E. Bill, *Fifty Years with the Baptist Ministers and Churches of the Maritime Provinces of Canada* (Saint John, 1880), pp. 110-127.

22. W. McCulloch, *op. cit.*, p. 183.

23. E. M. Saunders, *op. cit.*, pp. 180-181.

24. *Ibid.*, p. 275.

25. *Ibid.*, p. 263.

26. G. E. Levy, *The Baptists of the Maritime Provinces 1753-1946* (St. John, N.B., 1946), p. 121.

27. W. McCulloch, *op. cit.*, p. 182.

28. *The Speeches and Public Letters of Joseph Howe, op. cit.*, II, pp. 180-181.

29. Beamish Murdoch, *A History of Nova Scotia, or Acadia* (Halifax, N.S., 1867, 3 vols.), III, p. 577.

30. Cornelius O'Brien, *Memoirs of Rt. Rev. Edmund Burke* (Ottawa, 1894), p. 83.

31. Bishop Burke's retort to McCulloch's *Popery Again Condemned* is to be found in a postscript added to Burke's *Treatise on the First Principles of Christianity* (Halifax, 1808), pp. 401-449.

32. J. Emmet Mullally, *A Sketch of the Life and Times of the Right Reverend Angus Bernard McEachern* (Montreal, 1947), p. 13.

33. *The Catholic Diocesan Directory* (Halifax, 1935), p. 17.

34. T. W. Smith, *History of the Methodist Church: Eastern British America* (Halifax, Toronto and Montreal, 1890, 2 vols.), II, p. 394.

35. *Ibid.*, II, p. 398.

36. *Ibid.*, II, p. 390.

37. Joseph Holdich, *The Life of Wilbur Fisk, D.D.* (New York, 1842), p. 308.

38. Falconer and Watson, *op. cit.*, pp. 29-32.

39. C. O'Brien, *op. cit.*, p. 117.

40. G. E. Levy, *op. cit.*, p. 140.

XIII

The Reform Movement in the Canadas

THE STORY of the reform movement in the Canadas is somewhat more complex than in the Maritimes. An era of ill-feeling that ultimately exploded into two abortive rebellions arose out of more deeply rooted animosities than were manifest in the eastern provinces. Though the educational issue played an important role in stirring up antagonism, it never became the dominant theme as was sometimes the case in Maritime development. The variation in the two areas was probably due to the types of immigrant now entering the western provinces and to the more direct and constant influence of the United States upon the west as against its declining influence in the east.

Between 1815 and 1840 the population of British North America increased by over one-half million with the major portion settling in the Canadas.[1] A large proportion were Scottish Highlanders still mourning the exile of the Stuarts and the destruction of their clan system; next in numbers were the poverty-stricken Irish, with even more bitter memories against the British rulers. Insecurity and persecution were also part of the background of a later immigration from the United States of Quakers, Mennonites and Dunkers who sought in Canada a more tolerant rule than that which they had experienced either in Europe or America. This new flood of immigration, sharing a common experience of insecurity and persecution, was peculiarly susceptible to all egalitarian or reform appeals and in a remarkably short time produced a "western civilization" which challenged "by principle and practice" not only "the traditional social structure of the St. Lawrence valley"[2] but also the more recent social integration that had been established by the Loyalists. As was to be expected the representatives of the older societies were quick to resent the intrusion of what they considered an alien ideology into their so recently integrated social structure.

I

In the forefront of resistance to the revival of frontier democracy in Upper Canada was the Anglican Church. Its most influential strategist was John Strachan, who in 1827 had been made archdeacon of York. Though the recognized leader of the Family Compact, he had achieved his eminent position, not through the usual Loyalist status but because of his innate ability and his firm conviction in an aristocratically dominated society. As a matter of fact his was the saga of a poor immigrant boy who had made good in the new world. The son of an overseer of the granite quarries in the neighbourhood of Aberdeen, Scotland, he had worked his way through college, but was compelled through financial stringency to discontinue the study of divinity at St. Andrew's. Consequently, he decided to emigrate to Upper Canada (1799) in the hope of bettering his failing fortunes in an academic career. His first days in the new world were full of disappointment as he had been led to expect before leaving Scotland that he would become the head of a projected academy—"by and by to merge into a College."[3] Neither the academy nor the college materialized for the time being, so Strachan had to be content with the position of tutor in the household of a prominent Anglican layman in Kingston. During his stay at Kingston, Strachan met John Stuart, the bishop's official in Upper Canada, and was led by this energetic missionary to become ordained a deacon in the Church of England. After his ordination (1803) he conducted for a time a grammar school at Cornwall for the "sons of gentlemen"; here he trained in their most formative years a remarkable group of young men who were destined to become the second generation of the Family Compact society and to exert an unusual influence upon the social development of Canada.

The death of John Stuart in 1811 led to a great change in the career of Strachan; he had fully expected that he would succeed his friend and mentor as the bishop's official at Kingston, but this prize eluded him because, in the words of Dr. Bethune, his biographer, the widow of the late incumbent, Mrs. Stuart, "had intimated to several friends of her departed husband, her earnest desire that her son, Mr. George O'Kill Stuart, should take his father's place, and be removed there from York, his present charge."[4] The widow's desire seems to have prevailed over all other considerations and the result was that the younger Stuart received what seemed at that time the more important post at Kingston, while Dr. Strachan was given the lesser one at York. As it turned out, York, as the capital of the province, soon became the most influential city of Upper Canada and Strachan found a far greater outlet for his talents than if he had been elevated to the post of official at Kingston. No sooner had he entered upon his new duties than he was sworn in as a member of the executive council, where he was able to influence the direction of government, particularly during the eventful war years of 1812-1814. During this period he won great prestige by his forthright talk to American generals stationed in the occupied town of York; his courage and warm-hearted attention to the sick during a cholera epidemic also added lustre to his name which had become venerated among his devoted parishioners. At the conclusion of the war he toyed for a time with the idea of becoming the principal of McGill University at Montreal, but when that project became involved in protracted litigation he finally decided to abandon his oft-frustrated academic career and to give himself wholeheartedly to the task of shaping the religio-politico structure of Great Britain's second American empire. To this end he sought to provide a reasoned political philosophy for the rather theocratic state he had in view, as well as to furnish an alternative to the radicalism of the reform movement that had suddenly emerged in Upper Canada.

There were many elements in the reform movement that made it unacceptable to Archdeacon Strachan, not the least of these being its Scottish antecedents. The movement in its Canadian dress regarded Robert Gourlay, a professional Scottish reformer, as its founder. Gourlay had arrived in Upper Canada from Scotland in 1817, and immediately upon his arrival had circulated a questionnaire[5] among the settlers asking them to enumerate their grievances. Strachan, who prided himself on his expert knowledge of Scottish radicalism, denounced "Mr. Gourlay as a firebrand and a demagogue." Writing to a friend in Scotland in 1818, he said: "There had been here for about a year past, a Mr. Gourlay, from Fifeshire, trying to get us by the ears. He has done a good deal of mischief in the province by his seditious publications, exciting discontent amongst the people. I saw through him at once and opposed him with my usual vigour; upon which, the press groaned with his abuse of me. . . . A character like Mr. Gourlay, in a quiet colony like this, where there has been little or no spirit of inquiry, and very little knowledge, can do much harm; and notwithstanding the check he has received, he has already done great mischief."[6]

Another Scot who also excited the Archdeacon's displeasure, about the same time as the Gourlay incident, was Lord Selkirk, whom he accused of "abandoning justice and humanity," and of "hatching a deep laid scheme to ruin the trade of the North West Company,—an enterprise unworthy of a British peer."[7] The harsh attitude exhibited against this great Scottish benefactor is an unfortunate incident in Dr. Strachan's colourful career.   Nor is there much to be said in defence of his treatment of Robert Gourlay.   There seems little doubt that Gourlay was a troublesome individual[8]; but he had done nothing to merit the harsh strictures that were hurled at him by Dr. Strachan nor the imprisonment and exile that were meted out to him by the ruling authorities in Upper Canada. The only explanation of the partisan spirit displayed at York at this time was that it was an importation from Scotland: the leaders of the opposing parties were Scotch Whigs or Scotch Tories.   Gourlay and later William Lyon Mackenzie were ardent pupils of Cobbett and Joseph Hume, whose liberalism included the complete secularization of all social institutions; whereas Strachan and those whom he had trained for administrative posts belonged to the Tory school of Edmund Burke, which embraced a deep-seated fear of the popular democracy of the French Revolution.   As a member of the legislative council of Upper Canada, Strachan considered it his duty to expose the subversive nature of the doctrine of his fellow Scot.

II

Though Strachan succeeded in persuading his colleagues to bring about the banishment of Gourlay from the province, he was not so immediately successful in his duel with still another Scot, William Lyon Mackenzie.   The latter, a Dundee man, born of poor parents,[9] had never attended a university, but he had apparently received enough education to enable him to read with intelligence a prodigious number of books.   He was a Presbyterian, probably an Anti-Burgher, with a good knowledge of the finer points of Calvinistic doctrine; but his Calvinism was tinged with the romanticism of Burns, Scott and Byron; dominating all his other characteristics was his reforming zeal, that had been imbued in him by Joseph Hume.   In 1824 he became both publisher and editor of the *Colonial Advocate* in York, in which he set forth in great detail the principles of the reform movement.

The burning issue so far as the reformers were concerned lay in the Constitutional Act of 1791, in which the reality of power had been vested in the governor and an appointed executive and legislative council. An assembly elected on a restricted franchise was also an irritant; but even after elected it was little more than a debating society since none of its bills could become law without the concurrence of the appointed bodies.   Under this system public affairs in the province were controlled by an oligarchy, to a large extent under the dominance of Dr. Strachan. This represented to Mackenzie and his followers an intolerable ecclesiastical influence in state affairs; nor were they anywise reassured when the Roman Catholic bishop, Alexander Macdonnell, was made a member of the legislative council in 1831.

Though the constitutional issue was paramount for the genuine reformers, it was the issue of religious equality that caught the public imagination and generated the most heat in public debate; it also brought to Mackenzie's side a good deal of support that might otherwise have remained indifferent or fallen to the conservatives.   In the *Colonial Advocate* the editor laid great stress upon religious freedom, which he defined as the right of all the churches to carry on ecclesiastical functions such as baptismal and marriage rites, the right to hold property, and the right to education without religious distinction.[10]   One of the most contentious matters to receive full coverage in Mackenzie's paper was the clergy reserves.   These consisted of one-seventh of the land in the various townships and often lying waste in the most desirable places. They were also an irritating nuisance when they lay in the way of the construction of roads or other public utilities.   At first little notice had been given to them, but as they became more valuable through increased settlement the authorities of the Church of England began to visualize well-endowed rectories which would free incumbents from all voluntary or congregational financial support and thus restore a free and independent church pulpit.   For the reformers, however, a well-endowed church would mean a strengthening of ecclesiastical control in the social and political development of the colony; also they began to see in these lands a source of revenue for educational purposes; thus began the long agitation for the secularization of the clergy reserves.

III

It was not the reformers, however, so much as the Church of Scotland that frustrated the attempt to create a financially independent Anglican church. Like the latter, the Church of Scotland also abhorred the voluntary system of support, and even before the reserves had begun to yield any income, it had petitioned the government for financial aid in carrying on its work in Canada. It did this on the basis that it was also an established church and ought to be put on a basis of equality with the Church of England in the Colonies.[11] Nor was the government completely unresponsive to its plea, for in 1793 grants were made to its ministers in Montreal and Quebec. There was, however, considerable inequality in the grants to the two churches, for the Anglicans received over three thousand pounds whereas the Kirk ministers had to be content with a hundred.

Additional discrimination between the two churches was evidenced in the government's policy in the matter of erecting churches. The Anglican cathedral at Quebec had been built at the government's expense; but no such aid had been forthcoming for the Church of Scotland; on the contrary, legal obstacles had been put in the way of the latter securing title deeds to church property. Christ Church Cathedral at Montreal had been erected into a legally endowed parish in 1818, but it was not until twelve years later that St. Andrew's Presbyterian Church secured legal status.[12]

It was generally conceded by all that governmental grants out of direct revenue or even from more concealed sources were never going to be a satisfactory method of supporting an established church, so in 1815 and 1819 Anglican corporations were set up by the governor and executive council for the administration of the reserves. The general public seems to have been unaware of the existence of these corporations until some five years later. When at last they were publicly revealed a cry of anger went up from the Church of Scotland because it had neither been consulted nor represented in their formation.[13]

When the question of the reunion of Upper and Lower Canada was being discussed in 1822, the members of the Church of Scotland in Canada considered that this was an opportune time to get an established status for their church in a new constitutional act; consequently, they sent a petition to England asking for a provision in the proposed union bill that would give an unequivocal establishment to the Church of Scotland. In support of the petition the claim was put forth that the membership of the Church of Scotland in Canada was larger than that of the Church of England, a claim that was vigorously denied by Archdeacon Strachan.

It was about this time that a society for promoting the religious interests of Scottish settlers in British North America, more generally known as the Glasgow Colonial Society,[14] emerged upon the scene and began to play a rather decisive role in the relations of church and state in Canada. Its first secretary was Robert Burns of Paisley, later to become a national figure in Canada, while minister of Knox Presbyterian Church in Toronto[15]; its first patron was none other than Lord Dalhousie. Resistance to the exclusive claim of the Church of England to establishment and the clergy reserves was now being met on an organized basis, which was reflected at a meeting of the leading members of the Church of Scotland in Upper Canada at Cornwall in 1828, a meeting that led to the formation of the first Kirk synod in Upper Canada in 1832.

The immediate consequence of these Scottish agitations was the appointment by the British House of Commons of a select committee, later known as the Canada Committee, to investigate the religious situation in the Canadas. One of its first acts was to examine a chart that had been published by Dr. Strachan at the time of Bishop Jacob Mountain's death in 1825, in which was set forth the number of the Church of England clergy in Canada, with some observations on their increase from the time of Bishop Mountain's arrival until his death; this chart also gave a summary of the relative strengths of the various denominations in the colony, claiming that there were thirty-one Anglican clergy, while only two ministers represented the Church of Scotland, outnumbered by the secession churches three to one. It also included some very disparaging remarks about troublesome Methodist itinerants. It brought a storm of protest from nearly all the religious bodies in Canada and also came in for considerable criticism in Scotland; Dr. Lee, the moderator of the General Assembly of the Established Church of Scotland, pronounced it a tissue of misrepresentation; and in the Canadas also Dr. Strachan was charged with making false returns. His biographer, Dr. Bethune, concedes that there were some inaccuracies in the chart, but adds that it is not "always possible to avoid some exaggeration" while zealously pleading a good cause.[16]

The "cause" most on the mind of the Archdeacon at the time was the prevention of any of the revenue of the clergy reserves being diverted to the other denominations in the Canadas. A change in government policy in the administration of the reserves had greatly alarmed the Anglican authorities. In 1825 a Canada Corporation had been set up by the British government to administer crown lands; it had been permitted to buy a large block of the clergy reserves at a commissioner's valuation.

Other sales of the reserves followed under the direction of the governor-in-council, the proceeds of which were invested by the government with the *proviso* that the interest from such investments was to be used "for the purpose for which the said lands were reserved."[17]   All this was done without consulting the Anglican corporations that had been set up for the administration of the reserves, and as the Church of Scotland had already established its right to public support, it seemed rather inevitable that it would be receiving a share of the new income that had been made available for religious purposes.   This was something that Strachan was determined to forestall at all costs, hence his chart, which was followed by a personal visit to England in 1826 to plead the cause of the Anglican Church in Canada.   He seems to have had considerable success in his mission, for he not only prevented the Presbyterians from getting a share of the reserves at that time, but he also obtained a royal charter for a provincial university under Anglican control with an endowment of 225,000 acres of land and a yearly revenue grant of 1,000 pounds for a period of sixteen years.

On his return to Canada he found that the destruction of the reserves had become an important plank in the platform of the reform party.[18] At this juncture it would have seemed the part of wisdom for Dr. Strachan to have made some concession to the Kirk party, but in a speech in the legislative council he singled out the Presbyterians for his most biting sarcasm, saying that if they were let into the reserves, "there is no reason why any other denomination of Dissenters should not also be admitted."[19] This unfortunately for Strachan was a deduction drawn by the Canada Committee of the House of Commons, for it brought in a report (July 12, 1828) asserting the right of the Church of Scotland to participate in the revenue from the reserves, but added that the government had the "right to apply the money if they so thought fit, to any Protestant clergy."[20]

The Secession Presbyterians were not slow to take the hint and to put in a claim for a portion of the revenue.   In reply they were told by the governor of Upper Canada, Sir John Colborne, that it would clarify matters if all the Presbyterian clergy of the province were to unite into one synod for the purpose of receiving a consolidated grant.   In the meantime they were given a yearly grant from funds of the Canada Corporation as was also the Roman Catholic Church, thus leaving the contentious issue of the reserves themselves still an open question.

Not all the Secession churches at the time were in agreement on the question of receiving governmental grants.   There were those who regarded such grants as a repudiation of the voluntary system, particularly the members of the United Associate Synod of the Secession Church in Scotland. Because of this conviction they felt they could not unite with any of the Canadian synods, and in 1843 formed an independent presbytery which took the name The Missionary Presbytery of the Canadas in connection with the United Associate Synod of the Secession Church in Scotland. It soon became a vigorous denomination, forming a synod in 1843; shortly thereafter founding a Divinity Hall at London, with William Proudfoot as its first professor.[21]

IV

In 1831 there was presented to the British parliament a petition on behalf of an interdenominational committee of Upper Canada styled "The Friends of Religious Liberty." Among other things it petitioned that the clergy reserves be sold and the proceeds be used for educational purposes. Thus was initiated the great campaign for secularization of the reserves, a solution no more acceptable to the Presbyterians[22] than to the Anglicans. It had behind it, however, the energetic support of the Methodists, who under the leadership of a remarkable family, the Ryersons, were beginning to emerge as a powerful political force in Upper Canada. The petition of the Friends of Religious Liberty had been drafted by Jesse Ketchum, a reform leader, and Egerton Ryerson, a Methodist itinerant; and had been carried to England by George Ryerson, who also bore a similar petition from the Methodist Church in Canada, thus putting the Methodist denomination firmly behind the campaign for secularization, and identifying it with the principles of the reform movement in Canada.

This alliance of the Methodists with the reform movement began with the arrival of Egerton Ryerson on the York circuit in 1828, where he proceeded with the help of his brothers to give Methodism a new social status in the Canadas. As Egerton Ryerson's biographer, C. B. Sissons, has said, "Seldom has a Canadian home produced four such men as were George, William, John and Egerton Ryerson. Differing in character and talent, they all had upon them the mark of greatness."[23] Despite the fact that their father was a Loyalist and an Anglican with considerable suspicion of both democracy and Methodism, all the sons were attracted to the Methodist Church and its ministry.

Egerton's first interest was in law, but a period of illness accompanied by a religious experience impressed upon him "the uncertainty of earthly things" and he immediately began to direct his studies toward the Methodist ministry. He was preceded in this step by his brother William, who in 1823 had abandoned his farm to become an itinerant preacher. While visiting this brother on the Niagara circuit in 1825 Egerton was asked to conduct a Methodist service. He proved himself such a satisfactory preacher that he was persuaded to drop his studies and become a full-time itinerant at the age of twenty-two. Immediately, he was assigned to the York circuit, where almost overnight he became the best-known name in Canadian Methodism as well as a national figure, an eminence he sustained for some sixty years.

His sudden fame came through an attack upon a sermon preached by Dr. Strachan at the funeral of Bishop Jacob Mountain in 1825, in which the Methodist preachers were referred to "as American in origin and sympathies . . . ignorant persons who had forsaken their proper callings to preach what they neither understood nor cared to learn."[24] At a social gathering of Methodists in York, where the sermon was indignantly discussed, it was suggested that the "Boy Preacher," as Egerton had been dubbed, should prepare a reply to the Archdeacon's sermon, for publication in the *Colonial Advocate*. The reply began by challenging the truth of Strachan's aspersions on the education and loyalty of the Methodist ministers. These, he pointed out, followed a disciplined course of reading while on probation; furthermore, very few of them were Americans. His letter, which was published anonymously, closed with these ringing words: "I take my leave of the Doctor's Sermon at present. He may trust in Legislative influence; he may pray to 'the Imperial Parliament.' But we will trust in the Lord our God, and to Him will we make prayer."[25] The sensation caused by this letter was such that, in the words of Ryerson himself, "before every house in Toronto might be seen groups reading and discussing the paper."[26]

For the Methodists themselves, smarting under the criticism of Dr. Strachan, it came as a most invigorating tonic. Its effect has been most vividly recorded by Anson Green: he writes that the paper containing the letter reached him and his colleague, Franklin Metcalfe, at Hallowell (Picton) while we "were together . . . and we went into the field in the rear of the parsonage, sat down by the fence, and read the review. As we read we wept, and speculated about the unknown author. Again we read and wept; and then kneeled upon the grass, and prayed and thanked God for the able and timely defense of truth against the false-hoods that were then being circulated amongst the people. Little did we then think that the able reviewer was a youth who had been received on trial with myself at the previous Conference."[27]

William Lyon Mackenzie, whose paper had published the letter, now accepted the young minister as an ally in the cause of reform, but if he had read Ryerson's letter a little more carefully he might have recognized even then that this youthful preacher was fundamentally conservative in outlook, for his defence of Methodism stressed its respect for learning and its loyalty to British institutions. From the first Ryerson took great pride in his Loyalist ancestry, a pride which impelled him in later years to write in rich detail the sacrificial story of the United Empire Loyalists.[28]

Shortly after the discovery of Ryerson's literary talents he was made editor of the *Christian Guardian*, a paper founded by the Methodists in 1829. For a time Mackenzie and Ryerson worked harmoniously together as the editors of their respective papers. But this close alliance of the reformers and Methodists in Upper Canada greatly distressed the more conservative Methodists in Lower Canada, as well as the British Wesleyan Conference. The latter decided to break the agreement it had made with the American Conference to confine its missionary work to Lower Canada, and in 1831 it began to send missionaries into Upper Canada. Rather than continue the bitter rivalry that this invasion caused on the circuits, the Canada Conference sought corporate union with the British Conference. George Ryerson, who was in England at this time, was asked to attend a Conference meeting in England and sound it out on the question of corporate unity. George, however, was not impressed with English Methodists, who are, he wrote in a letter to Egerton, "generally either anti-reformers or half-hearted, lukewarm, hesitating reformers."[29]

A short time after penning these words George Ryerson left the Methodist church to join the Irvingites. C. B. Sissons considers it "difficult to overestimate the importance of the loss of George Ryerson to the liberal movement in Upper Canada."[30] From now on Egerton began to lean more heavily on his brother John for consultation and advice. The latter's primary interest was the establishment of Methodism as an ecclesiastical body on an equal footing with the traditional churches; and he was prepared to make terms with the conservatives in pursuit of his purpose. He had already achieved his goal to some extent when Sir John Colborne was persuaded to allot six hundred pounds to the Canada Conference for missionary work among the Indians.

In 1830 the Conference had embarked upon an educational project at Cobourg, and it was hopeful that if it achieved union with the British Conference the government would also make a grant to this project. Consequently, the negotiations opened by George Ryerson with the English Wesleyans were pushed with vigour by John and Egerton and union was achieved in 1833. The Canada Conference, however, was compelled to accept some extremely humiliating terms, not the least of them being the stipulation that "the English Conference shall have authority to send from year to year one of its own body to preside over the Canadian Conference." Another was the stipulation that "The Methodist Missionary Society in Upper Canada shall be auxiliary to the English Wesleyan Missionary Society, and the money raised by it shall be paid into the funds of the Parent Society."[31] The twelve English Wesleyan itinerants who left England under the leadership of Robert Adler to become itinerants in Upper Canada didn't help to make the union very popular, as they were constantly criticizing the Americanism of their Canadian colleagues; their animosity was directed towards William Ryerson to such an extent that "the great orator of Methodism" found himself in eclipse and poverty. Nevertheless, John and Egerton, who had been the foremost advocates of union, felt that they must at all costs retain the tie with the English Conference; consequently, they found themselves gradually alienated from their former radical friends and imperceptibly drifting into the Tory ranks. This inevitably led to a dramatic break in the once friendly relationship between Egerton Ryerson and William Lyon Mackenzie. It was precipitated by a series of articles by Ryerson in the *Christian Guardian* in which he criticized the philosophic foundations of British radicalism, including some harsh strictures upon Mackenzie's hero, Joseph Hume. This was too much for Mackenzie and he wrote bitterly in the *Colonial Advocate*: "The Americans had their Arnold and the Canadians have their Ryerson; and oppression and injustice and priestly hypocrisy may triumph for a time and wax fat and kick, but we yet anticipate the joyful day as not far distant in which the cause of civil and religious freedom shall win a great and lasting victory in this favoured land."[32]

V

Many a Methodist within the Canada Conference agreed with Mackenzie's characterization of Egerton Ryerson. Some of these found the British yoke intolerable and resolved to set up an independent conference of their own, in accord with the American system of church government. They called a conference in Toronto in 1834, and proceeded to elect John Reynolds as their bishop.[33] They revived the old name The Methodist Episcopal Church of Canada by which the Canada Conference had been known, and on this basis proceeded to lay claim to the property of the Canada Conference. Thus was precipitated an internecine strife on the circuits reminiscent of the days of the Ryanite schism. To this was added the humiliation of strife in the law courts— "decisions, appeals, decisions sustained and decisions reversed"[34]— protracted for years before the Canada Conference was confirmed in the legal possession of its property.

About the same time as the Episcopal schism took place, another branch of Methodism made its appearance in Canada: the Primitive Methodist Church, which had broken off from the Wesleyan Conference in England (1810) because of the latter's rejection of the camp-meeting institution. Among the first arrivals in Canada were William Lawson and his wife, who settled in York in 1829. Though not an ordained minister, Lawson began to preach in the market square and soon had gathered together a substantial following. The Primitive Methodist Conference of England took note of his success and sent out William Watkins as a licensed missionary.[35]

From York the movement spread rapidly into the rural parts, particularly during the unsettled period in Canadian Methodism following upon the union with the British Wesleyans. Other independent groups of Methodists also found this a favourable time for missionary work. The Bible Christians with John Glass as their first missionary began work in Upper Canada in 1831. They were followed by the Methodist New Connexion under the leadership of John Addyman in 1837, a fateful year both in the history of Canada and the Canada Conference. To add to the cup of woe of the much beleaguered Canada Conference was the return to Canada of George Ryerson from England to form an Irvingite Church at Toronto. This sect also cut deeply into Methodist membership in Toronto.[36]

These defections were not entirely due to the English connection nor the desertion of the reform movement; to a large extent they were caused by the repudiation of the voluntary system of church financing. The acceptance of a grant from Sir John Colborne by the Canada Conference for missionary work had caused grave misgivings on the part of a good many Methodists; a grant made by the government to the Cobourg Academy caused even greater apprehension, since it was difficult to distinguish this grant from the British government's contribution to the Anglican university at Toronto. It was also suspected that these financial grants were bribes to silence Methodist criticism of the oligarchy that was governing Upper Canada in its own selfish interest.

So great was the change taking place in the Canada Conference under Wesleyan leadership, that in the election of 1836 it found itself committed to the support of Sir Francis Bond Head, an eccentric lieutenant governor who had actually gone out into the hustings to speak in support of the Conservative party. Beside the Methodists his most vociferous supporters were Orangemen with "a wagon load of green shillelaghs brought to the grounds for the purpose of gently persuading the electors to vote for the government nominee."[37] So enthusiastic a Tory did John Ryerson become during this election that he boasted, that in his riding, the Bay of Quinte district, not a "ninny of them [the radicals] was elected."[38]

It **was** this strange reversal of political allegiance on the part of the Conference that left it unusually vulnerable to the attacks of splinter groups. While the government under the reckless leadership of Sir Francis Bond Head was for all intents and purposes goading the radicals into armed rebellion, the Canada Conference of 1837 which might have served as a check on extreme measures was asked to refrain from any criticism of Tory intransigence lest it embarrass Egerton Ryerson in his attempt to secure an additional subsidy for the Cobourg Academy. In the words of C. B. Sissons: "The grants to missions, the needs of the Academy, and the general attitude of the British preachers had combined to weaken the once sturdy independence of the Conference."[39]

The Rebellion of 1837 when it came, however, had many a secret Methodist sympathizer, not only among the schismatic groups but within the Canada Conference as well. Even the Ryersons began to have second thoughts about their new found Tory friends. John, in describing for Egerton the last days of Lount and Matthews, two victims of Tory fury, wrote, "Your benevolent heart, I am sure, will sink with horror at such barbarism in the 19th century."[40]

The dismay and shock experienced by both John and Egerton Ryerson at the government's treatment of the rebels was not shared by William Harvard, the Wesleyan president of the Conference, nor by his most energetic assistant, Robert Alder. Through the columns of the *Guardian* the president issued a pastoral letter asking each circuit preacher to go through class papers of societies to satisfy themselves fully of the loyalty of those who might be listed as members of the church at the forthcoming Conference. Anson Green, who remained neutral during the rebellion probably expressed the feelings of the majority of Canadian Methodists during the troublous year of 1837: "I could not be a rebel; my conscience and religion forbid it; and, on the other hand, I could not fight for the Rectories and Church domination."[41]

VI

It was the "Rectories" more than anything else that had made the Canadian Methodists regret their alliance with the British Wesleyans and the Family Compact. These have a rather complicated history going back as far as 1818, when the British government consented to the legal creation of endowed rectories in both Upper and Lower Canada.[42] In due course twelve rectories were created by letters patent in Lower Canada, but in no case were they endowed from the clergy reserves. Permission was granted, however, in 1826 by the Home Secretary to Lieutenant Governor Maitland and the executive council of Upper Canada to prepare certain glebe lands for occupation as rectories, but no action was taken at that time. It was not until 1836 when Sir John Colborne was about to relinquish his office that he established forty-four new Anglican rectories by letters patent, to each of which were assigned four hundred acres of reserved lands. When this became known during the opening days of Sir Francis Bond Head's ill-starred regime there was a spontaneous outburst of anger against both the government and the Anglican Church that may well have been the chief factor in precipitating the rebellion of 1837. Be that as it may, the rebellion for a time seemed to be a boon to the Anglican Church. None of its members were found among the rebels; and this raised its prestige in the public estimate in England. Consequently, the S.P.G. received enlarged contributions for the support of the Church in Canada. The authorities in England now decided that the time was ripe for the creation of a new Canadian diocese with Toronto, as York was now known, as the see city; and there was little question as to who should be the first bishop. In 1839 Archdeacon Strachan proceeded to England where he was consecrated bishop along with A. G. Spencer, who had been designated bishop of Newfoundland and Bermuda.

The delay in the creation of both these dioceses had been due to the lack of episcopal endowments. About this time there was established the Colonial Bishopric Fund under the direction of the archbishops and bishops of England. Subscriptions were opened for the new society and these were so generous that in a short time it was possible to establish three new colonial dioceses, including Fredericton, New Brunswick, to which John Medley was sent by the British government as its first bishop in 1845.[43]

On one matter, however, a grateful British government hesitated to yield to Anglican importunity: the clergy reserves still remained a contentious issue, and kept alive the spirit of agitation even while the rebellion was being suppressed. One of the last acts of the assembly of Upper Canada before it lost its identity in a reunited Canadian legislature was to pass an act for the distribution of the reserves among the various religious denominations. When the terms of this act became known, petitions began to circulate against it, but these soon became unnecessary as the British legal authorities declared the act *ultra vires*. The Imperial government then framed an act (1840) which forbade any future reservations, and at the same time authorized the governor in council to sell and distribute the reserves as follows: "The proceeds of previous sales should be distributed between the Churches of England and Scotland, to the exclusion of all other denominations, in the proportions of two-thirds and one-third respectively. All future proceeds were to be divided as follows: one-third to the Church of England, one-sixth to the Church of Scotland; and the residue to be applied by the Governor, with the advice of his council, 'for purposes of public worship and religious instruction in Canada'."[44] It was hoped by this last provision to still the cry for secularization by persuading dissenting congregations to accept a share of the reserves for educational purposes, thus overcoming their scruples in relation to the voluntary system of church support.

But the Imperial act also failed to meet the objections of the majority of the people who were now determined to prevent public funds being used for religious purposes. The reserves still remained a constant source of irritation, until finally a predominantly conservative government under the leadership of John A. Macdonald passed the Clergy Reserves Secularization Act (1854), which for all intents and purposes brought to an end the contentious era in the relations of church and state in Canada.

REFERENCES

1. *Vide* H. I. Cowan, *British Immigration to British North America: 1783-1837* (Toronto, 1938), pp. 16-17.

2. D. H. Gillis, *Democracy in the Canadas: 1759-1867* (Toronto, 1951), p. 181.

3. A. N. Bethune, *Memoir of the Right Reverend John Strachan, D.D., LL.D., First Bishop of Toronto* (Toronto, 1870), pp. 9-10.

4. *Ibid.*, p. 36.

5. R. F. Gourlay, *Statistical Account of Upper Canada* (London, 1822).

6. A. N. Bethune, *op. cit.*, p. 65.
   For a harsh judgment upon Strachan for this and other incidents in his career *vide* T. B. Roberton, *The Fighting Bishop, John Strachan, the First Bishop of Toronto, and other Essays in His Times* (Ottawa, 1926). *The John Strachan Letter Book: 1812-1834*, ed. by G. W. Spragge (Toronto, 1946), is also relevant to this and other issues in Strachan's controversial career.

7. Quoted by George Bryce, *Mackenzie Selkirk Simpson* (The Makers of Canada Series, Toronto, 1910), vol. V, p. 200.

8. For a study of Gourlay's career *vide* William Kingsford, *The History of Canada* (Toronto and London, 1888, 10 vols.), IX, pp. 207 *et seq.;* also W. R. Riddell, *Robert (Fleming) Gourlay as shown by His Own Records* (Toronto, 1916).

9. For biographical details *vide* Charles Lindsay, *The Life and Times of William Lyon Mackenzie* (Toronto, 1862).

10. *Ibid.*, pp. 20 *et seq.*

11. *Vide* W. S. Reid, *The Church of Scotland in Lower Canada; Its Struggle for Establishment* (Toronto, 1936), p. 37.

12. *Ibid.*, p. 49 or p. 91.

13. *Ibid.*, p. 48.

14. On the formation of this society *vide* R. F. Burns, *Life and Times of the Rev. R. Burns, D.D., Toronto* (Toronto, 1870), pp. 122-123.

15. *Vide infra.*, p. 211

16. Bethune, *op. cit.*, pp. 122-123. For an interesting comment on population estimates in early days of Upper Canada, *vide* Aileen Dunham, *Political Unrest in Upper Canada, 1815-1836* (London and Toronto, 1927), p. 85.

17. T. R. Millman, *The Life of the Right Reverend, the Honourable Charles James Stewart* (London, Ont., 1953), p. 71.

18. *Ibid.*, p. 72.

19. Quoted by Bethune, *op. cit.*, p. 125.

20. *Vide* W. Gregg, *History of the Presbyterian Church in the Dominion of Canada* (Toronto, 1885), p. 433.

21. *Vide* W. Gregg, *Short History of the Presbyterian Church in the Dominion of Canada* (Toronto, 1892), p. 146.

22. *Vide* Millman, *op. cit.*, p. 105.

23. C. B. Sissons, *Egerton Ryerson, His Life and Letters* (Toronto, 1937-1947, 2 vols.), I, p. 30.

24. *Ibid.*, I, p. 23.

25. *Ibid.*, I, p. 28.

26. *Ibid.*

27. *Ibid.*

28. Egerton Ryerson, *The Loyalists of America and Their Times* (Toronto and Montreal, 1880, 2 vols.).

29. Sissons, *op. cit.*, I, p. 138.

30. *Ibid.*, p. 166.

31. J. E. Sanderson, *The First Century of Methodism in Canada* (Toronto, 1908-1910, 2 vols.), I, pp. 306-307.

32. Sissons, *op. cit.*, I, p. 198.

33. Thomas Webster, *History of the Methodist Episcopal Church in Canada* (Hamilton, 1870), pp. 314-323.

34. *Ibid.*, p. 335.

35. R. P. Hopper, *Old-Time Primitive Methodism in Canada* (Toronto, 1904), p. 14.

36. John Carrol, *op. cit.*, vol. IV, p. 22.

37. Thomas Conant, *Upper Canada Sketches* (Toronto, 1898), p. 66.

38. Sissons, *op. cit.*, I, p. 349.

39. *Ibid.*, p. 381.

40. *Ibid.*, p. 446.

41. *Ibid.*, p. 396. *Vide* also *The Life and Times of the Rev. Anson Green, D.D., Written by Himself* (Toronto, 1877), p. 215.

42. A clear exposition of the rectories issue is to be found in T. R. Millman, *op. cit.*, pp. 138-143.

43. A description of the Colonial Bishopric Fund in relation to Canada is to be found in W. I. Ketchum, *The Life and Work of the Most Reverend John Medley, D.D.* (St. John, N.B., 1893), pp. 38-42.

44. J. M. Dent, *The Last Forty Years: Canada Since the Union of 1841* (Toronto, 1881, 2 vols.), II, p. 201.

XIV

Educational and Cultural Issues in the Canadas

AN AFTERMATH of the rebellions of 1837-1838 was the appointment
of Lord Durham, governor general of British North America, with a
special mission to investigate the causes of unrest in the disaffected
colonies. His famous *Report* highlighting the "gulf between the races"[1]
foresaw only two alternatives for Lower Canada: either it should be
completely left to the French or it should be completely Anglicized,
and since he regarded the French Canadians as "a people with no
history and no literature",[2] he had little compunction in recommending
the second alternative. To this end he urged that the two Canadas
be again reunited with a common educational system with English
as the only officially recognized language. By an act of Union in 1841
these recommendations were for all intents and purposes put into effect,
and it now appeared that the French Canadians had lost out in their
long struggle for cultural survival. That such an eventuality did not
come to pass was due to several factors, one of which was that French
Canada, as if to give the lie to the *Durham Report*, was now entering
upon its most creative literary period with Francis Xavier Garneau
writing a classic history of his compatriots and Octave Crémazie
originating a school of national poetry,[3]—something conspicuously
lacking in English-speaking Canada. Another important factor was
that Upper Canada, to which Durham had assigned the role of assimilating Lower Canada, was torn asunder by a class struggle in which
cultural issues such as primary and secondary education were prominently to the fore; until these were settled there could be no hope of
English-speaking Canada assimilating the more culturally united French-
speaking Canadians. Politicians like Louis Hippolyte Lafontaine and
Georges-Étienne Cartier were quick to recognize that the class struggle
in the upper province was far more bitter than any racial issue, and by

186

allying their followings with the political parties of Canada West they were able to modify the more dangerous provisions in the Act of Union in respect to the national identity of Canada East.

I

It was recognized, however, by all concerned that the crucial issue of assimilation or the continuation of a dual culture would be decided in the field of education; this consideration had received due recognition by the Durham Commission and to Arthur Buller had been assigned the task of outlining a general system of education which might contribute to a greater degree of cultural co-operation between the two races.   One of the first acts of the legislature of the reunited provinces was to enact a common school bill embodying many of Buller's suggestions such as the appointment of an ex-officio superintendent for the whole of Canada with working superintendents for its eastern and western sections.   The schools were to be financed partly through the sale of public lands and partly by permitting municipal corporations to become boards of education, with powers to tax for school purposes.

By a strange turn of events this school act with its professed purpose of making Canada East and West a cultural unity, actually achieved the opposite by re-establishing a dual culture on firmer foundations than ever before; it also contributed to the conception that education is a regional or provincial rather than a national concern.   The provision for two working superintendents was an obvious concession to a prevailing situation, but an even more significant concession was "a provision for dissent," permitting "inhabitants professing a religious faith different from the majority of the township or parish . . . to notify the school commissioners of their dissent and set up a board of their own to operate a minority school in the district."[4]   Though the divisive effect of this latter provision was recognized at the time, the framers of the bill were aware that any attempt to introduce a completely secularized education was going to meet with a stiff resistance not only from Roman Catholics but also from other religious bodies as well,[5] and that they would have to allow some leeway for separate schools if they were not to face a complete impasse.

Following upon the passage of the Act, the Honourable Robert Sympson Jameson was made chief superintendent of education (May,

1842), with Robert Murray, a Presbyterian minister, and Jean Baptiste Meilleur as his working superintendents in Canada West and East, respectively.[6] But despite the best efforts of the two working superintendents it soon became apparent that the previous educational development of the two sections was so diverse that no satisfactory compromise was possible between them. Canada West, now determined to have a liberal school system of its own, became so impatient with the School Act of 1841 that it sought a way out of the impasse by giving up any thought of assimilation with Canada East, thus undermining the whole conception of the Durham Commission in respect to the destruction of the separate national identity of Lower Canada. Consequently, the Act of 1841 was repealed insofar as it related to Canada West, which was now provided with a new common school act of its own (1843). Egerton Ryerson replaced Murray as superintendent of education and undertook with the co-operation of the Liberal government of Baldwin and Lafontaine to provide a secularized school system for Canada West. Even with Canada East out of the picture, it turned out to be a long struggle before Ryerson was able to work out a scheme acceptable to all the diverse elements of his own province; for the Roman Catholics under the adroit leadership of Bishops Charbonnel and Lynch with considerable support from other religious groups, particularly the Anglicans, fought and defeated several of Ryerson's earlier drafts, and compelled him to make provision for separate schools, somewhat along the lines indicated in the Act of 1841. Nor was Ryerson himself completely opposed to separate schools, since he was not fully in accord with many of his liberal supporters, who wished for a secularized school system from which all religious teaching should be excluded. The opposition from the churches and the persistent demand for separate schools made it possible for him to impress upon his liberal colleagues the need to include religious instruction in the public schools. So successfully did he achieve his purpose that he won from a notable English Liberal, the Earl of Elgin, a surprising tribute to the effect that he, Ryerson, had laid the foundation of the common school system "deep in the firm rock of our common Christianity."[7]

"The quest of a school system,"[8] to use C. B. Sissons' descriptive term for Egerton Ryerson's persevering school work in Canada West, was pursued with equal diligence by J. B. Meilleur in Canada East.[9] Meilleur at first applied himself to his task under the conditions of the Act of 1841 and he did succeed in lessening some of the Church opposition when he was permitted by the government to utilize the schools of the Christian Brothers. The letters of Charles Mondelet on "elementary and practical education"[10] which appeared in the press in 1841 explaining a system of education prevailing at that time in New York State, which he thought might be suitable to the peculiar needs of Canada East, were of considerable help in stirring up an interest in Meilleur's work. Nevertheless, after four years of experimentation under the Act of 1841, Meilleur suggested changes in the law to permit boards of school commissioners to be set up separately for Roman Catholics and Protestants. Other acts followed from 1846 to 1875, all of which were attempts to harmonize two very divergent philosophies of education in Canada East. The Act of 1875 has been described as the "charter of freedom for both Roman Catholics and Protestants."[11] This freedom is embraced in a significant provision that reads as follows: "Everything which, within the scope of the functions of the Council of Public Instruction respects especially the schools and public instruction generally of Roman Catholics, shall be within the exclusive jurisdiction of the Roman Catholic Committee of such Council. In the same manner, everything which within the scope of such functions respects especially the schools and public instruction generally of Protestants, shall be within the exclusive jurisdiction of the Protestant Committee."[12] With this awkward phraseology the attempt was given up to provide one school system for the province of Quebec, as Lower Canada became known after 1867. A dual system, under the direction of the churches in cooperation with the government was substituted. The decision on the part of the government to place education on a confessional basis was to a large extent due to the exertions of Cartier, who by this act restored to the Roman Catholic hierarchy the guardianship of the cultural heritage of French Canada, which since the Act of Union in 1841 had been the peculiar task of Liberal politicians.

III

As has already been intimated, the sharp divisions within the Protestant community precluded any possibility of imposing a secular educational programme upon the Roman Catholics either in Upper or Lower Canada. One of the chief causes of ill-feeling among the Protestant churches was, as in the Maritime provinces, the pressing need for a native ministry. This led to a well-organized political alliance on the part of non-Anglicans to wrest by legislative procedures from the Church of England the monopoly in higher education that had been granted to it in the royal charters of McGill University and King's College, Toronto.

The history of higher education in the Canadas, following upon the Conquest, begins with the passage of an act in 1801 by the legislature of Lower Canada, setting up a "Royal Institution for the Advancement of Learning" to which was entrusted the entire management of all schools and institutions of royal foundation in the province as well as the administration of all estates and property appropriated to these schools.[13] Because of the refusal of the Quebec hierarchy to co-operate in its administration, the Royal Institution was unable to achieve very much in the field of elementary education; perhaps an even more serious obstacle to its success than Roman Catholic intransigence was its lack of funds, as the government after a vague hint hesitated to put at its disposal the revenue from the sequestered Jesuit estates. A new lease of life, however, was given the Royal Institution in 1811, when James McGill willed it his Burnside estate along with 10,000 pounds for the purpose of founding a university. But a long period of litigation with McGill's relatives delayed any serious attempt to found McGill University until 1835 when the Privy Council confirmed the legality of the bequest. In the meantime, in order to comply with the conditions of the will, it was decided (1823) to allow Bishop Mountain to make "a *pro forma* appointment of professors."[14] The Bishop nominated his son, G. J. Mountain, as principal and professor of divinity, offices the latter continued to hold until his elevation to the episcopate, when they were entrusted to John Bethune, the dean of Christ Church, Montreal. Also during this period of uncertainty the proposed university received a royal charter (1821) which, though more liberal than that of King's College, Windsor, since it did not subject either the professors or students to religious tests, nevertheless did require that the faculty of divinity be under the control of the Church of England.

The stipulation with regard to the faculty of divinity early became a controversial matter impeding any real progress in setting up the university. At a Synod meeting of the Church of Scotland held at Kingston, in 1836, the Anglican monopoly of theological training in Canada was bitterly challenged by Robert McGill, a leading member of the Synod and also the editor of the *Canadian Christian Examiner*. In the columns of this paper McGill kept up a lively discussion of the topic and began to arouse public opinion against an exclusive faculty of divinity.[15] Further action was taken by the Kirk when it sent Alexander Mathieson, minister of St. Andrew's Church, Montreal, to England to ask the British authorities to set up a chair of theology for the Church of Scotland either at McGill or at King's College, Toronto. When these efforts failed to produce any satisfactory results, the Church of Scotland resolved to found a college of its own and it put so much vigour into the project that by 1842 it opened at Kingston a university, Queen's, which had received a royal charter in 1841 and became the first active university in the Canadas.[16]

Thus was set in motion a trend already moving strongly in the Maritimes—of putting higher education on a purely sectarian basis. Surprisingly enough the trend had been initiated by the Methodists of Upper Canada, with their Academy at Cobourg, which through an act of the legislature in 1841 had been transformed into Victoria College with Egerton Ryerson as its first principal.[17] The Roman Catholics had, as early as 1837, indicated their preference for sectarian higher education, when Bishop Macdonnell secured from the Upper Canada legislature a charter for an educational institution at Kingston, Regiopolis College; but it was not until 1851 that his co-religionists in Lower Canada began to give additional momentum to the trend, when Laval's seminary was transformed into Laval University.[18]

It was with considerable apprehension that the authorities at McGill watched the rapid narrowing of the constituency of their university by the multiplication of sectarian institutions. In 1838 they had tried to retain the support of the Church of Scotland with a compromise scheme on the faculty of divinity whereby "the Bishop of Montreal and the Presbytery of Quebec or the Synod of Canada on behalf of the Church of Scotland should be allowed to use lecture rooms for teaching their students theology and that these students be urged to attend classes on general education at McGill."[19] This compromise failed to satisfy either the Anglicans or the Church of Scotland; the latter refused to co-operate until the statute calling for an Anglican faculty of divinity was disannulled. When this was achieved in 1848, the Presbyterians of the Church of Scotland were so far committed to their own educational institution at Kingston that it made little difference to McGill's prospects for an enlarged constituency. As a matter of fact the constituency was narrowed still further when Bishop G. J. Mountain, despairing of securing a satisfactory faculty of divinity at McGill University, finally accepted a plan that had been put forward by Lucius Doolittle, the rector of Lennoxville and Sherbrooke, and founded Bishop's University at Lennoxville in 1845, to serve the Anglican community of Canada East. For principal of the new university he appointed an "uncompromising churchman"[20] Jasper Hume Nicolls, who, because of his ardent tractarian principles, soon became a controversial figure in Canadian church circles.

With the loss of Anglican support, the authorities of McGill University became impatient with Dr. John Bethune, who was still the principal and professor of divinity, and resolved to dismiss him (1846) and to entrust the administration of the university to a Montreal lawyer, whose first task was to secure a new charter free from all hampering religious clauses. At the same time it was decided not to appoint any professor to the faculty of divinity, an omission explained by Lord Elgin as the only way to carry out the spirit of James McGill's will which urged "that Christianity should be taught not in any single or inconclusive form, but in any and every form in which its great fundamental truths and precepts should be imparted."[21] In the partisan atmosphere of 1848 it was agreed that there was no immediate prospect of teaching Christianity in the universal form that the founder of McGill had desired, so it was decided that "the question respecting the religious and ecclesiastical principles to be inculcated were for the present to rest in a state of indecision as that in which the will of the founder and the Royal charter have left them."[22] This state of indecision continued for almost a century, until, in less partisan days, the faculty of divinity was reconstituted by the senate and the board of governors in cooperation with the affiliated theological colleges of the Anglican and the United churches.

But even after McGill had in 1848 freed itself from all church control it still continued to languish, as its possible constituency for the most part had been dissipated among the sectarian institutions. It was not until William Dawson, a former student of Thomas McCulloch, and a graduate of the famous Pictou Academy, became principal in 1855 that McGill University began to assume its present responsible position in the educational life of Canada.

IV

It was around King's College, Toronto, or Toronto University as it was later known, that the battle between secularism and sectarianism raged most fiercely. The struggle was a confusing one as the issues never remained clear cut because of the divided state of mind of many of the participants. Bishop Strachan, who had secured the charter for King's College, roundly denounced the Church of Scotland and the Methodists for setting up sectarian institutions, yet he in turn finally abandoned the idea of one provincial university and founded a church college; but not until he had made a serious attempt to give King's a broader basis than was possible under the original charter. In 1837 he had accepted some amendments to the charter to permit non-Anglicans to teach in the university, but he remained adamant on the faculty of divinity, which was confined only to those who would sign the Thirty-Nine Articles of Religion.

It was during this period that John McCaul, a graduate of Trinity College, Dublin, and principal of Upper Canada College, was made a member of the faculty of the university and in time became its principal. He began to deviate from the more rigorous position formerly maintained by the Anglicans, and during the tumultuous years that lay ahead for the university when he became its presiding genius, he contributed much in laying the foundation for a unique system of higher education, embodying as it were the principles of both the secularist and the sectarian.[23] It is an honour he shares with Egerton Ryerson, who also changed his mind frequently along the way, and Thomas Liddell, the first principal of Queen's University. Both these men took to heart some of Bishop Strachan's strictures and became concerned over the multiplication of small inefficient colleges; consequently, they began to discuss together a "scheme of college union in one university with as many separate colleges as the wants of the country may require."[24] Together they worked out a plan, finally embodied in a university bill presented to the legislature by Robert Baldwin in 1843. Baldwin's Bill, as it was popularly known, proposed to constitute a University of Toronto, consisting of King's, Regiopolis, Queen's, and Victoria colleges. The University of Toronto was to take over the entire endowment of King's, out of which it would provide 500 pounds annually to the constituent colleges for a period of four years; at the end of this period the maintenance of the colleges was to be provided from funds "set apart for religious purposes"—an oblique threat to the clergy reserves.

As was to be expected, when this bill was presented to the assembly there immediately arose a great storm of protest, particularly from the Anglicans. Bishop Strachan at once circulated a petition against it, accusing the bill of placing "all forms of error on an equality with truth, by patronizing equally within the same institution an unlimited number of sects, whose doctrines are absolutely irreconcilable: a principle in its nature atheistical, and so monstrous in its consequences that if successfully carried out, it would utterly destroy all that is pure and holy in morals and religion, and lead to greater corruption than anything adopted during the madness of the French Revolution."[25]

But with Ryerson and Liddell providing both Methodist and Presbyterian support for the bill it looked as if a federated university was to become an actuality in 1843; that it did not do so until thirty-five years later was due to the sudden intrusion of a constitutional issue into the political scene, throwing confusion into the ranks of the supporters of Baldwin's Bill. The constitutional issue arose out of the governor-general's refusal to admit that political patronage was the prerogative of the party in power and his refusal at the same time to sign a Secret Societies' Bill, aimed at the suppression of the Orange Order, until its legality had been passed upon by the imperial authorities. In the election campaign following upon this sudden assumption of personal rule by Sir Charles Metcalfe, accompanied by "scenes of violence and bloodshed,"[26] Egerton Ryerson was found to be on the side of his friend Metcalfe and it was felt that his writings had done much to contribute to the defeat of the Liberal government of Baldwin and Lafontaine.

With the return of the Tory party to power, there was an immediate move to shelve once and for all Baldwin's university bill. To W. H. Draper, the counsel of the Anglican petitioners, was entrusted the task of writing a new bill to be presented to the legislature of 1846. Draper's Bill in its final form was less of a departure from Baldwin's than had generally been expected, as it still retained the intention to provide the "highest academical and professional education" through a provincial university, but at the same time tried to appease the sectarians by providing for "an intermediate class of seminaries in connection with different religious groups." This bill, however, failed to pass because of the opposition of the Anglican Church, still unwilling to forego the endowments that Strachan had originally obtained for King's College. After the defeat of the Draper Bill, John A. Macdonald, who was beginning to emerge as an adroit politician, attempted to solve the impasse by one of those ingenious compromises for which he later became famous. The university question, however, proved too much even for his talents as a compromiser. His plan, presented to the assembly in 1847, would have returned King's College to the Anglicans along with a grant of $12,000 a year, and would also have provided the other three colleges with an annual grant of $6,000.[27] The "partition bill" as it was called, introduced a new element into the university question: up to 1847, there was considerable unanimity on the desirability of one single university; the establishment of separate colleges was regarded as a second best solution because of Anglican intransigence. Macdonald's Bill suddenly proposed to abandon the idea of a provincial university and to retain intact the existing universities and to provide them with an annual grant from the government. The issue was now similar to the one already dividing the Maritimes; the merits of one good provincial university as over against the value of several small church colleges. One of the most notable recruits to Macdonald's "partition bill" was Egerton Ryerson; to the charge of inconsistency he replied that "it satisfied his conviction of the need of religion as an essential part of all education."[28]

The new bill never reached maturity, for in the general election that followed shortly after its passage, it, along with the clergy reserves, became the most controversial issue before the electorate, and contributed to the downfall of the Tory party. With the return of the Liberals to power, with a stronger mandate than ever before, Baldwin no longer felt the need to rely upon Ryerson and Liddell for support, but proceeded to frame a university bill free from all ecclesiastical entanglements. In the new bill all reference to a faculty of divinity was eliminated; clergymen were prohibited from membership on the senate, nor could they hold the office of vice-chancellor. By richly endowing the university and providing it with educational advantages superior to any existing university in the province it was hoped to reduce all rival colleges to the status of mere theological institutions. It would seem, however, that Baldwin had gone too far to achieve his own aims; for a swelling tide of protest compelled the government to recede considerably from its extreme policy of secularization. In 1853, Francis Hincks, who had succeeded Baldwin as leader of the Liberal party in

Canada West, brought before the assembly a significant amendment withdrawing Toronto University from the work of teaching, which in the future was to be confined to those colleges that were willing to be affiliated with the university. To satisfy the needs of those who wanted to attend a non-sectarian college, he set up University College to become one of the affiliated colleges; other colleges were then offered privileges similar to those given to University College as one of the attractions of affiliation with University of Toronto.

Queen's and Victoria accepted the terms, along with the newly founded Knox College of the Free Church of Scotland. But it proved to be an unusually loose affiliation, leaving the separate colleges to go their own separate ways with little regard for the central university as the examining body. "It is not known that they ever sent up a student for examination."[29] Only the Presbyterians of the Free Church gave the new school their wholehearted support, for Knox College confined its teaching to theological subjects, sending its students to University College for arts.

Nor did the new arrangement retard in any way the multiplication of small colleges, but on the contrary seemed to increase them. After the secularization act of 1849, Bishop Strachan immediately proceeded to raise funds for the establishment of a new Anglican university and found enough enthusiasm for his project to enable him to open the doors of Trinity College in 1851. A year later the Basilian fathers under the patronage of Bishop Charbonnel set up a Roman Catholic arts college, St. Michael's, at Toronto. Some few years earlier (1848) the Roman Catholics at Bytown (Ottawa) had founded a college which ultimately became known as Ottawa University.[30] In 1857 the Baptists established a Literary Institute at Woodstock to provide both literary and theological training for Baptist youth, a venture in higher education that evolved into McMaster University at Hamilton.[31] All these new foundations arose, as it were, in defiance of the liberal tendency of the 'fifties; and new ones continued to spring forth in the following decades, because of a religious tension within the Anglican communion. Evangelical associations in revolt against the high church principles of Bishop's and Trinity, established Huron College at London in 1863, which in 1878 was transformed into the University of Western Ontario; and Wycliffe College at Toronto in 1877.[32]

Though the stream of development in the academic world seemed, despite the liberal triumph in the political field, to be overwhelmingly in favour of small colleges, yet there were other currents moving in the opposite direction. With the immense extension of university education in the latter half of the nineteenth century, particularly in the development of the physical and biological sciences, leading to increasing demands upon the provincial treasury, the government felt called upon to discontinue (1868) its largess to small institutions and to confine its grants to one provincial university; thus an era of effective federation was inaugurated. Representatives from nearly all the colleges took part in negotiations initiated by the government, and contributed something to the Federation Act of 1887, in which it was agreed that the federating colleges should co-operate in teaching arts and that they should have something to say on policy through representation in the senate of the university.[33] Yet at the last moment many of the colleges failed to take the final step and give up their own degree conferring powers; Victoria did not enter the scheme until 1890; Trinity held aloof until 1903; conspicuous among the absentees was Queen's. Nevertheless, there finally emerged a unique combination of sectarian and secular education in which nearly all the denominations, including the Roman Catholics through St. Michael's, were represented.

V

The final outcome was not unlike the original scheme that had been put forth by Baldwin in 1843; the endless delays that hindered its consummation until 1887 were due not so much to divisions within the academic community itself as to the entanglement of the university question with such matters as the clergy reserves and church establishment. It was not until these matters were finally taken out of the political field that there could be any sincere co-operation among the churches in a scheme of universal education. With the secularization of the clergy reserves in 1854, by an act of parliament, which at the same time put all the denominations on an equality as far as the government was concerned, the way was paved for a more harmonious era within the Protestant community; an act abolishing seignorial tenure passed in the same year as the secularization of the reserves also helped to remove one of the long outstanding irritants in the political life of Canada East.

Both these acts had been brought about by an alliance between Upper Canadian Conservatives and Lower Canadian Liberals, best exemplified in a remarkable friendship that grew up between John A. Macdonald, a member of the Orange Order, and Georges-Étienne Cartier, one of the Sons of Liberty under sentence of death following upon the rebellion of 1837. The friendship of these two men did much to solve many of the most difficult political and cultural issues of the Canadas and at the same time helped to raise the standard of political contests—long a glaring scandal in Canadian political life. During the election of 1841 "it was said that at least one-eighth of the members had been returned by violence or something worse," and it was feared that the general tendency in Lower Canada to accept open violence as part of electoral procedure would check the tide of immigration.[34] The election of 1857, following upon the removal of the clergy reserves and seignorial tenure as political issues, though badly marred by corruption and bribery was free from the more violent aspects of the previous contests.

Standards of honesty in relation to public funds still remained exceedingly low. Even a great churchman like Egerton Ryerson permitted himself to acquiesce in the questionable practice of the executive government of supplementing the inadequate salaries of its employees by allowing them to accept interest on public monies placed at their disposal for the administration of their departments.[35] But whatever blame rested upon Ryerson for following this method in the department of education was quickly forgiven because of his truly remarkable achievement in the field of primary education. A good many people in Upper Canada felt that they were living in a less stifling social atmosphere because of the work of Egerton Ryerson. The patient perseverance with which he personally supervised the setting up of a democratic school system, even in the most remote villages, and the persuasiveness with which he won over former adherents of the Family Compact to the view that educational advantages "belonged to every child irrespective of creed, wealth, and class,"[36] did much to dispel the "mutual jealousy and fear and petty gossip and mean rivalship"[37] which so marred the social intercourse of the Toronto through which Anna Jameson rambled in the 'thirties.

Another contributing factor to the amelioration of the "petty gossip and mean rivalship" that seems to afflict all pioneer communities was the close collaboration of heads of colleges during the era of university legislation. This collaboration began with the opening of a correspondence between Egerton Ryerson, while principal of Victoria College, and

Dr. Liddell, the principal of Queen's. The personal contact thus established between these two educators soon broadened to include Dr. John McCaul, University of Toronto, Adam Lillie of the Congregational Academy of Upper Canada, and Samuel Nelles, Ryerson's successor at Victoria. Thus was created a Canadian academic fraternity, dedicated to raising the cultural level of a nation yet to be born, through a confederation pact that greatly enlarged the bounds of intellectual companionship.

REFERENCES

1. Reginald Coupland, *The Durham Report: An Abridged Version with an Introduction and Notes* (Oxford, 1945), p. 15.
2. *Ibid.*
3. *Vide* Mason Wade, *The French Canadians 1760-1945* (Toronto, 1955), pp. 284-308.
4. *Vide* J. G. Hodgins, *Documentary History of Education in Upper Canada* (Toronto, 1897, 28 vols.), IV, p. 62.
5. *Vide* R. Coupland, *op. cit.*, p. 71.
6. J. G. Hodgins, *op. cit.*, IV, p. 301.
7. *Eighty Years' Progress of British North America*, by several contributors (Toronto, 1863), p. 417.
8. *Vide* C. B. Sissons, *Egerton Ryerson, His Life and Letters* (Toronto, 1937-1947, 2 vols.), II, Chapter III, pp. 76-104, entitled "The Quest of a School System."
9. J. B. Meilleur, *Mémorial de l'Éducation du Bas-Canada* (Quebec, 1876, seconde édition).
10. Charles Mondelet, *Letters on Elementary and Practical Education*, trans. by J. J. Williams (Montreal, 1841).
11. *Vide* W. P. Percival, *Across the Years, A Century of Progress* (Montreal, 1846).
12. *Ibid.*, p. 25.
13. *Eighty Years of Progress, op. cit.*, p. 493.
14. Armine W. Mountain, *A Memoir of George Jehoshaphat Mountain* (Montreal, 1866), p. 64.
15. W. Gregg, *History of the Presbyterian Church in the Dominion of Canada, op. cit.*, p. 394.
16. *Vide* W. E. McNeill, "The Story of Queen's," in *Queen's University, A Centenary Volume 1841-1941* (Toronto, 1941), pp. 8-24.
17. *Vide* C. B. Sissons, *op. cit.*, I, pp. 577-579. Also C. B. Sissons, *A History of Victoria University* (Toronto, 1952).
18. *Vide* Camille Roy, *L'Université Laval et les Fêtes du Cinquantenaire* (Quebec, 1903), pp. 1-29.
19. Cyrus Macmillan, *McGill and Its Story 1821-1921* (London, New York, and Toronto, 1921), p. 115.
20. D. C. Masters, *Bishop's University: The First Hundred Years* (Toronto, 1950), p. 11.
21. C. Macmillan, *op. cit.*, p. 199.

22. *Ibid.*

23. *Vide The University of Toronto and Its Colleges, 1827-1906* (published by the Librarian, Toronto, 1906), p. 20.

24. *Ibid.*, p. 28.

25. Quoted by Stephen Leacock, *Baldwin, Lafontaine, Hincks* (Makers of Canada series, Toronto, 1910), VIII, p. 196.

26. Nathanael Burwash, *Egerton Ryerson* (Makers of Canada series, Toronto, 1910), VIII, p. 130.

27. *Ibid.*, pp. 155-156.

28. *Ibid.*, p. 157.

29. *The University of Toronto and Its Colleges, op. cit.*, p. 38.

30. *Vide A Century of Catholic Education 1848-1948* (published by the secretariate of the Alumni Association, The University of Ottawa).

31. *Vide* J. E. Wells, *Life and Labors of Robert Alexander Fyfe, D.D., Toronto* (Toronto, n.d.), *passim.* Also *Concerning McMaster* (Hamilton, Ont., 1947).

32. *Vide* article by T. R. Millman, "The Church of England in Western Ontario, 1785-1857" in *Western Ontario Historical Notes* (issued by the Lawson Memorial Library, University of Western Ontario, London, 1955), vol. XIII, Nos. 1 and 2, pp. 14-15.

33. *Vide The University of Toronto and Its Colleges, op. cit.*, p. 57.

34. N. F. Davin, *The Irishman in Canada* (London and Toronto, c. 1877), pp. 439-440.

35. *Vide* C. B. Sissons, *op. cit.*, II; chap. XI, pp. 369-394, is entitled "The Interest Question."

36. N. Burwash, *op. cit.*, p. 172.

37. Anna Jameson, *Winter Studies and Summer Rambles* (ed. by J. J. Talman and E. M. Murray, Toronto, 1943), p. 30.

XV

An Era of Organization

THE TWENTY-FIVE YEARS preceding the confederation of the provinces of British North America were the most formative in the history of the colonies. Frontier conditions were passing away and "successful business men and well-to-do farmers" were providing the social leadership for a new "commercial agricultural society."[1] These years as well as those immediately following upon Confederation brought about a great transformation in the life of the churches in which the leaders of the new society took a prominent role; one conspicuous sign of their influence was the outward appearance of church property: "little wooden structures" were replaced by "handsome brick churches."[2] Another was the disappearance of boisterous camp-meetings. Improved educational facilities were beginning to show results, particularly among former sectarian churches, leading to an increase of home-trained ministers with definitely higher cultural attainments than their itinerant predecessors. These ministers were now settling down in well defined circuits or pastorates where they accommodated themselves to the secular institutions of the people among whom they dwelt.

Such radical changes did not come about without strong resistance on the part of those who still hankered after the old-time camp-meeting religion with its outward signs of grace and the "poor man" virtues of a puritanical society. This discontent very often produced new sectarian movements with a special emphasis upon "holiness."

The general tendency of the times, however, was away from the sect to the church type of religion, consequently it appeared as if the traditional churches like the Anglican, the Kirk and the Roman Catholic would find themselves very much at home in the changed social climate. But the era was also one of triumphant liberalism which had put all denominations upon an equality in the eyes of the law, thus creating some unusually difficult problems for those churches accustomed to a

superior legal status. Nor were the traditional churches less free from
internal strains than their sectarian rivals. The period of readjustment
following upon the cancellation of all government subsidy found the
members of the Church of Scotland rent asunder by the "Great
Disruption" of the mother church in Scotland, while the Anglicans
were constantly frustrated by the mutual suspicion of evangelical and
tractarian, and the Roman Catholics by the bitter enmity of liberal
and ultramontane.

Notwithstanding these disharmonies, the immediate decades before
and after Confederation were periods of rapid constitutional development
in all the churches that in many respects corresponded to the political development of the country.

I

For the Roman Catholic Church the new era was one of constitutional reorganization through provincial councils. The authority
for these lay in the bull creating the metropolitan see of Quebec, erected
in 1844, and consisting at first of three suffragans: Montreal, Kingston
and Toronto; three others were added in 1847: Newfoundland, Ottawa
and the North West. Though the Maritimes were not included in the
province they were to be "summoned to a provincial council, should
one take place."[3]

The first of these, summoned in 1851 by Archbishop Pierre Flavien
Turgeon, was a truly national assembly, in that it included delegates
from all the provinces of British North America representing a total
population of 1,084,342.[4] No far reaching decisions were made at
this council but it was a preliminary step towards liberation of the
church in Canada from its long tutelage under the Congregatio de
Propaganda Fide. For the time being, however, it confined its attention
pretty much to problems of discipline, morals and liturgy. One resolution
calling for the establishment of a Catholic university in Canada East
and a normal school for training teachers reflected the liberal spirit
dominant at this time. The resolution had an immediate effect in that
it led to the erection of Laval University.

It was not until the third council (1863) that important constitutional
questions began to emerge. At this council there was manifested considerable discontent with the rather cumbersome way in which bishops
were chosen for vacant sees. There seemed to be some confusion in the

minds of the members as to how preferences were conveyed to Rome, where the final decision was made, so the council asked from the papacy a firmly established rule for the election of bishops. However, the procedure remained indeterminate until 1908 when Canada was removed from the jurisdiction of the Propaganda and episcopal elections were then conducted "in accordance with the ordinary rules of canon law."[5]

The fourth provincial council (1868) ushered in an era of decentralization for the metropolitan see of Quebec, petitioning Rome for the erection of Toronto and St. Boniface into metropolitan sees. The petition was granted and Toronto assumed its new dignity in 1870, St. Boniface, of which more later, in 1871.

That Toronto rather than the older diocese of Kingston should have become the first metropolitan see of Ontario (the new name for Upper Canada after Confederation) was no doubt due to its importance as the capital of the province. But Toronto had also won ecclesiastical prominence because of the outstanding ability of its bishops. The first of these was Michael Power, a native of Halifax, Nova Scotia, who assumed office when the diocese, consisting of the western part of Upper Canada, had been separated from Kingston in 1841. He is perhaps best remembered for bringing to Toronto the nuns of Loretto whose convent schools quickly spread across Ontario and have imparted to their graduates a refinement and culture that has won for them general expressions of approval.[6]

Dr. Power's successor, Armand François Marie de Charbonnel, who came from France, also took a deep interest in Catholic education, bringing into his diocese the Christian Brothers, a teaching order dedicated to the education of the masses.[7] Thus the two first bishops of Toronto laid the foundations for separate Roman Catholic schools, making it possible for their successors to resist the strong demand in Ontario for a completely secularized system of education.

During Dr. Charbonnel's administration two new dioceses were created in Toronto: London in 1855 and Hamilton in 1856, preparing the way for the erection of a new ecclesiastical province. In 1860 Charbonnel brought his strenuous and eventful episcopate to an end by entering the Capuchin Order and handing over the diocese to Joseph Lynch, who became the first metropolitan of Toronto province embracing the whole of Ontario with the exception of a portion of the diocese of Ottawa, which still remained within the ecclesiastical jurisdiction of Quebec. The new province of Ontario had at the time a Roman Catholic

population of over 258,000, a remarkable increase from the days of
Bishop Macdonnell, whose flock according to an estimate compiled by
Dr. Thomas Rolph in 1834 numbered some 52,428 souls.[8]

Toronto, however, was not the first ecclesiastical province in
Canada to separate from Quebec; that honour belongs to Halifax which
became a provincial see in 1852, with three suffragan bishoprics: St.
John, Chatham and Charlottetown. A fourth was shortly added with
the creation of the diocese of Arichat (later known as Antigonish) in
the eastern section of Nova Scotia. It had been expected that Bishop
Fraser who held the see at Halifax at the time of the separation of Arichat,
would have become the first archbishop of the Maritimes, but Fraser
chose Arichat rather than Halifax as his diocese, so the dignity of metropolitan was conferred upon William Walsh, who called together his
first council[9] in 1857, representing a constituency of some 207,371
church members—almost as many as Toronto had when it became
a metropolitan a decade later.

No more ecclesiastical provinces were created in Canada until
1887 when Montreal was erected into a metropolitan with the dioceses
of St. Hyacinthe, Sherbrooke, Valleyfield and Joliette as its suffragans.
The long delay before Montreal reached the dignity of a metropolitan
see was probably due to internal feuds characteristic of this diocese from
the time it became a suffragan of Quebec. The Sulpicians who had
enjoyed unusual privileges as the seigneurs of Montreal resented the
fact that their first bishop, Lartigue, should be a mere auxiliary of
Quebec and they pushed their opposition to the extent of petitioning
the government to deprive Lartigue of his episcopate, but failed to achieve
their purpose. The quarrel between the Sulpicians and the episcopacy
was by no means lessened when Ignace Bourget assumed the full
administration of the diocese in 1837 and began to favour the Jesuits
over the Sulpicians whom he denounced as the last refuge of Gallicanism
and Catholic liberalism, and whose power he seriously undermined
by dividing the parish of Montreal.[10]

Another factor in the continuing subordination of Montreal to
Quebec was the bitter tension between the English- and French-speaking
inhabitants of the city. The passage of the Rebellion Losses bill (1849),
while Montreal served as the capital of Canada led to the burning of the
parliament buildings by an unruly Protestant mob. On another occasion
the address of an ex-Italian monk at Zion Church (1853) on the evils
of Romanism led to a street riot and caused troops to fire into the crowd,

killing five men.[11] Such displays of passion over racial and religious issues long kept Montreal the problem child of the hierarchy of Quebec.

There was, moreover, a serious cleavage between the two sees over a "new school of ultramontanism" greatly favoured by Bishop Bourget.[12] The new school was "more papal than the Pope" in its emphasis upon authoritarian rule and it was particularly embarrassing to Archbishop Baillargeon in his attempt to establish good relations with the predominantly liberal legislature. Nor was his task made any easier in mollifying a sensitive legislature when Bourget started a furious controversy with the very liberal *Institut Canadien*,[13] and persuaded the Pope to put it under an interdict. The quarrel was greatly embittered by the refusal of Bourget to allow one of the members of the *Institut*, Guibord, who died at the height of the controversy, to be buried in consecrated ground. Guibord's friends carried the case to the courts and after many years of litigation Bourget was compelled to yield to a decision of the judicial committee of the Privy Council ordering the interment of the body in the Catholic cemetery of Côte des Neiges, which was done under the escort of an armed guard. This was followed by the Bishop declaring "that the place where this rebellious child of the Church has been laid is now in fact separated from the rest of the consecrated cemetery to be no more anything but a profane place."[14]

Despite the resistance of the archbishops of Quebec to the new school of ultramontanism, its principles began to prevail in the provincial councils. After the fifth council (1873), presided over by a reputed liberal, Elzéar Alexandre Taschereau, who became Canada's first cardinal, pastorals were issued supporting Bourget on the Guibord issue and condemning Catholic liberalism and all its works.[15] At the sixth council (1878) the trend towards ultramontanism was even more pronounced: the rights of the Church as a perfect society were put forth in most uncompromising language; Catholics were warned against reading works written by non-Catholics and were forbidden to attend any Protestant religious services. Though this in part reflected the new mood of the papacy, following upon the decree of papal infallibility in 1870, it also reflected the desire of the Church authorities in Quebec to isolate the Catholic community from the Protestant as one means of preserving a distinct Roman Catholic culture now threatened by an increased minority position within the larger Canada after Confederation. One further step in this direction was taken at the seventh council of 1886, when it was decreed that ecclesiastical studies should be based upon the doctrine as set forth by St. Thomas Aquinas.

Opinion had now veered so far towards the new school of Bourget that in the following year Montreal was made a metropolitan see, and the completion of the Roman Catholic hierarchy proceeded apace. In 1899 it was given a regular apostolic delegate, and a plenary council was organized in 1909 attended by representatives from all the provinces of Canada, and embracing a constituency of 34 archbishops, bishops, vicars and prefects apostolic; 29 dioceses regularly established; 3 vicariates and 2 prefectures apostolic.[16]

II

While the Church of Rome in the years preceding Confederation was faced with the problem of decentralizing its topheavy rule at Quebec, the Church of England, on the other hand, was seeking for a central authority to bind together the distinct and separate dioceses of British North America. Such a search was stimulated by the fact that the church in Canada had long depended upon the imperial parliament as the source of its being in the colonies; when this support was withdrawn it had to find a new apologetic for its existence. There now emerged in many quarters a strong emphasis upon historical continuity with the primitive church, with a particular stress upon apostolic succession as the outward and visible sign of such continuity. Already this emphasis had been put forth in England by John Keble in his famous assize sermon (1833), out of which arose the tractarian movement with its "high" church views.[17]

The Anglican Church in the Canadas and the Maritimes in its prolonged contest with the sectarian movement had to some extent anticipated the tractarian or Oxford movement. John Strachan very early in his career had taunted the dissenters with their "low appreciation of the past" and the readiness with which they "cast off all regard for the forms and usages of the Church of the Apostles."[18] Bishop Strachan's high church views were shared by most of the bishops appointed by the Crown in the middle of the nineteenth century. Edward Feild in Newfoundland, John Medley in New Brunswick, and Hibbert Binney, who had succeeded John Inglis in Nova Scotia in 1851, were all convinced high churchmen. Many of their clergy and the laity for the most part had been attracted to the evangelical movement and were "bitter and strong" against what were termed "innovations."[19]

It was in the midst of the suspicions and recriminations of high and low church factions that the bishops had to face the crisis of disestablishment. The nature of the crisis was well expressed by Francis Fulford, who had been appointed by the Crown in 1850 to the newly-created diocese of Montreal: "We seem to have been deprived of the ecclesiastical law of England," he wrote to a friend shortly after his arrival in Canada, "and have not been provided with any recognized and effectual means of self-government for those who associate themselves together as members of our communion."[20]

To overcome this anomalous state of affairs, the bishop of Quebec, G. J. Mountain, called a conference of the bishops of British North America to meet with him at Quebec on September 23, 1851. Five of the seven bishops invited accepted the invitation and after a week's discussion drew up what became known as the "Declaration of the Bishops of British North America." It warned members of the Church of England that membership requires conformity to the rules and ordinances of the church, and involves the obligation to contribute to its maintenance; the declaration also affirmed the acceptance of Holy Scriptures as the rule of faith and the Book of Common Prayer as the "best help to members of the Church of England in the understanding of holy Scripture, and as the groundwork of the religious education of their children."[21] The most significant section of the declaration was a call to the clergy and laity to form synods both on a diocesan and provincial level; but this was something more easily said than done. Firstly, there was stiff opposition from diocesan church societies, some of which had been in existence since 1836; but an even greater obstacle was the difficulty experienced by the legal authorities in England to devise a bill to give colonial synods legal status. Finally, Bishop Strachan "having," in the words of Fennings Taylor, "proved himself to have been one of the most conscientious and law-abiding subjects . . . suddenly arrived at the conclusion that there was little virtue in the law;"[22] he then proceeded (1853) to organize a synod by the simple device of turning his annual visitation into such a body. This was done by a resolution saying, "That this meeting convened by the Lord Bishop . . . is the Diocesan Synod of this Diocese;" and that "we [the members of the Synod] now proceed to the transaction of the business we have commenced."[23]   An act of the legislature (1857) giving the synod legal status, was then submitted to the British government for examination, and was approved by a proclamation.   Thus the way was made clear for all the other provinces in British North America to proceed to the formation of diocesan synods.

Shortly after the organization of the synod of Toronto, a canon was passed providing for the election of bishops, which, according to Bishop Strachan, "excited wonder and astonishment and offended many as if it had been a new and unauthorized thing."[24]   The new canon was immediately put to the test in London, the see city of a proposed new diocese, Huron, carved out of Toronto.   Additional cause for astonishment was a long deadlock in the balloting between high and low churchmen, only broken by the withdrawal of Strachan's favourite candidate, A. N. Bethune, leading to the election of Benjamin Cronyn, a pronounced evangelical.   In the terminology of the day this was an "Irish victory, the consummation of the Irish Compact, or of Trinity College, Dublinism . . . cliqueism."[25]   When Bishop Strachan organized another diocese, Ontario, in 1862, the "Irish Compact" won again in the election of John Travers Lewis, a bishop who gained the distinction of being the first Anglican clergyman to be consecrated in Canada.   Such consecrations were now possible because the Anglican churches of British North America had at last succeeded in obtaining a primate of their own.

In 1859 the synods of Quebec, Toronto and Montreal had petitioned the Queen to appoint one of the Canadian bishops to preside over the general assemblies of the church in the province.   The following year the petition was granted and letters patent[26] were issued making Bishop Fulford the metropolitan of Canada with Montreal as the see city.   The province over which the new metropolitan presided included the dioceses of Nova Scotia and Fredericton as well as all the Canadian dioceses; Newfoundland though inclined at first to enter the new province later decided to remain under the jurisdiction of Canterbury, as did also Rupert's Land for the time being.

Following upon the creation of the ecclesiastical province of Canada the British government issued a statement to the effect that "where there is a responsible local government the crown should not interfere in ecclesiastical matters."[27]   Upon the death of Bishop Fulford (1868), the bishops of the province of Canada chose as their metropolitan Ashton Oxenden, the rector of a parish in England; the diocese of Montreal obligingly elected him as its bishop and thus was completed the final act in the drama of the separation of the Anglican Church in Canada from the Mother Church of England.

No sooner did the Canadian church gain its independence, than it sought once again some continuing tie with the see of Canterbury. Separation had come at a rather distressing time in the history of the Church of England. The Privy Council in the Gorham judgment had given a decision that seemed to undermine the church's teaching on baptismal rebirth; the question of higher criticism had been raised in an acute form by Bishop Colenso of Natal, and there had just been published an unusually outspoken book, *Essays and Reviews* by some younger theologians of the Anglican Church which had terribly outraged orthodox churchmen. All these had a disturbing effect on the newly organized Anglican Church in Canada, and so at the third provincial synod at Montreal, Bishop Lewis drew up a rather famous resolution expressing the alarm felt by Canadian churchmen over the unusual trends within the Anglican communion, and then went on to appeal to the Archbishop of Canterbury "to convene a National Synod of the Bishops of the Anglican Church at home and abroad, who, attended by one or more of their Presbyters or Laymen learned in Ecclesiastical law as their advisers, may meet together under the guidance of the Holy Ghost to take such counsel and adopt such measures as may best be fitted to provide for the present distress in such Synod presided over by Your Grace."[28] Though the Archbishop of Canterbury refused to call an imperial synod, he did as a result of this resolution invite all the bishops of the Anglican communion to meet with him at Lambeth Palace in 1867, thus inaugurating the decennial Lambeth conferences that have, without canonical jurisdiction, successfully fostered a world wide Anglican fellowship.

At the time of its organization the provincial synod represented a church population of some 479,136. After Confederation there was a considerable lull before it proceeded to bring into its membership the missionary dioceses of the north-west. In 1893, however, these were finally embraced in a General Synod of the Church of England in Canada reaching from the Atlantic to the Pacific and representing a membership of 661,608, about 13.7 per cent of the total population of the country.

III

The problem of organization during the era of secularization was far more difficult for the Presbyterians than it was for either the Roman Catholics or the Anglicans. It was necessarily preceded by a long series of church unions. These, however, were seriously retarded by the violent repercussions in the colonies following upon the disruption in 1843 of the established Church of Scotland.

From the first days of Scottish settlements in British North America there had been a keen awareness of the incongruity of several competing Presbyterian sects in the sparsely populated colonies. As early as 1818 the secession churches of Nova Scotia had started a trend towards church union, and in 1836 the Kirk synods of the Maritimes opened negotiations for a union of all branches of Presbyterianism. The Kirk of Nova Scotia "adopted a resolution to throw open the door of admission to ministers and members of the Secession Synod, and declaring its willingness, if the Synod did not immediately join as a united body, to receive without delay those ministers and congregations who might desire to join the Synod. . . ."[29] A similar offer was made in the Canadas to which the secession churches were not unresponsive. So it appeared that by the mid-century at least, Presbyterianism would become one united church in British North America. But the "Great Disruption" in Scotland soon changed such rosy hopes into the blackest despair. The immediate cause for the disruption was the intrusion by patrons of unwanted ministers upon protesting congregations, a quarrel that had little relevance outside of Scotland; but there was connected with it another issue that had long been disturbing an evangelical group within the established church, headed by Dr. Thomas Chalmers, namely, that the Kirk by its subservience to the state was failing to meet the challenge of the unchurched masses thrown up by the industrial revolution.[30] It was this issue that disturbed the more evangelical members of the Kirk outside Scotland and moved them to take sides in what appeared to be a purely local concern.

In the beginning there was general sympathy in British North America for the new Free Church that had emerged from the disruption, but after "deputies from both the Free Church and from the old Established Church visited Canada and set forth before the Canadian people their respective claims with passionate fervour,"[31] disruption of congregations became as widespread in the colonies as in Scotland.

Conspicuous among these delegates was Robert Burns, who as secretary of the Glasgow Colonial Society had been largely responsible for a new vigour and aggressiveness in the Church of Scotland both in the Canadas and in the Maritimes. After the disruption he threw in his lot with the Free Church and was chosen as its good-will ambassador to North America. Entering Canada from the United States by the way of Niagara, his journey from Toronto to Halifax developed into a triumphal tour. From Brockville to Prescott he was escorted "by a long train of men on horseback, and men, women, and children in all kinds of waggons and carriages, so that when the procession was joined by that from Prescott, it extended, it was said, for upwards of half-a-mile."[32] His stop at Kingston led to the disruption of Queen's College, and the establishment of a new Free Church college, Knox, at Toronto. At a later date, when Dr. Burns became pastor of Knox Presbyterian Church at Toronto, the development of Knox College became one of his chief responsibilities.

The disruption of Queen's College was the signal, as it were, for an intensified struggle for a reformed and purified Free Church. The root and branch nature of the more passionate reformers took its most extreme form at the St. Gabriel Street Church in Montreal. Even though the minister of this church, Henry Esson, had taken the lead in disrupting the Synod of Canada in connection with the Church of Scotland and had succeeded in leading all his flock into the Free Church, there still remained a group within the congregation who felt that the majority of the members were not seriously committed to the principles of Thomas Chalmers. A committee of twelve, with John Redpath, an influential layman, as its chairman "resolved to have a new congregation organized that would, as they regarded the matter, adequately represent the revived spiritual life of the Free Church, as well as its merely political views."[33] In the hope of avoiding a schism, Henry Esson resigned his pastorate; all the elders of the session offered to resign and make way for a new session; the congregation was willing to revise its constitution along lines desired by the twelve; but all was in vain; the purists remained adamant and organized a new congregation known as the Coté Street Church. To make sure that the evangelical principles of this church would survive in the future, John Redpath took the lead in founding a new Presbyterian college at Montreal, which opened its doors to students in 1864.

In a remarkably short time the spirit of separation began to abate and the movement towards union resumed its wonted course. It was revived in the Maritimes in 1860 when the Secession synod of Nova Scotia and the Free Church synod were united into the synod of the Presbyterian Church of the Lower Provinces of British North America. Six years later this synod was joined by the synod of the Free Church of New Brunswick. The Canadas followed a similar pattern with the union in 1861 of the synod of the United Presbyterian Church in Canada (Secession) and the synod of the Presbyterian Church of Canada (Free Church), taking the name, the Canada Presbyterian Church. Nine years later this body organized itself into the General Assembly of the Canada Presbyterian Church, made up at the time of four synods: Montreal, Toronto, Hamilton and London, embracing some seventeen presbyteries and showing a roll of two hundred and ninety-two ministers.[34]

The synods in connection with the established Church of Scotland remained on the side lines while these unions were taking place, partly because of bitter memories and partly because of the low estate of their membership. Though immediately after the disruption the Kirk exceeded the Free Church in numbers, it was not long before the latter had outstripped the former, not only in the number of its members but also in the enthusiasm and vigour of its activities. The synods of the Church of Scotland in Nova Scotia and Prince Edward Island remained dormant for ten years; the New Brunswick synod continued its regular meetings, but with a much diminished membership until it was united with the revived synod of Nova Scotia in 1868.

Not all virtue, however, had departed from the Kirk with the Free Church; some of its younger ministers were men of remarkable talents, who were destined to play an unusual role in moulding a Canadian national consciousness during the era of Confederation. Three names stand out in this field: firstly, there was John Watson, a professor at Queen's University, who along with George Paxton Young, the brilliant Free Church philosopher at Knox College, pioneered in Canada in facing the issues raised by modern Biblical criticism and sought to demonstrate that the "Idealism" which they both professed "was designed to transform Christianity into a rational faith;"[35] secondly, there was D. J. Macdonnell, one of Watson's students, who after a sojourn in Europe to complete his studies became minister of St. Andrew's Presbyterian Church in Toronto where he fought a battle for tolerance and boldly sought from the courts of his church some relief from confessional subscription[36]; and thirdly, there was George Monro Grant, the most influential churchman in the Canada of his day.

Grant requires more than a passing notice. A native of Pictou County and a graduate of that county's famous Academy, he proceeded to Scotland to complete his education. Here he came under the influence of the famous Scotch philosopher, John Caird, who strengthened him in his loyalty to the principles of the established church. Before going to Scotland Grant had been somewhat wavering in his churchmanship, being favourably disposed towards the Free Church, but closer contact with this church in Scotland had predisposed him towards the church of his fathers. Free churchmen he found "deeply filled—not with the enthusiasm which is pervasive and beautiful, but with the fanaticism which is stern and fierce."[37] On his return to Nova Scotia in 1861 he resolved to dedicate himself to a revival of the Kirk, which even at that time had hardly recovered from the disaster of 1843. After serving brief pastorates in Pictou County and on Prince Edward Island he became minister of old St. Matthew's in Halifax. Here he formed a close friendship with Archbishop Thomas Connolly of the Roman Catholic Church which "gave great offence to the narrow bigotry which in certain circles was rife."[38]

His friendship with the liberal and Catholic Thomas Connolly, and his revulsion for the denominational rivalry of the Protestant churches led him to take a strong stand against the sectarianism that had so long dominated the religious development of the colonies of North America. He also recognized that the Kirk in isolation from the other Presbyterian churches could only intensify the spirit of sectarianism. As a delegate from his synod to the Canadian synods he came in contact with men holding similar views to his own, such as D. J. Macdonnell in Toronto and D. M. Gordon from Winnipeg. So when Dr. William Ormiston, the moderator of the synod of the Canada Presbyterian Church addressed a letter in 1870 to the moderators of the rival synods calling for "Incorporation of all the Presbyterian Churches in the Dominion under one General Assembly,"[39] he found the synods of the Church of Scotland in a receptive mood. Committees representing four independent Presbyterian churches were immediately set up and after four years of negotiations these separate bodies were incorporated into the General Assembly of the Presbyterian Church in Canada.

In the basis of union there was included a re-affirmation of the Westminster Confession of Faith as the subordinate standard of the church as well as the Longer and Shorter Catechisms, "it being distinctly understood that nothing contained in the aforesaid Confession or catechisms, regarding the power and duty of the Civil Magistrate, shall be held to sanction any principles or views inconsistent with full liberty of conscience in matters of religion."[40] The united Assembly which met for the first time in 1875 represented a church population of 578,185, reaching from the Atlantic to the Pacific. Thus the long divided Presbyterians took the lead in building a territorial church that was coterminous with the national boundaries of the confederated provinces of Canada.

IV

First among the other churches to follow this example were the Methodists. They also faced the problem of disunity, and the path to unity was strewn with even more obstacles than those encountered by the Presbyterians. One of the worst was the ill-feeling that was continually evident between American and British Methodism, both of which were strongly represented in Canadian conferences. Hostilities reached a climax during a conference at Belleville (1840) when the Wesleyan Missionary Committee of England preferred charges against Egerton Ryerson on three counts: (1) Attempting to supersede the English Wesleyan Conference representative in Canada in communications with the government; (2) Attempting to secure for the Canada Conference the government's grant to the Wesleyan Missionary Society; and (3) "allowing the *Guardian* to become political."[41] These charges were followed by the withdrawal of the British Conference from union with the Canadian. The charges themselves did not bear close scrutiny, but the real reason behind the break was evident enough; it was a fundamental disagreement between the two branches of Methodism on the ultimate disposal of the clergy reserves. Ryerson's communication with the government to which the English Wesleyans had taken exception urged that the reserves be sold and that a fair distribution of the proceeds be made among the Canadian churches; the Canada Conference would then use its share for educational purposes. Such a solution had as its corollary a discontinuation of direct grants from the government to the churches, thus depriving the Wesleyan Missionary Society of the revenue it was using for its work among the Indians. In other words, Ryerson's suggestion would have enriched the Canada Conference's educational projects, but would have sadly crippled the missionary activities of the Wesleyan Missionary Society. For this reason the British Wesleyans were quite willing to see the proceeds of the reserves go to the Anglican Church which was in their estimation "the Established Church of all the British Colonies."[42]

The separation of the two conferences was of brief duration, as the rivalry that followed on the circuits created a climate favourable to the increase of new sects, and led to a renewed attempt at reunion, which was consummated in 1847, followed by "a season of mutual congratulation and pleasing reminiscences of former days before the unhappy estrangement."[43]

Reunion was in reality a preliminary step towards the creation of an autonomous Methodist Church in British North America. It was followed by the amalgamation of the work of Canada East and Canada West (1854). About this time the Primitive Methodist, the Bible Christian and the New Connexion churches, the latter affiliated with the Ryanites since 1841, began to organize annual conferences, thus preparing the way for organized negotiations among all the branches of Methodism in Canada. The first overtures for such an all embracing union were made by the Wesleyan Methodist Conference in 1866, in the form of a resolution calling for an end of Methodist divisions.

In the meantime, the Wesleyan Methodists in the Maritimes were becoming impatient with British rule and began to look upon union with Canadian Methodists as one way out of their subordination to the British Conference. Nor was the Wesleyan Conference of England loath to be relieved of its responsibility to the Methodists in the Maritimes, particularly as the latter were bitterly critical of the scale of stipends set by the Wesleyan Missionary Society. A preliminary step towards independence was the creation of a Maritime Conference. This had been first attempted by Robert Alder, a representative of the British Conference, in 1847, but his efforts proved fruitless.[44] In 1855, however, John Beecham, senior missionary of the British Conference, succeeded in setting up an Eastern British American Conference, embracing the Wesleyan Methodist churches of Nova Scotia, New Brunswick, New-foundland and Prince Edward Island,[45] paving the way for organic union with the Conference of the Wesleyan Methodist Church in Canada in 1874.

The man most responsible for the working out of this larger union was William Morley Punshon,[46] who in 1868 arrived in Canada from England to become president of both the eastern and western conferences. A man of "deep scholarship and moving eloquence", he led the larger conferences to a vision of the time "when, beneath the flag of that Dominion, there will be but one mighty Methodist organization with its voice of praise and prayer . . . reaching from the shores of the Atlantic to the Pacific Ocean"[47]; also he persuaded the New Connexion Church to co-operate in the attainment of this goal.

The inclusion of the New Connexion Church in the larger union involved considerable constitutional change for the Wesleyan Methodist Church, as the former insisted upon lay representation at conference meetings, something the British Conference and its allied conferences had long refused to tolerate in deference to John Wesley's fear of "too much democracy." Egerton Ryerson vigorously supported the New Connexion demand, and also made a motion favouring a president for the united conference elected by ballot, rather than a bishop or a general superintendent. "Thus," writes Sissons, "the man who had been absurdly accused of being the 'Pope of Methodism' made sure that the temporary head of the Methodist Church should be merely a presiding officer, invested with no such rank or duties as those germane to a Bishop or General Superintendent."[48] As a result of the negotiations there emerged in 1874 the Methodist Church of Canada, ruled over by a General Conference meeting every four years, and several regional annual conferences to look after administrative functions, supplemented by district meetings with local administrative powers, and congregational meetings under the control of a quarterly board.[49]

The new united church now represented a constituency of some 560,362 adherents or 16.3 per cent of the population of Canada. It had not yet reached its possible maximum strength as the Methodist Episcopal, the Primitive Methodist, and the Bible Christian churches still remained outside, but with their accession in 1884, the Methodist Church became the largest Protestant body in Canada with a membership at the time of the census of 1891 of 861,666, being 17.8 per cent of the population. The next largest group was the Presbyterian with a membership according to the same census of 770,119 or 15.9 per cent of the population. The

Anglicans came next with a membership of 661,608 or 13.7 per cent of the population. According to the same census the Roman Catholics numbered 2,009,201 or 41.6 per cent of the total population of Canada.

V

The next largest Protestant denomination in Canada after the Anglican was the Baptist, which also in the years before and after Confederation was busily engaged in trying to create a national church organization. The Baptists had a more serious problem of disunity than any of the other groups so far considered. The source of disunity lay in the conception of each local church as "in itself an independent democracy."[50] Nevertheless, the urgent demand for educational facilities to provide for an educated clergy, the desire for a Baptist paper, the need for pension schemes for the clergy and their dependents and the support of missionary projects, inevitably compelled the Baptists to seek for some kind of loose confederation of independent churches.

One of the most tireless advocates of Baptist unity was the missionary-minded Dr. R. A. Fyfe, who was described by a contemporary biographer as the "strongest worker and the ablest and most trusted leader" of the Baptist community in Canada.[51] He is best known as the founder and principal of Woodstock Literary Institute, but before going to Woodstock he had been associated with John Gilmour at Montreal in forming a Baptist Union in order to provide funds for the support of a Baptist college in Montreal. Also he was instrumental in bringing from England to Canada, Dr. J. M. Cramp to head the Baptist college; in so doing he secured a strong ally in the cause of Baptist unity. But even the combined efforts of Fyfe and Cramp failed to hold together the Baptist Union which foundered on the suspicion that the college it was supporting was not sound on the communion question. It was feared by the majority of Baptists that the authorities at the college favoured "open communion," and so they broke up the original union to form, in 1848, the Regular Baptist Union of Canada, only admitting those who adhered to "close communion" and refusing to give any further support to the college, thus forcing it to close its doors in 1849.

With the collapse of the college, Dr. Cramp turned to newspaper work to earn a living. He was, however, still destined to play a conspicuous role in shaping the policy of the Baptist Church in Canada, but in the Maritimes rather than in the central provinces. He had first visited the Maritimes in 1846 carrying with him letters from the Baptists of Canada with proposals for promoting union among the Baptists of the British provinces.[52] Though the proposals led to no tangible results, being frustrated by the formation of the Regular Baptist Union in the Canadas, the visit ultimately led to an invitation being extended to Dr. Cramp to become president of Acadia University, which he accepted. For almost a half century he "sought," in the words of one of his colleagues, "to lift his students out of the isolation and poverty of mere provincial life and enrich and ennoble them by a consciousness of vital relations as wide as humanity itself."[53]

"Isolation and poverty of mere provincial life" constantly challenged Dr. Cramp and all those who sought to create a unified Baptist community both in the Maritimes and in the Canadas to the extreme limits of their patience. Though the Baptist associations of Nova Scotia, New Brunswick and Prince Edward Island had become federated in 1846 into the Baptist Convention of the Maritimes, there still remained outside the Convention, the Free Baptists who kept alive the anti-Calvinistic principles of Henry Alline. These at first were divided into several groups because of certain variations in the definition of election and grace, matters that had first been debated with considerable fervour in New England. Almost simultaneously Asa McGray and Joseph Norton founded a Free Baptist Church and a free Christian Church at Argyle (1819) and Barrington (1821). Both these men were controversial preachers who were constantly making inroads into the membership of the Association Baptists. In 1837 McGray and Norton combined their followings into a conference called the Free Christian Baptists; shortly after the union, however, McGray with a small company of followers, broke away from the conference to form an independent church, again taking the name, Free Will Baptist. Thus the two bodies continued to quarrel bitterly for almost thirty years, often building rival meeting-houses "in small communities that could scarcely support one."[54]

A similar pattern developed in New Brunswick where several Free Will Baptist groups came together to form a Christian Conference Church in 1832, later known as the Free Christian Baptist (1847), and still later (1898) as The Free Baptist General Conference. When finally the conferences of Free Baptists, both in New Brunswick and Nova Scotia, drew up constitutions, they were found to differ little from the constitution of the Convention or Regular Baptists, except that the former, despite their name, did not allow as much local autonomy as the latter.

As the Free Will Baptists abandoned an itinerant ministry and adopted a settled pastorate there was the inevitable need to make greater provision for the minister and his family, leading many of the leaders of the conferences to consider union with the Baptist Convention of the Maritimes. Such a union had first been considered in 1846 at the time of the formation of the Convention, but it was not until 1887 that negotiations really began in earnest, only to precipitate a "heated controversy over the doctrine of Holiness."[55] The holiness emphasis brought about the formation of the Primitive and Reformed Baptist churches, some persisting to this day in New Brunswick. Despite these new schisms, the negotiations continued and a basis of union set forth by a committee in 1887 was finally accepted by a joint conference meeting in Saint John, New Brunswick, in 1905.

This basis of union was an unusual document since it achieved the miracle of bringing into fraternal association the Regular Baptists who believed in unqualified election, a limited atonement and close communion with the Free Baptists who held the doctrine of a general atonement, free will and open communion. Not unnaturally it was put forth as a plan for uniting all Free Baptists of Canada into one national church; but when it was submitted to the Baptist Convention of Ontario and Quebec in 1908, the reaction from the latter was far from enthusiastic,[56] nevertheless, the "plan" continued to be discussed year after year at successive meetings of conventions across Canada, until at last in 1944 a representative committee of Baptists under the chairmanship of Professor Watson Kirkconnell drew up a constitution for a federal union acceptable to all conventions and leading to the formation of the Baptist Federation of Canada in the same year. This national organization represented a constituency of some 443,944 adherents, or double the number reported in the census of 1871. But in the earlier census the Baptists constituted 6.8 per cent of the population, whereas by 1941 they had dropped to 4.2 per cent, a clear indication that the constant internecine strife had militated against the growth of the Baptist community in Canada.

Two other denominations that began to organize on a territorial basis both before and after Confederation were the Congregational and Lutheran. Both these churches had very frustrating careers in the early days of settlements; the former, as we have seen, losing most of its members to the Baptists in the Maritimes, and to the Presbyterians in the Canadas; the latter to the Anglicans in both areas. Nevertheless, there were pockets of survival of the two throughout British North America.

Although a Congregational Church was organized at Frome in Upper Canada by Joseph Silcox in 1819, nevertheless Congregationalism hardly appears as distinct from Presbyterianism in the Canadas until the establishment by Richard Miles of Zion Church at Montreal in 1832; two years later another Zion Congregational Church was founded in Toronto. Its pastor, John Roaf, achieved "considerable eminence as an advocate of reform in the stormy period of Canadian politics"[57]; however, Zion Church in Toronto had a very brief career. The stronghold of Congregationalism in British North America, after its collapse in the Maritimes was in Montreal under the vigorous leadership of Henry Wilkes, who in 1836 succeeded Miles as the pastor of Zion Church. Arriving from Britain with a grant from the London Missionary Society, he immediately made a tour of visitation throughout Canada reorganizing old and forming new Congregational churches, assisting them financially from the grant at his disposal.[58] At the conclusion of his tour he took up residence in Montreal, where for half a century he played a leading role in the religious and social life of that city. His interests extended beyond his small congregation, as he early became an advocate of a united Protestant fellowship for social and missionary action. He was the driving spirit in the formation in 1854 of the Canada Foreign Missionary Society (an undenominational body), and a ministerial association embracing "nearly all the non-Anglican evangelical clergymen of the city."[59]

Congregationalism, however, continued to be Dr. Wilkes' primary concern. Along with his many other responsibilities he acted as head of the Congregational College (removed from Toronto to Montreal in 1836), where he trained ordinands for the several Congregational unions of British North America. These unions, formed "to promote evangelical religion in connection with the Congregational denomination" originated in the Maritimes in 1846 and were based upon the constitution of the Congregational union of England and Wales. In 1853 a similar union was entered into by the churches of Canada, paving the way for the Congregational union of Canada founded in 1906. Like the Baptist convention it was a very loose federation; its constitution included a declaration to the effect "That this Union is founded on a full recognition of the distinctive principles of Congregational Churches, namely, the Scriptural right of every separate church to maintain perfect independence in its government and administration. . . ." Its function to a large extent was "to cultivate brotherly affection" and "to obtain accurate statistical information relative to the Congregational Churches throughout the British American Provinces."[60] At the time of its formation the union was representative of about 28,504 Congregationalists, being 0.5 per cent of the total population of Canada.

By this time the Lutherans who had organized their first synod in Canada in 1861 were well on their way to becoming a major religion in Canada, having attained by 1901 a population of 94,110, or over three times the number of Congregationalists. Lutheran revival in Canada was due in no small measure to the initiative of the Evangelical Lutheran Synod of Pittsburgh, which began in 1850 a regular Canada mission,[61] resulting in the formation of the Canada Conference of Pittsburgh (1853), to be known after 1861 as the Evangelical Lutheran Synod of Canada.

Continuous history of Lutheranism in Canada begins in Nova Scotia with the arrival from New York of Frederick Schultz at Lunenburg in 1772, but the Lutherans did not make much headway in the Maritimes until 1876 when they were organized into a conference, at first allied to the Pittsburgh Synod. In 1903 the Evangelical Lutheran Synod of Nova Scotia was set up, embracing thirty-two congregations with a total membership of 7,184.[62] The very vigorous and very conservative Missouri Synod began work in Canada when John Adam Ernst organized in 1879 the Canada District of the Missouri Synod in Ontario. In 1923 it changed its name to the Ontario District of the Missouri Synod. This was the beginning of an extension of the work of several American synods across the northern border, until today there are in Canada six distinct Lutheran synods. But the story of the growth and development of Lutheranism with its diverse ethnic backgrounds is so closely identified with the movement of populations into western Canada, that it will be deferred for a later chapter in this book.

VII

While the churches of Canada were busily engaged in organizational activities there was an evident lessening of denominational rivalry;

it became customary at national gatherings for the larger bodies to send fraternal greetings to one another, when their meetings coincided. Nevertheless, the new spirit of "live and let live" was frequently interrupted when some of the churches seemed to deviate too far from the established Canadian pattern. Evangelical churchmen of all denominations found it difficult to remain neutral over the matter of high and low church, so fiercely debated within the Anglican communion; nor were they happy about the unitarian tendencies of some of their brethren. In 1845 there was formed in Montreal the Canadian Evangelical Alliance to combat both tractarianism and unitarianism; under its auspices ministers of different faiths shared the pulpit of St. James Methodist Church to preach on "the great evangelical tenets," but because of differences of opinion on these tenets the Alliance was short lived.[63]

Underlying this alliance was a latent anti-Romanism never far from the surface in most Protestant denominations, and very often made evident in the form of Protestant missions to French Canadians. A French Canadian Missionary Society was organized in 1839 "to inaugurate a comprehensive effort" for the evangelization of French Roman Catholics.[64] It continued active for about forty years, but finally collapsed through lack of support as the churches became too much engrossed in their own denominational missions to the French to continue contributions to an undenominational society. One of the most notable of these denominational ventures was the Grande Ligne Mission founded in 1836 by Madame Henrietta Feller, whose romantic career as a missionary and teacher in French Canada has been told in great detail by J. M. Cramp in his story of the mission. Madame Feller looked to the public at large for financial assistance, but her chief support came from Baptist missionary societies both in Canada and the United States. The Grande Ligne mission seems to have been the most successful of all the missions to the French Canadians but even its support was not always secure. Dr. Cramp quotes from an article by J. N. W. Williams, one of the missioners, written in 1868, as follows: "The present state of the mission is a state of poverty and decline, while huge structures are reared like formidable fortresses all around us here to protect the interests of the corrupted Christianity which the Grande Ligne Mission and similar institutions are destined to overthrow."[65]

One of those similar institutions was an Anglican College at Sabrevois, founded in 1847 by the wife of Major William Christie as a teaching mission to French Canadian boys.[66] It also suffered from lack of financial support, though it had behind it an association known as "The Colonial Church and School Society for the Diocese of Montreal," incorporated in 1854 for the purpose of evangelizing the French. The work at first prospered and the Society expanded its activities to include a school for Indian boys at St. Francis; but it was never able to get its work officially accepted by the synod of the diocese of Montreal. The schools were later transferred to Montreal (1872), but were discontinued in 1911 when it was decided by the synod of Montreal that no further attempt should be made to proselytize among the Roman Catholics.[67]

Through the conversion of an Indian Chief, Joseph Onesakenarah, who also served as a parish priest for the Roman Catholics at the Indian reservation at Oka, the Methodists became involved in a very acrimonious mission to Roman Catholic Indians.   After his entrance into the Methodist Church Chief Joseph, who had also acted as secretary for the Sulpicians, immediately entered into a land dispute at Oka with his former employers.   The quarrel became intensified when Chief Joseph succeeded in getting a Methodist mission established at Oka (1869) under the direction of Xavier Rivet.   Several times the Chief found himself in jail and the mission itself became greatly depleted by the migration of large numbers of the Protestant Indians to Ontario.[68]

The Presbyterian mission to the French Roman Catholics under the direction of a Board of French Evangelization had an equally stormy career.   The work was first started in 1850 in a Mission House at Montreal; the following year a French Presbyterian Church, l'Église du Sauveur, was opened with A. B. Cruchet as pastor.[69]   In 1863 the Board received a remarkable recruit in the person of Father Charles Chiniquy, a former Roman Catholic priest who had led a French colony from Quebec to Kankakee County, Illinois.   Here he decided to abandon his Roman Catholic orders to enter the ministry of the Presbyterian Church; a large proportion of his flock followed his example. Shortly after his defection from the Roman Catholic Church he joined the Board of French Evangelization in Montreal and began to lecture on the evils of Catholicism, travelling widely throughout Canada and even beyond, creating riots and tumults wherever he went.[70]

Missions of this nature were disapproved by many Protestants, including some Presbyterians.   They were considered unnecessary irritants leading to a widening of the breach between the two races committed by a federation pact to work harmoniously together in creating a bi-cultural nation.

The Protestants themselves were not wholly free from similar "fringe sniping"; "queer sects" as they were called, were continually making inroads into the preserves of the new territorial churches, some of them originating within the framework of the churches themselves. Hence they could be regarded as heresies rather than sects. Groups like the Disciples of Christ were closely related to the Scotch Baptists in Canada; allied to them were the Campbellites who remained a critical group within the Baptist community as did the Brethren of Christ and the Christadelphians.

Irvingites, long a thorn in the side of the Methodists, were joined by the Mormons and Millerites in the middle of the nineteenth century, in harassing the former sectarian Methodists now settling down into a conventional parochial type of church life. Nevertheless, these new groups, as S. D. Clark has shown in his detailed study of the sects of Canada, "marked the final end of the great waves of religious revival which had been sweeping over the rural countryside of Central Canada and the Maritime Provinces for a half or three-quarters of a century."[71] Their day was not yet, as the great weight of social influences operating in Canada was towards the building of a unified nation and the religious response to this challenge was to create national or territorial churches.

REFERENCES

1. S. D. Clark, *Church and Sect in Canada*, *op. cit.*, p. 270.

2. J. Castell Hopkins, *Progress of Canada in the Nineteenth Century* (Toronto, 1900), p. 357.

3. *Vide* H. A. Scott, "The Roman Catholic Church East of the Great Lakes," Shortt and Doughty, *Canada and Its Provinces*, *op. cit.*, vol. XI, p. 95.

4. The population statistics throughout this chapter, unless otherwise stated, are taken from *Census of Canada 1870-71* (Ottawa, 1876), vol. IV, containing "the summaries of Census taken at different periods, in and for the territories now constituting the British North American Provinces" or from the *Ninth Census of Canada, 1951* (Ottawa, 1953), vol. I, table 37, containing "numerical and percentage distribution of the population by religious denominations" from 1871 to 1915.

5. *Vide* H. A. Scott, *op. cit.*, p. 101.

6. R. W. Harris, *The Catholic Church in the Niagara Peninsula* (Toronto, 1895), p. 306.

7. A good account of the origin and purpose of the Christian Brothers is found in W. J. Battersby, *De La Salle, A Pioneer of Modern Education* (London, New York and Toronto, 1949), pp. 48-124.

8. Thomas Rolph, *A Descriptive and Statistical Account of Canada* (London, 1841, 2nd ed.), pp. 268-269.

9. H. A. Scott, *op. cit.*, p. 82.

10. For a sympathetic account of Bourget's conversion to ultramontanism *vide* Léon Pouliot, S. J., *La Réaction Catholique de Montréal, 1840-1841* (Montreal, 1942), *passim*.

11. J. M. McMullen, *The History of Canada from Its First Discovery to the Present Time* (Brockville, Ont., 3rd ed., 1892, 2 vols.), vol. II, p. 228.

12. For a critical account of the rise of the new school of ultramontanism *vide* C. Lindsey, *Rome in Canada* (Toronto, 1877), p. 158 *et seq.*

13. *Dernière Correspondance entre S. E. Le Cardinal Barnabo et L'Hon. M. Dessaulles* (Montreal, 1871). A discussion on the aims and purposes of the *Institut Canadien* (a copy in Divinity Hall Library, McGill University).

14. *Vide History of the Guibord Case* (Montreal, "Witness," 1875), p. 122.

15. *Mandements Lettres Pastorales et Circulaires des Evêques de Québec*, *op. cit.*, vol. IV, pp. 320-336.

16. H. A. Scott, *op. cit.*, p. 102. The Canada Census for 1911 gives 2,841,881; 39.4 per cent of the total population.

17. *Vide* R. W. Church, *The Oxford Movement, Twelve Years, 1833-1845* (London, 1891), pp. 82-83.

18. A. N. Bethune, *Memoir of the Right Reverend John Strachan*, *op. cit.*, p. 229.

19. W. Q. Ketchum, *The Life and Work of the Most Reverend John Medley*, *op. cit.*, p. 64. *Vide* also H. W. Tucker, *Memoir of the Life and Episcopate of Edward Feild, D.D., Bishop of Newfoundland, 1844-1876* (London, 1877), pp. 128-129.

20. Fennings Taylor, *The Last Three Bishops Appointed by the Crown for the Anglican Church of Canada* (Montreal, 1869), p. 57.

21. A. W. Mountain, *A Memoir of George Jehoshaphat Mountain, D.D., D.C.L.* (Montreal, 1866). The complete declaration is given from pp. 292-299.

22. F. Taylor, *op. cit.*, p. 94.

23. *Triennial Visitation of the Lord Bishop of Toronto and Proceedings of the Church Synod of the Diocese of Toronto, October 12 & 13, 1853* (Toronto, 1853), p. 7.

24. A. N. Bethune, *op. cit.*, p. 275.

25. J. I. Cooper, *Irish Immigration and the Canadian Church before the Middle of the 19th Century* (*The Journal of the Canadian Church Historical Society, Toronto, 1955*), vol. II, p. 15.

26. The letters patent is printed in the *Journal of the Proceedings of the Second Provincial Synod of the United Church of England and Ireland in Canada* (Montreal, 1862), pp. 6-16.

27. *Ibid.*, *vide* appendix to the *Journal*, pp. 83-89.

28. *Journal of the Proceedings of the Provincial Synod etc.* (Montreal, 1865), p. 34.

29. W. Gregg, *Short History of the Presbyterian Church in the Dominion of Canada* (Toronto, 1892), p. 35.

30. Robert Buchanan, *The Ten Years Conflict: Being the History of the Disruption of the Church of Scotland* (Glasgow, 1857, 2 vols.). *Vide* especially vol. I, ch. VII, pp. 296-338, "The Fruits of Evangelical Ascendency."

31. Charles W. Gordon, "The Presbyterian Church and Its Missions," *Canada and Its Provinces*, *op. cit.*, p. 273.

32. R. F. Burns, *The Life and Times of Rev. Robert Burns, D.D.* (Toronto, 1872), p. 186.
33. R. Campbell, *A History of the Scotch Presbyterian Church, St. Gabriel Street, Montreal* (Montreal, 1887), p. 391.
34. W. Gregg, *op. cit.*, p. 159.
35. *Philosophy in Canada, a Symposium*, ed. by J. A. Irving (Toronto, 1952), p. 10.
36. J. F. McCurdy, *Life and Work of D. J. MacDonnell* (Toronto, 1897), p. 257.
37. Grant and Hamilton, *George Monro Grant* (Toronto, 1905), p. 37.
38. *Ibid.*, p. 81.
39. W. Gregg, *op. cit.*, p. 189.
40. *Ibid.*, p. 191.
41. J. E. Sanderson, *The First Century of Methodism in Canada* (Toronto, 1910, 2 vols.), vol. II, p. 16.
42. *Ibid.*, vol. II, p. 16.
43. J. Carrol, *Case and His Cotemporaries, op. cit.*, vol. V, p. 3.
44. T. W. Smith, *History of the Methodist Church Within the Territories Embraced in the late Conference of Eastern British America* (Halifax, 1890, 2 vols.), vol. II, p. 444.
45. *Ibid.*, p. 447.
46. *Vide* F. W. Macdonald, *The Life of William Morley Punshon, LL.D.* (London, 1887), pp. 310-360.
47. *Minutes of the Forty Eighth Annual Conference of the Wesleyan Methodist Church in Canada* (Toronto, 1871), p. 117.
48. C. B. Sissons, *op. cit.*, vol. II, p. 610.
49. *Journal of Proceedings of the First General Conference of the Methodist Church in Canada* (Toronto, 1874), pp. 21-27.
50. *Memoir of Daniel Arthur McGregor, Late Principal of Toronto Baptist College:* (published by the Alumni Association of the Toronto Baptist College, 2nd ed., Toronto, 1891), p. 156.
51. Quoted from Professor J. E. Wells by C. C. McLaurin, *Pioneering in Western Canada: A Story of the Baptists* (Calgary, 1939), p. 41.
52. T. A. Higgins, *The Life of John Mackett Cramp, D.D.* (Montreal, 1887), p. 98.
53. E. M. Saunders, *History of the Baptists of the Maritime Provinces, op. cit.*, p. 369.
54. G. E. Levy, *The Baptists of the Maritime Provinces 1753-1946, op. cit.*, p. 240.
55. *Ibid.*, p. 263.
56. *Ibid.*, p. 288.
57. R. J. Hutcheon, "Miscellaneous Religious Bodies in Canada," *Canada and Its Provinces, op. cit.*, p. 382.
58. *Canadian Congregational Year Book for 1877-8* (Toronto, 1877), p. 29.
59. J. Wood, *Memoir of Henry Wilkes, D.D., LL.D., His Life and Times* (Montreal, 1887), pp. 109-159.
60. *The Congregational Year Book* (Toronto, 1908), p. 23.
61. *Lutheran Cyclopedia*, ed. by Erwin L. Lueker (Saint Louis, Missouri, 1954), p. 161.
62. *Ibid.*, p. 160.
63. *Vide* J. Wood, *op. cit.*, pp. 127-128.
64. *Ibid.*, p. 108.

65. J. M. Cramp, *A Memoir of Madame Feller* (London, n.d.), p. 254.
66. The story of Sabrevois College is found to a large extent in the *Minute Book of the Ladies Committee of Sabrevois Mission* (L'Église du Redempteur, Montreal).
67. *Vide Proceedings of the Fifty-Third Annual Synod of the Diocese of Montreal* (Montreal, 1912), p. 42.
68. *Vide* F. C. Stephenson, *One Hundred Years of Canadian Methodist Missions 1824-1924* (Toronto, 1925, 2 vols.), vol. I, pp. 132-133.
69. *Vide* J. T. McNeil, *The Presbyterian Church in Canada 1875-1925* (Toronto, 1925), p. 99.
70. *Vide* C. Chiniquy, *Fifty Years in the Church of Rome* (Montreal, n.d.), pp. 822-829.
71. S. D. Clark, *op. cit.*, p. 328.

XVI

The Churches and Confederation

CONFEDERATION HAS been described as "the child of political deadlock."[1] Fundamental to this deadlock were the racial and religious antipathies which seemingly had paralyzed the functioning of representative government in the Canadas. Nevertheless, there arose at this time in both French- and English-speaking Canada a desire for nationhood so strong that even religious controversy was stilled in its presence.[2] Such a desire had for some time been freely expressed at Montreal among the English-speaking section of the city, often coupled with a threat to seek annexation with the United States. There was also in Toronto a "Canada First" group under the leadership of W. A. Foster, expressing a similar sentiment and whose growing resentment at colonial status was startlingly expressed by Edward Blake in a famous "Aurora Speech," when he described Canadians as "four millions of Britons who are not free."[3] In Canada East the same thought was put forth by Joseph Cauchon in a much publicized brochure (1865) in which he said: "No, we do not always wish to remain in the colonial state—we must be one day a nation, since that is necessarily our destiny and the end of our aspirations."[4]

Union of all the self-governing colonies in British North America was seen as a preliminary step towards nationhood, but even then Canada would remain small both in population and in wealth in comparison to her expanding neighbour to the south. There was one obvious way that this disparity might be overcome—by the opening up of the northwest to colonization under the control of a federal government at Ottawa; western expansion also was seen by some as a means of reconciling Canada's two cultures through enlarged boundaries and greater national responsibilities. Such a prospect was first put forth by Georges-Étienne Cartier in a speech advocating the assumption by the Canadian government of the administration of the Hudson's Bay Company's territories:

228

"Then," he said, "our Canada will extend as it did in the days when it was explored on all sides by our Fathers of the French race from the Atlantic to the Pacific. We will restore the national boundaries as the historical emergencies gradually are straightened out. From ocean to ocean a new life will reanimate all this part of North America."[5] After accompanying Sandford Fleming's survey party to the Pacific coast, George Monro Grant wrote a book, *Ocean to Ocean*, to assure the Canadian public that Cartier's vision of a new and reanimated Canada through the acquisition of the north-west was fully justified. What he had seen on his trip led him to affirm: "Thank God, we have a country. It is not our poverty of land or sea that shall ever urge us to be traitors."[6] Although a large portion of this book is taken up with a detailed description of the national resources of the new land Canada had acquired, Grant as his wont was, closes his survey in a more idealistic vein: "But the destiny of a country," he warned, "depends not on its material resources. It depends on the character of its people." Here, too, he found full ground for confidence. "We in everything 'are sprung of earth's first blood, have titles manifold.' We come of a race that never counted the number of its foes, nor the number of its friends, when freedom, loyalty, or God was concerned."[7]

Ocean to Ocean helped Canadians in no small measure to emerge from the universal pessimism that seized upon the country in the great depression of the 'seventies by creating a feeling of national destiny, which survived the religious and racial discords that continued with even greater intensity after the federation pact of 1867.

I

During the first federal election campaign in the newly created nation, leaders of the churches vied with one another in their support of the coalition government that had achieved Confederation; and it would seem doubtful that the administration of Sir John A. Macdonald would have survived its first appeal to the people if it had not been for the churches' intervention into the political field. In both Quebec and Nova Scotia there were strong Liberal parties determined to secure the repeal of the British North America Act; nor was Ontario very happy about the separate school law that had been practically forced upon her in the old union legislature by the votes of the Quebec members.

In Quebec there was great suspicion among the Liberals and nationalists that the French minority in the new Dominion was now in a less strategic position to retain its cultural privileges than in the old province of Canada. Even young Wilfrid Laurier, who was to become the great prophet of Canada's national destiny, was at first hostile to the prospect of Confederation, declaring it "false in its conception, iniquitous, immoral and cruel in its details."[8] But when some of the more fervent nationalists began to push their resistance to violent extremes all the bishops of the province issued mandements supporting the new constitution. Archbishop Baillargeon, who had been closely consulted by Cartier during the negotiations for Confederation, sternly rebuked the agitators, declaring: "Before Confederation had been decreed by the Imperial Parliament, and while it was a project it was permitted us, without doubt to discuss and even to use all possible means to prevent it from becoming law . . . But today discussion is no longer possible; the law is promulgated; the work of authority must be respected."[9] As a result of this clerical support the coalition government gained an overwhelming victory in the province of Quebec in the first federal election.

Egerton Ryerson also had played his part in contributing to the victory in Quebec by working out the separate school act in consultation with Archbishop Lynch of Toronto and with government officials in Quebec.[10] It was the embodiment of the principle of this Act into the British North America Act that made the Quebec hierarchy enthusiastic supporters of Confederation.

Not only in Quebec, however, was Ryerson's influence felt. Like Archbishop Baillargeon he deemed it incumbent upon him to take an active role in the first federal election. In support of the Liberal-Conservative government under the leadership of Sir John A. Macdonald he wrote an election pamphlet entitled, *The New Canadian Dominion: Dangers and Duties of the People in regard to Their Government.* How much this pamphlet contributed to the government's victory in Ontario (not as sweeping as in Quebec) it is difficult to say, but it did show that Ryerson, in the words of his biographer, "had read the conscience of the province."[11]

Two other prominent churchmen who took an active part in the first momentous federal election were Archbishop Thomas Connolly and George Monro Grant, but with less satisfactory results than that of their colleagues in Quebec and Ontario. Both of them spoke publicly in support of the coalition government; Connolly also wrote a long letter to the *Morning Chronicle*, Halifax, setting forth the thesis that a union of the provinces is a necessary defence "against an ambitious expansive neighbour, emerging from the civil war";[12] this letter was given wide publicity throughout Canada and tracts from it were contained in *The Union*, a leaflet issued in Hamilton for distribution among Roman Catholics to win support for the government.[13]   Both Connolly and Grant were prophets for Confederation "not without honour" save in their own province of Nova Scotia; but even here they paved the way for an ultimate reconciliation of Nova Scotia with the rest of Canada, as was recognized during the election by one of the leaders of the anti-confederate forces, who is reported to have said: "We shall win this immediate election, win easily, but we shall lose in the end." When asked, "How so?" he replied, "The men with ideas and ideals are against us.   Look at Archbishop Connolly, and that young Presbyterian minister, young Grant, in Halifax.   Those are the men of the future, and they are all against us."[14]

The close personal friendship between Connolly and Grant was not without its ultimate effect on the cultural relations of Quebec and Ontario, for when Grant became principal of Queen's University and somewhat of a Canadian oracle he constantly supported the Roman Catholics on the separate school issue, as Connolly had convinced him that if Roman Catholics were permitted separate schools there would be "no more of Catholic and Protestant in our political fights and then indeed we would have a country that will last in spite of all opposition."[15] To have such a country Grant was willing to allow the Catholics separate schools, even though his own personal preference was for a more unified system of state education.

II

Needless to say, this compromising attitude was the exception rather than rule in the first days of the new nation, and the separate school issue upon which both Protestant and Catholic felt so deeply soon put the Confederation *entente* to its most severe test.   The re-emergence of the school issue came rather unexpectedly in New Brunswick where the Liberals under the leadership of a prominent Methodist layman, George King, undertook in 1870 to provide their province with a provincial school system comparable with that of the other provinces of Canada. Under a confessional system, it was apparent that New Brunswick's schools were of an inferior standard to those of the public school systems prevailing in Ontario and Nova Scotia. One of the most enthusiastic advocates of a provincial system was Lemuel Wilmot, a Liberal reformer, who became the first lieutenant governor of the province. Immediately he threw the full weight of his influence behind George King; the latter had in 1870 formed with George Hatheway a coalition government which came to power with the "firm resolve . . . to obtain direct taxation and free schools."[16] In this resolve it was supported by spokesmen for the Methodist, Baptist and Presbyterian church schools; these schools had been established in defiance of the Anglican monopoly of education, but the churches were now anxious that they should be integrated into a unified public school system.

The Roman Catholics, on the other hand, had been greatly pleased with the confessional school system that had evolved in New Brunswick, particularly as it allowed them with little interference to conduct French language schools among the Acadians. Bishop Sweeny in a bitter sermon at Saint John denounced non-sectarian schools as irreligious and immoral; Protestant feelings were further acerbated when a Roman Catholic paper, the *Morning Freeman*, called the governor "Pope Wilmot" and referred to his council members as "Methodist Cardinals."[17] Despite Roman Catholic protests throughout Canada, accompanied with a warning that Confederation itself was being endangered, the Free School Act was passed by the New Brunswick legislature (1871), and the federal government now found itself involved in the first of a series of constitutional crises over separate schools. When the Roman Catholics of New Brunswick failed to get the Privy Council to declare the school act unconstitutional they turned to the Canadian parliament for the remedial legislation provided by the B.N.A. Act to protect minority school rights. Though the appeal was strongly supported by the Quebec hierarchy, Cartier himself urged his compatriots not to press for such legislation lest a direct intervention into a field assigned to the provinces might some day tempt "the Protestants of Quebec to invoke the intervention of Ottawa to modify the Quebec school system."[18]

Fortunately, the bitter resentments arising out of New Brunswick's suppression of separate schools were greatly reduced when the King government negotiated a "gentlemen's agreement" somewhat similar to one that had been worked out in Nova Scotia, where Roman Catholics were left undisturbed with certain schools in which religious education was carried on outside school hours.

III

The more serious repercussions from this bitter controversy occurred not in New Brunswick but in the Province of Quebec; here it gave a renewed vigour to an ultramontane party, which since the proclamation by the Pope in 1864 of a Syllabus of Errors, condemning all things liberal, had been growing in political influence, and was creating a serious tension between English- and French-speaking Canada. Even after 1864, however, the ultramontanes who favoured a complete isolation of Quebec from the rest of Canada, had been held in check by the liberal elements within the Roman Church, particularly by the hierarchy at Quebec and by the Sulpicians at Montreal. But the failure of George-Étienne Cartier, the trusted adviser of this liberal church party, to obtain remedial legislation for the Catholic minority in New Brunswick had greatly undermined his leadership in Quebec, and prompted Bishop Bourget to organize the *Programme Catholique* to work within the Conservative party for ultramontane legislation. The *Programmists* put forth a manifesto urging all Catholic electors to give their votes only to men who pledged themselves to full allegiance to Roman Catholic doctrines and were ready to bring about any changes in the laws demanded by the church, particularly in matters relating to marriage, education and the erection of parishes.[19] This manifesto was publicly endorsed by Bishop Bourget and by his most enthusiastic colleague Bishop Lafléche at Three Rivers. Archbishop Taschereau, Baillargeon's successor, repudiated the *Programme* as did also the bishops of Rimouski and St. Hyacinthe, but this opposition was suddenly halted by a rebuke from Cardinal Patrizi representing the Propaganda. Bishop Bourget who had enthusiastically greeted the declaration of papal infallibility in 1870 and had also, at the same time, received from the Pope a decree outlawing the liberal *Institut Canadien*[20] was now encouraged by Rome to defy his superior at Quebec. Just before the provincial election (1875) he issued a pastoral informing Catholic voters not only "who are the candidates for whom you ought to vote on account of their good principles" but also instructing them "as to who are those who do not merit your confidence." Among the latter were those "who support doctrines which are condemned by the Syllabus; who oppose all intervention by the Pope, Bishop or Priests, in the affairs of the Governments, as if these Governments were not subject to the principles that God has revealed to the Church for the good government of the people. . . ."[21] In another pastoral issued during the federal election of 1876 Bourget outlined a simple formula for creating the good society by declaring, "each one of you can and ought to say in the interior of his soul, 'I hear my Curé; my Curé hears the Bishop; the Bishop hears the Pope; and the Pope hears our Lord Jesus Christ, who aids with his Holy Spirit to render them infallible on the teaching and government of His Church'."[22]

In this same year, however, the Liberals struck back strongly by protesting the election of several Conservative members because of the undue pressure exerted by the priests during the campaign. One particularly glaring incident was the election of Hector Langevin, the brother of the bishop of Rimouski, whose case was heard before Judge Routhier. Routhier summarily dismissed the charge of "undue influence" by asserting "that the clergy were immune from questioning or control by the State of their actions on such moral questions as voting."[23] An appeal to the new supreme court of Canada reversed this judgment and declared the election void—a unanimous decision rendered by Justice Taschereau, the brother of the archbishop of Quebec. By this time the papacy, alarmed over the growing discontent throughout Canada at the activities of the *Programmists* sent an apostolic delegate, Bishop Conroy, to Quebec to inquire into the divisions among the Catholics. Bishop Conroy came to the conclusion that the ultramontane attack against the Liberal party had gone too far and he condemned unreservedly clerical interference in political elections, pointing out that the Pope in condemning liberalism did not mean to condemn any political party.[24]

Conroy's visit to some extent put a damper upon clerical influence in the elections, but it did not bring to an end what has been designated the "holy war" between the liberal and ultramontane factions within the church itself, particularly over university policy. In Montreal there was constant agitation for a university free from "taint" of liberalism attaching to Laval University.

Though Archbishop Taschereau seemed at times to have capitulated to ultramontane principles, particularly when he issued a mandement making it "a mortal sin for the faithful"[25] to read the *Montreal Witness*, he ultimately came to be regarded as the champion of Canadian unity and a bulwark against the more extreme policies of the *Programmists* and their successors the *Castors* (Beavers), a new Catholic party dedicated to weeding out liberals from the educational life of Quebec.[26]   When in 1886 Taschereau was made the first Canadian cardinal, the ultramontane cause received its most serious blow, for by this time the Archbishop was considered a sound liberal.   According to his own testimony he had in his earlier days looked upon toleration as a weakness but subsequent experience had taught him "that when properly exercised, toleration is a force."[27] In other words, the new cardinal had developed into a statesman who now recognized that only through "give and take" could Confederation be preserved.

Confederation also had enlarged the responsibilities of the church in Quebec to include its co-religionists in the provinces of Canada; it had led to a rediscovery of the Acadians and their need of Quebec's support in their struggle for cultural survival; it had also led to the discovery of the *métis* and the north-west and of its obligation to extend "Canadian civilization into those immense regions."[28] These larger responsibilities of leadership Taschereau felt could only be adequately discharged within the framework of Confederation, not simply as a sullen obstructive minority but as a co-operating partner with English-speaking Canadians in all the affairs of Canadian public life.

It was this larger view that Wilfrid Laurier had attained after his first youthful outburst against Confederation.   In a famous speech in 1876, which, it has been said, made him prime minister of Canada in 1896, he addressed the isolationists as follows: "You wish to organize a Catholic party.   But have you not considered that, if you have the misfortune to succeed, you will draw down upon your country calamities of which it is impossible to foresee the consequences? You wish to organize all Catholics into one party, without other bond, without other basis, than a common religion; but have you not reflected that, by that very fact, you will organize the Protestant population as a single party, and that then, instead of the peace and harmony now prevailing between the different elements of the Canadian population, you will throw open the door to war, a religious war, the most terrible of all wars?"[29]

Laurier's fear that Protestants would be provoked into forming a single party was fully justified; at the time he uttered his warning there was already in being in Montreal a Protestant Defence Association, organized in opposition to the *Programmists*. Sir Alexander Galt, long regarded as the Protestant strategist in Quebec, though he did not join the association, gave it moral support. Nevertheless, he recognized that it was just as dangerous for the good of the country for the Protestant minority in Quebec to isolate itself from the Roman Catholic majority, as it was for Quebec to isolate itself from the rest of Canada. Consequently he wrote a pamphlet entitled *Civil Liberty in Lower Canada* in which he appealed for both Roman Catholics and Protestants to range themselves on the side of freedom. He wrote: "With a plain and unmistakable declaration on the part of the Protestants that they will, equally for their Roman Catholic fellow-citizens, as for themselves, resist the encroachments of the Church upon the State, it may be possible to arrest the arrogant course of Bishop Bourget and his confrères."[30] In furtherance of this object he wrote a second and larger pamphlet on *Church and State*, again appealing "to all good citizens, whether Catholic or Protestant, to resist the present attempt of the Roman Catholic Hierarchy to control the Local Government of Quebec."[31] As neither of these appeals seemed to have achieved very much, Galt wrote to Sir John A. Macdonald expressing his fears for the future of freedom in Quebec because of the close alliance of the Conservative party with the *Programmists*, to which he received the rather unhelpful reply: "Use the priests . . . for the present election, but be ready to fight them in the Dominion Parliament."[32]

After the election Galt invaded the province of Ontario in search of allies in his struggle with Bourget. He now pressed boldly for a new course of action which was to put pressure upon the leaders of both political parties to "lay aside their mutual jealousies, and unite in a declaration to the Hierarchy, that their interference must absolutely cease, or that all would unite in legislation to check it effectually."[33] Galt's speeches in Ontario led Archbishop Lynch of Toronto to give a very closely reasoned address on the Roman Catholic point of view on the relations of church and state; at the same time he tried to assure Protestants that the Roman Catholic Church was not inimical to political freedom. The speech received public commendation from Galt and helped to remove a great deal of the religious tension that was building up in the Canadian parliament, threatening to produce the same sort of political deadlock that had preceded Confederation.

Shortly after Archbishop Lynch's speech, one of the younger leaders of the English-speaking group in the Conservative party of Quebec issued a pamphlet in which he pointed out that the Roman Catholics were not infringing upon Protestant privileges in Quebec and that with regard to quarrels in the French Canadian family the best interest of

Protestants "will be secured by preserving that position of neutrality which has hitherto marked their conduct."[34]   Galt, on the whole, was inclined to agree with his younger colleague and not long after this the Defence Alliance ceased to exist.

IV

Not so in Ontario.   Here an Equal Rights Association had been formed in opposition to Archbishop Lynch's Catholic League; it was felt that the League by its support of Sir Oliver Mowat's government was gaining undue privileges for the Roman Catholic Church.[35]   Under the persuasive eloquence of D'Alton McCarthy the Equal Rights Association began to interest itself in Roman Catholic encroachments throughout Canada, and to regard Ontario as the protector of Protestant rights in all parts of the Dominion.   Soon the members of the Equal Rights Association became concerned over the fact that Ontario, the champion of Protestant freedom in Canada, was fostering within her own provincial boundaries, not only separate religious schools, but French language schools as well.   A particularly bitter attack was made upon the latter by D'Alton McCarthy, who had become seriously alarmed over the danger of racialism to national unity.   As racialism, he felt, was being fostered in the separate schools of Ontario, he launched a vigorous attack upon them.   "With the Separate School Law," he declared, "there is but one thing to be done, there is but one amendment that can be satisfactory, and that amendment is to repeal the different clauses that have been passed ..."   Forgetting for a moment his abhorrence of racialism he made a racial appeal to his British audience: "Let us see that our Protestant money," he declaimed, "is not, against our will, diverted to the separate schools . . . We want no treason taught in our public schools.   We want the history of England fairly written, so that our children may have some admiration for the great old land."[36]   If McCarthy was not indulging in racialism he was proclaiming an imperialism just as unpopular in French-speaking Quebec as French nationalism was in Ontario.

The Equal Rights Association's agitation against the danger of French racialism led to the promulgation in 1911 by the Ontario government of Regulation 17, which placed severe restrictions upon French language schools.   Regulation 17 was bitterly resented in Quebec and no doubt contributed much to cool Quebec's ardour for the Allied cause during the First World War.[37]

Be that as it may, extremists both in Ontario and Quebec during the 'eighties seemed determined to avail themselves of every incident to acerbate tensions to the breaking point. The clamour in Ontario from the Equal Rights Association, now firmly allied with the Orange Order, for the execution of Louis Riel, in revenge for his execution of Thomas Scott in 1870, was matched by Quebec's compensation of $400,000 to the Jesuits for the loss of their estates after the British Conquest. McCarthy added fresh bitterness to the religious quarrel by carrying his crusade to the west where he helped to persuade the government of Manitoba to pass an act in 1890 abolishing separate schools of the French-speaking minority,[38] thus raising for a second time the most contentious issue in Canadian national life.

It was at this low point in the political life of Canada that Wilfrid Laurier, now leader of the federal Liberal party, decided to attempt to bridge the gap between the two races, by supporting Manitoba's right to frame her own school system, but at the same time to plead with the province for "a tenderness towards minority scruples."   In pursuit of a common patriotism he invaded Ontario and won the hearts of Orangemen with his plea for "an inclusive rather than a hyphenated Canadianism,"[39] thus forestalling the formation of a predominantly anti-Catholic government at Ottawa.

V

Though Laurier succeeded during his fifteen years as prime minister of Canada in achieving marvels "in bridging the gap" between French- and English-speaking populations, nevertheless, the ancient fears and prejudices, symbolized in the terms "papist" and "heretic" remained, and prevented the development of any true cordiality between the two peoples. The French Canadian clergy remained convinced that there is in Protestantism a spirit of anarchy, corrupting to all good social institutions; they even opposed, for example, any mingling of Protestants and Catholics in labour unions, feeling that such collaboration would destroy the social homogeneity of interests that should prevail in such an organization.[40]

On the other hand, the Protestant minority in Quebec, try as it might, could never be rid of the feeling expressed by Sir A. T. Galt, that Roman Catholic dogmas "leave no common standing-ground, as fellow citizens for those who are in, and those who are out of the pale of the Roman Church," and they always remained under the fear that the Church of Rome would, whenever opportunity provided, "grasp the civil government as a means of compelling obedience to their dogmas."[41] Consequently the Protestant Churches for the most part refused to abandon their missions among the French Canadians, being convinced of an obligation to free Canada from an ever present threat of Roman dominance. An outstanding spokesman for this point of view was the first principal of the Presbyterian College at Montreal, Dr. D. H. McVicar, who never wearied of urging the necessity of "French Evangelization." In seeking support for his favourite mission he warned his Protestant compatriots that the Church of Rome "viewed in reference to its rich endowments, thorough organization, increasing political influence, growing ultramontanism, and especially in reference to the strong hold which her unscriptural dogmas and idolatrous practices have upon her adherents, should alarm and arouse all to the serious consequences to us and to our children, which history shows to result from such power and influence as well as to excite deeper sympathy for our beloved fellow-subjects more immediately under her sway."[42]

Not all Protestants shared his pessimistic view. George Monro Grant was optimistic enough to hope that "the Head of the Church will find a way of uniting the two great historic Confessions of Christianity, that have so long stood face to face as enemies, in a church of the future grander than any existing church." To which he added as an expression of his sincere friendship towards French Canadians: "Who that has once sailed up the St. Lawrence from Quebec, in the daylight, can help having it borne in upon him that there is there, in the very centre of our country, a Christian civilization that is not of our type, but that is altogether beautiful from some points of view."[43]

REFERENCES

1. Goldwin Smith, quoted by Sir John Willison in *The Federation of Canada 1867-1917*, by several authors (Toronto, 1917), p. 41.
2. *Vide* O. D. Skelton, *The Life and Times of Sir Alexander Galt* (Toronto, 1920), p. 444.
3. *Ibid.*, p. 446.
4. Honoré Mercier, *L'Avenir du Canada* (Montreal, 1893), p. 16.
5. Quoted by Thomas Chapais, *Cours d'Histoire du Canada* (Quebec, 1934), vol. VIII, p. 212.

6. G. M. Grant, *Ocean to Ocean* (Toronto, 1877), p. 363.

7. *Ibid.*

8. Quoted by Robert Rumilly, *Mgr. La Flèche et Son Temps* (Montreal, n.d.), p. 37.

9. *Mandements . . . des Evêques de Québec, op. cit.*, vol. IV, p. 580.

10. C. B. Sissons, *Egerton Ryerson: His Life and Letters, op. cit.*, vol. II, pp. 465-470.

11. *Ibid.*, p. 553.

12. F. J. Wilson, *The Most Reverend Thomas L. Connolly* (reprinted from the Annual Report of the Canadian Catholic Historical Association, 1943-1944), p. 6.

13. *Ibid.*

14. Quoted by Grant and Hamilton, *George Monro Grant, op. cit.*, p. 103.

15. F. J. Wilson, *op. cit.*, p. 8.

16. J. B. Lynham, *Educational Institutions in New Brunswick 1830-1871* (an unpublished thesis, McGill University, 1947), p. 250.

17. *Ibid.*, p. 259.

18. L. Groulx, *La Confederation Canadienne* (Montreal, 1918), p. 180.

19. R. Rumilly, *op. cit.*, p. 60.

20. *Vide supra*, p. 205.

21. Quoted by A. T. Galt, *Church and State* (Montreal, 1876), p. 22.

22. *Ibid.*, p. 23.

23. *Vide* Mason Wade, *The French Canadians 1760-1945* (Toronto, 1955), p. 367.

24. *Ibid.*, p. 369.

25. *Mandements . . . des Evêques de Québec* (nouvelle serie, Quebec, 1899), vol. I, p. 273.

26. *Vide* M. Wade, *op. cit.*, pp. 376-377.

27. Quoted by Oliver Mowat in *Men of the Day; A Canadian Portrait Gallery*, ed. by Louis H. Taché (Montreal, 1894), p. 137.

28. T. Chapais, *op. cit.*, vol. VIII, p. 212.

29. V. Barthe, *Wilfrid Laurier on the Platform* (Quebec, 1890), p. 72.

30. O. D. Skelton, *op. cit.*, p. 485.

31. A. T. Galt, *op. cit.*, p. 37.

32. O. D. Skelton, *op. cit.*, p. 482.

33. A. T. Galt, *op. cit.*, p. 41.

34. O. D. Skelton, *op. cit.*, p. 487.

35. *Ibid.*, p. 482.

36. *Men of the Day, op. cit.*, pp. 213-216.

37. *Vide* M. Wade, *op. cit.*, p. 680 *et seq.*

38. *Vide infra.*, p. 267

39. M. Wade, *op. cit.*, p. 426.

40. *Vide* A. B. Latham, *The Catholic and Labour Unions of Canada* (McGill University Economic Studies—No. 10, Toronto, 1930), pp. 41-42.

41. A. Galt, *op. cit.*, p. 36.

42. J. H. MacVicar, *Life and Work of Donald Harvey MacVicar* (Toronto, 1904), pp. 150-151.

43. Quoted by John Oxley in *Men of the Day, op. cit.*, pp. 89-90.

XVII

Missionary Development

MISSIONARY ACTIVITY on the part of the Canadian churches was a late development, due to the fact that most of them were daughter churches of missionary societies. Before they could take up the task of missionary work both at home and abroad, they had first to achieve independence of their fostering societies. Nevertheless, there were some stirrings even before the days of "independence from control abroad," since the Canadian churches did not remain unaffected by American activism.

American activism, according to W. W. Sweet, is based upon "the disinterested benevolence emphasis suggested by Jonathan Edwards" and is responsible for more Christian activity than any other "theological emphasis in modern times."[1] To it may be assigned the origin of the social-gospel emphasis in American Protestantism, reflected in Canada in many reform movements and temperance crusades. Its most evident influence, however, has been in the field of missionary enterprise, particularly in the missionary expansion into the north-west.

I

The beginnings of missionary activity in British North America can perhaps be dated with the formation of Bible Societies. As early as 1804 a society was organized at Quebec through the initiative of Francis Dick, a minister of the Congregational Church; another was formed at Pictou, Nova Scotia, in 1813; and in the same year under the auspices of Sir John Cope Sherbrooke there was organized "The Bible Society of Nova Scotia and Dependencies" which, within four weeks of its formation had collected and sent two hundred pounds to the British and Foreign Bible Society.[2] This marks the first occasion that the

Canadian church population began to take an interest in missionary work beyond the shores of what is now Canada, but it still remained a rather indirect interest.

More direct interest in foreign missions arose first among the Baptists of the Maritime provinces, stimulated no doubt by their close association with the Baptists of the New England states. In 1827 the Baptist Church at Saint John, New Brunswick, "formed itself into a missionary society to aid the [New England] Baptist mission in Burmah."[3] At a meeting of the Nova Scotian Baptist Association at Cornwallis in 1832 a resolution was put forth to form a combined society of Home and Foreign missions to solicit money for the American Baptist Missionary Board in Boston. Within a short time one hundred and forty pounds had been collected, much of it through canvassing by "Female Mite Societies." The general enthusiasm thus manifested led to a resolution at a later meeting of the Baptist Association to solicit funds for the "education and maintenance of some one suitable person as a missionary in some foreign land."[4] It was this provision that enabled Richard Burpee and his wife to go to Burma in 1844 to share in the work being carried on there by the American Baptist and Foreign Mission Board, and gave the Baptist Church of the Maritimes the distinction of being the first religious body in British North America to send missionaries overseas.

Almost simultaneously (1844) the Synod of the Presbyterian Church in Nova Scotia appointed a Board of Foreign Missions "to select a field and choose a missionary."[5] The field selected was one of the New Hebrides Islands and the missionary was John Geddie, a minister at Cavendish, Prince Edward Island. Accompanied by his wife, Geddie left Nova Scotia (1846) in the depth of the winter and established his mission at Aneiteum, where he laboured for many years. At the end of his ministry he was able to say: "When I landed on Aneiteum there was not a Christian, and before I left there was not a heathen, on the island."[6]

Interest in foreign missions in the Canadas lagged somewhat behind that in the Maritimes. A visit of Dr. Duff of the Free Church Mission in India to Montreal in 1854 stirred up considerable enthusiasm and led to the formation of an interdenominational group called the Canadian Foreign Missionary Society "intended to be a truly Canadian Catholic Association."[7] A provisional committee debated for a time whether to send a missionary either to Arabia or to Mongolia but finally decided to concentrate on Labrador. As this was not strictly speaking a foreign mission, the name of the society was changed to "The Labrador Mission."[8] Most of the churches lost interest in this non-denominational venture and the upkeep of the mission fell to the Ladies' Missionary Association of Zion Congregational Church; still later it became embraced in the Grenfell Mission in Labrador.

The early dissolution of the Canadian Foreign Missionary Society was indicative of the fact that it was born out of due time; the nearby challenge of home missions, particularly in the north-west compelled foreign missions, for the time being, to take a secondary place.

II

Up to the time of the founding of the Red River Settlement by the Earl of Selkirk (1812) at the forks of the Red and the Assiniboine rivers, the north-west remained of little concern to Canadians, except for the fur traders. But suddenly it became evident both to church and state that there was growing up in close proximity to Canada a far western culture, outside the pale of Christendom. The larger portion of the population was made up of aborigines, who were to a large extent being debauched by white traders, and no one seemed to care.

On the prairies these consisted of roving bands of buffalo hunters speaking Algonquin, Sioux and Athabascan dialects. Though migratory they had advanced a stage further than the migratory bands of eastern Canada, as the band in the west was a stable body governed by an informal council. These Indians had also formed societies or fraternities which sometimes acted as a police force, "regulating the life of the camp on the march"[9]—a precursor of the Royal Mounted Police. At the time they first made contact with white men, their way of life had been revolutionized by the horse which had been introduced into the prairies from Mexico. Among the changes was the introduction of class distinctions; also the tribes had been put permanently on a war footing so that "peace was a rare interlude in their lives."[10]

To the north of the prairies, tribes of Athabascan speech were on a more primitive basis, while on the Pacific coast a great intermingling of tribes due to immigration from various parts of North America seemed to have produced a more advanced cultural development in comparison to the other Indians of Canada; at least there was more "colour to their social and material life,"[11] though they were not, perhaps, so ingenious in inventing artifacts as their arctic and sub-arctic neighbours the Eskimos.

The way and manners of these Indians were not unknown to the outside world in the middle of the nineteenth century, for the famous Belgian priest, Father Pierre-Jean de Smet, had visited both the plains and the Pacific Coast Indians as early as 1840, and published a book on them in 1843 in which he dealt extensively with their supernatural beliefs.[12] According to de Smet they believed in a Supreme Deity or the Great Spirit; but it is the opinion of a recent student of British Columbian Indians that "religion in the orthodox sense did not exist among them," or at least "the concept of a Supreme Being did not bear heavily on their native mind."[13] The same, however, cannot be said of the Eskimo whose sea-goddess was very difficult to propitiate and whose religion was so gloomy "that it hindered more than it helped in the bold struggle to exist."[14]

During the French regime in Canada there had been a few spasmodic attempts to convert the Indians of the north-west to Christianity. On his first trip to the Rockies in 1731 the intrepid explorer Pierre Gaultier de la Vérendrye took along with him Father Meisiager, a Jesuit missionary, but before the latter succeeded in establishing a permanent mission ill-health compelled him to return east. A Father Coquart is reputed to have established a mission at the forks of the Red and Assiniboine rivers in 1743, but this was abandoned when la Vérendrye gave up his explorations in the north-west.[15]

These explorations, however, were not without their results for the future of the Canadian west. French Canadians, associated with the various posts along la Vérendrye's route into the Rockies, who had become entangled in matrimonial unions with the daughters of the soil, preferred to stay with their new friends.[16] Thus originated a race of half-breeds, to add to the colour and variety of the north-west.

The ostensible ruler of these vast territories was the Hudson's Bay Company through its trading posts established along the water routes leading from Hudson's Bay to Lake Winnipeg and to the Pacific coast. Little had been done by the Company to care for the religious needs of the workers at these posts beyond an instruction "to its officers to the effect that the liturgy of the Church of England be read regularly at all the posts of the Company"; even less had been done for the Indians under their supervision.

For a century and a half there were neither churches nor schools in Rupert's Land, as the country was then called. It is true that the Company had brought out some teachers from England to teach the half-breed children that were becoming quite numerous through the cohabitation of Company clerks with native women, but these soon gave up pedagogy for the more lucrative fur-trade. Marriage was unknown, liquor trade flourished and the degradation of the Indians went on apace.[17]

The Hudson's Bay Company, however, was not the only offender in this regard. The Northwest Fur Trading Company, founded by some merchants at Montreal (1784), had entered into competition with the Hudson's Bay Company for the furs of Indian trappers and they also found that liquor was an inducement in securing pelts. Also these Montreal traders discovered that the French-Indian *métis* were most useful middlemen in the fur-trade, and they made it a policy to be represented in the north-west by as many French-speaking Canadians as possible, so that it came to pass that French was "for over fifty years, the official and universally spoken language in the Canadian West outside of the Hudson's Bay Company factories."[18]

This policy of using French Canadians was so successful that it compelled the Hudson's Bay Company to establish posts along the Red River and throughout the prairies in an endeavour to regain their lost trade. The competition was so bitter that it ushered in a lawless era as the struggle increased in intensity for a monopolistic control of the territory, which the Hudson's Bay Company claimed in virtue of a Royal Charter, and the Northwesters as part of Canada by virtue of the British conquest of 1759.[19]

It was in the midst of this struggle that Thomas Douglas, Earl of Selkirk, purchased a commanding number of shares in the Hudson's Bay Company, after which he planted his famous Selkirk Colony at the forks of the Assiniboine and Red rivers. His motives in establishing the colony have long been a subject of controversy; some commentators have insisted that it was to help the Hudson's Bay Company in its struggle with the Northwesters; others have regarded it as a purely philanthropic venture.[20] Be that as it may, the Northwesters and their French Canadian allies assumed the former motive and urged the *métis* to harass in every way possible the settlers that the Earl of Selkirk was bringing out from the Highlands of Scotland and from Ireland. Their rather irresponsible agitation led to an armed encounter (the Battle of Seven Oaks) in which the first governor of the colony, Robert Semple, was killed. Selkirk then proceeded to enlist a private army in the Canadas, made up chiefly of disbanded soldiers called Meurons, from the name of one of the colonels of their former regiment. He then took them to the Red River to provide protection for his settlers. Peace was finally achieved for the district by a union of the two companies in 1821, but retaining the older name of Hudson's Bay Company. Selkirk then urged his Meurons, consisting chiefly of Germans, but also of French, Italians and Swiss to settle down in the Red River area. Not all were willing, but a minority did, thus adding to the racial admixture of the new colony.

III

Although Selkirk had promised in his prospectus a Gaelic-speaking clergyman for the Highlanders from Scotland, his more immediate concern after reaching the north-west was to secure a Roman Catholic priest to exercise some discipline over the more volatile members of the Red River settlements. He presented his need to Bishop Plessis at Quebec, urging upon the latter "the infinite good which might be effected by a zealous and intelligent ecclesiastic among those people, among whom the sense of religion is now almost entirely lost."[21] In response to this request Plessis dispatched Pierre Tabeau to the Red River to look over a situation that was receiving a bad press in the Canadas. Tabeau, whose sympathies were with the Northwesters, reported unfavourably on the future of the struggling colony and suggested that "periodic visitations would be sufficient under the circumstances."[22]

Under further urgings from the colonists themselves, Plessis sent Joseph Norbert Provencher, upon whom he bestowed the powers of a vicar-general; he also provided him with two assistants, as he was now convinced that the church in Lower Canada had a strategic interest in the religious and cultural development of the north-west. Consequently, in 1822 Provencher was made a bishop that he might be free to act with dispatch in creating a Roman Catholic policy in relation to western development.

The new bishop's first concern was to preserve the French Canadian cultural tradition from being absorbed within the Anglo-Saxon. To this end he built his residence and a church across the river from Fort Douglas (now Winnipeg) where he attempted to weld together a "new nation" composed of *métis*, French and Meurons. He then placed his little colony under the patronage of St. Boniface, "in order to draw God's blessing on the German Meurons, Catholics none too fervent, through the intercession of the Apostle of their nation."[23]

One of his most serious problems was manpower since it was impossible to persuade French Canadian priests to settle down in the north-west. At a critical moment the problem was solved when the Oblates of Mary undertook to supply the necessary clergy for his diocese. One of the first of the Oblates to arrive was Brother Alexandre Antonin Taché, whom Provencher greeted with the exclamation: "What! I have asked for men, and they send me a child."[24] The child was destined to become Provencher's successor and one of the most notable figures in the founding of the Province of Manitoba.

With the arrival of the Oblates, Provencher was able to proceed on a most ambitious plan of expansion. The importance of the north-west in the eyes of the Roman Catholic Church was made further evident when Provencher's diocese was transformed into a separate apostolic vicariate in 1844. Work among the Indians and Eskimos in the north was given a prominent place in the scheme of expansion by the appointment of Taché as Provencher's coadjutor with episcopal headquarters at Ile à la Crosse. When Provencher died in 1853 Taché became bishop of St. Boniface, as the diocese of the north-west became known, and Vital J. Grandin, who had conducted a very successful mission among the Chippewyan Indians and Eskimos became his successor in the see of Ile à la Crosse.

The real stimulus behind this rapid expansion was the spirit of self sacrifice of the Oblates of Mary, a nineteenth-century foundation, full of the romantic zeal of the century and which won from Pope Pius IX the encomium, "the Martyrs of the North."[25] Nor was their interest confined solely to the north; they had also learned to endure without complaint the loneliness of the prairies in their fervent earnestness for the conversion of the Indians. Father Lacombe, one of the most romantic figures of the order, proceeded westward from St. Boniface and built a mission about nine miles from where Edmonton now stands. Here he lived an adventurous life trying to bring about peace between the Crees and the Blackfeet.

From St. Boniface also two French Canadian priests, Norbert Blanchet and Modeste Demers, were sent out to the west coast in 1837 where it was known that some French Canadians had accompanied

Alexander Mackenzie of the Northwest Company on his trip to the Pacific and had made their homes there. Demers immediately upon his arrival began a mission among the Salish Indians around Fort Vancouver, the principal post of the fur-traders; while Blanchet proceeded further south into what is now the state of Washington. Owing to the distance of these missions from any episcopal authority, Father Blanchet was consecrated archbishop of Oregon while Father Demers was made his suffragan (1847) with his see at Victoria on the southern tip of Vancouver Island. Though Demers was consecrated bishop of Vancouver Island his diocese also extended to the mainland and included New Caledonia and Alaska or Russian America.[26] At the time of his consecration Bishop Demers did not have a priest at his disposal, but in 1857 he was greatly cheered by the arrival of Joseph d'Herbomez, who established an Oblate mission at Esquimault with himself as its head.[27] He had arrived just in the nick of time, as between 1858-1860 thousands of white men of almost every race invaded British Columbia in search of gold.

The story of the work of the Oblates among the Indians of British Columbia is one of the great chapters in the annals of Christian missions.[28] It was made doubly difficult by "unscrupulous whites who swarmed into British Columbia in the early sixties" and "revelled in an infamous traffic of poisons which they called liquors, alcohol with a mixture of camphor and tobacco juice." A missionary particularly successful in combatting "the twin vices of debauchery and intemperance" was Paul Durieu, who arrived on the Pacific coast in 1859. His missionary system included Eucharist watchmen who rendered for communicants "the same services as the chiefs did formerly to common people,"[29] and involved sharp discipline, often accompanied by physical punishment. Though it was condemned as an undue exercise of priestly authority, it did achieve wonders in preventing Indian converts from falling back into their former moral degradation.

After the arrival of the gold miners in great numbers, Bishop Demers found it impossible to cope with the problems of his unwieldy diocese from his see city of Victoria, and he persuaded the head of the Oblates, Joseph d'Herbomez, to become the first vicar-apostolic of British Columbia. The consecration was performed in 1864 by Archbishop Blanchet of Oregon City "being assisted by Bishop Demers and Father Fouquet who, by special dispensation, acted as third bishop."[30] D'Herbomez established his see at New Westminster, where for a quarter of a century he guided the destinies of his church on the mainland in the most turbulent period in the history of British Columbia.

Among the white settlers there was a great confusion of tongues, particularly during the first days of the gold rush, and also a great variety of religions. It was a population that regarded Roman Catholicism with suspicion and was particularly unfriendly to any conception of a church directed society. Though there were a great variety of sects with their own ministers, yet these tended to cancel one another out, making British Columbia the most secularly minded province in British North America. This soon became a matter of serious concern to the Roman Catholic Church, as it precluded the possibility of securing separate schools. Bishop d'Herbomez never ceased to urge upon the authorities the value of religious schools, and the constant rebuffs he received from the legislature were to darken the final days of his episcopate, as it did that of his colleague at St. Boniface.

IV

The Anglicans, like the Roman Catholics, were particularly fortunate in having at their disposal an unusually zealous missionary society for the work of evangelization in the north-west. This was the Church Missionary Society, founded at the opening of the nineteenth century. Like the Oblates it shared in the romanticism of the age.[31] But it was also a child of the evangelical movement within the Church of England and very anti-Catholic; so that when the paths of the Oblates and the C.M.S. missionaries crossed in the far away places of the north-west it was only to create considerable confusion in the minds of the Indians on the relative value of beads and New Testaments.[32]

The entry of the C.M.S. into the north-west was somewhat accidental. At the time of the death of the Earl of Selkirk in 1820, the Presbyterians of his colony were still without their promised clergyman, so the authorities of the Hudson's Bay Company decided to discharge the unfulfilled promise by appointing an Anglican clergyman, John West, a chaplain to the Company with instructions "to reside at the Red River Settlement." Upon his arrival (1821) West, who "had expected a willing co-operation from the Scotch settlers" was soon "disappointed in his sanguine hopes of their cheerful and persevering assistance, through their prejudice against the English Liturgy." Despite the chilly reception he received from the Highlanders, West writes: "I visited them, however, in their affliction and performed all ministerial duties as their Pastor."[33] He was also much shocked at the blasphemy of the Scotch at the Red River Settlement which, he said, "proved a degeneracy of character in an Indian country."[34]

Although he set about at once to provide a school for the settlers, his deeper interest seemed to lie in the conversion of the Indians and Eskimos, and he at once attempted to persuade the Church Missionary Society to enter upon a vast scheme of missionary work among the Indians of the north-west. The Society agreed and West proceeded to work out a plan of action. He was convinced that the only way to teach Christianity to the Indians was by removing them from their native environment into a boarding school and there to give them a general education in preparation for their understanding of Christian doctrine and practice. He himself initiated one such school and one of his pupils, Henry Budd, who became an ordained minister in the Church of England and a devoted missionary to his own people, provided in time tangible evidence of the wisdom of West's plan.

West remained only three years in the north-west, yet his influence upon Anglican development in western Canada has been quite remarkable, since his association with the C.M.S. gave western Anglicanism its strong evangelical colouring; he also laid down a church policy towards the Indians and Eskimos from which there has been little deviation to this day.

This first C.M.S. missionary was shortly followed by a long line of devoted priests from England, whose adventurous careers were closely followed by their evangelical friends and supporters at home. West's immediate successor was David Jones "whose administration to the Scotch was preferred by them because of his less strict adherence to the Anglican ritual." In 1825 Jones was joined by William Cochrane who, as the Archdeacon of Assiniboine, became a renowned personage in the area. It was said of him that "as regards his methods of handling the Indians," he might "be called the Father of all such as handle the plough and the hoe, or the prince of farm instructors."[35]

Anglican work in the north-west received a tremendous boost by a bequest from the estate of James Leith, formerly a chief factor of the Hudson's Bay Company, of 12,000 pounds. This money was invested in an endowment for a bishopric and in 1849 David Anderson was consecrated as its first incumbent, receiving the title Bishop of Rupert's

Land by royal patent. The following year the S.P.G. began to contribute men and money to the newly created see and the Church of England now seemed well on its way to becoming the dominant religious force in the north-west, as the C.M.S. continued to send out from England men of unusual calibre. Among these were James Hunter and William Kirkby, by whom the Gospel was carried for the first time within the Arctic circle.[36] Even more notable was John Horden, who arrived at Moose in 1851 and in a very short time (eight months) was able to preach to the Crees in their own language. This remarkable linguist also mastered Ojibway and Eskimo and carried on a vigorous mission to the Eskimo on Whale River on the east coast of James Bay.[37] Directing these missions and following his clergy into their remote stations for confirmations and counsel was Bishop Anderson.[38] In 1864 Anderson resigned his see to Robert Machray, whose long episcopate and great administrative ability was to overshadow the work of his predecessor.

Not the least of Bishop Anderson's contributions to Anglican development in the north-west was a sermon he preached in England in 1865, during which he told of a missionary, Robert McDonald, "sinking in rapid decline" but still trying to carry on his mission to the Tukudh Indians. "Shall no one come forward," he asked, "to take up the standard of the Lord as it falls from his hands, and to occupy the ground?"[39] In answer to his plea William Carpenter Bompas offered his services. Leaving England in July 1865 he reached Fort Simpson on the Mackenzie River the following Christmas, an unheard-of feat of travel in the depths of winter.

Like the Oblates the C.M.S. also decided to search out the Indians on the other side of the Rockies. Their interest in this area was first stirred by a Canadian merchant who, as early as 1819, made a plea in England on behalf of the Pacific coast Indians; nothing happened, however, until twenty years later when Captain James Prevost offered a free passage to the Pacific Coast to a C.M.S. missionary, William Duncan. The latter arrived at Esquimault Harbour in 1857, whence he proceeded on a four-hundred-mile journey northward to Port Simpson where he began a mission among the Tsimshean Indians. On November 9, 1858, he wrote in his journal: "Through the mercy of God, I have begun school today. It has been a strange day to me, and the Lord helped me through."[40]

There were to be many strange days in the career of William Duncan. He soon came to the conviction that it was impossible to make real conversions among the Indians as long as they remained in contact with whiskey-selling whites on the Pacific coast; so on May 27, 1862, he left Port Simpson with fifty Indians for Metlakahtla to found an Indian Christian community; shortly afterwards three hundred more Indians joined the colony and Duncan soon had a flourishing and prosperous settlement in which law and order prevailed as nowhere else on the Pacific coast. The cultural and spiritual transformation in Indian life was attested by all those who visited the colony, even its critics. But Duncan was an eccentric genius who would brook no interference in his direction of the colony, not even from the evangelical Bishop Ridley of Caledonia, under whose jurisdiction he was finally placed. Most embarrassing to the Bishop was Duncan's refusal to allow him to conduct a communion service for the Indians. The upshot of the controversy was the removal of the whole colony to Alaska, to a new Metlakahtla provided by the American government.

Apart from this dispute with the bishop over church discipline, Duncan was highly displeased with the Indian Act of the British Columbia legislature which he felt was "based upon the fallacy that the Indians are a set of irresponsible beings, ignorant alike of what is good for them and how they can obtain this good. . . ."[41]

But what may have had an even more deleterious effect on the issues involved at Metlakahtla was a serious dissension within the Church of England at Victoria between the bishop and his dean, in which the social hierarchy of the Hudson's Bay Company were deeply involved.

As a matter of fact, Anglicanism seems to have got off to a very bad start in British Columbia. Its origin may be traced to the appointment by the Hudson's Bay Company of Herbert Beaver in 1836 as chaplain west of the Rockies. Beaver's relations with the chief factor McLaughlin were unhappy. In 1837 they "ceased to communicate with one another even on paper."[42] Irregular marital relations of most of the Company's officers and men at Fort Vancouver, including the chief factor himself, was the cause of the friction. During the height of the controversy the chief factor administered a "caning" to his troublesome chaplain. After McLaughlin's departure, to be replaced by James Douglas, there was established a certain amount of harmony between the chaplain and the Company, evidenced by the fact that the first entry in Beaver's marriage register is "the union of James Douglas and Amelia Connolly."[43]

On Beaver's return to England in 1838 there seemed no great

hurry on the part of the Company to replace him, for it was not until 1849 that another chaplain was appointed to the area. Beaver's successor, Robert John Staines, was no more pleased with what he found around Fort Victoria where he took up residence, than was his predecessor at Fort Vancouver. Besides stirring up resentment over his condemnation of irregular marriages he greatly antagonized the Company by associating himself with a group of dissidents on Vancouver Island who were very critical of the Company's policy towards settlers. On a journey to England to present the grievances of the settlers directly to the colonial office, the ship on which he sailed foundered and Staines was drowned.[44] Not until 1853 was a third chaplain appointed, this time Edward Cridge, who proved to be far more satisfactory in the estimation of the Company than his predecessors, but not as far as the Anglican officialdom was concerned.

Vancouver Island had become a crown colony in 1849, and Cridge regarded himself as the representative of an established church and he looked forward to becoming the first bishop of the Island. But following upon the gold rush of 1858, the mainland west of the Rockies, British Columbia, was also created a crown colony and when British officials got around to appointing a bishop for the Pacific area, they choose George Hills, whose diocese of Columbia with Victoria as its see city included both Vancouver Island and British Columbia. It was hoped to mollify Cridge's chagrin by making him dean of the cathedral that was now established at Victoria.

Soon friction broke out between the bishop and his dean. When the former abandoned all idea of an established church and began to follow the Canadian pattern of rule by synod, Dean Cridge insisted that he was placing his church outside the Anglican fold.[45] He also publicly denounced the Bishop's high church sympathies, and so interfered with the conduct of the cathedral services that Hills brought him before the courts of British Columbia. In the ensuing trial in which the Dean was judged guilty of insubordination[46] the Company was solidly behind Cridge "their own man," regarding Hills as a rank outsider who had been imposed upon them by British officials. When Cridge abandoned the Church of England to form a branch of the Reformed Episcopal Church at Victoria, of which he became a bishop in 1876,[47] many of the old stalwarts of the Hudson's Bay Company society, including the governor, Sir James Douglas, transferred their allegiance to the new church. This schism from the Church of England is an interesting side-light on the "persistance, (sic) even as late as 1874, of the family-company-compact influences in Victoria."[48] It also helps to explain the defiance of episcopal authority by William Duncan at Metlakahtla, whose side of the argument was always vigorously supported by Cridge and his following at Victoria.

Despite the discords and schisms, however, the Anglican Church became for a time the largest denomination in British Columbia, a distinction it had failed to achieve in any of the other provinces of Canada. This was due in part to the support it received from the Hudson's Bay Company in its early days, and also to the fostering care of English missionary societies, but above all to the unusually dedicated priests that these societies sent out from England. Some of these missionaries, no doubt, indulged at times in unseemly controversy, such as occurred at Metlakahtla, yet it can be said of Bishop Ridley and most of his colleagues that "they gave the last full measure of devotion" to the cause they had most at heart.[49]

In tracing the origins of Anglicanism in the north-west we have been digressing somewhat from the main theme of this chapter, namely the development of missionary activity within the Canadian churches themselves; Anglicanism in Canada, however, with the exception of Bishop G. J. Mountain, who visited Rupert's Land under the auspices of the C.M.S. in 1844,[50] showed little interest in western missions. But the Church of England in Canada was ultimately to take over the responsibility for these missions and the pioneer work of the British missionary societies is in a real sense part of the story of Canadian Anglicanism in this area.

V

The first purely Canadian Protestant Church upon the scene in the north-west was the Methodist. But even in the case of the Methodists the pioneer work was done by the British Wesleyan Missionary Society. It has been suggested that Sir George Simpson, the chief factor of the Hudson's Bay Company, who is supposed to have been impressed with the work the Methodists were doing among the Indians in Canada West, had recommended that an invitation be extended to the Wesleyan Missionary Society to extend its activities to the north-west. It is questionable, however, that Simpson, who was known to be opposed to educating Indians, was the moving spirit in bringing Methodist missionaries into the Company's territories. A more probable explanation is that the request came from Benjamin Harrison, a deputy governor of the Company and a member of the evangelical Clapham sect. Harrison may well have met Peter Jones, an Ojibway Indian and a Methodist preacher, who on a visit to England in 1832 had created a tremendous interest among evangelical circles in Indian missions,[51] and been impressed with what he conceived to be the superiority of the Methodist way of converting the aborigines of Canada. Be that as it may, an invitation was extended by the Company to the Wesleyan Society, and the latter began a mission in 1840 under the superintendency of James Evans, with Robert Terrill Rundle, George Barnley and William Mason as his assistants, all of whom were assigned to various posts of the Hudson's Bay Company.[52]

The leader of the mission, James Evans, is one of the great figures of missionary history. Perceiving that his first task was to raise the cultural level of the Indians before any sound Christianity could be taught to them he undertook to provide them with a literature of their own. Consequently he invented a syllabic system for the Cree language, easily adaptable to allied languages. It consisted of "less than fifty characters" and can be mastered "by any intelligent white man in less than an hour."[53] With blocks of wood, lead from old tea chests, ink made from soot and sturgeon oil and an instrument used by the Hudson's Bay Company for baling furs he set up a printing press and was able to turn out in his remote post at Norway House in the Cree syllabic, portions of the Scriptures and several hymns. His invention was a great boon to all the missionaries of whatever denomination among the Indians. It now appeared that this most creative genius was about to lead a great crusade for the cultural advancement of the long-neglected Canadian aboriginal population.

But Evans was a man of uncompromising temperament and he soon aroused the enmity of his sponsor, the Hudson's Bay Company, particularly by his insistence on Sabbath observance and his denunciation of the liquor traffic. False accusations were trumped up against him leading to a trial and recall to England. In this way the man "who made one of the greatest literary inventions in the wide sweep of civilization"[54] was cut short in his missionary career; for shortly after his return to England (1846) he died at the early age of forty-five, fortunately not before the false charges made against him by the authorities of the Hudson's Bay Company were admitted to be pure fabrications.

Evan's colleagues also had their differences with the Company. Robert Rundle, reputed to be the first white man to visit the site upon which the city of Edmonton now stands, was also insistent on a strict observance of the Sabbath, with the result that the Company began to give its preference to Roman Catholic missionaries. These were continually winning Rundle's converts away from him; nevertheless, the Methodist missionary seems to have won a goodly following, as he succeeded in establishing two residential Indian schools, and taught his pupils to read and write by means of the Cree syllabic.[55] At the end of eight years, ill-health compelled him to return to England. Shortly after his departure (1853) Methodist missions in the north-west were transferred by the Wesleyan Society of England to the Canada Conference.

In 1854 John Ryerson was sent by the Canada Conference to the various missions to report on their progress and needs. His journal written during this journey, like G. J. Mountain's, is an invaluable source of information on the social and religious life of the north-west in the middle of the nineteenth century. He records that at the time of his visit there were only eighteen Protestant missionaries in all this vast area: thirteen Anglicans, four Methodists and one Presbyterian.[56] This interesting report stirred up a great deal of enthusiasm in the Canada Conference in favour of Indian missions and led to the dispatch of two quite famous Methodist missionaries, whose names are greatly venerated in western Canada, George McDougall and his son John, both of whom settled among the Indians in the Edmonton area.[57] They were followed by Egerton R. Young, who went to Norway House, and George Young, who became a well-known personage in the Selkirk settlements.

After its entrance into the prairies, the Canada Conference became concerned about conditions west of the Rockies. The fact that many Methodists had arrived in British Columbia during the gold rush and were without Methodist ministrations was called to the attention of the Conference by the superintendent of the Wesleyan Methodist missions in Canada, Enoch Wood. As a result of his plea, Ephraim Evans, Edward White, Ebenezer Robson and Arthur Browning volunteered their services for this distant field and arrived in Victoria in 1858, where they were welcomed by Edward Cridge.[58]

At first the work of these ministers was confined to the "swirling crowd of adventurers from all lands,"[59] who were taxing the ingenuity of all the missionaries on the west coast. Dr. Ephraim Evans, the chairman of the group, established his headquarters at Victoria, while his colleagues proceeded to Nanaimo, New Westminster and Hope on the Fraser River. At the latter place Ebenezer Robson, one of the best known of the pioneer ministers of British Columbia, started a school for Indian children; thus Methodism began to play its distinctive role in the evangelization of the aborigines in the far west.

VI

Strangely enough the last of the major churches of Canada to enter upon missionary work in the north-west was the Presbyterian; this despite the fact that Presbyterians were in a majority among the Protestants settled in the Red River area. Part of the reason for the long delay before these first settlers received a pastor of their own faith was their insistence upon a Gaelic-speaking preacher; another was the divided state of Presbyterianism in the Canadas which long frustrated any vigorous missionary work in the north-west.

After repeated requests by the Selkirk settlers to the Free Church in Canada West, Dr. Robert Burns in 1851 undertook to find a suitable man for what was considered a very difficult congregation. His choice fell upon John Black, one of the first graduates of Knox College, who at the time was engaged in a mission to the French Canadians at Montreal. Black, a Lowlander, could not speak Gaelic, but he was very proficient in the French language and it was hoped by Dr. Burns that he might be able to win some of the *métis* into the Presbyterian Church.[60] Although this was a vain hope, it soon became evident that he was going to be very acceptable to the Scotch settlers who after their long endurance of the Anglican liturgy were ready to forgive Black his deficiencies in the Gaelic tongue. On his arrival three hundred of them left the Church of England to worship in the manse provided for Black until a church could be built. As a matter of fact, he "found a congregation ready made, and it arose like Minerva, fully armed and scarcely needing equipment."[61] In seven weeks after the first Presbyterian service was held in Kildonan parish, as it was now called, six elders were chosen by ballot and Presbyterianism was well on its way to becoming the most formative factor in the cultural development of the north-west, despite its slow start.

Black, himself, had no intention, when he first arrived at Red River, of staying on permanently, as he was anxious to be back to his first love, the French Canadian missions in Lower Canada. But he stayed on for thirty years, being for the first eleven the only Presbyterian minister on the prairies. A series of letters to his brother, preserved in the archives of the United College at Winnipeg, attest to the loneliness this pioneer minister felt on the prairies, arising, says his biographer, "from a strain in his nature rendering him liable to depression."[62] But how could he leave a people who had declared that "the greatest occasion ever known in Kildonan was the day when we had our own church and minister again,"[63] when no other minister was forthcoming. Also he was concerned over the fact that his was the only major church in the west not engaged in missionary work among the Indians.

Finally, after persistent appeals to Toronto, a second minister, James Nisbet, was sent by the Foreign Mission Committee of the Presbyterian Church in Canada in 1862 to Kildonan to carry on a mission among the Indians in the Red River area. After prolonged negotiations between Black and the Committee it was agreed to allow Nisbet (1866) to proceed with a party of ten, including his wife and child, into the wilderness to found a mission at Prince Albert on the north branch of the Saskatchewan River.[64] Here with the assistance of George Flett, a Cree guide, who later became an ordained missionary, an amicable property arrangement was made with the Crees; an establishment was set up, including a school for the Indians, and the Presbyterians were now engaged like the other denominations, not only in converting Indians, but also in preparing the way for a peaceful settlement of the prairies, when the north-west would be opened up to white immigration.

About this same time the Canadian Presbyterians also began to show some interest in the work being done in British Columbia by an Irish Presbyterian, James Hall, who in 1861 had organized a congregation at Victoria.[65] About this time the Canada Presbyterian Church sent out Robert Jamieson, who reached New Westminster in 1862, and laboured for twenty-two years on the Lower Mainland and in Nanaimo. Hall, at Victoria, was followed, first by Thomas Somerville, and then by Simon McGregor from Nova Scotia. There does not, however, seem to have been much enthusiasm for these distant missions in Canada, and Presbyterianism on the west coast came under the care of the Colonial Committee of the Church of Scotland, until it was ultimately embraced in the General Assembly of the Presbyterian Church of Canada.

Presbyterians on the west coast, like those of the eastern churches, failed to evince much interest in Indian work; nor did Nisbet's mission at Prince Albert have a very long career. This was probably due to the fact that the Presbyterians began their Indian missions in an age of transition from a hunting to an agricultural era. Already in 1866 it was evident that the buffalo upon which the Indians depended for their livelihood were disappearing, and that white settlers were destined to move ever westward into the prairies, forcing the Indians to adopt a less nomadic way of life. This forced missions like the one at Prince Albert to close down. Particularly was this the case after the government adopted the policy of forming treaties with the Indians and settling them on reservations.

VII

From the outset the Red River settlements were the spearhead in the transition from a hunting to a "commercial agricultural society." All the tensions of such a profound change of economy were enacted in miniature there, and the churches were permitted to play a quite unusual role of reconciliation. They did not attempt, as at a later date, to follow the "melting pot" policy, but rather the emphasis was upon separate cultural development with as little friction as possible.

The local subdivisions of the community were based upon nationality and religion, and the inhabitants were allowed to follow the old familiar patterns of their homelands. French Canadians occupied land strips along the river after the fashion of Lower Canada; Scots established a typical Scottish parish community, while the English followed the Anglican parochial system. The *métis* were encouraged by the Hudson's Bay Company to continue hunting in order that the pemmican, a staple food made from buffalo meat, might be kept in good supply. On the White Horse Plains the devotees of the chase were kept in good order by Cuthbert Grant, a *métis*, who bore the title "Warden of the Plains."[66]

Although no local self-government had been permitted in the settlements before their acquisition by Canada, yet the Hudson's Bay Company had organized the Assiniboine Council (1835) composed of fourteen leading clergymen and laymen nominated by the Company. To it was assigned the responsibility of maintaining law and order and upon it fell the task of ironing out the disputes that arose from time to time among the cultural groups, or between the Company and its subjects. One of the most thorny of these issues was the demand of the *métis* for free trade between the growing American towns to the south and the settlers. This trade was looked upon with disfavour by the Company as an infringement upon its monopoly and it tried to stop it by imposing an import duty on American products. In this dispute in which the *métis* began to produce some adroit political leaders the churches exercised a moderating influence in the interests of peace; but they were not always partisans of the Company. A young Roman Catholic priest, Antoine Belcourt, is reputed to have been the strategist behind the *métis* agitation for free trade.

The welfare of the Indians was always a constant concern of the clergy. Belcourt tried to win them away from their nomadic ways by establishing a school at St. Eustache on the Assiniboine for members of the Saulteaux nation, but because of their strong vagrant habits he had little success. Archdeacon Cochrane, who also undertook to establish an Indian settlement at Netty Creek (1832), seems to have had better success in his objective; by dint of great perseverance he taught his colonists the art of agriculture.

In the field of education there seems to have been complete harmony among the cultural groups. Parish or separate schools with the assistance of a council grant were the accepted pattern; these in turn became feeders for more advanced institutions: an Anglican College at St. John's, a Roman Catholic at St. Boniface and a Presbyterian at Kildonan. Out of these institutions was created in 1877 the University of Manitoba, in which each college still retained control of its own teaching but with common standards and examinations for degrees to be conferred by the University. To Father Forget, whom Bishop Machray characterized as the "lovable Rector"[67] of St. Boniface, belongs considerable credit for the harmony accompanying the negotiations for a federated university.

A rich satisfying multicultural life on a confessional basis was apparently developing in the Red River community, justifying the fondest hopes of its founder, the Earl of Selkirk. But it could only survive on such a basis with a large amount of goodwill and religious toleration. Unfortunately, the spirit of goodwill evaporated suddenly after the community was integrated as the Province of Manitoba with the Dominion of Canada, but that does not seem to have been the fault of the first settlers, whose original policy, if it had been adhered to, might well have saved Canada from some of its most acrimonious political contests.

REFERENCES

1. W. W. Sweet, *The American Churches* (New York and Nashville, 1948), p. 121.

2. E. C. Woodley, *The Bible in Canada* (Toronto and Vancouver, 1953), p. 19.

3. E. M. Saunders, *History of the Baptists of the Maritime Provinces, op. cit.*, p. 227.

4. G. E. Levy, *The Baptists of the Maritime Provinces 1753-1946, op. cit.*, p. 138.

5. W. Gregg, *Short History of the Presbyterian Church, op. cit.*, p. 85.

6. J. M. MacLeod, *History of Presbyterianism on Prince Edward Island* (Chicago, 1904), p. 24.

7. *Circular of the Provisional Committee of the Canadian Foreign Missionary Society* (Montreal, May, 1854). A copy in the archives room, Divinity Hall, Montreal.

8. J. Wood, *Memoir of Henry Wilkes, op. cit.*, p. 165.

9. D. Jenness, *The Indians of Canada, op. cit.*, p. 128.

10. *Ibid.*, p. 131.

11. *Ibid.*, p. 361.

12. *Vide* Helene Margaret, *Father DeSmet* (New York, 1940).

13. *Our Native Peoples* (British Columbia Heritage Series, prepared by the Provincial Archives, Victoria, B.C., 1951), vol. I, p. 30.

14. D. Jenness, *op. cit.*, p. 418.

15. *Vide* A. G. Morice, *History of the Catholic Church in Western Canada* (Toronto, 1910, 2 vols.), I, pp. 33-52.

16. *Ibid.*, I, p. 54.

17. *Vide* E. H. Oliver, *The Winning of the Frontier* (Toronto, 1930), pp. 169-170, for a quotation from D. W. Harmon, *A Journal of Voyages and Travels in the Interior of North America*, p. 34.

18. A. G. Morice, *op. cit.*, I, p. 59.

19. *Ibid.*, I, pp. 56-58.

20. *Vide* Grace L. Nute, ed., *Documents Relating to Northwest Missions 1815-1827* (Saint Paul, 1942), pp. xii and xiii; also R. G. MacBeth, *The Making of the Canadian West* (Toronto, 1905, 2nd ed.), pp. 6-7.

21. G. Nute, *op. cit.*, p. 6.

22. A. G. Morice, *op. cit.*, I, p. 92.

23. *Ibid.*, p. 107.

24. *Ibid.*, p. 193.

25. *Ibid.*, p. 309; *vide* also Alex Taché, *Vingt Années de Missions dans le Nord-Ouest de l'Amerique* (Montreal, 1866), pp. 97 *et seq.*

26. F. W. Howay and E. O. S. Scholefield, *British Columbia from Earliest Times to the Present* (Vancouver, 1914, 2 vols.), vol. II, p. 610.

27. *Vide* A. G. Morice, *op. cit.*, vol. II, p. 303.

28. *Vide* F. W. Thomas, *An Account of the Missionary Work done by the Oblates in St. Joseph's District, Cariboo, B.C.* (MSS. in Library of the University of British Columbia, n.d.).

29. A. G. Morice, *op. cit.*, II, p. 351.

30. *Ibid.*, II, p. 328.

31. *Vide* Eugene Stock, *The History of the Church Missionary Society* (London, 1899-1916, 4 vols.), especially vol. III, pp. 238-253.

32. *Vide* A. G. Morice, *op. cit.*, I, pp. 342-343.

33. John West, *The Substance of a Journal During a Residence at the Red River Colony* (London, 1824), p. 27.

34. *Ibid.*, p. 16.

35. A. C. Garrioch, *The Correction Line* (Winnipeg, 1933), p. 86.

36. *Vide* H. A. Cody, *An Apostle of the North* (London, 1910, 2nd ed.), pp. 53 *et seq.*

37. *Vide* A. R. Buckland, *John Horden, Missionary Bishop* (London, 7th ed., n.d.), *passim*.

38. *Vid* David Anderson, *The Net in the Bay or Journal of a Visit to Moose and Albany* (London, 1854), *passim*.

39. H. A. Cody, *op. cit.*, p. 20.

40. William Duncan, *Ten Years Work among the Indians* (London, 1867), p. 39.

41. Henry S. Wellcome, *The Story of Metlakahtla* (London, 1887), p. 475.
For an interesting discussion of the personality of Duncan *vide* Bertal Heeney, "William Duncan," in *Leaders of the Canadian Church* series, ed. by B. Heeney (Toronto, 1943), pp. 175-191.

42. G. Hollis Slater, "New Light on Herbert Beaver" (*British Columbia Historical Quarterly*), vol. VI, No. 1, p. 20.

43. *Ibid.*, p. 23.

44. *Ibid.*, p. 28.

45. P. M. Johnson, "McCreight and the Church" (*British Columbia Historical Quarterly*), vol. XII, pp. 297-309.

46. *Vide Trial of the Very Reverend Edward Cridge Rector & Dean of Christ Church Cathedral, Victoria* (Victoria, 1875). Copy in the Archives of the University of British Columbia.
For an outline of Cridge's doctrinal views *vide* E. Cridge, *As It was in the Beginning* (Toronto, 1909).

47. *Vide* F. Vaughan, *A History of the Free Church of England, otherwise called the Reformed Episcopal Church* (Bath, 1936), p. 110.

48. P. M. Johnson, *op. cit.*, vol. XII, pp. 297-309.

49. *Vide* D. Wallace Duthie, ed., *A Bishop in the Rough* (London, 1909). This journal of John Sheepshanks gives a vivid picture of the work of Anglican clergymen in the mining camps; *vide* also Mrs. Jerome Mercier, *Father Pat, A Hero of the Far West* (Gloucester, 1909, 2nd ed.).

50. *Vide* G. J. Mountain, *The Journal of the Bishop of Montreal During a Visit to the Church Missionary Society's North-West American Mission* (London, 1845).

51. *Vide* Peter Jones, *Life and Journals of Kah-ke-wa-quo-na-by* (Toronto, 1860), especially pp. 305 *et seq.*

52. *Vide* J. H. Riddell, *Methodism in the Middle West* (Toronto, 1946), pp. 15 *et seq.*

53. John McLean, *James Evans, Inventor of the Syllabic System of the Cree Language* (Toronto, 1890), p. 164.

54. J. H. Riddell, *op. cit.*, p. 22.

55. Alfred Carter, *The Life and Labours of the Reverend Robert Terrill Rundle, Pioneer Missionary to the Saskatchewan, Canada* (an unpublished thesis in the Library of Union College, B.C.), p. 161.

56. John Ryerson, *Hudson's Bay or A Missionary Tour* (Toronto, 1855), pp. 61-75.

57. *Vide* John McDougall, *George Millward McDougall the Pioneer, Patriot and Missionary* (Toronto, 1888), especially pp. 179-201.

58. *Vide* F. W. Howay and E. O. S. Scholefield, *op. cit.*, II, p. 637.

59. E. A. Davis, ed., *Commemorative Review of the Methodist, Presbyterian and Congregational Churches in British Columbia* (Vancouver, 1925), p. 3.

60. *Vide* George Bryce, *John Black, the Apostle of the Red River* (Toronto, 1898), p. 60.

61. *Ibid.*, p. 67.

62. *Ibid.*, p. 77.

63. E. H. Oliver, *His Dominion of Canada* (Toronto, 1932), p. 130.

64. *Vide* article by George Boyle, "The Foreign Mission Committee of the Presbyterian Church in Canada," *The Bulletin, Records and Proceedings of the Committee on Archives of The United Church of Canada* (Toronto, 1955), No. 8, pp. 37-41.

65. *Vide* J. T. McNeil, *The Presbyterian Church in Canada 1875-1925* (Toronto, 1925), p. 103.

66. For an interesting study of the cultural life of the Red River Settlements, *vide* G. H. Dowker, *Life and Letters in Red River 1812-1863* (an unpublished thesis, University of Manitoba, 1923).

67. Robert Machray, *Life of Robert Machray* (Toronto, 1909), p. 276.

XVIII

Western Expansion

IT WAS IMPOSSIBLE for the north-west to remain forever under the rule of the Hudson's Bay Company, particularly after permanent settlements began to take place. However small these might remain, a demand was sure to arise among the settlers for a better social status than that of being the merely tolerated wards of a commercial company. In response to this desire the British government had quickly established the two crown colonies of Vancouver Island and British Columbia on the Pacific coast.

Because the Red River settlements were so largely the creations of the Hudson's Bay Company itself, there was a prolonged delay before the demand for citizenship on the part of these settlers received adequate consideration. During this period of hesitation they themselves began to discuss various ways whereby they might "become clothed in the garments of citizenship."[1] Thus arose three distinct parties: one favouring the status of a crown colony, another absorption into Canada, and a third (very small) advocating annexation with the United States. It is beyond the limits of this study to enter into the details of the Red River uprising (1870) that was finally provoked by the deepening tensions of this partisan spirit; or to attempt to assess the blame for the unfortunate incidents that led to the shooting of Thomas Scott, an Ontario Orangeman, on the order of the *métis* leader, Louis Riel. Neither will it be possible to make more than a passing mention of the later uprising of *métis* on the banks of the Saskatchewan River about a decade later (1885) which led to the execution of Louis Riel. Suffice it to say that these two executions considerably dampened the rosy hopes that had been foreseen for the cultural reconciliation of French- and English-speaking Canadians, as they applied themselves to the common task of creating a great nation reaching from ocean to ocean.

Nor was the prospect of national survival much improved after

Canada had secured at great expense a transcontinental railway (1886) as the price of British Columbia's entry into Confederation. The slow filling up of the west with settlers, due to the collapse of the boom that had accompanied the building of the railway and the discouraging accounts that had been circulated about the harsh climatic conditions of the prairies, made many despair of Canada's future.[2]

But with the advent of the Laurier regime (1896) accompanied by increased economic prosperity stimulating an intensive drive to fill up the vacant lands of the west, hopes were again revived that Canada could become a great nation. During the next fifteen years the population of the country was increased from five to eight millions, as people from every quarter of the globe began to move into the north-west. The greatest variety of racial groups was to be found on the west coast where the frequent "gold rushes" brought swarms of people not only from Europe and America but from the Orient as well; so that by 1910 British Columbia contained twenty-one nationalities, professing forty-seven different religions.[3] On the prairies also the complexity of races and faiths was hardly less confusing.

I

During this period of mass immigration the Canadian government depended upon the churches not only to help in the assimilation of the new settlers into the Canadian way of life, but also to co-operate in ironing out the tensions that inevitably arose between the old and new citizens. In the beginning it turned hopefully to the Roman Catholic hierarchy for counsel and advice in dealing with the suspicious *métis*. When the Red River uprising got completely out of hand urgent messages were sent to Archbishop Taché, who was in Rome attending the Vatican Council, to hurry home and help to restore order in Canada's newly acquired territory. Though Taché arrived too late to save the life of Thomas Scott, there seems little doubt that his influence over his former pupil and protégé, Louis Riel, helped to make the transfer from the Hudson's Bay Company's authority to the Canadian government far less turbulent than it might otherwise have been.[4]

Again during the era of treaty-making with the Indians, preliminary to settling them on reservations, the government's commissioners were always accompanied by missionaries both as advisers and interpreters.

When in 1899 it was decided to extend the treaty policy into the north country where mineral discoveries were attracting explorers, the chairman of the commission, David Laird, asked Father Lacombe to accompany him into the Athabasca area in an advisory capacity; also travelling with the commission, unofficially, was the Roman Catholic bishop of Athabasca and Mackenzie River, whose headquarters were at Fort Chipewyan.[5]

The preponderant influence which the Roman Catholic Church seemed to exercise over the government in the opening days of Canadian rule soon began to wane with the newer waves of immigration. Protestant Ontario sent more settlers than Catholic Quebec, and the majority of the European immigrants were Protestant. Also it became difficult for the Church to provide services for those Catholics who did not understand French. Archbishop Taché and his Oblate fathers were particularly hard pressed to find priests for the Irish Roman Catholics who were flocking into the prairies in large numbers. Taché made an earnest plea to eastern Canada for English-speaking priests, but the response he received was very disappointing. The arrival of the Jesuits in 1885 to take over the work at St. Boniface College relieved the situation somewhat, as it freed the Oblates for missionary work among the Indians for which they were peculiarly adapted; it also put new zest into Roman Catholic educational activity in Manitoba.[6]

In British Columbia the Oblates were also embarrassed with a multitude of duties; they had arrived for the purpose of concentrating on Indian work, but were soon involved in diocesan organization and the supervision of very diverse groups of people. It was not until the opening of the twentieth century that they received any reinforcements, when the Benedict fathers arrived and established an industrial school for Indians at Clayoquot on Vancouver Island; further badly needed help was furnished when the Marist fathers in 1903 took charge of the mission of Comichan. In this same year the see of Victoria was elevated to an archbishopric with New Westminster and Athabasca-Mackenzie River as suffragans.

The establishment of a separate province of British Columbia had been the result of a plea from the first provincial council of St. Boniface in 1889. Already the Roman Catholic Church was aware of its lessening influence in the west, and Taché had summoned the council in order to plan a reorganization of his too widely scattered province. Besides asking for the establishment of a separate metropolitan for British Columbia, the council also asked that St. Albert "the territory east of the 169th degree of longitude should become a separate vicariate-apostolic,"[7] a suggestion that was duly carried out. In order to safeguard the needs of the church in the west, the council provided for a representative to be stationed at Ottawa.

There were several causes for the decline of the Roman Catholic Church in the west from its former impregnable position. The uprising on the Saskatchewan was a serious blow to its prestige in this area. Though the Roman Catholic priests were in sympathy with the *métis'* grievances, yet their vigorous stand on the side of law and order, resulting in the martyrdom of three of their priests at Frog Lake, had alienated the half-breeds from the church. But a far more serious threat to the work of evangelization was an agitation against separate schools led by D'Alton McCarthy, who as representative of the Equal Rights Association of Ontario, was touring the west and urging its citizens to overthrow the school acts of both Manitoba and the North West Territories.[8] As a result of this agitation a Liberal government under the leadership of Thomas Greenway came to power in Manitoba in 1888, on a platform which called for the overthrow of separate schools. One of the first acts of the new government was the cessation of the French version of the *Official Gazette*; then followed the most cruel blow of all, the creation of a Department of Education which refused to recognize any responsibility for the separate schools in Manitoba.[9] This new act was made doubly bitter from the fact that it was given the force of law by the signature of Lieutenant-Governor Schultz, Riel's arch-enemy during the uprising of 1870.

These untoward events darkened the final years of Archbishop Taché, who died in 1894.[10] It remained for his successor Archbishop Langevin, long identified with the ultramontane party of Quebec, to face the full impact of the Liberal regime at Winnipeg. He resolved to resist by every legal and legislative means available to him the new Manitoba School Act, and in this he had the hearty co-operation of the hierarchy of Quebec. His first move was to challenge the constitutional legality of the Act before the Supreme Court of Canada. Here he was successful, but this decision was overthrown by the Privy Council.[11] On a second appeal (1894) by the church authorities before this final tribunal, the Council conceded that the Roman Catholic minority had a real grievance, but suggested that it could be righted by remedial legislation in the Canadian parliament as provided for in the B.N.A.

Act.[12]   Such legislation was almost secured from a Conservative government at Ottawa in 1896.

At this juncture, however, Wilfrid Laurier, the leader of the Liberal opposition began to re-echo the warning expressed by Georges-Étienne Cartier during a similar controversy over the New Brunswick School Act, namely, that the overthrow of provincial autonomy in any one province in relation to school acts might well lead to the overthrow of Quebec's own school laws. As an alternative to remedial legislation, Laurier asked that he be given an opportunity to negotiate personally with Premier Greenway an amicable settlement of the question. Neither the Quebec hierarchy nor the authorities at St. Boniface were willing to entrust this task to Laurier, but in the election of 1896 the Liberals came to power in Canada and Laurier was launched on his great career of racial reconciliation. Though his victory was much deplored publicly by the Quebec hierarchy, he had not lost complete contact with his own church, for the archbishop of Montreal, Mgr. Bruchesi, had kept in close touch with him believing "that sunny ways and personal pressure would go further than the storms and thunderbolts of the doughty old warrior [Mgr. Laflèche] of Three Rivers."[13]

Immediately after the election Laurier tried his sunny ways with Premier Greenway and negotiated a settlement whereby the teaching of French was permitted in Manitoba schools if parents so desired when there were at least ten French-speaking children in attendance; religious instruction for Roman Catholic children was also granted after school hours. The Church was far from satisfied with this settlement and Laurier himself was somewhat chagrined with the final result; for when later the separate school question again came to the fore with the creation of the new provinces of Alberta and Saskatchewan, he tried to secure better terms for his co-religionists than had been obtained in Manitoba.

Before the provinces had been carved out of the North West Territories, the Territorial government under the proddings of D'Alton McCarthy, had considerably modified the autonomy of the separate schools, provided for in the Territorial Act of 1874, by some ordinances of 1892 and 1901.   Laurier, in submitting to the House of Commons the bills creating the provinces of Alberta and Saskatchewan had ignored the later ordinances and attempted to retain the school system of 1874.[14] Opposition against the old system, however, had become so strong that Laurier was compelled to bring in an amendment to his own bill which simply guaranteed to the Catholic minority the separate schools as they existed under the ordinance of 1901. Once again the Roman Catholic hierarchy felt keenly aggrieved, since their schools were now under the control of the public school boards of the provinces. What was particularly resented in Quebec was that the final settlement had followed the pattern of Ontario rather than that of their own province. The controversy perhaps left deeper scars in the relations of Ontario and Quebec than it did in the prairie provinces and intensified the racial feeling between the two original provinces of Canada.[15]

About this time Ontario began to put severe restrictions upon her French schools; this in turn caused a reaction in Quebec against Laurier's policy of reconciliation and gave considerable impetus to the formation of a national party. The leader of the new party, Henri Bourassa, declared: "To wish to obtain the esteem, the confidence, and the goodwill of our English fellow citizens in sacrificing our incontestable rights, in consenting ourselves to the rupture of the national compact which guarantees these rights and in accepting thefts, infringements, and insults in the same manner as we welcome fair dealing, is to doom ourselves in advance to scorn and slavery."[16]

This deepening tension between Ontario and Quebec was a rather ironical commentary on the high hopes that had been voiced by Georges-Étienne Cartier and George Monro Grant, that the inclusion of the north-west within the Dominion of Canada would contribute to the peaceful co-existence of French- and English-speaking Canadians.

II

While the Roman Catholics were predominantly concerned over the retention of French Canadian culture in the north-west, so the Anglicans were equally anxious for the preservation of British ideals and institutions in the same area. As early as 1867 Bishop Machray, realizing that the whole of the north-west was going to be opened up for white settlement, laid his plans accordingly. He foresaw, rightly, that as soon as his diocese became an integral part of the Canadian nation, that the fostering societies in England would wish to withdraw their grants. Consequently he made inquiries about what help he might receive from the old dioceses of Canada "and the answer was chilling and discouraging in the extreme."[17] Such being the case he resolved to see what could be done to make his own diocese better prepared for the expected inrush of settlers. Taking a leaf out of Archbishop Taché's book, he decided to turn his diocese into a metropolitan province and divest some of his responsibilities upon diocesan bishops. Writing to the Church Societies in England he pleaded for their co-operation in securing endowments for the contemplated sees. On a visit to England in 1871 he appeared before the Council of the Colonial Bishopric's Fund to present his plan for the division of his diocese and for additional financial help in setting up the new episcopates.[18]

His plea on the whole was eminently successful; Rupert's Land was made into a metropolitan see and the Archbishop proceeded to the creation of new dioceses and the consecration of new bishops. For the north country around the Hudson Bay he chose John Horden who, with his assistant, James Peck, had laboured for twenty years among the Indians and Eskimos, to become bishop of Moosonee (1872).[19] For the Athabasca-Mackenzie district the inevitable choice was William Bompas.

In 1874 Bompas was consecrated bishop of Athabasca, but this was only the first of three enthronements for "the Apostle of the North," who "set his face steadfastly towards the frozen north, as far as possible from the restraints of civilization,"[20] becoming successively bishop of the Mackenzie River Diocese in 1881, and of Selkirk (Yukon) in 1891. Nearer home Machray chose John McLean, formerly the archdeacon of Assiniboine, for the bishopric of Saskatchewan.

While in England the Archbishop made a strong plea for St. John's College, urging its importance in keeping the west for the Church of England. "The thought," he said, "of this coming multitude, this new nation of white men, mainly, doubtless, of Anglo-Saxon blood— with all their struggles for this world, carrying with them the common human burden of sin with all its sorrows—may well fill the mind with anxiety and bid it be alive and active in preparing."[21] The response on the part of the Anglican communion was fairly good, but not as great as Machray had expected.

British Columbia was not included in the new province, as Machray felt that Canada west of the Rockies should have a metropolitan of its own; but the unfortunate divisions among churchmen in this area and also the temporary nature of British Columbia settlements in the mining areas prevented any metropolitan status until it was integrated into the General Synod of Canada.

Bishop Hills of Columbia faced even more difficult tasks than Machray in trying to meet the needs of his flock in the mining settlements of British Columbia. His responsibilities were somewhat lightened by the consecration of William Ridley for the diocese of Caledonia in 1879 and Acton Sillitoe for New Westminster in 1880. The latter's chief work was among the miners of the Kootenay area where with the co-operation of Henry Irwin (Father Pat) he achieved considerable success in ministering to a most diverse population, including Indians and Orientals.[22] It soon proved impossible for Bishop Sillitoe, because of the obstacles to travel in British Columbia, to administer his diocese effectively, and so in 1899 the diocese of Kootenay was carved out of New Westminster, but lacking any episcopal endowment, it remained for many years under the supervision of neighbouring bishops.

Because of the crying need for men and money both in the prairies and in British Columbia, Machray resolved once again to make an earnest plea for help before the churches of eastern Canada. In 1881 he journeyed to Montreal to present the needs of the west to the central committee of the province of Canada, but again with little success, as the eastern dioceses felt that the missionary diocese of Algoma (founded in 1861) was a sufficient charge upon their home mission funds. It was after this fruitless trip that Archbishop Machray reached the conclusion that the only way the eastern churches could be persuaded to accept some responsibility for the extension of Anglicanism in the west would be through a national synod for all Canada. Previously, Machray had refused to agree to the formation of such a synod lest it endanger the evangelical foundations of the province of Rupert's Land; but the need for expansion in the west was so great that he put his fears aside, even to the extent of permitting a pronounced Tractarian, J. R. Anson, to become bishop of Assiniboine (now Q'Appelle) in 1884.[23]

By this time most Anglican churchmen were agreed on the desirability of the union of the various branches of the Church of England into one general synod. Delegates from the diocesan synods met at Winnipeg in 1890, and drew up a plan for a national synod, consisting of a house of bishops and a house of delegates chosen on a proportionate basis from the clergy and laity of the member dioceses. The president of the synod, to be elected by the bishops from among the metropolitans, was to be styled the Primate of All Canada. Out of the Winnipeg scheme emerged the General Synod of the Church of England in Canada, first called together at Toronto in 1893; an early message of the upper house to the lower was the announcement of the election of Archbishop Machray as the Primate of All Canada.[24] Thus through western leadership and pressure, the Church of England in Canada had at last become a national or territorial church.

Following upon the consummation of the General Synod the Primate's first aim was to set up one missionary society to consider objectively all the missionary needs of the church. Again he was greatly alarmed by eastern indifference to his plan, as the dioceses were still inclined to retain their own diocesan societies. After considerable agitation on the part of the west the provincial Synod of Canada agreed to merge (1901) its Diocesan and Foreign Missionary Society into the Missionary Society of the General Synod, for which the Primate wrote a canon committing to the Anglicans of Canada responsibility for a vigorous missionary campaign in the west.[25]

The immediate results were far from satisfactory, as the Church of England, by virtue of its close association with the established Church of England, has been constantly frustrated in attempting to meet the peculiar needs of the west, since the era of mass immigration. This sense of frustration has never been more poignantly expressed than in a book written by William Newton, the pioneer missionary of the S.P.G. at Fort Edmonton, where he arrived in 1875.[26] Writing after twenty years' experience on the Saskatchewan he said: "It seems almost impossible for church ideas to take root and thrive in our colonies. The people have no historic sense. There is nothing in which it can grow. Their notions are of today or at most yesterday; their hopes and thoughts are in the future; their dreams are of coming times, so the Church of England is at a disadvantage. Her ideas and methods are not new; they are ancient; what therefore have they to do with young America?" But lack of historic sense on the part of the settlers was not the most serious problem the church faced in the west; there was the lack of personnel. Nor was this overlooked by Canon Newton. In his characteristic pessimistic vein he writes: "For many years now it has been evident that we have neither the men nor the means to cope with the difficulties of large, sparsely-settled districts. At present we shut our eyes to the fact, by making a so-called 'mission' cover fifty or a hundred or two hundred miles, and supply it with a solitary priest or deacon, or lay-reader, and even such missions are often vacant, or cannot be supplied continuously. The missioner's health breaks down, or the solitude oppresses him, or the apathy of the few who belong to the Church discourages him, or the zealous sects around undermine his work, or his inexperience leads him into difficulties which he is unable to overcome, or his sanguine hopefulness at starting leads him to make glowing reports which cannot be sustained, and the Church authorities are disappointed because he cannot do impossibilities, and tell him so."[27] Such experiences, however, were not peculiar to the Church of England; all the churches in the west faced the same problems of isolated families and loneliness; the Roman Catholics were able to mitigate the latter to some extent by settling religious orders in remote areas; the others sought to meet some of the difficulties by pooling their resources. Along this path they ultimately arrived at the conclusion that only by church union could the needs of the west be adequately met.

III

Church union as a solution of western problems was first initiated by the Presbyterians, and was due to the unusual missionary expansion that occurred under the leadership of a most energetic superintendent of missions, James Robertson. Robertson himself was not an advocate of church union, but during his era he had involved his church in so many and great responsibilities that his successors felt compelled to lessen some of their burden through co-operation with other churches.

To John Black of Kildonan must go the credit for the appointment of Robertson to an office that was new to Presbyterian Church polity. After thirty years' service in the north-west Black had journeyed in 1881 to the General Assembly of the Presbyterian Church, meeting at Kingston, where he made an eloquent plea for the appointment of a superintendent of missions, and suggested James Robertson, then minister of Knox Church, Winnipeg, for the post. The appointment was made, though with some hesitation, as the word "oversight" "in the terms of his appointment was protested by certain of the brethren as smacking of Episcopacy."[28] The brethren were not far wrong, for during the next twenty years the Presbyterian Church in the north-west was under the close personal direction of a vigorous administrator, but who at the same time was a veritable father-in-God to both clergy and people committed to his care. The energy which he gave to his task is partly to be explained by his educational background.

As a student of theology at Princeton and later at Union Seminary,

New York, he had become thoroughly imbued with the spirit of "disinterested benevolence" and its corollary "American activism" with its "stress upon life rather than a creed."[29]   His affinity with this American school of thought is evidenced by one of his own famous expressions: "I would rather have a man know less Latin and more Horse."[30]   It was also seen in his constant journeyings to the most remote outposts of the north-west, living, as it were, "on the trail."   On his first journey westward he proceeded to Battleford, the original capital of the North West Territories, where he planned to build a Presbyterian church in anticipation of the expected settlers, but with the transfer of the railway from the north to the south and the selection of Regina as the new capital, Dr. Robertson quickly adjusted his plans to the new situation, so that a Presbyterian Church was immediately erected in the prospective city to welcome the future citizens on their arrival.   A Church and Manse Building Fund which he had launched upon assuming his new office made it possible for him to start building operations wherever he foresaw the possibility of a future town or city.   Under his vigorous leadership the Presbytery of Manitoba soon grew into three presbyteries, Winnipeg, Rock Lake and Brandon, "together constituting the Synod of Manitoba and the North West Territories,"[31] of which Dr. Robertson became the first moderator.

In 1890 he visited British Columbia and was greatly shocked to learn of the neglect of the interior of that province by the Presbyterian Church.[32]   Soon the responsibility to overcome this neglect rested upon his own shoulders, when the Columbia Presbytery sent a resolution to the General Assembly asking that their presbytery be allowed to come under the direction of Dr. Robertson.   One of his first acts was to organize (1892) the presbyteries of Vancouver Island, Westminster and Kootenay, along with the Presbytery of Calgary, into the Synod of British Columbia. By 1896 he had founded the Presbytery of Edmonton, and then proceeded on a journey through eastern Canada to Great Britain in search of missionaries to work in those northern areas where, he lamented, "there were 25,000 Presbyterians somewhere in the west uncared for by the Church."[33]

The following year he was back in the west on an adventurous journey to the Yukon where a gold rush was in full swing.   Observing that some ten or twenty thousand people had moved into the placer beds of the Klondike "and with them had gone the rum-seller, the gambler, the courtesan, the pimp, the vile parasitic vermin from the city slums, but not a single missionary,"[34] he rushed back to Winnipeg to find the right kind of missionary for this most difficult assignment. The only suitable man available appeared to be a young Irishman, R. M. Dickie, who was in his second year of theology at Manitoba College. As the need was so urgent, Dickie was withdrawn from his classes, ordained and hurried into the Yukon.

Dickie's handling of the miners more than justified the confidence that had been bestowed upon him, with the result that the Yukon Mission soon caught the imagination of the Presbyterian public and contributions began to pour in for its continued support.[35] The Yukon has been designated Robertson's last great adventure, for he died in 1902 at the age of sixty-three, worn out by his super-human efforts, having started 642 missions and 121 augmented charges.[36]

The responsibility for carrying on his work was shared between two men: J. A. Carmichael, who became superintendent of the Synod of Manitoba and the North West Territories, and Dr. J. C. Herdman, holding a similar position in relation to the Synod of British Columbia. Due to the prevailing prosperity of the time and the spirit of optimism associated with the Laurier regime, the era of expansion continued unabated under the new leadership. Missions were now attempted among the Ukrainians and Hungarians, with the purpose as expressed by Dr. Carmichael of assimilating these people into "our social and national standards, as well as to our religious ideals."[37] Dr. Herdman, however, was not fully in agreement with the broader aspects of this policy. "While it is very proper and worthy," he said, "to emphasize the national side of the work and the importance of welding all classes together into one loyal Canadian national life, yet we dare not forget first principles, that the Church herself exists for the bringing of men to the Saviour."[38]

Dr. Herdman represented a conservative evangelical point of view, confining the church's work largely to personal conversion, while his colleague was thinking in terms of social and national responsibility. In this he was following in the tradition of Dr. Robertson, whose reports are full of references to railway building, the problem of racial admixture and immigration policy as part of the church's concern. Here was a definite approach to the social gospel that was to become so prominent in the preaching of a later generation of clergy in the west, particularly in the Winnipeg area.

With the appointment of J. H. Edmison as Home Missionary

Secretary of the General Assembly, Dr. Carmichael received a strong ally, who was also eager to co-operate with other churches to build up "homogeneous and thoroughly Christian communities." In furtherance of this objective, particularly when an economic depression began to bring the work of expansion to a halt, he became "one of the most eager and most earnest advocates of Church Union,"[39] a phase of Canadian church development to be pursued further in the following chapter.

IV

Like the Presbyterians, the Methodists by the energy and vigour of their superintendent of missions in Manitoba and the North West Territories, James Woodsworth, became deeply involved in the social political development of the west. Woodsworth had been preceded by George Young as the first superintendent of missions (1868), but Young's task to a large extent was confined to supervising Indian missions.

For some years after Confederation Methodist growth in the north-west seemed to lag behind the Anglican and Presbyterian, but after the final union of the Methodist Church in Canada (1884), a more vigorous missionary policy was pursued, of which the appointment of James Woodsworth to the post of superintendent was tangible evidence. For Woodsworth, like Dr. Robertson, was an activist, deeply influenced by the liberal and optimistic preaching of Henry Ward Beecher,[40] a precursor of the social gospel in America, whose philosophy he made his own. But he never allowed his liberal optimism to dull his critical faculties, nor did he hesitate to speak out against what he believed to be the mistakes of either church or state.

Like his predecessor he found a good deal of his time taken up with visiting Indian missions and schools. On his first missionary tour he was accompanied by John McDougall whose life since the early 'seventies[41] had been identified with these missions and who had won a well deserved tribute from General Strange for his performance of dangerous duties[42] during the uprising of the *métis* in 1885. The Methodists naturally took great pride in their Indian work, but Dr. Woodsworth began to have some doubts on the policy being followed by his church and the government in relation to Canada's original population. "It may be," he wrote, "a question whether a too liberal paternalism on the part of both state and church has not been a mistaken kindness, the effect being to pauperize instead of to produce independence of character."[43]

In 1894 he proceeded to Port Simpson, British Columbia, where Thomas Crosby was carrying on Indian missions pretty well in the tradition of William Duncan of Metlakahtla fame. During his thirty years of dedication to Indian work Crosby had transformed a pagan village "built after the old-style, large wooden houses without either grace or conveniences," into "a modern town, with good houses, many of them well furnished, even to sewing machines and musical instruments."

Though Dr. Woodsworth was greatly impressed by the physical and material improvements that had been achieved under Crosby's administration he was rather startled when he was besought by the Indians for a preacher "who would build them a cannery or a steamboat or a saw mill or do some thing else to help them along material lines."[44] It was his fear as well as Crosby's himself, that such preoccupation with material artifacts on the part of the preachers might leave a spiritual vacuum in the lives of the Indians which "peculiar sects" would try to fill.

Nor were his alarms without their justification, for the Salvation Army had already arrived at Port Simpson and were conducting startling evangelical revivals, much to the consternation of the Methodists. In an endeavour to counteract the Salvation Army's growing influence in his mission, Crosby had organized a "Band of Workers" to revive the old-fashioned revivalistic methods of the Methodists. At the time of his visit Woodsworth records that "feeling ran high between the Salvation Army and Crosby's 'Band of Workers'."[45]

For some reason the Methodist ministers in western Canada eschewed "the earlier typical evangelism" that had served their predecessors so well in the pioneer days of eastern Canada, and had adopted a rational presentation of the Gospel with an emphasis upon the works of Christ rather than his salvation.[46] Quite early they had established a theological college at Winnipeg (Wesley) where the emphasis according to its principal, Dr. J. W. Sparling, was upon a professionally educated ministry to carry on a settled pastorate. Such a policy did not go unchallenged by those who felt that the conditions of the west called for the training of itinerant evangelists. In reply Dr. Sparling said that he was not unaware of the need and that he had a plan to meet such a situation: "The Church," he wrote, "has entered upon a new era in her methods of work, which is not a new departure but a revival of the old plan of the early days of Methodism.   There hardly ever was a time when there was such a demand for lay-workers or when there was such a force in the field as now.   The peculiarity of the times seems to have created the very necessity for this demand.   And while every pastor does indeed fulfil the command 'Do the work of an evangelist,' yet owing to the peculiarity of his work as a pastor he cannot enter fully into the work of an evengelist. . . ."[47] Sparling's plan was simply to pass over revivalistic work to laymen, very much in the manner that Wesley had organized lay preachers, but like Wesley's preachers they also were inclined to start an independent sect of their own, so that the plan was hardly a success from the Methodist point of view.

As a matter of fact, Dr. Sparling was trying to have the best of two worlds by making the Methodist Church both a church and a sect type of religion.   After the union of 1884, the Methodists were firmly resolved to be a national church rather than a sectarian movement, but the pioneer conditions of the west called for sectarianism or at least for the techniques of social reorganization that come so easily to a sect type of religion.

But it was not simply the desire to be recognized as a church that led the Methodists away from sectarianism in the west.   Both her missionaries from eastern Canada and the great number of preachers that Dr. Woodsworth had brought over from Great Britain were seriously concerned to preserve or to establish Anglo-Saxon institutions in the north-west; and so they initiated practical measures for transforming the heterogeneous people moving into the west into good Canadian citizens.   Thus they became involved in social service work among non-Anglo-Saxon peoples, and began to pioneer in social welfare activities.[48] Work among "European Foreigners" was carried on from two centres, Pakan, Alberta, and from All People's Mission, Winnipeg. The latter emerged from a Sunday School class conducted by Dolly Maguire in 1889 for some neglected German boys.   Under the direction of J. S. Woodsworth, the son of James Woodsworth, it evolved into a significant social service activity that was to be imitated by the Presbyterians with their Robertson Memorial Institute and the Anglicans with their King Edward Settlement, both at Winnipeg.[49]

With social service added to its task of preaching the Gospel the Methodist Mission Board, like the Presbyterian, found its commitments in the west an impossible strain both on its man power and finances. Consequently, there arose within the Methodist community a strong desire to lighten the burden through church union. One enthusiastic supporter of such a solution was Alexander Sutherland whom Dr. Oliver described as a "Missionary Statesman in an imperial, if at times imperious, manner,"[50] another was Dr. C. E. Manning, who worked closely with Dr. Edmison of the Presbyterian Board in co-ordinating the work of their two churches in the west to such an extent as to make church union almost inevitable.

V

In contrast to this tendency towards a united Christendom on the part of the traditional English-speaking churches, there was an opposite tendency among the foreign-speaking European churches; this was particularly the case with the Lutherans, who not only revived many of the divisions associated with their European backgrounds but also imported more recent divisions from the United States. The oldest Lutheran congregation of western Canada was organized by the Icelanders at Gimli in Manitoba in 1876. Its first pastor, Paul Thorklaksson, had been educated in a conservative theological school in the United States, and his preaching was very conservative in tone. This seems to have been unacceptable to a minority group in his congregation. These dissenters secured within the first year of Thorklaksson's pastorate a more liberal pastor from Europe, Dr. Jon Bjarnson. Thus early in its history the small colony at Gimli was divided into two competing Lutheran congregations, known respectively as the Icelandic Synod of America and the Icelandic Congregation in New Iceland.[51] A similar division took place in an Icelandic community at Selkirk after its organization into a congregation in 1889. Here the dissidents broke away to form a Unitarian Church.[52]

The oldest German-speaking Lutheran church was founded in Winnipeg in 1888 with Heinrick C. Schmielder as its first pastor; he also organized a congregation at Edenwold in what is now the Province of Saskatchewan. In 1896 he returned to the United States, but during his absence at Edenwold the Winnipeg Lutherans had secured a pastor, Martin Ruecius, from Germany (1892) who wisely sought to associate the western congregations with the Canada Synod. He was also successful in getting four pastors from this Synod to join him in missionary work in the north-west and together they brought into being the Evangelical

Synod of Manitoba and the North West, later changing its name to the
Evangelical Synod of Western Canada.[53] Unfortunately, an internal
division caused a split in the newly organized synod, with the minority
group attaching itself to the Ohio Synod of the United States.

From now on American synods began to add to the variety of
Lutheranism in western Canada. In 1905 the Ohio Synod, after a brief
missionary campaign, was able to form a Canada conference in affiliation
with the mother synod in the United States.[54] Swedish settlers became
the particular concern of the Minnesota District of the Augustana Church,
forming its first congregation in Stockholm, Saskatchewan, in 1889.

The Norwegian Lutheran Church of the United States began
missionary work in Vancouver and New Westminster in 1889, and from
British Columbia extended its activities into the prairie provinces. Its
scattered congregations were in time incorporated into the Norwegian
Lutheran Church of Canada, which now directs three institutions of higher
learning in western Canada.[55]

The Danish United Evangelical Lutheran Church, the Lutheran
Free Church and the Slovak Evangelical Lutheran Church hardly begins
to exhaust the varieties of Lutheranism in Canada. With the exception
of the Missouri Synod they are now all associated, fraternally at least,
in the Canadian Lutheran Council. This council has asserted an extremely
conservative position, accepting "the canonical scriptures of the Old
and New Testaments as the inspired Word of God and as the only
infallible rule and standard of faith and practice,"[56] supplemented
by the unaltered Augsburg Confession as the true interpretation of
Christian doctrine.

Despite this very orthodox statement, the Missouri Synod refuses
to associate itself with the Council, having been originally organized
in Chicago (1947) in protest against modernist tendencies within
American Lutheranism,[57] and insists upon the acceptance of scriptures,
without reservation as the written word of God. Its fundamentalist
outlook makes a strong appeal in the west, and the Missouri Synod now
has the second largest membership among the organized groups of
Lutherans in Canada.

VI

Two religious groups, the Congregationalists and the Baptists,
so prominently to the fore in the religious development in the Maritimes,

take a very secondary place in the religious history of western Canada. The former was very early upon the scene in British Columbia when W. F. Clarke, representing the Educational and Home Missionary Society of Montreal, organized a congregation in Vancouver in 1858. But the white members of Clarke's congregation took umbrage at the presence of coloured folk in the same meeting house, so the congregation was dissolved and Clarke devoted himself exclusively to work among negro refugees from the southern states.[58]

No other Congregational Church appears in British Columbia until Hugh Pedley organized a second church at Vancouver in 1887; it had a very uncertain existence, largely because of frequent change of ministers, and was only saved from complete disintegration by its absorption into The United Church of Canada.[59]

A Congregational mission was started in Winnipeg in 1879 by William Ewing, who, with the help of the Colonial Missionary Society of Great Britain, attempted to open up new centres at Brandon and Portage la Prairie. These remained very small in numbers; even with the addition of the United Brethren of Christ (1907) and a rather hopeful mission among some German-speaking settlers from Russia, Congregationalism was unable to obtain any significant following in the west, as its sophisticated presentation of the Gospel was hardly suitable for a pioneering community; also its failure to unite effectively in the years of expansion in the west was to prove a great handicap to its growth, a failure shared by the Baptists.

The Baptists, though they laboured under all the constitutional defects of the Congregationalists as a missionary religion, usually, because of the more informal preaching of their ministers, gained a larger following in pioneer communities. Their rather slow start as an organized religion in Canada's newer provinces was due to the fact that there were few Baptists among the first settlers in the north-west; furthermore, there was no missionary society in the older provinces that felt any special obligation towards this undeveloped region. But after Manitoba had become part of Canada some Baptists in Ontario, under the proddings of Dr. Fyfe, organized an *ad hoc* committee in order to send a delegate into the new province to investigate the prospect of organizing congregations in the north-west. The delegate chosen was Alexander McDonald, who visited Winnipeg in 1873, only to learn that Baptists were few and far between in the Red River area. Two years later he returned and succeeded in organizing a church at

Winnipeg "with a membership of seven, including the pastor."[60]   Shortly
after, two other congregations sprang up, one at Emerson (1876) and a
third at Stonewall (1878).

By this time the Ontario Convention had given an official approval
to the venture and appointed Thomas L. Davidson secretary of a Home
Missionary Society with the direction to give special emphasis to western
expansion.   The Baptists were now moving into the west in greater
numbers, so that by 1880 it became possible to form a Red River
Association with Alexander McDonald as its first moderator.[61]   The
newly formed association early received a cruel blow when its founding
father removed to the United States shortly after he had been appointed
field secretary for the north-west.   Constantly the Baptists were to be
frustrated by the loss of their ministers to the United States, but this
was compensated somewhat by the financial help they received from
American sources.

American missionary societies early came to the aid of a few
struggling Baptist churches on the Pacific coast.   The first of these had
been founded by William Carnes from Ontario, at Victoria in 1876; it
constituted at the time, a congregation of seven white and seven negro
members.   Lack of good leadership and of harmony between whites and
blacks almost wrecked this church at its inception.[62]   With the arrival
of Walter Barss from Nova Scotia in 1884 and with the financial aid
of the American Home Mission Board, Baptist expansion in British
Columbia became more marked.   By 1897 there were enough churches
to justify the formation of the Baptist Convention of British Columbia.
Then came the withdrawal of American support, and some very lean
years.

In 1907 the Convention entered into union with the Manitoba and
North West Convention in the hope of strengthening its failing fortunes,
but the larger body, known as the Baptist Convention of Western
Canada hardly prospered more than the two separate conventions due
to the fact that it was formed in a time of extreme financial depression.
During this era, a young minister, Alex Grant, arrived from the east,
and by introducing new revival techniques into Baptist preaching he
brought about a considerable increase in church membership.[63]

This revival led to an attempt to found a Baptist College at Brandon
in order to secure a native ministry.   But it was soon discovered that
the college was overtaxing the resources of the churches, and it was only

saved from complete extinction when it was turned over in 1938 as an undenominational institution to the Manitoba government.[64]

A brighter aspect to Baptist work in western Canada has been its missions among the non-Anglo-Saxon peoples; but even this work was marred when differences arose between the German- and English-speaking Baptists over the type of theological teaching at Brandon College. The Germans feared that the College was under the dominance of modernist teachers and withdrew from the Convention. This fear was not confined to German Baptists, so that there were numerous schisms from the Convention, leading to the formation of several fundamentalist sects, a phase of Baptist development in the west to be considered in a later chapter in this study.

VII

This survey of the historical development of the major denominations in western Canada would hardly be complete without some reference to the churches allied in spirit to eastern orthodoxy and the Mennonites. The Russian Orthodox Church, strongest in Alberta, is greatly confused at the present time because of political divisions. The old Orthodox autonomous church which refuses to recognize the patriarch at Moscow has its representatives in Canada, as well as a pro-Soviet group. There are also Russian emigrés who are in communion with the patriarch of Constantinople. Much larger than either of these is the Ukranian Greek Orthodox Church which has arisen out of great travail. Being originally a *uniat* church, it owed allegiance to the Pope, but early came into conflict with the Roman Catholic authorities in the west because of its insistence upon having married priests. Its members were also subject to vigorous missions among them by Presbyterians and Methodists, and the Greek Orthodox Church. In 1918 some Ukrainian leaders resolved to retain their cultural unity by organizing an autonomous church on a democratic basis. They first tried to get some candidates ordained to the priesthood by the bishop of the autonomous Russian Orthodox Church in the United States, but without success. Finally they succeeded in persuading the Metropolitan Germanos of the Assyrian Church to comply with their request. He ordained several young Canadian students, including Samuel W. Sawchuk, the present president of the executive council of the Ukrainian Church of Canada. Under Sawchuk's vigorous leadership the church secured as bishop,

Hilarion, a Ukrainian emigré who had been consecrated in Europe, and is now styled the Metropolitan of the Ukrainian Church of Canada. There has been considerable criticism of the nationalistic emphasis of this new branch of Orthodoxy, but the Ukrainians reply that they were dissatisfied with the authoritarian emphasis of the Roman Catholic Church and with the quality of the Protestant clergy in charge of the Ukrainian missions; they are convinced that the present democratically based church admirably suits the Ukrainian temperament, and they are hopeful it will make its own unique contribution to the cultural life of Canada.[65]

The divisions within the Mennonite community are even more complicated than within the Orthodox, as there are to be found in Canada six varieties of Mennonite religions; but there are two major Mennonite bodies, the General Conference Mennonite Church and the Mennonite Brethren, the latter a more evangelical group than the former, which are fast developing a church type of religion. From the beginning the Mennonite history in Canada was a stormy one, particularly after the Manitoba government began to interfere with the conduct of their sectarian schools; but after the removal of the hard "sectarian core"[66] to Mexico there has been less resistance to the secular state. Also there is an increasing contact with other religious denominations and a growing similarity in their church architecture and their formalized service to the conventional churches of Canada. The two major groups have their own theological colleges where they are producing an educated ministry, while their conferences are promoting cultural welfare activities along the conventional Canadian pattern.[67]

VIII

We have now reached a stage in our story of religion in Canada where the western missions are maturing and making their own contribution to the religious and cultural development of the Dominion. At the same time they are showing some sharp contrasts to eastern development. One conspicuous contrast is in the relative strength of the various churches. In eastern Canada the Roman Catholics have remained the largest religious group, but according to the census of 1911 they had fallen from first to third place in western Canada, with a total population of 291,487. First place had been assumed by the

Presbyterians with a membership of 350,511, followed by the Anglicans with 316,511. The Methodists, the largest Protestant denomination in central Canada came fourth in the west with a population of 260,346. Next in order came the Lutherans, numbering 152,512; the Ukrainians and Orthodox together made up some 77,729, followed by the Baptists with a population of 70,253; the Mennonites numbered about 31,713 and last of all the Congregationalists with a following of some 10,791.[68]

Although the major denominations in the west had by the opening of the twentieth century become embraced in the territorial churches of the east, yet there were considerable differences of cultural outlook. The spirit of Loyalism which played such a prominent role in eastern development had little influence in the west; absent also were the historic memories of the War of 1812 and the antipathy it had created towards things American.

The mixing of a greater variety of nationalities in the west has enforced a necessary toleration of creeds and cultures creating an impatience with eastern prejudices and emphases. Thus the west became a fruitful soil for novel religious experiments and provided an arena for one of the most significant developments in Canadian church history, the creation of The United Church of Canada.

REFERENCES

1. R. G. MacBeth, *The Making of the Canadian West* (Toronto, 1905), p. 18.

2.. *Vide* Goldwin Smith, *Canada and the Canadian Question* (Toronto, 1891), p. 59.

3. R. E. Gosnell, ed., *The Year Book of British Columbia* (Victoria, B.C., 1903), pp. 314-331.

4. *Vide* A. G. Morice, *History of the Catholic Church in Western Canada* (Toronto, 1910, 2 vols.), vol. II, p. 57 *et seq.*

5. *Vide* Charles Mair, *Through the Mackenzie Basin* (Toronto, 1908), pp. 25, 26.

6. *Vide* A. Bernier, *Les Dates Mémorables du Collège de Saint-Boniface* (St. Boniface, 1945), pp. 16, 17.

7. A. G. Morice, *op. cit.*, II, p. 214.

8. *Vide* J. W. Dafoe, *Clifford Sifton in Relation to His Times* (Toronto, 1931), p. 36 *et seq.*

9. *Ibid.*, p. 41.

10. A. G. Morice, *op. cit.*, II, p. 233.

11. *Ibid.*, II, pp. 234-240.

12. *Vide The Manitoba School Case, 1894* (ed. for the Canadian Government by the appellant's solicitors in London, 1895), p. 286.

13. O. D. Skelton, *Life and Letters of Sir Wilfrid Laurier* (Toronto, 1921, 2 vols.), II, p. 44.

14. *Vide* C. C. Lingard, *Territorial Government in Canada* (Toronto, 1946), p. 175 *et seq.*

15. For an interesting commentary on "the conflicts over the schools" *vide* Andre Siegfried, *The Race Question in Canada* (London, 1907), p. 80 *et seq.*

16. Quoted by M. Wade, *The French Canadians, op. cit.*, p. 544, from H. Bourassa, *Les Écoles du Nord-Ouest* (Montreal, 1905), pp. 1-3.

17. Robert Machray, *Life of Robert Machray* (Toronto, 1909), p. 216.

18. *Ibid.*, p. 226.

19. *Vide* A. R. Buckland, *John Horden, Missionary Bishop* (London, n.d., 7th ed.), pp. 68, 69.

20. H. A. Cody, *An Apostle of the North* (London, 1910), p. 229.

21. R. Machray, *op. cit.*, p. 229.

22. *Vide* Mrs. Jerome Mercier, *Father Pat, A Hero of the Far West* (Gloucester, 1909, 2nd ed.), especially p. 68.

23. *Vide* R. Machray, *op. cit.*, p. 314.

24. *Ibid.*, p. 391.

25. *Vide Journal of the Proceedings of the Third Session of the General Synod of the Church of England in Canada* (London, Ont., 1902), pp. 218-221.

26. For history of Anglican Church in northern Alberta *vide* F. A. Peake, *Anglican Beginnings In and About Edmonton, Alberta* (unpublished thesis, University of Alberta, Edmonton, 1953).

27. William Newton, *Twenty Years on the Saskatchewan* (London, 1897), p. 155.

28. J. T. McNeill, *The Presbyterian Church in Canada 1875-1925* (Toronto, 1925), p. 107.

29. W. W. Sweet, *The American Churches, op. cit.*, p. 116.

30. Quoted by E. H. Oliver, *His Dominion of Canada* (Toronto, 1932), p. 183.

31. *Ibid.*, p. 186.

32. *Vide* C. W. Gordon, *The Life of James Robertson* (Toronto, 1908), p. 332.

33. *Ibid.*, p. 333.

34. *Ibid.*, p. 354.

35. *Ibid.*, p. 364.

36. E. H. Oliver, *op. cit.*, p. 213.

37. *Ibid.*, p. 199.

38. *Ibid.*, p. 205.

39. E. H. Oliver, *op. cit.*, p. 215.

40. *Vide* James Woodsworth, *Thirty Years in the Canadian North-West* (Toronto, 1917), p. 6.

41. *Vide* John McDougall, *On Western Trails in the Early Seventies* (Toronto, 1911), *passim.*

42. J. Woodsworth, *op. cit.*, p. 95 *et seq.*

43. *Ibid.*, p. 85.

44. *Ibid.*, p. 193.

45. *Ibid.*, p. 194.

46. *Vide* S. D. Chown, *Some Causes of the Earlier Typical Evangelism* (Ryerson Essay, No. 43, Toronto, 1930), p. 6 *et seq.*

47. Quoted by S. D. Clarke, *Church and Sect in Canada, op. cit.*, p. 412, from the *Christian Guardian*, Nov. 9, 1887.

48. *Vide* J. S. Woodsworth, *My Neighbour, A Study of City Conditions, A Plea for Social Service* (Toronto, 1911), *passim.*

49. *Vide* James Woodsworth, *op. cit.*, p. 243.

50. E. H. Oliver, *op. cit.*, p. 164.

51. *Vide* J. J. Eyelands, *Lutherans in Canada* (Winnipeg, 1945), p. 157, *et seq.*

52. *Ibid.*, p. 182.

53. E. L. Lueker, ed., *Lutheran Cyclopedia* (Saint Louis, Mo., 1954), p. 162.

54. *Ibid.*, p. 163.

55. *Ibid.*

56. W. A. Mehlenbacher, *The Lutheran Church in Canada* (Pamphlet, available from the Canadian Lutheran Council, Winnipeg).

57. *Vide* E. L. Lueker, *op. cit.*, p. 606.

58. E. H. Oliver, *op. cit.*, p. 106.

59. *Minute Book of the First Congregational Church, Vancouver* (Archives, Union College, Vancouver), p. 254.

60. C. C. McLaurin, *Pioneering in Western Canada* (Calgary, 1939), p. 78.

61. *Ibid.*, p. 94.

62. *Ibid.*, pp. 247-248.

63. *Ibid.*, p. 259.

64. *Ibid.*, pp. 295-314.

65. Based on personal interview with Samuel W. Sawchuk, Principal of St. Andrew's College, Winnipeg, and President of the Executive Committee of the Consistory of the Ukrainian Greek Orthodox Church in Canada.

66. *Vide* C. A. Dawson, *Ethnic Communities in Western Canada* (Toronto, 1936), p. 110.

67. *Vide* C. H. Smith, *The Story of the Mennonites* (Newton, Kan., 1950, 3rd ed.), p. 702 *et seq.;* also *Jahrbuch der Konferenz der Mennoniten in Canada* (Abbotsford, B.C., 1954), especially "Report of the S.M.Y.O. given at the C.M.Y.O. Business Meeting held July 6, 1954, at Abbotsford, B.C." for welfare and cultural activities, pp. 194-196.

68. Figures based on the *Fifth Census of Canada, 1911*, II, p. 2.

XIX

Church Union

THE GREAT architect of the Canadian nation, Sir John A. Macdonald, designed a country with a railroad "as its principal axis."[1] It remained for his younger contemporary, Sir Wilfrid Laurier, to complete the design by bringing peoples from all over the world to live along this and another transcontinental railroad that he himself initiated. Thus the north-west was colonized by railroads; hundreds of small communities sprang up along these arteries of trade between east and west, and people of very divergent cultures were immediately challenged to create a new communal life that might in some sense fit into the Canadian pattern. The churches were expected to give the lead in this task, and the cultural development of the new Canadians became one of the most pressing problems of the home mission boards.

At first these boards insisted upon perpetuating sectarian exclusiveness with the result that "Everywhere in the North-West can be found little Match-box churches, built by the English-speaking, all poorly equipped, poorly heated, lighted and ventilated, the congregation small and struggling, and the minister inadequately paid."[2] As was to be expected, the inhabitants of these railroad towns became impatient with a sectarian system which not only prevented them from enjoying adequate church facilities but also from entering into full communal life with their neighbours; never had sectarianism appeared more incongruous than in these sparsely settled towns and villages where the paramount need was to break down cultural and racial barriers. Accordingly these railroad communities took it into their own hands to create a church adequate to their needs[3] and were to stop at nothing short of a national church for Canada. In doing so they involved their country in one of the most unusual emotional crises of its history.

I

To Principal Patrick of Manitoba College, Winnipeg, belongs the honour of launching the "frail bark of organic union on the calm sea of ecclesiastical politics—a sea destined to become rough with the waves of opposition to the proposed merger."[4] During the opening session of the Presbyterian General Assembly meeting at Winnipeg in 1902, a committee was appointed of which Principal Patrick was a member, to convey greetings to the Methodist General Conference also meeting in Winnipeg. In the course of his remarks to the Conference, Patrick, on the spur of the moment made a dramatic plea for the organic union of the Methodist and Presbyterian churches of Canada.

The speaker had sounded the right note as far as the Methodist Conference was concerned, for it immediately passed a resolution favouring organic union among the Protestant churches of Canada, but added that in view of the fact that the relations of the Congregational, Methodist and Presbyterian churches had been "marked by a great deal of spiritual unity . . . the time is opportune for a definite, practical movement concentrating attention and aiming at the practical organic union" of these three denominations.[5] This was followed by the appointment of a committee of influential clergymen and laymen to be ready to confer with similar "union committees" that might be set up by other church bodies. The following year the Congregational Union of Ontario and Quebec formed a similar committee.

It took the Presbyterians two years to make up their minds to respond to this practical overture from the Methodists and Congregationalists; but at a meeting of the General Assembly held at Saint John, New Brunswick, a church union committee was appointed as tangible evidence of the willingness of the Presbyterian church to confer with other churches on the subject of organic union. Not unrelated to this decision was the spontaneous formation by laymen of church union societies with the purpose of "collecting and disseminating, either by the press or otherwise, all information that will tend to advance the cause of Church Union in Canada." The societies were pledged "to enlist the sympathies and services of as many people as possible to carry out the above idea."[6] As their members were for the most part drawn from the Presbyterian, Methodist and Congregational churches there was a tendency for them to emphasize the immediate union of their respective churches as the most feasible first step in setting up a united church of Canada.

In a remarkably short time they had created a strong climate of public opinion in favour of immediate action on the part of the governing bodies of the churches; furthermore, community churches were springing up all over the west; so that when the three union committees met together for their first conference at Knox Church, Toronto (December 21, 1904), to form a Joint Committee of Union there seemed to be little occasion to discuss either the merits or feasibility of church union:[7] the task of the Joint Committee was for all intents and purposes to regularize a situation that was rapidly getting out of hand, particularly on the prairies.

II

As the Committee got down to the great task in hand only one serious obstacle to unity seemed to loom on the horizon, and that was a rather violent theological controversy over Biblical studies in the theological colleges, started by no less a personage than the general superintendent of the Methodist Church, Dr. Albert Carman. Although Dr. Carman had long been the revered head of the united Methodist Church, he had also been the last bishop of the Methodist Episcopal Church, and represented an older generation of circuit riders who had little patience with modern Biblical scholarship which seemed to them to be undermining the very foundations of belief. It soon became evident after some of his more violent attacks upon the "modernists" in the public press that Dr. Carman also had many sympathizers in other churches as well as his own.[8] His inflammatory verbal assaults upon the new school of theology were extremely annoying to the younger theologians who had welcomed the prospect of church union as an excellent opportunity for a restatement of Christian doctrine in the light of modern scientific knowledge and recent Biblical research.

The findings of modern Biblical research and historical studies had been slow in reaching Canada, but at the opening of the century they were being eagerly studied in both universities and theological colleges; at Victoria University, Dr. George Workman had dared to say "that no scholar of repute today accepts the 'dictation' theory of inspiration."[9] His students were apparently in a mood also to throw over the older conception of Biblical inspiration as was the Chancellor of the University, Dr. Nathanael Burwash; nevertheless, through the efforts of Dr. Carman, Workman was forced to retire from his chair in 1899. He was then invited to become a member of the teaching staff of the Wesleyan College; but here he was challenged once again by Dr. Carman on his theological views and in 1907 was dismissed from his post.[10] Despite these dismissals and the disapproval of church authorities, his views continued to have wide dissemination and were being taken for granted by the younger clergy and a good many intelligent laymen within the Methodist Church.

A similar development was taking place at Queen's University under the leadership of Dr. W. G. Jordan, where, through the tactful support of Principal Grant, it met with far less opposition than in the Methodist colleges.[11] Also at the Congregational College in Montreal, Principal John Frederick Stevenson, during his term of office from 1878 to 1886, had familiarized the rising generation of Congregational youth with contemporary European theological scholarship.[12]

Parallel with liberal Biblical studies there was developing a new interest in philosophical research. This had been initiated by Professor John Watson at Queen's and Professor George Paxton Young at Knox College, Toronto, and was an attempt on the basis of Kantian-Hegelian idealism to bridge the gulf between science and religion.[13]

In view of this wide-spread interest in the reconstruction of belief at the opening of the twentieth century in Canada, there was some justification for the intellectuals in the churches to believe that now was the opportune time to revise the classical creeds of the church. As the most serious opposition to any such revision was expected from the Methodists, the modernists were greatly cheered when Dr. George Jackson, an English Wesleyan minister, well versed in the new exegesis of the Bible, was asked in 1905 to occupy the influential pulpit of the Sherbourne Street Methodist Church, Toronto. His public lectures on the early narratives of Genesis, to the effect that those chapters could no longer be regarded as "literal history,"[14] were so well received by Toronto audiences that it seemed quite probable that the sub-committee on doctrine, representing the Joint Committee of the negotiating churches, would produce a very "modern document." However, such hopes were soon turned to despair and the whole project of union was jeopardized by the redoubtable Dr. Carman, who at a critical point in the negotiations resorted to the press[15] to denounce Dr. Jackson and all his works in terms of withering scorn. Though many influential Methodists such as Chester D. Massey and Newton W. Rowell entered the controversy on Jackson's side,[16] yet Dr. Carman was still able to rally strong support for his stand at the General Conference of 1910.[17]

In such an intellectual atmosphere as this it was indeed optimistic to expect any radical restatement of the creeds of the church, and even if Dr. Carman had not stirred up the fundamentalists, there was little probability that the members of the sub-committee on doctrine would have attempted any far-reaching revisions of the churches formularies, for they were for the most part well advanced in years and quite conservative in outlook. Furthermore, their terms of reference were not revision, but rather to find a formula that would not trespass too harshly upon the particular confessions of faith of the three negotiating churches; and in this they succeeded admirably, as the preamble to their doctrinal statement makes clear. It reads as follows: "We further maintain our allegiance to the evangelical doctrines of the Reformation, as set forth in the doctrinal standards adopted by the Presbyterian Church in Canada, by the Congregational Union of Ontario and Quebec, and by the Methodist Church." Appended to the preamble was a statement of faith, closely fashioned from the Brief Statement of the Reformed Faith as put forth by the Presbyterian Church, U.S.A., in 1905, and supplemented from the Articles of the Faith as prepared in 1890 by the Presbyterian Church in England.[18] There was also an attempt to create a delicate balance between the Calvinism of the Westminster Confession and the Arminianism of John Wesley. It is a document to which very few conventional Protestant churches can take exception, and was admirably conceived for the purpose in view.

III

The sub-committees on the ministry and on polity were to find their assignments far more difficult than the sub-committee on doctrine. The nature of the ministry itself involved little discussion as all three churches assumed the validity of one another's orders; nor did church government present any insuperable obstacle to unity. It was soon discovered "That while the officers and courts of the negotiating Churches may bear different names, there is a substantial degree of similarity in the duties and functions of these officers and courts."[19] Accordingly, it became a matter of redistributing a plurality of familiar names to the officers and courts of the united churches. The highest court was to be known as the General Council (a Congregational term), presided over by a moderator (a much venerated Presbyterian title). Next in order were to be eleven territorial conferences to be made up of three or four hundred ministers and an equal number of laymen, elected from the sessions and official boards of local congregations, exercising authority over the ministry in the matter of admission and discipline; below the conference was to be a presbytery to maintain oversight of pastoral charges, to superintend the education of candidates for the ministry and to license, induct and to have oversight of ministers within its area.[20]

There were two matters of great importance that caused serious disagreements—the imposing of tests upon candidates for the ministry and the placing of ministers in their pastoral offices. On the first all three churches represented varying points of view: the Congregationalists were in the habit of examining their candidates on their theological beliefs and their religious experiences, but objected to submitting them to any formal subscription to creeds; the Methodists were inclined to inquire carefully into the personal habits of a candidate to the ministry, whether he smoked or indulged in intoxicating liquor and such like things; while the Presbyterians, less concerned with personal habits, have always laid great emphasis upon an "oath of fealty to the doctrine and courts of the church." After much discussion it was finally agreed that "the duty of inquiry into the personal character, doctrinal beliefs, and general fitness of candidates for the ministry, shall be laid upon the Presbytery, District Meeting or Association."[21]

Much more prolonged debate took place over the matter of formulating definite questions to be put to the candidates at the time of ordination. J. K. Unsworth, a one time Congregationalist, is credited with having blocked for over a year any formal subscription to doctrine on the part of would-be ministers. Ultimately the following provision was accepted by all concerned: ". . . candidates shall be examined on the Statement of Doctrine of The United Church, and shall, before ordination, satisfy the examining body that they are in essential agreement therewith, and that as ministers of the Church they accept the statement as in substance agreeable to the teaching of the Holy Scriptures."[22] This was supplemented in the ordination service with three brief questions: on belief in Christ, a divine call and belief in the Holy Scriptures.

Even more contentious was the matter of devising a suitable method for placing a minister in his pastoral charge. The Methodists were determined to retain the stationing committee so closely associated with an itinerant ministry which they still regarded as of the essence of Methodism. The Presbyterians and Congregationists were equally wedded to a call system, whereby a congregation sought out a minister for itself and made its own arrangements on the length of tenure, stipend and such like matters, directly with the minister concerned. This system appeared to the Methodists to be leaving the minister too much at the mercy of the congregation; while the Presbyterians and Congregationalists were equally convinced that a dictatorial stationing committee was a most undemocratic procedure. As neither side was inclined to yield on what seemed to be a matter of principle, the sub-committee attempted a synthesis of the two systems which worked out as follows: the individual congregation should have the right to call a minister, but the appointment of the minister should be vested in a settlement committee. As this appeared to be creating a future impasse, the following explanatory note was added: "while the right of appointment shall rest with the Settlement Committee it shall comply as far as possible with the expressed wishes of ministers and pastoral charges."[23]

IV

By 1908 the Joint Committee had completed its Basis of Union, and looked forward expectantly to quick approval from the supreme governing bodies of the three churches concerned. Two of these gave almost immediate confirmation but in the third there was to be an acrimonious debate for almost two decades before the final consummation of church union could be achieved. The Congregationalists were most expeditious; in 1910 their Union sent the Basis to its congregations where it received an overwhelming approval and from that time on the Congregational Union held "itself in readiness to take all necessary constitutional and legal steps when these should be called for"[24] to enter into the United Church of Canada. In the same year the General Conference of the Methodist Church, after voicing its approval of the Basis, sent it on to district meetings and annual conferences for adoption or rejection; these also gave a very substantial vote for its acceptance. Two years later the Methodists arranged for their congregations to express their opinion on the Basis by a popular vote. This showed the Methodist communion at large as overwhelmingly in favour of union, so that from 1912 on the General Conference was fully prepared to consummate the proposed union.

With the Presbyterians matters were not so simple as with the other two churches; there was a definite procedure to follow in relation to the Barrier Act which provided that "no prepared law or rule relative to matters of doctrine, discipline, government or worship shall become a permanent enactment until the same has been submitted to Presbyteries for consideration."[25] In 1910 the General Assembly by a majority vote approved the Basis and then in accordance with the Barrier Act transmitted it to the presbyteries for their judgment, after which, if the presbyteries approved, it was to be sent on to the sessions and congregations to test the general opinion of the rank and file of church membership. The result of the vote in the presbyteries was fifty for the Basis, twenty opposed. The plebiscite among the congregations held in 1912 showed a similar cleavage of opinion: about 67% were in favour of the Basis, while 32% registered their opposition.[26] Because of the considerable minority opposed, it was decided by the General Assembly to ask the Joint Committee to accept some changes in the Basis; though these were rather minor, it was decided after submitting the changes to the presbyteries to test popular opinion once again. This was done in 1915, only to reveal "a growth of sentiment against the union,"[27] but with still a large majority in favour. Consequently, the General Assembly meeting in Winnipeg in 1916 resolved that at the end of the war it would "unite with the Methodist Church of Canada and the Congregational Churches of Canada to constitute 'The United Church of Canada'."

As soon as this decision was made there arose such a storm of protest within the Presbyterian family that at the meeting of the General Conference of 1917 a resolution was passed calling for a truce in propaganda activities until the end of the war.[28] Comparative peace reigned within the Presbyterian Church until 1921, when the Assembly by a vote of 414 to 107 decided to consummate the union and directed the Joint Committee on Law and Legislation to proceed to the preparation of the necessary legislation. In doing so it knew it was going to create a schism within the Presbyterian Church; but if it failed to act it also faced an even larger schism, since there were in Canada by 1923 local church unions amounting to more than 1200 pastoral charges, including in them not less than 3000 congregations or worshipping units.[29] As many Presbyterians had entered these unions with the approval of the General

Assembly it was felt that to fail to consummate the union would be a breach of faith on the part of the supreme governing body of the Presbyterian Church of Canada.

The legislation called for by the Assembly was finally approved by that body in 1923, and enacted into law in 1925. The years between the irrevocable decision of 1921 and its consummation in 1925 were used by the opponents of union to rally all their forces for a last ditch stand, and proved to be the most tumultuous in the religious history of Canada.

IV

Nor were these opponents confined to the Presbyterian Church alone. As a matter of fact all the major churches of Canada watched the consummation of Church Union with considerable trepidation, as they feared the attraction of what might well come to be a national church of Canada. The one that might appear least concerned, the Roman Catholic, was seriously troubled over the prospect of a united Protestantism, particularly in western Canada. George Thomas Daly, the rector of the Cathedral of Regina, wrote extensively on the subject, and though he arrived at the conclusion that "this movement of Church-Union [indicated] the complete disintegration of Protestantism and the open condemnation of its fundamental principles,"[30] nevertheless, he was at the same time constantly urging upon his co-religionists more generous support of the Catholic Church Extension Society as the best means of meeting the combined strength of Protestantism on the western frontier.

Not unrelated to church union was the removal of·the very able Bishop McNeil from St. George's, Newfoundland, first to British Columbia to become the archbishop of Vancouver (1910) where he began to organize Roman Catholic propaganda suitable to western conditions, and then in 1912 to the very important see of Toronto from where he began to direct Roman Catholic strategy in the west towards the new Canadians and the English speaking community generally. The reason for this obvious transfer of the direction of western work from the see of Montreal to Toronto was no doubt due to the former's loss, through inept handling, of a large portion of the Ukrainian Uniat Church, from the Roman Catholic communion. As the newer Canadians were showing a preference for the English rather than the French language it had been decided by the hierarchy to erect at Toronto St. Augustine's

Seminary for training English-speaking priests, and to Archbishop McNeil had been entrusted the task of "breathing a soul"[31] into the new institution. Also he was given the responsibility of directing the policy of the Catholic Extension Society in combatting the inroads of Protestant missions among Roman Catholic racial groups in the west. Appeals for the Society became the more urgent as church union and more aggressive Protestant missionary activity loomed on the horizon.[32]

Enthusiasm for church union in western Canada was to create a more serious problem for the Anglicans and Baptists than for the Roman Catholics; both of them received pressing invitations from the Joint Committee of the negotiating churches in 1906 to participate in the negotiations to bring about a more inclusive union, and there was no inconsiderable desire from their constituencies to make some friendly response to this invitation. The Baptists, however, were seriously handicapped in giving any definite response, as they had not yet succeeded in organizing a Canadian federation of their regional associations. In the Maritimes the Regular and Free Baptists had in 1906 formed the Maritime Convention and were inclined to confer with the Joint Committee, but the Baptist Convention of Ontario and Quebec finally arrived at the conclusion that Baptist principles compelled them "to maintain a separate organized existence . . . to propagate their views throughout the world,"[33] and the Maritimes ultimately concurred with their position. Part of the reason for this abrupt dismissal of the Joint Committee's invitation may have been due to a smouldering dispute within the Convention of Ontario and Quebec over Biblical inspiration which, by the time church union was achieved, had split the Convention into two factions, Union and Regular Baptists, causing many Baptists, particularly in the west, to revert to the sectarian type of religion.[34]

For the Anglicans the invitation was not as easily dismissed as for the Baptists, since they had long been advocates of a united national church of Canada. As early as 1881, Canon (later Bishop) Carmichael had urged that the church "should face infidelity and heathenism unitedly" and "march as an army rather than as independent regiments, and in some way, as yet undefined, for the love of Jesus and the good of souls, be united."[35]

Five years later (1886) the Anglican Synod sent out an invitation to other Christian bodies for a conference looking towards the reunion of the churches to which there was an immediate response from the Presbyterian and Methodist churches. While these conferences were being

initiated the famous Lambeth Quadrilateral appeared upon the scene
(1888) and there was for a time a deepened interest in the prospect of
a united Protestant church in Canada. But the insistence of the
Quadrilateral upon the acceptance of the historic episcopate as the
guarantee of a valid ministry was something the non-episcopal churches
refused to accept, and the Quadrilateral proved ultimately to be more
of a hindrance than a help to the project of unity in Canada, as the
Anglicans felt that they must negotiate within its terms of reference.

When in 1906 an invitation was extended to the General Synod
to join in the work of the Joint Committee, it appointed a committee for
that purpose, but with the stipulation that it must confer "along the
lines laid down by the Lambeth Conference of the present year."[36]   As
this stipulation was unacceptable to the Joint Committee, the overtures
were soon abandoned, but there was continued apprehension in western
Canada as to the ultimate effect upon the Anglican missions in the north-
west if a distinctively Canadian church appeared upon the scene, particularly as the Church of England with its rather parochial name was being
more and more ignored by new Canadians who were looking for a church
of Canada as their passport to full Canadian citizenship.   Upon Archbishop Mathieson of Rupert's Land, who became primate of the Anglican
Church in 1912, fell the chief responsibility of leadership during the
critical years leading up to the final consummation of church union;
and as a westerner he was perhaps more apprehensive as to its effect
upon the fortunes of the Church of England in Canada than were his
eastern colleagues.

A second Lambeth Appeal for church union in 1920 with less
emphasis upon the historic episcopate appeared as a godsend to the
Canadian Primate, and he hastened to get a committee appointed by
General Synod (1921) to open negotiations with the union committees
of the other churches. He then sent a letter to the Joint Committee
asking it to consider on the basis of the new Lambeth Appeal a more
inclusive union than the one they then had in view. This letter of the
Anglican Primate was somewhat of an embarrassment to the members
of the Joint Committee as they were now determined to complete the
projected union before getting involved in further negotiations which
might lead to even greater divisions within their own churches. By the
same token they were disinclined to appear unresponsive to the larger
vision that Archbishop Mathieson was urging upon them with considerable
persistence; a curt refusal could well have been used by the opponents

of the smaller union as evidence of the lack of a sincere ecumenical spirit on the part of the Joint Committee.[37] Nevertheless, they frankly admitted that they did not wish to introduce a distraction into negotiations that had been going on for almost two decades and respectfully suggested "that any further steps in the direction of a still larger union be postponed until the three churches could take action as a united body."

But by this time there was a rather firm determination on the part of some Anglicans not to be left out of a union that might well become the most significant event in the religious development of Canada; also there were some Presbyterians who felt that somehow the approaching schism in their own church might be avoided if the Anglican Church were included in the final consummation of church union. In Montreal a group of Anglicans and Presbyterians attempted a local union on the basis of the Lambeth Appeal and in May 1922 a rather startling manifesto appeared in the *Gazette*[38] signed by five Anglican and five Presbyterian clergymen offering to accept at once mutual ordination as a first step in creating an all embracing Protestant church for Canada. A conspicuous member of this "Group of Ten" was Dr. Richard Roberts of the American Presbyterian Church. For some reason the offer was ignored by the governing authorities of the two churches concerned.

One final attempt to get the Joint Committee to reconsider its decision to unite only three churches was made by J. E. Ward, the rector of St. Stephen's Anglican Church, Toronto, who on his own initiative issued a call in January, 1923, for "a national organization expressing the soul of Canada with a clear single tone big enough to embrace all the varied forms of worship existing in the Dominion."[39] This seems to have been the last effort of any of the non-participating churches to impede the final consummation of church union; from now on they became the interested spectators, though not always neutral, of the far more vigorous efforts of the non-concurring Presbyterians to prevent their church from entering into the union.

V

This opposition first began to assume an organized form after the General Assembly in 1910 gave its approval to the Basis of Union. In that same year there was formed the Presbyterian Association for the Federation of the Protestant Denominations.[40] It was hoped that by propagating the idea of a federal council of churches, such as existed in the United States, the proponents of the Basis might be persuaded to give up the idea of organic union. As the appeal did not get much response, the Federation was abandoned to be replaced by the Presbyterian Church Association,[41] formed shortly after the General Assembly voted in 1916 to enter into union with the Methodists and Congregationalists as soon as the war was over.

The new Association frankly proclaimed that it was determined to prevent organic church union, but the wartime truce of 1917 impeded at first any vigorous propaganda, and it was not until the General Assembly in 1921 again reasserted its intention to enter the union that the Association really got into its stride. At a meeting called at Toronto in September, 1922, with Dr. D. J. Fraser in the chair, it solemnly pledged its members to work for "the continuance of the Presbyterian Church in Canada."[42] The fury of its campaign so alarmed Dr. D. R. Drummond, the chairman of the General Board of the Presbyterian Church and a supporter of union, that he began to waver on the wisdom of going to parliament for enabling legislation. In the hope of preventing a schism within his own church he wrote a pamphlet entitled: "Is There Not a Way Out?" It was Dr. Drummond's opinion as expressed in a letter to the newspapers that "A union rooted in disunion is no union at all. Certainly it is not the union for which our people and General Assembly had voted." In his pamphlet he suggested that the negotiating churches should give up the idea of uniting themselves into a legal entity, and simply become an ecclesiastical entity to be called "The Federal Church of Canada . . . or any other name agreed upon."[43] There were several things of a practical nature that this ecclesiastical organization might do, but it would avoid the complete integration of work and worship as envisaged in the Basis of Union. Dr. Drummond was well aware that it was the union churches of the west, already well integrated with a council of their own, that were compelling the union Presbyterians to push on with all possible speed to the final legal enactments, and so he suggested that these churches might accept the Basis of Union as their fundamental charter and enter as a separate church into the federated churches of Canada.

Some prominent Presbyterian unionists like Dr. Clarence Mackinnon of Pine Hill College, Halifax, were inclined to give Dr. Drummond's plan a favourable hearing, but Dr. George C. Pidgeon, the alert strategist of the church union forces, declared the plan no way out of a "most solemn obligation and trust." It was designed as he recognized to avoid a schism and while he deeply sympathized with its purpose he was certain that its adoption would create a far more serious schism, in which all three churches entering union would be involved. Before a congregation which taxed the capacity of Bloor Street Presbyterian Church he declared: "The people who sacrificed their denominational identity at their church's bidding expect her to keep her word; they look to the Anti-Unionists to keep their word. There is nothing to do but to go forward; it is impossible to split these causes up again, and it is impossible to keep them as they are."[44] Dr. Pidgeon's arguments prevailed, and the waverers were won back.

The Presbyterian Association then proceeded to the serious business of organizing a continuing Presbyterian Church. For this task it employed a general organizer who was directed to set up anti-unionist committees in every synod, presbytery and congregation in Canada. One of his duties was to create and distribute literature pointing out the evils of church union; the general tenor of this literature was to the effect that "the certainty of proved Presbyterianism is preferable to the uncertainty of the organic union experiment"; that "Presbyterians want and will demand their own church as the best outward expression of their own inward convictions."

But while preparing for the continuance of a Presbyterian Church, after union became an established fact, the Association did not cease to hope that they might be able to block either in the courts or in legislature the final consummation of the United Church of Canada. When finally the enabling legislation reached the Dominion Parliament there was staged, as one writer put it, "the great ecclesiastical battle of the century so far as Canada is concerned."[45] Its dramatic interest was highlighted by the fact that the prime minister, W. L. Mackenzie King, was the chief spokesman for the anti-unionist forces while the leader of the opposition, Arthur Meighen, was the skillful champion of the unionist cause. It is generally conceded that Meighen's logical presentation of the unionist case was the decisive speech of a long-drawn-out debate. He pointed out that, "To the utmost of their power they [the three churches seeking legislation] have formed a union—indeed they have consummated the union—but, as all agree, legislation is necessary because of the civil rights involved." He then dared anyone "to deny them [the three churches] the consummation of the union which they themselves have effected."[46] It was a contention impossible to deny, so the bill setting up the United Church of Canada received royal assent on July 19, 1924.

With the passage of the enabling legislation the battle passed from parliament to the congregations, as the Church Union Bill provided an opportunity for any congregation, if it so desired, to vote itself out of the union.   It was now the aim of the Presbyterian Association to force a vote wherever possible.   As might be expected the controversy between the two Presbyterian factions became exceedingly acrimonious during the last frantic days of voting, dividing not only neighbour against neighbour, but even creating tension within family units.

Because of the various methods of voting in the different provinces and the innumerable ballot disputes that arose during the counting, it has been impossible to get a reliable estimate of the result of the voting. Dr. C. E. Silcox, who has made an exhaustive study of the returns, thinks there was a grand total of votes in favour of union of 178,630 as over against 114,289 opposed; but as there were many congregations where voting did not take place, these figures have little meaning.   More reliable is the Canada Census of 1931 which reports a Presbyterian population of 872,428, indicating that the continuing Presbyterian Church had acquired during the days of readjustment more than half of the members of the former Presbyterian Church in Canada.[47]

Following upon the voting came the difficult task of dividing the property which was assigned to a neutral award commission.   Out of the total assets of some ten and a half million dollars, around three million, two hundred and fifty thousand dollars, or approximately thirty-one per cent were assigned to the continuing Presbyterian Church; included in the award were two theological colleges, Knox at Toronto and the Presbyterian College at Montreal.[48]

At the final session of the General Assembly of the Presbyterian Church in Toronto, the last act of separation was replete with drama. When the Assembly was about to adjourn, Dr. Ephraim Scott rose to protest an adjournment with the "object of blotting out the Presbyterian Church" and claimed the right of "seventy-nine members of that Assembly . . . to continue in session."   His request was refused, but according to his own version, "When the moderator pronounced the benediction and declared the Assembly closed, the seventy-nine loyal members immediately chose one of their number, an ex-moderator, to preside, and, amid the thunders of the organ, which blared its loudest to drown the proceedings, the Assembly was reconstituted with prayer, and then adjourned to meet at 11.45 that same night in Knox Church."[49] The following day Dr. Scott was elected moderator of a reconstituted assembly and immediately entered the pulpit to denounce church union as "our country's greatest national crime."[50] In this grim mood the continuing Presbyterian Church prepared "to face the duties of the present and to plan for the future."[51]

VI

On the same day (June 10, 1925) in Toronto arena "three great streams of religious life met and merged,"[52] sealing their union in an immense communion service. All were aware they were present at an historic occasion: one of the most significant and far-reaching church unions since the Reformation, drawing people from every corner of the country, from the United States and overseas. One enthusiastic correspondent described the scene as follows: "Rivalling in intensity of religious fervour and attendance any Protestant revival which the world has ever witnessed, yesterday morning's gathering will live long in the memories of those fortunate enough to be present. Beneath the lofty arched roof of the great Arena, the sacred covenant of union was signed on sheep-skin parchment by the leaders of the three uniting Churches, the while a sea of upward of seven thousand upturned faces gazed on the spectacle in silent reverence and prayer."[53]

Very little difficulty was experienced in fusing the three distinct strains that came together to form one church. Probably because of the violence of the attack upon the united church by its critics the actual fusion took place so readily—they had "to stand together for the cause of union on a dozen fronts."[54] The universal testimony of those who stood together in those formative days is that the union is a great success, not perhaps so much from a material point of view as a spiritual, through a cross-fertilization of ideas and an enlargement of vision.

But there was also some bitter aftermath. Because so many of the Presbyterian clergy entering the union had at the end of the balloting found themselves without churches, there was for a time a surplus of ministers; furthermore, many of the more prosperous Presbyterian congregations had thrown in their lot with the continuing Presbyterian church, while the overwhelming majority of the poorer or mission churches had joined the union, creating a financial embarrassment at a time when it was expected that the United Church would embark on a great missionary campaign among the new Canadians of the west.

Even more disappointing was the decline in Canada of the ecumenical spirit that had been so prominent in the opening days of the negotiations and enshrined in the Basis of Union as one of the chief objectives of the prospective church. The objective reads as follows: "It shall be the policy of The United Church to foster the spirit of unity in the hope that this sentiment of unity may in due time, so far as Canada is concerned, take shape in a Church which may fittingly be described as national."[55]   At the first meeting of the General Council the United Church ratified a resolution adopted by the General Assembly of the Presbyterian Church in Canada on June 5, 1924, expressing "the hope that the present union to which our beloved Church has committed herself . . . may under the Providence of God pave the way for further unions of the Churches of Christ."[56]   To this invitation little heed was given, as the spirit of unity animating the Protestant churches at the beginning of the century had been largely dissipated before the end of the first quarter.   What was peculiarly frustrating was the sectarian spirit being engendered by the bitter rivalry between the continuing Presbyterian Church and the United Church, as they feverishly began to organize competing congregations in almost every city, town and hamlet across Canada.   This new sectarian war on the circuits, so characteristic of the pioneer days of Canada, was surely an anti-climax to the twenty years of negotiations for a national church of Canada.   With the passing years the bitterness between the estranged branches of the former Presbyterian Church began to abate, so that by 1937 Dr. George C. Pidgeon was ready to allow the continuing Presbyterian Church the legal right to call itself the Presbyterian Church in Canada, though the name was still enshrined in the complete title of The United Church of Canada.[57]   During the Second World War the spirit of unity once again became manifest and was given a new impetus when the General Synod of the Church of England extended in 1943 an invitation "to any Christian communion which shares its hopes and aspirations for a reunited Christendom to meet with representatives of the General Synod to discuss a basis of union."   The invitation was eagerly accepted by The United Church of Canada and negotiations have been in progress ever since for an even more inclusive national church.

REFERENCES

1. Donald Creighton, *John A. Macdonald, The Old Chieftain* (Toronto, 1955), p. 475.

2. E. Lloyd Morrow, *Church Union in Canada* (Toronto, 1923), p. 63. Quoted from Professor Dyde, "The Journal of Relig.," Chicago, March, 1922.

3. *Ibid.*, p. 62.

4. *Ibid.*, p. 14.

5. *Journal of Proceedings of the Sixth General Conference of the Methodist Church* (Toronto, 1902), p. 172.

6. Pamphlet: *Montreal Laymen Organize to advance the Cause* (Archives of The United Church of Canada, Victoria University).

7. *Vide* R. J. Wilson, *Church Union in Canada After Three Years* (Ryerson Essay, No. 39, Toronto, 1929), pp. 14-15.

8. *Vide* C. B. Sissons, *A History of Victoria University* (Toronto, 1952), pp. 235-236.

9. G. C. Workman, *The Old Testament Vindicated* (Toronto, 1897), p. 36.

10. G. C. Workman, *For Members of the Montreal Conference of the Methodist Church* (Montreal, 1908); copy in the Archives, Victoria University.

11. *Vide* N. Micklem, "A Hundred Years of Theology," in *Queen's University: A Centenary Volume: 1841-1941* (Toronto, 1941), especially p. 105.

12. *Vide* C. E. Silcox, *Church Union in Canada* (New York, 1933), p. 134.

13. *Vide* John Watson, *Christianity and Idealism* (New York and London, 1897), especially pp. 121-152; also George Paxton Young, *The Ethics of Freedom* (Notes selected, translated and arranged by his pupil, J. G. Hume, Toronto, 1911), especially p. 586.

14. George Jackson, lecture on "The Early Narratives of Genesis" (delivered before the Young Men's Association, Toronto, 1909); copy in the Archives of Victoria University.

15. *The Globe* (Toronto, Feb. 26, 1909). A second letter entitled "Dr. Carman Holds His Course" appeared on the front page of the *Globe* on March 1, 1909. In the same issue Chester D. Massey wrote, "I desire as a layman of the Methodist Church to express my sincere regret at the unbecoming attack made by Dr. Carman on the Rev. George Jackson. . . . His letter is as intolerant as an encyclical of a medieval pope."

16. N. W. Rowell wrote to Dr. Carman on March 10, 1909. ". . . if the union of the churches, in which we have been so deeply interested, is delayed or rendered impossible for many years to come, I with great respect and with the greatest possible regret feel compelled to suggest to you that you will be largely responsible for the result because of instituting an ecclesiastical controversy." (Copy in the Archives of Victoria University.)

17. *Vide Journal of Proceedings of the Eighth General Conference* (Toronto, 1908), especially p. 374; a new paragraph inserted in the Discipline for disciplining a Professor, Lecturer or Teacher.

18. *Vide* E. L. Morrow, *op. cit.*, pp. 114-121; also T. B. Kilpatrick and K. H. Cousland, *Our Common Faith* (Toronto, 1928), p. 57, *et seq.*

19. *Basis of Union Together with a Brief Historical Statement* (Toronto, 1922), p. 18.

20. *Ibid.*, pp. 20-22.

21. *Ibid.*, p. 26.

22. *Ibid.*

23. *Ibid.*, p. 24; *vide* also C. E. Silcox, *op. cit.*, p. 144, *et seq.*

24. *Basis of Union, op. cit.*, p. 10.

25. Quoted by C. E. Silcox, *op. cit.*, p. 136.

26. *Ibid.*, p. 169.

27. *Ibid.*, p. 173.

28. On the truce of 1917 and its consequences *vide* George C. Pidgeon, *The United Church of Canada* (Toronto, 1950), p. 51, *et seq.*

29. C. E. Silcox, *op. cit.*, p. 228.

30. G. T. Daly, *Catholic Problems in Western Canada* (Toronto, 1921), p. 114.

31. George Boyle, *Pioneer in Purple: The Life and Work of Archbishop Neil McNeil* (Montreal, 1951), p. 145, *et seq.*

32. *Vide* G. T. Daly, *op. cit.*, p. 147, *et seq.*

33. *Canadian Baptist*, Sept. 12, 1907.

34. *Vide* W. C. Carder, *Controversy in the Baptist Convention* (Thesis, Baptist Historical Collection, McMaster University, 1950), p. 23, *et seq.*

35. C. E. Silcox, *op. cit.*, p. 106.

36. *Journal of Proceedings of the Fifth Session of the General Synod of the Church of England in Canada* (Kingston, 1909).

37. *Vide* Letter of Dr. J. E. Edmison to Dr. G. C. Pidgeon, Jan. 25, 1923 (Archives of The United Church of Canada, Victoria University).

38. *Gazette* (Montreal, May 22, 1922).

39. *Mail and Empire* (Toronto, Jan. 30, 1923).

40. *Vide* G. E. Silcox, *op. cit.*, p. 189, *et seq.*

41. *Vide* Ephraim Scott, *"Church Union" and the Presbyterian Church in Canada* (Montreal, 1928), p. 56, *et seq.*

42. *Resolution of Presbyterian Convocation* (Toronto, Sept., 1922), Copy in Archives of The United Church of Canada, Victoria University.

43. *Vide* D. R. Drummond, *Is There Not a Way Out* (Memorandum published by St. Paul's Church, Hamilton, Ont.).

44. G. C. Pidgeon, *The Church Union Situation in Canada*, p. 8. (Pamphlet distributed by the Publicity Department of the Joint Union Committee, Toronto, 1924.)

45. C. E. Silcox, *op. cit.*, p. 263.

46. *House of Commons Debates* (Ottawa, June 26, 1924).

47. Population per Canada Census of 1921 . . . Presbyterian, 1,411,792; Methodist, 1,161,165; Congregationalist, 30,788; 1931 . . . Presbyterian, 872,428; The United Church of Canada, 2,021,065. It may be that some members of the United Church through habit reported that they were Presbyterians during the 1931 census.

48. For "Division of Property and Legal Adjustments" *vide* C. E. Silcox, *op. cit.*, pp. 347-379.

49. E. Scott, *op. cit.*, pp. 65-66.

50. *The Toronto Daily Star* (June 11, 1925).

51. E. Scott, *op. cit.*, p. 64.

52. *The Globe* (Toronto, June 11, 1925).

53. Quoted by S. D. Chown, *The Story of Church Union in Canada* (Toronto, 1930), p. 120.

54. C. E. Silcox, *op. cit.*, p. 464.

55. *Basis of Union, op. cit.*, p. 3.

56. *Record of Proceedings of the First General Council* (Toronto, 1925), p. 214.

57. *Vide* Correspondence between G. A. Sisco and G. C. Pidgeon, 1937 (Archives of The United Church of Canada, Victoria University).

XX

Persistence of Sect Movements

THE YEAR the Methodist Church of Canada completed its process of consolidation (1884) Dr. George M. Grant wrote an article for the *Canadian Methodist Magazine* in which he paid a tribute to denominationalism as the weapon whereby liberty had been gained in the church, but now that liberty had been won he felt the Methodists like the Presbyterians were justified in laying the weapon aside. As an afterthought he added, "Or must the sword devour forever?"[1] The pessimism implied in this question was due to a new outbreak of sectarianism in Canada that would in time prove as embarrassing to the United Church of Canada in its attempt to create a national church as sectarian Methodism had been to the Anglican Church when it aspired to become the national church of British North America.

Although modern sectarianism bears many resemblances to earlier frontier movements there are significant differences which it will be the purpose of this chapter to set forth. One resemblance that seems to persist in Canadian history is the paradoxical alliance of other-worldly religions with a this-worldly political party; but even in this alliance the contrast between earlier and later sectarian development in Canada is most evident; for sectarianism in this century seems to be on the side of authority rather than liberty. A further contrast is the failure of twentieth-century sectarianism to achieve the same mass conversion as was common in the opening decades of the eighteenth century; still another striking contrast, for a time at least, was the pre-occupation of modern sects with urban rather than rural groups; but in more recent years the sects in Canada have become active in rural work, even invading the Indian reservations, long the sheltered preserves of designated churches, and the remote fishing villages of Newfoundland, where for almost two centuries three major denominations had dominated the religious life of England's oldest colony.

I

For the origin of this latest sectarian revolt against the conventional churches it is necessary to look beyond the borders of Canada, as it is part of a world-wide movement arising in Europe around the close of the Napoleonic wars. The pioneer of the revolt was the Catholic Apostolic Church (Irvingite) with its emphasis upon charismatic gifts and millenarian speculation; also the Plymouth Brethren with their insistence upon "sound doctrine" in conformity with a literal interpretation of the Bible played a remarkable role in creating discontent within prevalent eighteenth century "rational" religion.[2] The emphasis upon "sound doctrine" became more clamorous with the advent of the Darwinian theory of the origin of the species and the new school of Biblical criticism. Millenarian theories, however, soon began to dwarf the importance of "sound doctrine" among the modern sectarians, who were in revolt against the industrial revolution which was creating a depressed class whose only hope of the amelioration of their hard lot was through a divine intervention.[3]

There are innumerable millenarian sects, but for the most part they fall under two general categories: post-millenial and pre-millenial. The former expects the Gospel to permeate the whole world after which begins the millenium; at the end of the millenium Christ himself will return to the earth, then comes the resurrection of the dead followed by judgment, the destruction of the old world by fire and finally will be revealed a new heaven and a new earth. A more popular doctrine, as far as the dispossessed of this world are concerned, is the pre-millenial, which looks for an immediate return of Jesus, who will come before the millenial kingdom is established upon earth; His coming, however, is in two stages: the first in pre-millenial literature is known as the "Rapture" when He comes in the air to translate the "believers" from earth to heaven, including those who have already died. In the second stage He comes back with His people to the earth, overcomes Satan who is cast into the abyss; then follows a thousand years of bliss, after which Satan will be unbound and allowed to make one more effort to regain his rule upon earth, but he will be subdued once more and judged along with all lost souls and cast into the lake of eternal fire, while Christ and His true church will soar to heaven.[4]

This latter form of millenialism became very popular among American sectarians in the first half of the nineteenth century with a veritable rash of date-setting for the end of the world. One over-enthusiastic prophet, William Miller, a Baptist licentiate in New York State, decided that "the cleansing of the sanctuary" would occur some-time between March 21, 1843, and March 21, 1844. When this prophecy failed, others tried to improve upon Miller's calculations; among them "Pastor" Charles Russell who set forth his ideas in *The Divine Plan of the Ages* and Judge J. F. Rutherford who coined the phrase "millions now living will never die."[5]   To propagate these ideas there was formed the International Bible Students' Association, more commonly known as Jehovah's Witnesses.

Most of these adventist sects (to use a covering term) found their way to Canada during the middle of the nineteenth century, but circumstances at the time were hardly propitious for them and it was not until the opening of the twentieth century that they began to build up any substantial following.[6]

Another sectarian movement within the membership of the Methodist Episcopal Church of the United States, was at first to receive a more cordial welcome in Canada. It is known as the Holiness movement based upon John Wesley's doctrine of perfection.   It began at the end of the Civil War in the United States in reaction to an evident deterioration of moral and spiritual values during the post-war era. At first Methodist conferences were inclined to give their official approval to this attempt to improve the moral standards of their people.   Holiness associations were formed for the purpose of bringing about "the sanctification of the second blessing" or "the eradification from the heart of the believer of the natural depravity of inborn sin."   Soon, however, the "respectable" members of the Methodist Church found it increasingly difficult to tolerate the more extreme forms of "sanctification" which often involved rolling on the floor (Holy Rollers) or speaking with tongues (Pentecostals).   Also disturbing to the general membership of the church was a tendency on the part of holiness groups to indulge in pre-millenial speculation of the adventists.[7]

When finally the church decided to impose some restraints on the extremists, little groups here and there broke away from the Methodist discipline; out of these dissidents arose two new denominations: the Nazarenes and the Pilgrim Holiness Church. The former was from the beginning less demonstrative than the latter in its forms of worship and is now well on its way to a church type of religion.

II

It was not until after the Methodists in Canada had completed their union that the Holiness movement began to emerge north of the border; for a time it appeared to be entirely distinct from the American variety. The union of 1884 was a signal, as it were, for the long smouldering revolt of the disinherited against what they considered to be the abandonment of the simple frontier virtues of revivalism.

The leader of the revolt was Ralph Horner, whose meteoric rise to fame as a revivalist preacher resembles that of Henry Alline's a century earlier in Nova Scotia.[8]   A native of Shawville, Quebec, he was converted in 1872 at a Methodist camp-meeting near his home.   Immediately he began to preach to his neighbours and soon discovered he had an unusual talent for arousing strong religious emotions.   Like Alline he compared with amazement his new found way of life to the one he had abandoned.   In his *Reminiscences* he commented as follows: "A number of times I had drunk and danced all night . . . with the people of the community.   They having known me in my sinful life were now anxious to hear the new preacher."   It was because of an "experience of entire sanctification giving him perfect fitness for heaven that he felt clothed with power for soul winning."[9]

In 1883 he proceeded to Victoria University where he studied theology for two years, but during this time he was also engaged in organizing Holiness meetings and building up little groups similar to those that had been organized within the Methodist Episcopal Church of the United States a decade earlier; at the same time he was having grave misgivings about the kind of teaching he was receiving at Victoria University.   "It was," he writes, "a great trial to college professors to have me look them in the eyes and ask them if they had the experience of entire sanctification."[10]

His break with the Methodist Church began in 1886 when he refused to accept a circuit assigned to him by the Montreal Conference and proceeded on an evangelistic tour of his own devising.   For several years the Conference tolerated his free-lance revivalism, but a mounting torrent of protest against the confused noise of "speaking with tongues" and the rather terrifying prostrations that occurred during his preaching, compelled the Montreal Annual Conference in 1895 to depose him from its ministry.[11]   Accordingly, he organized his followers into a Holiness Movement Church; a convention was held the same year at Ottawa attended by sixty evangelists who arrived from Ontario and the western provinces as well as from Quebec. One of his first projects was the establishment of a college at Ottawa for training evangelists.

For a time the new sect entered upon a very expansive period, organizing conferences throughout Ontario, Manitoba, Saskatchewan, Alberta and even down into the state of Michigan. Like all modern sects it became very missionary-minded and carried the doctrine of entire sanctification to Ireland, Egypt and China.[12] The movement, however, was seriously retarded by internal dissensions over the true interpretation of sanctification. Ralph Horner had at the first conference of the new church been elected bishop, a position he held until 1916. In that year, after a disagreement with some of his colleagues, he abandoned the Holiness Movement Church to found the Standard Church of America. In 1918 this new church opened a college at Prescott, Ontario, and soon rivalled its parent body in its missionary zeal. But after Horner's death in 1918, both these Holiness churches declined rather rapidly in numbers and influence. At the present time the Holiness Movement Church has a membership of a little over 1,600, while the Standard Church has a slightly higher number of adherents.

III

A major contribution to the decline of the Hornerites, as they were popularly called, was the appearance in Canada in 1883 of the Salvation Army. It made a strong appeal to uprooted people in the urban centres of the Dominion. As S. D. Clark has emphasized in his study of the sectarians,[13] the Holiness movement coincided with the rise of the Canadian city during the last two decades of the nineteenth century. It was Ralph Horner who originated the use of a large tent for revivalistic services, being the urban equivalent for rural camp-meetings. The Salvation Army, however, dispensed with the tent and proceeded to hold open air services in the city streets, and thus made an even more immediate contact with the nomadic and unattached people of the cities. Its warm personal religion with an emphasis upon individual salvation, accompanied by such mystical incantations as "saved by the blood", soon gave it a far larger following than even the Hornerites were able to mobilize.

At first municipal authorities were horrified at its very unorthodox methods of preaching the Gospel and tried to suppress out-of-doors religious services; in some cases the Army was met with angry mobs who indulged in missile throwing. In both Montreal and Quebec there were mass arrests; but this form of persecution only seemed to add to the popularity of the Salvation Army among the social outcasts, and within a short time after its arrival in Canada there were few urban centres where a local body had not been organized.[14]

The Methodist Church which had for so long been the spiritual home of the poor and lowly felt its impact most severely, particularly when the more evangelically-minded of the Methodist ministers, in revolt against the new respectability of their church, became officers and preachers for the new sect. Seriously alarmed at this untoward development, the Methodist Church tried to save the situation by sending out teams of evangelists to conduct urban revivalistic services; one of the most famous of these was the Crossley-Hunter team which toured Ontario and the west during 1887 and 1889.[15] Such evangelists, however, seemed to contribute more to the sectarian than to the church cause, as they were inclined to set up their own Gospel halls independent of central supervision.

Another attempt on the part of the churches to meet the sectarian challenge was to imitate Salvation Army techniques. The Methodists instituted the Gospel Band movement, out of which evolved the Epworth League; and the Anglicans organized the Church Army, but neither of these ever became serious rivals to the Salvation Army.[16]

The latter, however, was not without its own internal problems. In 1891 P. W. Philpott led a revolt against what he considered to be too much centralized control by International Headquarters, and carried out of the Army a large number of officers who began to found independent mission halls. Fundamentally the schism was a protest against a policy of creating a new kind of social welfare church. This policy was more firmly adopted by Headquarters after the Army had gained tremendous popular approval for its canteen work during the First World War. In peace time it continued to receive large contributions as it had during the war from the wealthier members of society, whom it no longer wished to offend.[17] Its mass appeal as a conversion religion has considerably diminished in recent years, nevertheless, it still has a following of some ninety-two thousand members or about 0.5 per cent of the population, which is a very high proportion in relation to the other sects of Canada.[18]

IV

With the decline of the Salvation Army and the Hornerites as evangelizing forces, the way was opened for a large influx of smaller sects from the United States just when western Canada was undergoing rapid urbanization. Among the new arrivals were several varieties of Holiness sects, the most conspicuous being the Nazarenes, who quickly spread across Canada and now have a membership of 8,000, the largest concentration being in Alberta.[19]

The Holiness movement was soon to meet a serious rival in Pentecostalism, which is a composite of many groups that sprang up in America and Great Britain between 1900 and 1916.[20] Baptism by the Holy Spirit attested by the gift of tongues is set forth as the distinguishing mark of the Pentecostals; some of them place a strong emphasis upon the outpouring of the "Latter Rain" as an additional gift of the Holy Spirit; they are also enthusiastically pre-millenial. A Pentecostal revival occurred in 1907 at All Saints Anglican Church in Sunderland, England,[21] and this has led several Anglican clergymen to identify themselves with the Pentecostal movement in Canada.

Although the Pentecostals differentiate themselves sharply from Holiness sects by their rejection of the "second work of grace," nevertheless they are eclectic enough to include in their services such cultic practices as the gift of healing, clairvoyance, and revelations. One of the most eclectic of the Pentecostal sects is the Four Square Gospel of Aimée Semple McPherson; it is four square in that it is fundamentalist, perfectionist, adventist and charismatic.[22] Four Square tabernacles are to be found in most of the major cities of western Canada.

The Pentecostals, like the Holiness sects, lean heavily upon Bible colleges to spread their peculiar and very complicated beliefs; in this they have had considerable assistance from Anglican clergymen. One such leader prominent in the movement in western Canada is Dr. J. E. Purdie, who has served for twenty-five years as principal of the Western Bible College; he has been described by the General Superintendent of the Pentecostal Assemblies of Canada as "the dean of all our Bible Colleges and Institutes."[23]

Pentecostal growth and expansion has been more spectacular than any of the other sects: in 1911 it had a membership of 515, by 1961 it had grown to 143,877. The extent of the expansion is indicated by the fact that there are 11,237 Pentecostals in Newfoundland—clear evidence that Pentecostalism is no longer confined to urban centres but is now spreading to the most remote rural areas.[24]

V

Although Ontario still continues to lead all the other provinces of Canada in the variety and number of sect religions,[25] nevertheless, the sects exercise a greater influence in the social and political life of western Canada, simply because they represent a higher percentage of the total population.   This to some extent is due to the break-up of those homogeneous groups of " 'peculiar peoples' who have sought in *bloc* settlements to preserve their religion and their ways of life."[26]   While the settlements remained isolated from the outside world they were immune to the inroads of modern day sects, but once their isolation was broken into by the building of railroads and modern highways they soon became receptive to the latest refinements of pre-millenial and Pentecostal theories.

It is not surprising that they turned to the sects rather than churches when making a painful break with their old way of life, for most of them had descended from the apocalyptic wings of the Reformation churches. The most numerous were the Mennonites, originating from the Swiss Brethren, one of the oldest of the sixteenth-century Anabaptist sects. They ascribe their peculiar "separated" way of life to Menno Simons, who in 1536 broke from the Medieval Church to form an egalitarian and pacifist society.[27]   His followers were drawn from Switzerland, Germany and Russia, and within the general framework of Mennonism there has been from earliest times a variety of religious expression ranging from Unitarianism to millenialism.   After their arrival in America the same divisive tendency soon manifested itself and there are now at least sixteen varieties of Mennonites[28] in the United States, and five in Canada.

Closely allied to the Mennonites in doctrine and polity are the Hutterites who also originated from the Swiss Brethren, but remained "untouched by the Menno Simons' influence."[29]   They share with the Mennonites strong pacifist and egalitarian views, but they carry the principle of equality to far greater lengths, in that they insist upon a complete sharing of goods and eat at a common table.

With the introduction of general conscription in Russia, where they had been domiciled since 1771, they along with the Mennonites began to emigrate to America in 1874 upon condition that they would be exempt from military service. When this exemption was withdrawn by the Americans in 1918, they crossed the border into Manitoba and Alberta.[30] With their firmly knit communal government[31] they are less susceptible to the invasion of novel sects than are the other "bloc" settlements of religious groups, but occasionally a Hutterite does leave his colony and integrates himself into the secular world, usually with the help of one of the more cosmopolitan of the minor sects.

Less successful than the Hutterites in maintaining their own peculiar way of life are the Doukhobors, who with the help of the Quakers began to arrive in western Canada directly from Russia in 1899. Settled at first on some rich farmland in Saskatchewan they proved themselves capable farmers; unfortunately, their religious convictions made it impossible for them to qualify for patents for individual homesteads. A large number, incensed by the treatment they received in Saskatchewan, moved on to British Columbia into the Kootenay area.[32] Here during the painful process of readjustment to the difficult conditions of this region they began to indulge in bizarre protests against their hard lot. Often these took the form of nude parades symbolizing the "discard of man-made laws and authorities in favour of an 'inner voice' reflecting the 'laws of Christ'."[33] They are now broken up into many rival groups such as the Independents, Sons of Freedom, Union of Christ Colony and Sharing Doukhobors. Part of the cause of this fragmentation was a revolt against the drab and repressed life imposed by the original Doukhobor religion.[34] A good many have sought greater freedom from their taboos by identifying themselves with the secular world, but in doing this they have not found their way into the conventional churches, but rather have helped to swell the ranks of the Pentecostals and Jehovah's Witnesses.[35]

Still another religious group that shows a high degree of segregation as settlers, but is also becoming integrated into the secular life of the Canadian west are the Latter Day Saints or Mormons. Their greatest concentration is at Cardston, Alberta, where they have a Mormon Temple, the only one in Canada. Although Charles Ora Card, the founder of this community, fled from the United States (1880) in order to avoid conviction as a polygamist,[36] there is no attempt at present to defy the marriage laws of the province of Alberta. Despite the fact that the Mormons are increasingly playing an influential role in the political and social life of Canada, they are definitely on the sectarian side of the great religious divide. They identify themselves with the ancient tribes of Israel and believe they are a "chosen people" engaged in building a new Zion; like many of the sects they indulge in adventist prophecy based on a literal interpretation of the Bible as well as their own *Book of Mormon*. Although their economic life is dominated by Canada, culturally it is subsidiary to Utah.[37] According to the latest census they are about 50,000 strong, and firmly held together by the Mormon doctrine of obedience to those who have been placed in authority over the Mormon communities.

This Mormon doctrine of obedience to authorities finds its counterpart in other sects in what might be described as the cult of leadership. The leadership principle develops very naturally in the modern sects, since their origin and growth depends upon a preacher's ability to win converts away, not only from the traditional churches, but from other sects as well. Consequently sectarian colleges and Bible schools devote a great deal of time to courses in public-speaking which include all the devices of mass appeal, so that their graduates may be able to win a personal following.[38] Such techniques of evangelization, however, have had the effect of conditioning people to follow rather uncritically those sect leaders who are adept in the art of mass appeal. Thus the way was prepared for the emergence of a predominantly strong personality to unite the sects of western Canada into a compact political party, particularly, if he were able to secure the use of the modern media of mass communication.

In point of fact that is what occurred when William Aberhart, a Calgary high-school teacher, began to broadcast in 1925 a series of "prophetic lectures" from a Calgary theatre. Out of these broadcasts emerged the Prophetic Baptist movement which Aberhart transformed into a political party.

VI

The success of the Prophetic Baptist movement in winning converts for a new political party was not entirely due to the rhetorical gifts of William Aberhart. A quarrel over fundamentalism within the Baptist Convention provided him with his first congregation and it also gave him the opportunity to secure many former Baptist Convention ministers who helped him in organizing his new sect.

The fundamentalist controversy out of which arose the Aberhart movement is a rather late development in the Baptist communion. While the Jackson case[39] was disturbing the unity of the Methodist Church (1908), a leading Baptist theologian at McMaster, Toronto, was able to tell newspaper reporters that the matter of modernism had already been decided in his church and that "the doctrine taught at McMaster was essentially the same as Jackson's."[40] The professor, however, had spoken out of turn, for even then some Baptist ministers were manifesting great discontent over the "modernist" views of Professor H. T. Matthews of McMaster University.

The question of Matthew's orthodoxy was raised at the Ontario-Quebec Convention in 1910, and in the ensuing debate Professor Matthews was vindicated,[41] but this was by no means the end of the matter. Within the Baptist Church in Canada there had for some time been a strong tendency to indulge in pre-millenial speculation due, perhaps, to the intimate association of Baptists with the Plymouth Brethren. During the First World War there had been a marked resurgence of such speculation, and as pre-millenialism depends upon a literal interpretation of the Scriptures, there was an increased discontent with the modernist teachings of Dr. Matthews at McMaster.

The leader of the dissidents, Dr. T. T. Shields, founded in May 1922, the *Gospel Witness* which he designated as an "organ for criticism of 'modernism' and McMaster University."[42] In the first issues of this fundamentalist magazine the main target for criticism was Professor Matthews. For four years Dr. Shields continued his vehement attacks upon both Professor Matthews and McMaster University, until the Ontario-Quebec Convention in 1926 felt compelled to pass a vote of censure upon him; Dr. Shields then withdrew from the Convention and organized an Ontario-Quebec Association of Regular Baptist Churches, of which he became the first president. To his new association flocked a great many Baptist ministers, especially those "without university training, and practically all of Plymouth Brethren tendency."[43] The most devastating results of Shields' schism were felt in the Western Association, already flooded with pre-millenial literature from the Moody Bible Institute and its allied Bible schools in the United States. As Dr. Shields was opposed to the peculiar Moody form of pre-millenialism, he began to denounce it quite roundly and gave offence to a good many of his would-be followers in western Canada, with the result that they broke away from the Regular Baptist Association to form an Independent Baptist Fellowship more in accord with the "dispensational" doctrines of the Moody Bible Institute.[44]

It was out of this fragmented Baptist community that William Aberhart recruited the pioneer members of his own Prophetic Institute. A native of Ontario, where he began his teaching career, he had before his arrival in Calgary in 1910 become identified with the fundamentalist party within the Ontario-Quebec Baptist Union. In Calgary he became a Bible teacher under the sponsorship of the Westbourne Baptist Church. It was not long before his teaching on familiar pre-millenial themes, spiced with what he called "dispensational revelations" attracted a large following, compelling him to abandon the library of the Westbourne Baptist Church for one of the largest theatres in Calgary. From the theatre he began to broadcast his talks (Nov. 25, 1925) to a province-wide audience.[45] These consisted of a series of lectures entitled "God's Great Prophecies," in which he divided the world's history into four dispensations of time: (1) the beginning of things, (2) the time of the Hebrews, (3) the times of the Gentiles, and (4) the dispensation of grace.[46] The various parts of the scriptures were assigned to one or other of these periods, or as he put it, some revelations were for the Jews alone, others for the time of the Gentiles and still others applied only to those within the dispensation of grace; in this way Aberhart was able, to his own satisfaction, to make plausible the verbal inspiration of every word of scripture.

It soon became evident that a great many people on the prairies had been disturbed by modernist preaching and were hungering for the kind of infallible Bible that Aberhart was proclaiming. The popularity of his message led him to contemplate building an institute for the purpose of training young men and women as evangelists for his "dispensational" interpretation of the scriptures. Shortly after a radio appeal (1927) for funds for his contemplated college he was enabled to build the Calgary Prophetic Bible Institute, of which he became the first dean. He then invited the members of the Westbourne Baptist Church to use the auditorium of the new Institute as their place of worship.

At this point Aberhart's denominational allegiance becomes a bit confusing. Up to the time of the construction of the Institute he had been a lay member of the Westbourne Baptist Church which had formerly been affiliated with the Western Baptist Conference; but when it became noised about that Brandon College, supported by the Union, had gone modern, he persuaded the Westbourne Church to repudiate its membership in the Union and become an independent congregation.

The arrangement with the Institute, however, proved unsatisfactory to most of the members of the Westbourne Church, so they decided to move to the east end of the city of Calgary and reassume the name Westbourne Baptist Church.[47] Shortly after they sought affiliation with the Regular Baptist Association; as this association adhered to Shields's interpretation of the pre-millenial hope, the Westbourne Church had now cut itself off from Aberhart's movement, and the Dean of the Calgary Prophetic Bible Institute was compelled to build up a new congregation based upon his own pre-millenial doctrines.

His new following became known as the Bible Institute Baptist Church,[48] and was constituted out of his radio audience who listened faithfully to his lectures every Sunday; he also offered at the Calgary Prophetic Bible Institute a three-year course of training for any young people who wished to equip themselves for service in fundamentalist churches.

In his broadcasts of religious instruction on pre-millenial theology Aberhart often mingled prophesies on current political and economic events, revealed to him so he affirmed, by his study of the Old Testament prophesies. During the depression years of the 'thirties these political and economic references became more frequent and more popular. Looking around for economic ideas to suit the needs of the time he came upon Major C. H. Douglas' book on Social Credit, which seemed to serve his purpose admirably. Although the connection between Social Credit and pre-millenial theories is not too obvious, nevertheless, there are certain esoteric overtones in both that made a tremendous appeal to people who were caught in an unrelenting economic depression. Since Aberhart's economic doctrine offered them not only a new heaven but also a new earth here and now, he soon had a political as well as a religious following which swept him to power as premier of Alberta with an avalanche of votes[49] on August 22nd, 1935. Thus was repeated once again that strange anomaly in Canadian religious development—a sectarian religion of a most other-worldly type creating a very this-worldly political party. Such a feat, however, had not been achieved by the Prophetic Baptist Church alone; fundamentalist sects of most diverse views had found a common meeting ground in the political philosophy of Social Credit.

VII

A major contribution to the growth of the Social Credit movement is the Bible college, now a prominent feature in the cultural development of western Canada.   In some respects these colleges or institutes resemble the folk high schools of Denmark, as they enroll youth after they have had some experience in the work-a-day world and endeavour to inculcate a definite philosophy of life.   Consequently they are producing a great many lay leaders who are not only able to assist in the expansion of their respective sects, but also become active in the political field as well.   At his Bible school in Calgary Premier Aberhart was able to train politicians, some of whom became members of his cabinet, and one of them, E. C. Manning, assumed the mantle of leadership upon the death of his leader in 1943.

A very significant development among Bible schools in recent years is an emphasis upon the undenominational character of their teaching; thus they are creating a sense of unity among the sects, which contributes to greater political unity as well.   The Winnipeg Bible Institute and College of Theology founded, significantly enough, the same year as the United Church came into being (1925), took the lead in proclaiming a variant form of church union.   According to its catalogue it "stands for the unity of all true believers in Christ, irrespective of denominational affiliation or non-essential doctrinal views"; furthermore it proclaims itself "part of a movement which God has raised up in the past half-century for the preservation and proclamation of Bible truth."   But this new union, as the sectarians see it, in contradistinction to the union of the United Church, is to be based upon "the full divine authority and inerrency of the Holy Scriptures."[50]

The most famous of the undenominational schools in the west is the Prairie Bible Institute at Three Hills, Alberta.   Now in its thirty-fourth year it has an enrolment of over 1200 students, including those in elementary and high schools.   During its comparatively brief life it has sent some nine hundred missionaries into the foreign field as well as supplying a large number of the preachers for the Gospel halls and tabernacles of Canada and the United States.[51]   On its campus are to be found huge dormitories, an immense library of sectarian literature, an elementary school, a high school, a printing press, a saw mill, a fire station, garages, shops, barns, stores, playing fields, a hangar and a plane to transport speakers and choirs to various parts of the continent.   Many farmers about Three Hills have deeded their land to the Institute and have now become voluntary labourers, as members of the Institute's staff.   It is the boast of this institution that all its workers from principal to janitor receive an equal remuneration in the form of allowances and gifts.   Quite recently it acquired a tract of timberland at the foothills of the Rockies to provide lumber for an ever-expanding building programme.[52]

Although the college seems to have had a close association with the Christian Missionary Alliance Church in its founding days, it now claims to be strictly undenominational, a claim fully supported by the fact that its student body is drawn from over fifty different religious denominations from Canada and the United States.[53]

VIII

The success story of Three Hills Bible Institute serves to illustrate both the growing strength and the increasing unity of the sectarian movement in western Canada.   None of the traditional church theological colleges can begin to match the achievement of the sectarian colleges either in enthusiasm or in the number of their students.   Between 1922-1947 students at fundamentalist institutions increased steadily, while the theological colleges of the churches faced decreased enrolment. In Alberta alone the total number of students at the Bible schools "increased from 800 in 1940 to 2,100 in 1947".[54]   Nor have the sectarian congregations lacked for ministers, while all the long-established churches, including the Roman Catholic, were depending for the most part upon eastern Canada to keep them supplied with clergymen; these very often found western conditions too difficult and either returned to eastern Canada or moved across the border to the United States.

Although pre-millenial religion was born out of the travail of hard-times, the prosperity of recent years has not caused any diminution in its popularity.   In point of fact, it seems to be taking on renewed vitality and becoming part of the established pattern of western Canada. This may be due to the fact that the sects as well as the churches are sharing in the general religious interest that has arisen both in the United States and Canada in the post-war years.   If, as has been suggested, this renewed interest in religion has been stimulated by a desire for supernatural security in a world threatened by nuclear destruction it can well be that fundamentalist doctrine offers, on the face of it, greater security than the more sophisticated theology of the traditional churches. There is evidence that many congregations in the established churches are highly critical of the modernist views of their clergy,[55] and are inclined to give a sympathetic hearing to sectarian doctrine constantly proclaimed over the radio.

Along with the sects there are now springing up throughout Canada innumerable cults which specialize in the art of freeing man from his neurotic fears, and whose colleges are concentrating upon techniques of mental healing.[56] In this field of psychical comfort or "peace of mind" religion, there are many different forms of religious expression, ranging from Father Divine's Peace Mission Movement with its "Peace everyone, good health, good appetite, good fortune"[57] to Baha'ism, stressing the oneness of mankind, world peace and universal language. Both these cults along with Christian Science, Unity Truth, Church of Truth, Divine Science, Spiritualists, Rosicrucians and several others have their missions in Canada and are attempting to convey "peace of mind" through an eclectic combination of spiritual healing, mysticism, metaphysics and various other comforts.

At first sight this cultic development might be regarded as an alternative religion to the sectarian, but very often it appeals more strongly to the middle class, whose normal place is in the established churches, reflecting these churches' neglect of the art of pastoral counselling. Be that as it may, the statistics available on these cults do not seem to indicate that they are a serious threat to the sectarian movement in western Canada,[58] as most of the sects are adding to their fundamentalist appeal many of the cult techniques, such as affirmations and prayers for health and mental well-being, which are intended to give release from neurotic disturbances. The cults in the west as well as the modernist churches are under the suspicion that they are not sound in doctrine, since they are not usually fundamentalist and some of them favour an orientalist rather than a Christian theory of salvation.

For the present, at least, fundamentalism offers greater security to disturbed people in western Canada than cultic theories, and is creating a sense of unity among the sects, not enjoyed by the cults, particularly in the political field. It was on this common interest in an inerrant Bible that William Aberhart with his slogan "Back to the Bible" was enabled to become premier of Alberta. It is with this same common interest that his successor, Premier Manning, is holding the Social Credit

THE CHRISTIAN CHURCH IN CANADA

party together and upon which he expatiates every Sunday afternoon in a nation-wide broadcast from the Calgary Prophetic Bible Institute.

The effectiveness of the "Back to the Bible" slogan has been more recently demonstrated in British Columbia, when Philip Garlardi, a Pentecostal preacher from Kamloops, who became the minister of public works, made the Bible an issue in an election campaign and is acknowledged to have made a major contribution to the success of the Social Credit party in his province.

REFERENCES

1. Quoted by G. C. Pidgeon, *The United Church of Canada* (Toronto, 1950), p. 18.
2. *Vide* Edward T. Vernon, *Beliefs of Today: A Review of Modern Cults and Creeds* (London, c.1925), p. 47, *et seq.*
3. *Ibid.*, p. 15; also p. 116, *et seq.*
4. J. E. Purdie, ed., *What We Believe* (published by the Pentecostal Assemblies of Canada, Toronto, n.d.), pp. 28-32.
5. *Vide* E. T. Clark, *The Small Sects in America* (Nashville, 1937), pp. 43-62.
6. *Vide* S. D. Clark, *Church and Sect in Canada, op. cit.*, pp. 366-367.
7. *Vide* E. T. Clark, *op. cit.*, p. 76, *et seq.*
8. *Vide supra*, p. 119.
9. A. E. Horner, ed., *Ralph C. Horner, Evangelist, Reminiscences from His Own Pen, also Reports of Five Typical Sermons* (Brockville, Canada, n.d.), p. 13.
10. *Ibid.*, p. 46.
11. *Ibid.*, p. XIV.
12. *Ibid.*, p. XVI.
13. S. D. Clark, *op. cit.*, p. 371.
14. *Vide* Robert Sandall, *The History of the Salvation Army* (London, 1947-1950, 2 vols.), II, p. 254-260.
15. S. D. Clark, *op. cit.*, p. 406; *vide* also reference to Crossley and Hunter in J. Woodsworth, *Thirty Years in the Canadian Northwest, op. cit.*, p. 156.
16. On the difficulties of the traditional churches in down-town areas *vide* J. S. Woodsworth, *My Neighbour* (Toronto, 1913), pp. 155-174.
17. S. D. Clark, *op. cit.*, pp. 427-430.
18. *Canada Census*, 1961.
19. Population statistics for the smaller sects and cults of Canada are based upon a report secured by the author from the Dominion Bureau of Statistics.
20. *Vide* E. T. Clark, *op. cit.*, p. 139.
21. *Vide* J. E. Purdie, *op. cit.*, p. 2.
22. E. T. Clark, p. 186.
23. J. E. Purdie, p. 1.
24. *Census of Canada*, 1951. The Canadian census figure lumps together all varieties of Pentecostal groups and probably omits some whose names do not indicate that they belong to the Pentecostal movement.
25. Cf. Dominion Bureau of Statistics.

26. C. A. Dawson, *Group Settlement: Ethnic Communities in Western Canada* (Toronto, 1936), p. ix.

27. *Vide* C. Henry Smith, *The Story of the Mennonites* (Newton, Kansas, 1950, 3rd ed.), p. 89.

28. *Vide* F. S. Mead, *Handbook of Denominations in the United States* (New York and Nashville, 1951), pp. 124-128.

29. John Horsch, *The Hutterian Brethren* (Studies in Anabaptist and Mennonite History, 1931), p. 6.

30. *Ibid.*, p. 115.

31. For the Faith of the Hutterites *vide Account of Our Religion, Doctrine and Faith, Given by Peter Rideman of the Brothers whom Men call Hutterians* (Bungay, Suffolk, 1950).

32. *Vide* J. P. Zubek and P. A. Solberg, *Doukhobors at War* (Toronto, 1952), p. 73, *et seq.*

33. C. A. Dawson, *op. cit.*, p. 18, *et seq.*

34. *Ibid.*, p. 29.

35. *Ibid.*, p. 82.

36. *Ibid.*, p. 29.

37. *Ibid.*, p. 37.

38. *Vide* W. E. Mann, *Sect, Cult and Church in Alberta* (Toronto, 1955), p. 102, *et seq.*

39. *Vide supra.*, p. 291.

40. *Toronto Daily Star*, March 1, 1909.

41. *Vide* W. C. Carder, *Controversy in the Baptist Convention* (Thesis, McMaster University, 1950), p. 17.

42. *Ibid.*, p. 23.

43. *Ibid.*, p. 84.

44. R. L. Whan, *Pre-millenialism in Canadian Baptist History* (Thesis, McMaster University, 1945), p. 34.

45. *Vide A Tribute to William Aberhart* (published by the Calgary Prophetic Bible Institute, n.d.).

46. *Vide* W. Aberhart, *God's Great Prophecies* (Calgary, n.d.), Lecture No. 2, p. 10, *et seq.*

47. Personal Interview.

48. *Vide A Tribute, op. cit.*, p. 9.

49. *Ibid.*, p. 10.

50. *Catalogue, Winnipeg Bible Institute and College of Theology*, 1955-1956, p. 5.

51. *Vide Catalogue Prairie Bible Institute*, 1955-1956, p. 7.

52. Based on a conversation with Mr. A. H. Muddle, Secretary of the Institute.

53. Records of the Prairie Bible Institute.

54. *Vide* W. E. Mann, *op. cit.*, p. 91.

55. *Ibid.*, p. 54.

56. *Ibid.*, p. 111.

57. C. A. Braden, *These Also Believe: A Study of Modern American Cults* (New York, 1949), pp. 4 and 464.

58. Most of the cults are so small in membership as to be omitted from the *Canada Census* of 1951. Christian Science is included, having a membership of 20,795. According to the Dominion Bureau of Statistics the Christadelphians number 2,244; Unity, 697; Baha'i, 375; Rosicrucian, 92; I am, 76; Father Divine, 31.

XXI

Modern Problems

IT WAS NOT until after the First World War that the full impact of the industrial revolution was felt in Canada. Two events revealed rather startlingly to Canadians for the first time the deep seated *malaise* of modern society. The first was the formation of "One Big Union," organized by the Industrial Workers of the World; the second, which followed shortly after, was the Winnipeg strike, called on May Day, 1919.[1] Both these events pointed up sharply the divisions among churchmen over such matters as social reconstruction, industrial democracy, collective bargaining and international order.

The source of confusion was due to the fact that the Canadian churches for the most part had conceived their social responsibility in terms of individual conversions, and their customary response to a disintegrating social situation was to call for a religious revival. This, as has been noted in previous chapters, had been a very effective means of social reform in the individualistic society of the open frontier; consequently, there was a great reluctance on the part of church leaders to abandon the well-tried methods of pioneer days for a new social gospel that was being proclaimed by some younger clergymen at the time of the Winnipeg strike.

I

The new social gospel asserted strongly the right of the church "to make its voice heard in matters of politics and economics." From one point of view the "right of intervention," so much debated by European churches at the opening of the twentieth century was hardly an issue in Canada, as there has rarely been a period, as in Europe, when the churches were absentees from history.[2] In point of fact the right of the churches to exercise political influence has been a constant factor in Canadian social and political development. It had been asserted by the Roman Catholic Church from earliest times and hardly less so by the Anglican, particularly during the period when the latter was propagating the political philosophy of Loyalism. Similarly, the sectarian churches in their long struggle for religious freedom and equality had learned all the arts of political pressure.

These attempts to exercise political influence, however, were chiefly concerned with the constitutional and ecclesiastical structure of the nation rather than with its economic and social development; nevertheless, they did pave the way for church-sponsored legislation for overcoming social evils.

The most glaring social evil of frontier days was over-indulgence in alcoholic beverages. At first the churches sought to counteract this evil by organizing temperance societies, whose members were urged to sign a pledge of total abstinence; when this method failed in its purpose there arose within several churches a demand for a prohibition of the liquor traffic. Gradually the whole political influence of the Methodist, Baptist and Presbyterian churches, with some support from the Anglican, was mobilized behind a crusade for prohibition. So successful was this crusade that all the provinces of Canada, Quebec excepted, between the years of 1916 and 1921 adopted some form of prohibitory legislation.[3]

Among the Protestant churches there was also considerable unanimity in seeking legislation to enforce "keeping the Sabbath." Presbyterians of Scotch descent were particularly horrified at the desecration of the Sabbath by industrialists trying to speed up production with a seven-day week,[4] and took the lead in placing some restraint on unrestricted industrialization.

II

Behind such interventions there was, however, no political or social philosophy upon which the churches based their action; nor did the advocates of reform legislation feel called upon to include in their political activity matters appertaining to the broad field of social welfare, such as the care of the needy and unfortunate members of society. To some extent this was due to a divergence of opinion among the churches as to where the responsibility towards the needy rested. The Roman Catholic hierarchy of Quebec has never wavered in its social philosophy, transplanted from France to the new world, and based upon the French tradition of charity, in which the chief reliance for welfare services is placed upon the parish and religious orders, with governmental subsidy when necessary. Care for the needy in the English speaking provinces was for the most part based upon the English poor law, with its deterrent overtones, such as work houses and residence settlement laws, and reflects a more harsh attitude towards the indigent and unemployed than does the Quebec system.[5]

Strangely enough, the churches allied with liberal parties supported harsh measures towards the poor more vigorously than those allied with the conservatives. The Anglican church in Nova Scotia seems to have had a greater concern for the poor than the sectarian denominations. In the early days of Halifax it was taken for granted that the rector of St. Paul's parish and the churchwardens should assume responsibility for distributing relief to the poor; but there developed strong opposition among the dissenters when the legislative council attempted to subsidize this welfare work.

The most consistent opposition to public relief measures appears to have come from the secession Presbyterians. During a period of very serious distress in Pictou County, Nova Scotia, when some people were pleading for governmental assistance, the *Presbyterian Witness* (March 10, 1849) editorialized as follows: "We are decidedly opposed to anything in the shape of Governmental Grants, for such purposes, except in cases of extreme emergency, and after all private channels of Christian charity have been drained."[6]

The Wesleyan Methodists of the Maritimes also were reluctant to become entangled with any state relief. William Black, the reputed father of Methodism in the Maritimes, "believed that the work of the minister was on a plane so high that it made no contact with such things as government."[7] In Upper Canada, however, the Methodists displayed no such qualms about contact with the government and under the leadership of Egerton Ryerson they early began to make their influence felt in the realm of social welfare, particularly in their vigorous championship of the welfare of the Indians.[8]

The Baptists, despite their vehement emphasis upon the separation of church and state, were sometimes more urgent than other denominations in seeking public assistance for the poor, but this varied among different associations. According to the "Articles of Practice" of one Ontario church, it was primarily the duty of the Baptist community to look after their own poor and "not cast them on the mercies of the (sic) publick," but there was also a reservation to the effect that "in cases of long extended need publick (sic) help was not to be refused."[9]

On one important issue all the churches were in accord; they agreed unanimously in condemning slavery as an inhuman institution. The most successful co-operative venture among the clergy was the formation of an Anti-Slavery Society (1851) of which Principal Michael Willis of Knox College was the president and William McClure, a minister of the New Connexion Church, was the secretary.[10] In the Anglican diocese of Huron, the Colonial and Continental Church Society carried on a mission to fugitive slaves under episcopal patronage.[11]

On another matter of grave concern, the care of the criminal and the insane, the clergy displayed unusual insensitivity. Until very recently the treatment of criminals in Canada was nothing less than shocking,[12] and what protests were voiced came from secular rather than clerical sources. When a boy of fifteen was executed in Toronto as late as 1848, the Anglican *Church* in reporting the event raised no question of the right of society to inflict the extreme penalty upon a minor, but was deeply concerned over the appropriateness of the hymn chosen for the occasion. "To introduce upon the gallows," it commented, "verses appropriate only to the quiet death-bed of a sincere Christian, is to our mind, an act of shocking profaneness."[13] Equally slow were the churches to advocate any improvement in the treatment of the insane, whose asylums are still a blot on the Canadian landscape.

Since organized Christianity in Canada was so little concerned over the welfare of the criminal and the insane, it was hardly to be expected that church leaders would react very kindly to labour unrest. In point of fact they reacted very strongly against the first signs of labour unions. When in 1847 a strike was called by the shoemakers of Toronto and London, the church papers all agreed in condemning the strikers, and most of them considered the efforts of Robert Owen to improve the conditions of labour in England as those of "a downright mad man."[14]

III

Our consideration of church attitudes on social problems thus far has been confined to the first half of the nineteenth century: towards the end of the century there began to emerge the idea that the church ought to exercise some moral control in social and political development, an idea based on theological presuppositions. Two prominent Canadian churchmen who pioneered in this field were George M. Grant and D. J. Macdonnell. Both of them were influenced in their thinking by the transcendental philosophy of Dr. John Caird of Scotland, who was inclined to dwell upon the practical aspects of Christianity "and to pay less attention to questions of doctrine."[15]   It was this emphasis upon practical Christianity that led D. J. Macdonnell to attempt to meet the challenge of slum conditions in Toronto by organizing (1890) mission houses with night school classes for working girls, not unlike the Girls' School of Industry, initiated by Dr. John Caird in Scotland some decades earlier.[16]

G. M. Grant's role as a social reformer was enacted on a larger stage than Macdonnell's, as he sought the improvement of political morality rather than civic slums, but like Macdonnell his interest in social affairs was based upon the inspiration he had gained from Caird's fundamental views of Christianity; also he was not immune to Henry Ward Beecher's "emotional optimistic theology."[17] Although he deprecated some of the humanistic aspects of Beecher's teaching he was in absolute accord with one of the famous American preacher's dicta, that "it is the duty of the minister of the Gospel to preach on every side of political life."[18] With a vision of Canada as a nation based upon Christian principles, Grant never hesitated to denounce politicians whom he felt were betraying his vision.[19]

Two other Canadian churchmen far more deeply moved than Grant by the social philosophy of Beecher were the famous missionary superintendents of the north-west, James Robertson and James Woodsworth. Both of them had also accepted wholeheartedly the American theological emphasis of "disinterested benevolence" responsible for so much Christian activity in the United States. It was this doctrine of disinterested benevolence, as has already been observed,[20] that led them to dedicate their lives to missionary work.

These precursors of what came to be known as the social gospel, like their mentor Beecher, saw social and economic problems as essentially simple. "Protect the rights of the individual, support morality, and everything in this fortunate country would go more than well"[21] is probably a fair summary of the social outlook of Robertson and Woodsworth as it is of Henry Ward Beecher's.

But just as a later generation of social thinkers in the United States, like Washington Gladden and Walter Rauschenbusch,[22] felt compelled to go a step further and advocate a form of Christian socialism, so in Canada a later generation of churchmen began to see that social problems were not so easily solved as their predecessors thought. C. W. Gordon (Ralph Connor) who wrote a biography of James Robertson, made a slight departure from the optimistic faith of his hero in demanding more rigid control of the acquisitive instinct, while his son King Gordon embraced in its entirety the socialistic doctrine of Walter Rauschenbusch.[23] An even more drastic break with the past was made by J. S. Woodsworth, the son of James Woodsworth, who became one of the founders and leaders of a socialistic political party, the Co-operative Commonwealth Federation (C.C.F.).

It was while serving as the superintendent of the All Peoples' Mission, Winnipeg, that he learned first-hand the needs and despairs of the city proletariat in Canada. What he learned did not come as a great surprise, for while a student at Oxford he had visited Mansfield House in the east end of London, where he had gained a considerable knowledge of the dark side of city life; and he conceived it his task to prevent "the spread of the blight to Canada."[24] His experience at the All Peoples' Mission only strengthened this resolution and he proceeded to make the Canadian public aware of the challenge before them in two books: *Strangers within our Gates* and *My Neighbour*, both published shortly before the First World War. They consisted of earnest "pleas to responsible citizens to create constructive social organizations that would overcome the forces of disorganization and greed." The scientific approach of Dr. Woodsworth, with its stress upon the concrete and practical was to have far-reaching effects upon the development of the social gospel in Canada, and to give it a more permanent footing in Canadian national life than has been the case in the United States.

The philosophical formulation of the social gospel, however, was not the work of Dr. Woodsworth, but of Professor Salem Bland, who fired the imagination of several generations of theological students both at Winnipeg and Toronto with his proclamation of a religion for a new age. Dr. Bland foresaw the new age as one of socialism, but his socialism was still coloured by the optimistic liberalism of an earlier age which believed in an inevitable progress towards a better day for all mankind. "Mankind," he wrote, "is in the grasp of divine currents too strong to be resisted." One of these divine currents was the coming to power of labour, but a labour that would become Christianized since "labour and Christianity were bound up together." It was his conviction that if labour should "turn away from Christianity now" it would be turning "away from the throne" that God was preparing for it.[25]

IV

By the turn of the century the social gospel was making a deep impression upon the organized life of the churches; this is evidenced by the fact that most of them were transforming their committees on moral reform into councils of social service. In 1902 the standing committee on Temperance, Prohibition and Moral Reform of the Methodist Church was given the status of a General Conference board and Dr. S. D. Chown became its first general secretary. As Dr. Chown was very sympathetic towards the views of the new school of social reformers he immediately widened the scope of his board to include what he designated "applied Christianity." He also acted as chairman of a special committee on sociological questions which reported to the General Conference of 1906 "that the present social order is far from being an ideal expression of Christian brotherhood, and that the spirit of much of our commercial life is alien to that of the Gospel."[26] The same report recommended "the establishment of fellowships on sociology in our colleges for the investigation of Canadian economic conditions and tendencies, and for the development of a widely progressive sociological literature." Under the leadership of Dr. Chown the old cumbersome name of his board—Temperance, Prohibition and Moral Reform—was changed to Evangelism and Social Service. Although the primacy of evangelism was still recognized in the new title, nevertheless the General Conference of 1918 was very specific in directing the Board "to give effect to the many recommendations concerning the application of the principles of the Gospel to the economic, political, social and moral relations of life."[27]

A similar evolution from moral reform to social service also occurred in the Presbyterian Church. In 1907 the General Assembly set up a department of Temperance and other Moral and Social Reforms, but this was quickly replaced by a Board of Moral and Social Reform, with Dr. G. C. Pidgeon as its first chairman. In 1911 the name of the board was changed to that of Social Service and Evangelism, which indicates an even more drastic change of emphasis than within the Methodist Church, since social service came first in the new title.   For some reason this board was hardly set up before it was merged with the Home Mission Board,[28] where it remained as a sub-committee until the formation of The United Church of Canada. This subordination to the Home Mission Board did not, however, indicate any diminution of interest in social service in the Presbyterian community, as J. H. Edmison, its secretary, remained vehement in urging that the church's severest test was in trying to bring its message of redemption to the most neglected areas of the great city centres. In his first report to The United Church of Canada he quoted the warning words of Dr. Charles Thompson of the American Board of National Missions, that "The battle of the Gospel with the massed populations will prove the Gettysburgh of Missions."[29]

The Anglican Church remained somewhat tardy in adjusting itself to the new currents of social thinking, but in 1915 the General Synod replaced its old committee on Moral and Social Reform with a Council of Social Service.   The man most responsible for this change of name was Dean L. N. Tucker, who had taken to heart the admonition of the Lambeth Conference (1897) that "a Christian community as a whole is morally responsible for the character of its own economic and social order."   In urging the formation of the new council Dean Tucker said that "Social Service must take its place by the side of Missions and Religious Training for the Young."   In 1918 it achieved such equality when Canon C. W. Vernon was appointed its full time general secretary.[30]

About this time both the Baptists and Congregationalists also set up similar councils, thus displaying a rather unanimous Protestant interest in Christian social service.[31]

The Roman Catholic Church had even extended its interest further than the Protestant churches by actively participating in the most delicate of all social problems: collective bargaining between capital and labour. In justification of the church's intervention in the field of industrial welfare, Father Joseph-Papin Archambault wrote in 1911: "The social question, it cannot be denied, exists in Canada; by tomorrow it may become so acute as to produce a fatal crisis."   According to Father Archambault the Church must meet such a crisis by the formation of Catholic labour unions, inspired by Christian principles; and he was greatly cheered by the fact that in 1911 Church sponsored syndicates or labour unions had a membership of 350,000.[32]

V

The crisis, however, must have seemed remote in 1911, and the Canadian people on the whole felt they lived "in a country whose future prospects gave good grounds for the most optimistic dreams."[33] Nor did the outbreak of the First World War greatly disturb this complacency, and it was not until some time after its close that the full implications of the disaster that had befallen western civilization made their impress upon the Canadian mind. For a time the social problem fell into the background, as the people bent all their energies to winning a war that was in their minds to end all wars. The cause of the war to Canadians was simple: they blamed it upon Kaiser Wilhelm II and his docile subjects. Church leaders for the most part never questioned the justice of the Allied cause. At the General Synod of the Church of England in 1915, the Primate, Archbishop Mathieson, proclaimed that his church "preached courage, loyalty and patriotism . . . for the cause for which we have been rallying support is one about which no follower of Christ need entertain qualms of conscience."[34]

Within the Methodist Church there was some questioning. J. S. Woodsworth objected to the Church lending her support to war in the name of Jesus, and was particularly shocked at churches being used as recruiting centres.[35] His protests ultimately led to his dismissal from the Bureau of Social Research of which he had become the secretary in 1916.

In French-speaking Quebec some of Woodsworth's sentiments were re-echoed by Henri Bourassa, who questioned the theory that the war was due solely to Germany. At first he was roundly denounced by the French press and also by Archbishop Bruchesi of Montreal who "declared that it was the duty of the faithful to give the mother country, dragged into the war in spite of herself, the loyal and hearty support demanded both by religion and patriotism."[36] For a time Bourassa was a voice crying in the wilderness, but after the introduction into Canada of compulsory military service, his compatriots began to rally around him, and to look upon the war as something inflicted upon them by Britain's imperialistic ambitions. This in turn led to a deepening animosity between English- and French-speaking Canadians, which is one of the bitterest fruits for Canadians, at least, of both world wars.

From the point of view of the churches, the war created a spirit of religious optimism. Many of the clergy served as chaplains and were delegated important tasks by the government which leaned heavily upon them to help maintain public morale both at home and at the front.   One of the most lauded heroes of the war was Canon F. G. Scott, the senior chaplain of the first division in France.[37]   All active church members felt they were occupied in a great cause.   Women met in halls to knit for the soldiers or to engage in many forms of relief work. Laymen helped to organize campaigns for selling war bonds.   It was confidently expected that the end of the war would bring a new and glorious era in which justice and right would reign more strongly than ever before, and that the social crisis which loomed so large before the war would be quickly solved.

VI

It was indeed a bitter disillusionment for the Canadian people to find that the long agony of the war had solved no problems but rather intensified them.   Racial antagonism, so long Canada's major problem, was more bitter than ever; but even more serious was the deepening rift between capital and labour, which came to a head when a strike was called by the metal trades of Winnipeg on May 1, 1919, followed shortly thereafter by a general sympathetic strike called by the Trades and Labour Council.   The strike had originated out of the swift closing down of war plants at the close of hostilities, creating a serious unemployment situation, and had been preceded by a series of lesser strikes during which agents of the Industrial Workers of the World had been agitating for the creation of one big union as the only way for labour to gain an influential voice in the industrial development of the country.

As Winnipeg divided into two camps, a Citizens Committee of One Thousand and a Strike Committee of the Trades and Labour Council, with the strikers gaining for a time complete control of the city and the possibility that the general strike would spread to other cities, all Canada became emotionally involved in what appeared to be a social revolution. The strike lasted about six weeks and was characterized by riots and bloodshed, resulting in some very repressive labour legislation in the Canadian parliament.[38]   It ended in failure for the strikers, whose leaders were arrested for sedition and were subjected to protracted trials, which continued to keep the political life of the country sharply divided on the social issue.

For the churches it was a time of reassessment of their own social philosophy.   During the strike a good many prominent churchmen had closely identified themselves with the cause of labour. Playing a prominent role in keeping up the morale of the workers was a Labour Church, founded by William Ivens, a Methodist minister who had been having difficulties with his church because of his pacifist views. In the midst of the strike a meeting was called by the leaders of the Labour Church in Victoria Park to provide a forum for the expression of the grievances of the strikers. One of the speakers at this meeting was the beloved Canadian padre, Canon F. G. Scott. Although Canon Scott was never particularly interested in political systems or social theories, he had an affectionate interest in people and he had rushed to Winnipeg because he had heard that some of his boys (returned soldiers) were in trouble.[39] He voiced very earnestly the right of these boys to find jobs and establish homes in post-war Canada.

Also present at the meeting was J. S. Woodsworth whose ideology had by this time driven him out of the Methodist ministry to become a longshore workman, but who had organized a Sunday School at Vancouver where he taught a doctrine partaking "of the elements of both Christianity and Socialism."[40] Both Canon Scott and J. S. Woodsworth were highly regarded in a large section of the Christian community of Canada because of their obvious sincerity and their fearless advocacy of the rights of the underprivileged. Church leaders, even under the pressure of leading laymen, were loath to denounce them publicly for their part in the strike.

These leaders were also concerned over the disappearance of the workers from their congregations, but were at the same time aware that the solid membership of the churches was closely identified with the economic and cultural interests of the owning classes, who were unwilling to tolerate any longer clergymen who, in their minds, were attempting to overthrow the established order of things. The serious question that now faced the responsible leaders of the church, following the Winnipeg strike was simply this: Was there a place in the organized structure of the church for the new proletariat of the cities, or must they be abandoned either to pre-millenial sects or to the new secular humanistic institutions that were now coming to the fore?[41]

VII

During the great depression of the 'thirties and after the outbreak of the Second World War, this question became ever more insistent, and for a time the churches made a determined effort to put religion to work to reform the social structure in order that they might gain the allegiance of the proletariat. The Board of Evangelism and Social Service of the United Church took the lead in calling for a new approach to the social question. At the United Church General Council in 1932 it put forth an actual indictment of personal evangelism as a method of reforming society. "A Christianity," it proclaimed, "whose message has historically been one of personal salvation is face to face with what is very clearly, not just a personal, but a mass or collective problem, and for this it finds its resources inadequate." After paying tribute to what evangelical Christianity had accomplished in the past, it went on to say that its former sufficiency "has little bearing on the major causes of the present emergency" and "only attests the need for a fresh interpretation of Christianity."[42] At the same time it warned against any salvation made on a purely secularist plane or through merely external adjustments; this, it held, would be "just as futile as to talk piously of changing men's inner life without changing the social and economic environment into which children are to be born."[43]

Similar expressions of disillusionment with mere evangelism as a method of reforming society, accompanied by a call for a fundamental social change, could be duplicated from the proceedings of nearly all church gatherings during the depression years.

VIII

With the outbreak of the Second World War the churches became even more explicit in their social doctrines. This second holocaust was an occasion for a far more profound meditation on the structure and constitution of Western society than had been the first. A Commission on the Church, Nation and World Order, set up by the General Council of The United Church of Canada in 1940, deprecated strongly the characterization of the war as "a war in defence of our Christian civilization." "There is much in our civilization," it stated, "which is not and never has been Christian, and which cannot possibly be defended by Christian leaders." It then asserted that "so far as it is our Christian civilization for whose defence we have fought, it is incumbent upon the Church to declare what are the basic elements in a

Christian civilization and to point out where we have failed to incorporate such elements in the body politic."[44]

Spokesmen for the Anglican Church were equally forthright in calling for a reappraisal of our so-called Christian civilization. A *Bulletin* published by the Council for Social Service of The Church of England in Canada devoted one issue in 1941 to a discussion of "Religion, Revolution, and Restoration." Taking the findings of the Malvern Conference of English Churchmen, held that same year in England, as its guide, it informed Canadians that this Conference proclaimed that "a way of life founded on the economic motive is contrary to the will of God." The Conference itself was regarded as "nothing less than a revolution in England" and the moral to be drawn from it was that "We cannot be content with the *status quo* within our own country. It will not stand the test after the war."[45]

The Roman Catholic Church also took a lead in urging social changes along collectivist lines. As early as 1939 Father M. M. Coady, Director of Extension of St. Francis Xavier University, proclaimed in *Masters of Their Own Destiny*, issued under the imprimatur of the bishop of Antigonish, that "Group action is the great wave that is breaking over society today. The evolution from individualism to some form of collectivism is nearing its completion."[46]

He hoped to see its completion by way of consumers' co-operatives, but in Quebec Bishop Dauville of Saint-Hyacinthe hoped to see it by way of corporatism. At the twenty-second annual convention of the Catholic syndicates at Granby in 1944 the Bishop urged "simultaneous development of workers' and employers' syndicates as a prelude to the economic corporatism which we consider essential to the future of labour and employers as well."[47]

IX

Towards the close of the war, it became evident that any serious reform of the social order was going to meet stiff opposition from many quarters. Sharp divisions on the nature of the reform necessary began to appear among all denominations. The provincial government of Quebec, becoming alarmed at the growing agitation for corporatism in clerical circles attempted to appease it by setting up a post-war Economic Council to bring in suggestions for improving economic conditions. Corporatist sympathizers like Father Georges-Henri

Levesque of Laval University and Eugène L'Heureux of *L'Action Catholique* were given representation on the Council, but the chairman, Jules Brillant, a utility magnate, was expected to exercise a moderating influence upon his more ebullient colleagues.[48] The supporters of corporatism, however, met more serious opposition than the government, because it was practically impossible to persuade businessmen to organize into syndicates, a necessary complement to labour syndicates if the corporate state was to be brought into being. The Quebec hierarchy also discovered considerable discontent with its sponsorship of labour syndicates as well as such groups as the Jeunesse Ouvrière Catholique (J.O.C.). The former became particularly offensive to middle-class congregations after they began to adopt militant strike procedures. Consequently, the hierarchy sought to lessen the tension by keeping the syndicates as well as the J.O.C. outside the parochial organizations.[49]

No such easy solution of avoiding the deepening tension between management and labour was possible for the Protestant churches. In 1944 the Commission on the Church, Nation, and World Order of the United Church reported "an underlying hostility on the part of prominent laymen towards the pronouncements of Church Courts in the economic and social field."[50] At the end of the war this hostility became far more vocal and influential in the council of the churches, provoking a counter-hostility among the proponents of the social gospel, particularly those who believed with Dr. Salem Bland that the "Great Christianity" of the twentieth century might well solve "the unparalleled problems of social and political reconstruction."[51] A good many of these followers of Dr. Bland had become experts in various fields of knowledge in the hope that they might use their skills in the field of social reconstruction. Under the leadership of J. S. Woodsworth they attempted to be scientific and practical in achieving their goal of a Christian civilization; many of them enrolled in the League for Social Reconstruction, founded in 1932, for the "promotion of research, the education of public opinion and the development of political organizations seeking the establishment of a planned and socialized economy in Canada."[52] As time went on and they experienced a growing coolness on the part of the churches towards their social and political activities, they became more absorbed in the purely secular aspect of their work and less in its theological presuppositions. Many of them became research experts in such matters as labour codes, banking, taxation and other secular concerns;[53] several became members of parliament and one became the premier of Saskatchewan.

X

With the loss of this militant wing of the social reformers, a good deal of the enthusiasm for a Christian social order began to wane in the churches; nevertheless, it was still asserted by church councils that the churches should have something to say on the direction and goals of a continuing industrial revolution, so much more dangerous for the human race in view of the latest scientific discoveries. At the same time it was recognized that in a highly specialized society church pronouncements in this field of industry must be based on the research of competent experts. As it was difficult for the separate churches with limited budgets to secure such services, it was decided to emulate the churches of the United States and set up a central church council similar to the Federal Council of Churches in the United States (recently renamed the National Council of Churches in the United States). Thus came into being the Canadian Council of Churches, which was commended to the Anglican General Synod in 1943 on the basis "that we must have sufficient organization to examine more closely into industrial and economic matters."[54]

Up to the present the Canadian Council has not obtained the same recognized status as the mouthpiece of Canadian Protestantism on national and international affairs as has the National Council in the United States, nor has it, like the latter, worked out a "co-ordinated programme for a continued impact upon national life."[55] Unfortunately for the Canadian Council it had to effect its organization at a time when there was a definite trend away from the ecumenical spirit of the war years towards a "hardening of denominational positions."[56]

XI

The evident decline of the popularity of the social gospel in recent years has not been entirely due either to "the hostility of prominent laymen" or to the defection of the scientific reformers from the churches. Many socially conscious clergymen have abandoned the optimistic outlook of the social reformers and are giving guarded approval to the pessimistic redemptive theology of continental Europe. Religious teachers in Canadian theological colleges have criticized sharply the scientific and humanistic aspects of the social gospel, founded, as it has been expressed, on a "secular instead of a religious hope."[57] Also among these critics is a renewed emphasis upon "the lonely decision of a life commitment within the individual soul."[58]

It is questionable, however, if the average Canadian Christian is yet in a mood to comprehend a pessimistic theology born out of the anxieties of a disillusioned Europe. If there is anguish in Canadian Christianity it consists of the loss of the Bible as a "unitary and authoritative revelation."[59] This is well authenticated by the growing sectarian movement which has for all intents and purposes established two Social Credit governments in Canada.

No doubt the typical Canadian is well aware that the liberal interpretation of Christianity with its "faith in progress and evolutionary providence" has received rough handling by history in recent years, but it would seem that the fading of liberalism's dream has not yet caused the typical Canadian to embrace the quietism which "stresses man's impotence to transform the world." One of them at least, a scion of Methodist frontier Christianity, after voicing many doubts and fears for the future of the church, finally pins his hope on converted scientists to rally the Christian forces of society.[60] Thus it would seem that activism, born of frontier revivalism, is still the authentic note of Canadian Christianity. It has in recent years received a new lease of life, due to the fact that Canada has entered upon one of the most expansive periods of her history. As expansion is now the watchword of Canadian national life, so it has become the predominant theme within the churches as they bend themselves to the old familiar task of providing social integration for uprooted and displaced persons moving into city suburbs and the new mining towns of the northlands.

REFERENCES

1. The significance of this strike is commented on in *The Cambridge History of the British Empire, op. cit.*, VI, p. 768, *et seq.*

2. William Temple, *Christianity and Social Order* (A Penguin Book, 1942), p. 1.

3. *Vide* A. Thomson, *Alcohol or Christ* (Toronto, 1947), for the story of the churches' struggle for prohibition, especially pp. 26-31.

4. *Vide* W. H. Jamieson, *The Nation and the Sabbath* (Toronto, 1901, 2nd ed.), especially "Canada and the Sabbath," pp. 135-148.

5. *Vide* E. S. L. Govan, "The Social Services" in *Canada* (The United Nations Series), *op. cit.*, pp. 390-407.

6. Quoted by W. H. Elgee, *The Social Teachings of the Canadian Churches*, *op. cit.*, p. 279.

7. *Ibid.*, p. 283.

8. *Ibid.*, p. 292.

9. *Ibid.*, p. 277.

10. *Vide* Fred Landon, "Abolitionist Interest in Upper Canada," *Ontario History*, XLIV (1952), No. 4.

11. *Vide* T. R. Millman, "The Church of England in Western Ontario" (Western Ontario Historical Notes, London, Can., 1955), XIII, Nos. 1 and 2.

12. *Vide Report of the Royal Commission to Investigate the Penal System of Canada* (Ottawa, 1938), especially pp. 12-24.

13. Quoted by W. H. Elgee, *op. cit.*, p. 302.

14. *Ibid.*, p. 320.

15. *Vide* John Caird, *The Fundamental Ideas of Christianity* (Glasgow, 1915, 2 vols.), I, p. xv.

16. *Ibid.*, p. xxv; also J. F. McCurdy, *Life and Work of D. J. Macdonnell*, *op. cit.*, p. 296.

17. Henry F. May, *Protestant Churches and Industrial America* (New York, 1949), p. 68.

18. *Ibid.*, p. 40.

19. *Vide* Grant and Hamilton, *George Monro Grant*, *op. cit.*, especially p. 98.

20. *Vide supra.*, pp. 274, 276.

21. H. F. May, *op. cit.*, p. 72.

22. *Ibid.*, p. 231, *et seq.*

23. *Vide Social Planning for Canada*, by the Research Committee of the League for Social Reconstruction (Toronto, 1935), especially pp. 37-39.

24. Grace MacInnis, *J. S. Woodsworth, A Man to Remember* (Toronto, 1953), p. 38.

25. S. G. Bland, *The New Christianity* (Toronto, 1920), p. 100.

26. *Journal of Proceedings of the Seventh General Conference of the Methodist Church of Canada* (Toronto, 1906), p. 274.

27. *Journal of Proceedings of the Eleventh General Conference of the Methodist Church* (Toronto, 1922), p. 233.

28. *Vide* J. T. McNeil, *The Presbyterian Church in Canada 1875-1923*, *op. cit.*, p. 65.

29. *Record of Proceedings of the First General Council of The United Church of Canada* (Toronto, 1925), p. 101.

30. *Vide* C. W. Vernon, *The Old Church in the New Dominion*, *op. cit.*, p. 191.

31. *Vide* G. E. Levy, *The Baptists of the Maritime Provinces, 1753-1946*, *op. cit.*, p. 299.

32. J. P. Archambault, *Une Digue Le Bolchévisme: Les Syndicats Catholiques* (Montreal, 1919), pp. 7-10.

33. Jean Bruchési, *A History of Canada* (trans. R. W. W. Robertson, Toronto, 1950), pp. 192-193.

34. *Journal of Proceedings of the Seventh Session of the General Synod of the Church of England in Canada* (Toronto, 1916), pp. 20-21.

35. G. MacInnis, *op. cit.*, p. 104.

36. M. Wade, *The French Canadians 1760-1945*, *op. cit.*, p. 645.

37. *Vide* A. F. Duguid, *Official History of the Canadian Forces in the Great War 1914-1919* (General Series, Ottawa, 1938), I, p. 420: "Major (Canon) F. G. Scott on the evening of the 22nd encouraged an advancing battalion with the words, 'A great day for Canada, boys—a great day for Canada,' and he was in their midst when they charged the wood." *Vide* also F. G. Scott, *The Great War as I Saw It* (Toronto, 1922), p. 62.

38. *Vide* D. C. Masters, *The Winnipeg General Strike* (Toronto, 1950), *passim*.

39. *Ibid.*, *op. cit.*, p. 91.

40. G. MacInnis, *op. cit.*, p. 125.

41. For a detailed discussion of this problem *vide* H. R. Niebuhr, *The Social Sources of Denominationalism* (New York, 1929), especially p. 18, *et seq.*

42. *Record of Proceedings of Fifth General Council of The United Church of Canada*, 1932, p. 286.

43. Quoted by Ernest Thomas, *The Church and the Economic Order* (pamphlet of the League for Social Reconstruction, Toronto, 1934), p. 20.

44. *A Report of the Commission on Church, Nation and World Order* (The United Church of Canada, London, Ontario, 1944), p. 11.

45. *The Bulletin* (The Council for Social Service, The Church of England in Canada, Toronto, Ontario, February 25th, 1941), pp. 1-8.

46. M. M. Coady, *Masters of Their Own Destiny* (New York and London, 1939), p. 27.

47. M. Wade, *op. cit.*, p. 979.

48. *Ibid.*

49. E. C. Hughes, *French Canada in Transition* (London, 1946), p. 104.

50. *A Report of the Commission on Church, Nation and World Order, op. cit.*, p. 11.

51. S. G. Bland, *op. cit.*, pp. 158-159.

52. E. Thomas, *op. cit.*, cover page.

53. *Social Planning for Canada, op. cit., passim.*

54. *Journal of Proceedings of the Fifteenth Session of the General Synod of the Church of England in Canada* (Toronto, 1943), p. 264.

55. *Yearbook of American Churches* (New York, 1952 edition), p. 268.

56. *Vide* article by W. J. Gallagher, "The Canadian Council of Churches," in *The Anglican Outlook* (Gardenvale, P.Q., April, 1952), vol. 7, No. 6, pp. 8-9.

57. D. R. G. Owen, *Scientism, Man, and Religion* (Philadelphia, 1952), p. 190.

58. J. S. Thomson, *The Hope of the Gospel* (London, 1955), p. 162.

59. W. A. Gifford, *The Seekers* (Boston, 1954), p. 268.

60. *Ibid.*, p. 285, *et seq.*

INDEX

345